Language in the Visual Arts

Language in the Visual Arts

The Interplay of Text and Imagery

LESLIE ROSS

McFarland & Company, Inc., Publishers
Jefferson, North Carolina

Library of Congress Cataloguing-in-Publication Data

Ross, Leslie, 1956–
Language in the visual arts : the interplay of text and imagery / Leslie Ross.
p. cm.
Includes bibliographical references and index.

ISBN 978-0-7864-6795-2 (softcover : acid free paper) ♾
ISBN 978-1-4766-1625-4 (ebook)

1. Writing and art. 2. Words in art. I. Title.
N72.W75R66 2014 701'.08—dc23 2014008165

British Library cataloguing data are available

Front cover image: The Hours of Jean Lallement, ca. 1524
(courtesy Walters Art Museum)

Printed in the United States of America

McFarland & Company, Inc., Publishers
Box 611, Jefferson, North Carolina 28640
www.mcfarlandpub.com

Dedicated to my parents

Table of Contents

Preface and Acknowledgments

This book has been a long time in the making—I might be embarrassed to admit *how* long—although I hasten to add that I have happily pursued and completed a number of academic publishing and other creative projects during the several years since I first began to visualize this current text. Hopefully, the aging and maturing process has affected this work positively and this present volume represents a much finer version of the study I initially began some years ago.

This study concerns text/image relationships in the history of art, admittedly an extremely wide-ranging topic but an extremely logical outgrowth of my long-developed and specialized interests in medieval art and manuscript illumination in particular, my long-standing interests in modern and contemporary art, and my great enthusiasm for all the many areas of art history that I have been privileged to teach and write about during my several decades as a faculty member at Dominican University of California. Far from shying away from any fields strictly "outside my academic specialty," I feel that I have been very lucky indeed to have been able to develop course materials at Dominican that, in addition to those many courses involving traditional and necessary coverage of specific time periods or geographic ranges, have also included courses that represent materials and themes from wider, cross-cultural, and deliberately interdisciplinary perspectives.

Without this background and enthusiastic openness to the larger world of art history and the humanities, I doubt very much that I would ever have visualized, let alone undertaken, this study. There is certainly no rule, after all, that dictates that a scholar of medieval illustrated hagiographic manuscripts cannot also delve enthusiastically and quite profitably into the realms of modern and postmodern language-based art; indeed, there are many connections to be made and similarities and differences to be noted—much "more than meets the eye"—in all the periods in which artists have combined written texts and visual imagery, or have used words *in* art and words *as* forms of visual art. From ancient times to the contemporary period, text/image combinations have been creatively pursued and explored in many ways by visual artists and writers. This study is designed to highlight not only the diverse but also the similar ways in which text/image relationships have long served as fodder for creative explorations.

There are many dangers to be easily and more than well anticipated in such a wide-ranging and thematically-based study as this present book. As stated also in the introduction to this text, my goals and intentions from the very beginning have never been to provide any sort of comprehensive survey of text/image relationships throughout the history of art, but rather to gather together and describe highly selected examples, arranged around specific themes, which represent particular forms or genres of word/picture combinations. Naturally, scholarly specialists in any of the many areas that I delve into in this book may find my coverage less than appropriately detailed. I am more than well aware of the many very significant gaps in this book. There are so many more artworks, artists, and examples that could well have been included that I simply do not mention at all, as well as so many other examples of highly fascinating text/image relationships that could or doubtless should have been afforded coverage or more detailed mention here. I offer my sincere apologies for these most egregious *lacunae*. Hopefully, the notes and extensive bibliographic references will serve as at least partial mitigation for these gaps in coverage in the text itself. In spite of these obvious and highly objectionable gaps in coverage, I trust and hope that among the many examples that are included in the study at least some colleagues will find some of this material eye-opening and "new" (or newly encountered) as well.

During the several years that I have worked on this study, so many people have assisted and supported me in various capacities that the task of appropriately acknowledging them all is really a quite daunting challenge in itself.

I have greatly appreciated my lengthy communications with and assistance from Robbi Siegel of Art Resource in New York, from which source I obtained many of the images included in this book. I thank her so much as well for her patient guidance in assisting me through the often highly complex navigations and negotiations involved with image-sourcing and permissions.

I have also benefited greatly from my contacts with many other helpful people such as the staff members at ARS, VAGA, and the Bridgeman Art Library, as well as Sue Palmer at Sir John Soane's Museum in London, whom I first met many years ago, Ruth Bowler at the Walters Art Museum in Baltimore, and the staffs of the Bibliothèque Nationale in Paris, the British Library in London, the Pierpont Morgan Library in New York, the New York Public Library, and the Bodleian Library in Oxford for graciously facilitating several of my image requests. I sincerely thank Valeska Soares for allowing me to include an image of her work; Dr. Mamoun Sakkal for sending me an image of his work; Wanda Hansen for sending me digital images of William T. Wiley's work; John Baldessari's studio for allowing me to reproduce one of his works; Xu Bing's studio for sending me excellent copies of the images I requested; Shelley Lee (the estate of Roy Lichtenstein) for her generous assistance; the studio of Claes Oldenburg and Cossje van Bruggen in New York for providing me with a wonderful image; the archivist at Regen Projects in Los Angeles for facilitating my requests for images from Glenn Ligon and Jack Pierson; Martha Rosler for granting me permission to reproduce one of her works after a highly fruitful and engaging discussion; the Gladstone Gallery in New York for the image by Shirin Neshat; Mary Boone Gallery in New York for the image by Barbara Kruger; the White Cube Gallery in London for the image by Gilbert & George; and the Gagosian Gallery in New York for Ed Ruscha's images included here.

I am deeply indebted as well to many others who have read, offered comments upon, and assisted me in various ways with this study. I have discussed portions of this text with several academic colleagues, including Dr. John Lowden of the Courtauld Institute in London whose comments, years ago, upon "shaped texts" in medieval Byzantine manuscripts were most helpful. Dr. Ilana Tahan of the British Library in London also took much enthusiastic care, some years back, in allowing me access to rare Hebrew manuscripts with micrographic writing and in discussing my research interests. The staff members at the Fisher Landau center in New York gladly offered me an appointment to view the collection a few years ago; many thanks to Dr. Peter Williams for facilitating this appointment. I owe great thanks to Dr. Marvin Sackner, too, for more recently assisting me with some image-obtaining details from his remarkable collection (The Sackner Archive of Concrete and Visual Poetry).

I have also been so delighted with the research assistance offered by graduate students at Dominican University of California, including Victoria Sheridan, Robin Pryor, Karen McGuinn, Barbara Luttig-Haber, and most recently, Anne Tignanelli and Andrea Triolo—for proofreading and diligent assistance with photo-sourcing. I also want to convey my deep appreciation for my many students, undergraduate and graduate, who have taken my course "Language in the Visual Arts" at Dominican University of California during the past several years. Many of these students have found the course materials quite inspirational, resulting in several BA and MA theses of which I am very proud (as are their authors, and deservedly so).

This book has indeed been a long time in the making, and I also want to thank many other friends who have so patiently listened to me over the years, who have offered their support and good wishes throughout this project, who have listened diligently to my accounts of book-work, and who have expressed their support. Most of all, I want to thank my dear parents—to whom I dedicate this book.

INTRODUCTION

Visual Wordplay: A Thousand Words

"A picture," according to the old saying, "is worth a thousand words." "Show me a picture," people say, when they want clear information and easy-to-understand directions. These sayings indicate that written language and visual imagery are generally understood to be two quite separate and distinct, albeit closely related, genres of human communication. The activities of writing and reading written words are different from the activities and processes involved with the creation and viewing of pictorial images. Reading texts and viewing images require different sets of skills and indeed involve different functions of the human brain.[1]

Before the advent and development of alphabetic writing systems, the earliest examples of human communication systems appear in pictorial forms. These largely consist of relatively simple graphic indications of common and recognizable natural phenomena such as plants, animals, human beings, the sun, moon, stars, and so forth. Written language might thus be said to ultimately derive from pictures.[2] The necessity and desire to communicate increasingly more complex information gradually resulted in the development of various forms of nonpictographic writing systems that employ agreed-upon markings to indicate phonetic sounds. Alphabetic writing systems in particular use specific symbols/letters to represent the sounds of spoken languages. One must be conversant with the spoken language in order to interpret the written symbols. This requires training, a knowledge of the alphabet system used, and an ability to translate the symbols into words (whether spoken aloud or heard internally).

Similarly, while the ability to recognize and identify pictorial imagery is also culturally conditioned and requires visual training as well, even so, a single visual representation of a person, or an animal, or a common object may suffice and substitute for many different vocabulary words in a variety of spoken and written languages. In that sense, images are often seen as having a greater impact, immediacy, and legibility for a wider audience than written words. Pictures may thus be "worth" many words indeed.

Although the written and pictorial modes of human communication are distinctly different and function well independently of each other, this book is concerned with what happens when the two modes are directly and deliberately combined, when actual written texts appear in visual imagery, or when visual imagery actually consists of written words. This book is not about written descriptions of works of art, artworks that are based on textual sources, or artworks that evoke literary themes, but rather with works of visual art that include or consist of written language. From the inscriptions liberally strewn in Renaissance paintings; to the words flowing through, around, and out of medieval art; to contemporary language-based art, written language in the guise of captions, inscriptions, declarations, signatures, indications of spoken dialogue, and so forth appear in the pictorial arts throughout history and in diverse cultures.

The vast range of possibilities for word/picture combinations in the visual arts inspires and at the same time challenges strict categorization. The materials included in this book are, however, arranged in loose thematic groupings. Allowing for overlaps and fully admitting the possibilities of multiple intentions and variable "readings," the categories proposed here are designed not so much to create boundaries or limitations but rather to stimulate appreciation for the diversity of word/picture combinations as they appear in the art forms of many historical and contemporary cultures.

By no means does this book propose or intend to be a complete catalogue of examples. Such a task would not only be herculean in scope but would run the grave risk of attempting to condense (and thus dangerously oversimplify) a vast amount of previous and excellent scholarship by professional specialists in a great number of fields. Casting out a wide but by no means comprehensive net into this fascinating territory, one can see that throughout history written words have been combined with visual imagery in forms which range from the explanatory to the enigmatic, from the constructive to the contradictory, from the iconic to the irreverent, and even from the zealous to the zany.

The thematic rather than strictly chronological organization of the materials in the following chapters is also designed to point out how the many various forms of word/picture combinations really cannot be placed in a linear, sequential development for "easy reading." In fact, word/picture combinations developed in the ancient world and medieval period often bear remarkable similarities to later and present day examples. Although the creation and reception of texts and images differs vastly from the pre–Gutenberg medieval era to postmodern cyberspace communications, general types and formats of word/picture combinations are repeated through the centuries, not so much in an evolutionary progression but in a consistent exploration of related forms. The comparison and grouping of these similar formats cuts across the centuries and the different cultures considered in the book, emphasizing shared modes and purposes.

A great deal of excellent scholarship has already been devoted to the development of appropriate descriptive terminology for the categorization of word/picture relationships in the history of art. Ranging from general studies to highly focused concentrations in specialized areas, much of this scholarship has involved the development of classification systems—categories into which the many divergent forms of word/picture relationships may be placed.

Some of these scholarly classification systems are highly detailed. For example, Dario Covi's masterful and extremely useful studies cataloguing inscriptions in fifteenth-century Florentine painting detail several major categories or formats in which written words can be found in Renaissance painting.[3] Covi's classification categories include: artists' signatures, titles, explanatory texts that aid in the identification of figures or subjects, and invocations, speeches, and exegetic inscriptions that aid in conveying the significance of the work of art or contribute to its interpretation. Within each of these larger categories, Covi also listed numerous subcategories. For example, inscriptions generally representing "speech" in paintings may be further subclassified into indications of dialogue taking place between the figures who are represented in the painting, or indications of speeches, declarations, or exhortations addressed to the viewer of the painting by a person or persons represented in the painting.

Some inscriptions in paintings, again using Covi's categories, serve to enhance the realistic appearance of an object or scene depicted the work. Such is the case, for example, when an inscription is placed on an object represented in the painting and the writing appears to be integral to the object depicted rather than "floating" on the picture's surface. Other inscriptions do appear to "float" on the surface of the picture; these types of inscriptions (often names, titles, captions, labels, signatures, and speeches) serve primarily to contribute information about the painting but are not necessarily designed as elements that contribute to any sense of pictorial realism.

This distinction between "internal" and "imposed" inscriptions formed the partial basis for the categorization systems developed by John Sparrow in his 1969 study, *Visible Words*.[4] Concentrating primarily on Renaissance and Baroque art, Sparrow defined "internal" inscriptions as those that appear to be integral to the scene and that can be read as elements of realism. "Imposed" inscriptions, in contrast, do not appear to be integral to the scene. They may provide useful information, but they may also be perceived as "alien and intrusive" elements.[5] Acknowledging, however, that the distinction between "internal" and "imposed" inscriptions "must not be pressed too hard,"[6] Sparrow further categorized inscriptions into two additional types: "labels" and "messages." "Labels" provide basic descriptive information (such as names, titles, and dates), whereas "messages" suggest deeper or more sophisticated meanings or references conveyed by the artist to the spectator. The information contained in "labels" is of a purely descriptive nature, whereas "message"-type inscriptions (such as quotes from scripture in religious works) provide added dimensions and deeper significance. Both "labels" and "messages," can, of course, appear as either "internal" or "imposed" elements in works of art.

Yet another categorization system for defining inscriptions in paintings was proposed by Mieczyslaw Wallis in 1973.[7] Describing all inscriptions in paintings as "semantic enclaves,"[8] Wallis identified four major formats/functions of inscriptions in paintings, plus several subcategories within these larger distinctions. Initially beginning his analysis with medieval art, Wallis's categories include (1) inscriptions that convey information (such as labels of names that identify figures or scenes); (2) inscriptions that indicate speech or dialogue (either between the figures in the painting, or statements addressed to the viewer from figures represented in the painting); (3) invocations (prayers addressed by spectators to holy figures in the painting); and (4) artist's statements "not connected with the subject matter of the painting"[9] (such as signatures). Using these fundamental four categories, Wallis expanded his discussion from medieval to twentieth century painting. He noted the decline, for example, of speech-type inscriptions in Renaissance and post–Renaissance art, and the apparent rise in popularity of undecipherable "pseudo-inscriptions" in twentieth-century art. Wallis's discussion also touched briefly on the use of inscriptions in Chinese painting and in ancient Egyptian art. He concluded that "in various epochs and in various culture areas, semantic enclaves in the form of inscriptions in paintings performed different functions of varying importance for the interpretation and response to the work of art."[10]

Apart from these general studies, much additional scholarship has been devoted to the study of particular types of inscriptions, such as artists' signatures[11]; the form and placement of signatures by specific artists[12]; and the categorization of inscriptions and signatures found on specific media such as ancient Greek pottery, Roman mosaics and wall paintings,[13] and Flemish Renaissance period tapestries[14] and manuscripts.[15] An interest in creating classification systems characterizes much of this focused scholarship as well. Artist's signatures on paintings, for example, may be classified as being on the margin or frame of the pictorial space (separated), included in the pictorial space but not integrated in the composition (floating), or included in the pictorial space as an integral/realistic element (integrated).[16] Painted or incised inscriptions on Greek pottery have been usefully classified into several different types as well: caption (names of figures represented and indications of speech), signatures (of potters and painters), mottoes, dedications, and owner's names.[17]

The development of classification systems for describing text/image relationships has also proven extremely attractive to and useful for scholars of modern art. For example, the *Word as Image* exhibition held at the Milwaukee Art Museum in 1990 gathered together a vast number of works created by American artists between 1960 and 1990, all of whom featured or included words in some forms.[18] The exhibition and accompanying catalogue impressively divided these divergent works, in many different media, into five major categories: (1) Words from the Environment (works that include signs, logos, and recognizable representations or fragments of everyday or popular culture); (2) Words as Sign and Structure (works that investigate the relationship of written and visual language systems and symbols); (3) Words as Juxtaposition and Association (works that evoke multiple associations and fluid readings); (4) Words as Narrative (works that include written language with a storytelling emphasis); and (5) Words as Socio-Political Commentary (works that use written language to challenge, criticize, or otherwise comment directly on current social or political issues).

The skillful, prescient, and thought-provoking classification system developed for the *Word as Image* exhibition functions very well indeed for the diversity of materials and messages conveyed by later twentieth-century and contemporary artists who include written language in their works. Similarly, Dario Covi's painstaking categorization of inscriptions in fifteenth-century Florentine paintings is impressively appropriate for the materials with which he was concerned. One would not find Covi's categories as useful and applicable to twentieth-century art, nor were they, of course, ever intended to be applied to modern art.

Most recently, John Dixon Hunt has proposed another impressive categorization system, describing four broad categories into which text/image relationships may be placed: explicitly, implicitly, additively, and collaboratively.[19] Examples of explicitly related words and images are those where pictures and writing appear in the same visual field. Implicit relationships are those in which the visual images invoke or depend upon written sources but do not include any actual text. Additive (or supplementary) relationships are those in which, for example, titles or other explanatory information or commentary are placed near to or even on the artwork. Finally, collaborative relationships involve cases where the texts and images depend so closely upon each other that meaning is lost with the removal of either written or pictorial elements.

However, a common dilemma facing all developers of systems to categorize text/image relationships is the fact that these can ultimately be rather "evanescent" distinctions, as John Sparrow noted.[20] The authors of the *Word as Image* exhibition catalogue were faced on many occasions with works of art that could have been placed into several of their different "frequently overlapping, but clearly definable categories of intent."[21] Scholars who have attempted to use previously developed category systems to approach different media and periods in the history of art have been frequently frustrated by the inapplicability if not irrelevance of many of the terms. For example, there is no "accepted pictorial vocabulary" for describing the appearance of the text scrolls that appear so frequently in medieval art, wrote Alison Flett.[22] In her impressive analysis of the functions and significance of text scrolls in several late medieval manuscripts, Flett found the classification systems of both Wallis and Sparrow to be useful to only a limited extent. Text scrolls can function as "labels" and as "messages" simultaneously, she demonstrated, and the "often multiple and overlapping functions of text and image in text scrolls" can place them into more than one or two categories at the same time.[23]

It is abundantly clear that word/picture relationships provide endless fascination and virtually endless possibilities for analysis. This present book is designed to offer a contribution to this extremely rich topic by approaching the material thematically in a series of chapters that investigate the various ways in which words in artworks may function.

Chapter One, "Pictures in Words/Words in Pictures: Working Together," concentrates upon word/picture combinations in which texts and images are coordinated in mutually elucidating manners and in which written language and visual imagery are utilized in conjunction with one another to clarify or contribute information. The first section of this chapter, "Pictures in Words," introduces a discussion of medieval manuscripts which display extremely creative and uniquely close associations between words and images. In the illustration and decoration of medieval manuscripts, words may be constructed of pictures, pictures may include words, letters may function as pictures, and pictures may be created of words. Especially in their apt coordination of letters and images, "historiated" initials in medieval manuscripts function both as text elements and as fields or containers for illustrations relevant to the text. They maintain their textual function as letters while also providing fields for visual imagery illustrating the text.

The second section of this chapter, "Words in Pictures in Words," offers a short discussion of labels and "speech scrolls" (indications of spoken dialogue) as found in medieval manuscripts, especially in connection with the illustrated letter form. In these cases, additional texts are included within enlarged letters that themselves also contain illustrated scenes. These added texts are designed to contribute more information about the images, whether in the form of identifying labels or speeches made by the figures illustrated. The final sections of this chapter, "Words in Pictures" and "Talking Art," further concentrate on complementary text/image combinations from a diversity of periods when written texts are added to works of art primarily to contribute to the viewer/reader understanding of the visual images. These artful combinations of words and pictures may indeed "speak" to the audience directly and provide clear directions as to the subject matter and the meaning of the work of art.

Contrasting with these relatively straightforward word/image combinations, Chapter Two: "Word/Picture Puzzles," considers examples where texts and pictures create puzzles, challenges, and perhaps even offer counter-messages for the audience. In these cases, viewers must engage in a process of careful decipherment to extract the less-than-immediately-obvious layers of meaning in these textual and visual combinations. The first section of this chapter, "Mixed Messages," concentrates on the pictorial device known as the *cartellino*, a little fictive piece of paper that usually bears artists' signatures, dates, and other textual information, frequently found in Renaissance and later paintings. *Cartellini* can appear to be both *on* and *in* paintings. They challenge the viewer's perception of the spatial relationships between their inscribed texts and the pictorial images they accompany. The second section of this chapter, "Hidden Texts," focuses on the snippets of texts found in the works of the nineteenth century American *trompe l'oeil* masters, such as Harnett, Peto, and Haberle, whose images often include illusionistic depictions of paper ephemera in various states of legibility. Although painstakingly rendered, the impression of clarity is frequently belied by the fragmentary nature of the texts displayed. Worn and torn labels, and folded and overlapping letters, business cards, and other scraps of paper create a sense of partially hidden information, or partially obscured clues as to the meanings of these works. This section also discusses the use of fragmentary texts in Cubist and later collage works and the manipulation of painted words and word fragments in the works of artists such as Stuart Davis. The word-laden paintings by Stuart Davis are often filled with optical puns and fragments of texts and frequently have clever alliterative titles. An understanding of Davis's own theories about art and language as well as his interest in creating "Word-Shapes" are critical to the decipherment of these pieces.

The second part of this chapter additionally considers examples of the creation of images superimposed on grids or patterns containing words. This form was popular in late antiquity and later notably employed by the ninth-century monastic author, Hrabanus Maurus. His intertextual image-poems are stunning correlations of verbal and visual information. The base texts retain their legibility while images and intertexts are woven through the compositions. Viewers/readers of these pieces engage in a process of discovery through increasingly deeper levels of understanding, gradually unearthing the hidden texts contained in these ingenious word/picture puzzles.

The third chapter, "Picture/Word Puzzles," contains two sections: "Crossed Purposes" and "Enigmas." The first section focuses on the intellectual and visual challenges posed by the language-art contradictions of twentieth-century artists such as René Magritte. Magritte's remarkable series of word pictures explores the ambiguous nature of written language and pictorial imagery, challenging the viewer with paradoxical combinations of images and written accompaniments, names, or labels. The disruption of traditional meanings and the vagueness and ambiguity of written and pictorial symbol systems are prevalent themes in his highly influential work.

The second section of this chapter begins with an exploration of the intriguing displays of cryptic and enigmatic letters and phrases in some late medieval manuscripts. Scattered or geometrically configured letters appear in the margins of several late medieval prayer books and the exact symbolism and meanings of many of these have yet to be fully understood. These mysterious letter combinations may be secret codes or formulae. They remain absolutely fascinating and thought-provoking word/picture enigmas.

This section also explores the artistic creation of "pseudoscripts"—forms that either attempt, with varying degrees of fidelity, to emulate foreign or ancient writing systems, or, forms that represent wholly invented artistic constructions. From the "pseudo-Arabic" writing commonly found in medieval and Renaissance art to the enigmatic cipher writing developed by modern artists such as Max Ernst, the potential for graphic markings to be read both as pictures and as words is discussed here.

Chapter Four, "Words as Images," considers the creation and display of texts alone, largely without any accompanying pictorial imagery. The language paintings of twentieth-century artists such as Edward Ruscha and Robert Indiana are discussed in the first section of this chapter, "Artful Words." The literary references, social commentary, and hard-edged word-images of Robert Indiana often contain terse statements with dramatic impact. In the word-based works of Edward Ruscha, words and phrases range from the banal and familiar to the ironic and witty to the disturbingly evocative. Ruscha's "imaged word"[24] works tend to present texts with no contexts; the significance, sense, or meaning of the words seems lost, in spite of their legibility.

"The Art of the Alphabet," section two of this chapter, considers images that are created of texts. These range from the artfully shaped texts of the ancient and medieval world to the shaped poetic constructions of the Renaissance and early modern eras to the calligrams of Guillaume Apollinaire and the diverse forms of modern "Concrete Poetry." The long-popular and related artful shaping of individual alphabet letters into embellished, symbolic, and pictorial forms is also discussed in this section.

The final section of this chapter, "Words About Words," covers the word-and-idea-based language art typical of Conceptual and other postmodern art movements. Artists such as John Baldessari and Joseph Kosuth are discussed. In many of their works, texts stand alone, without any accompanying pictorial imagery, largely serving to draw attention to language itself as a conventional symbol system. The exploration of language systems, and their use as powerful signifiers in social and cultural contexts, is also considered with the works of contemporary Chinese artist, Xu Bing. This discussion leads directly into the following chapter.

Chapter Five, "The Power of the Word," is organized into two sections: "Awful Words" and "Awe-Filled Words." The first section concentrates on works of art that use words to comment on the use or abuse of language in social and political contexts. A great many twentieth-century and contemporary artists, such as Glenn Ligon, Barbara Kruger, Gilbert & George, Martha Rosler, and Shirin Neshat, have created works that use words, often alone or in conjunction with visual imagery, to produce strident comments about, as well as challenges to, the ways in which language can be used to manipulate, control, dominate, and influence perceptions. The power of words—their use and abuse—is explored in diverse ways by these artists.

The second section of this chapter also concentrates on powerful words; however, attention is directed here to examples of sacred texts and reverential writing traditions in a variety of world cultures. Artfully presented words designed to inspire and to create awe are considered, ranging through a diversity of both western and Asian faith traditions. Special attention is given to Islamic calligraphic art and the development of extremely ornate and decorative examples of shaped texts and letters/words that form significant symbols. In some cases, the legibility of the texts appears subsumed to the larger desire of presenting the letters, words, and phrases as visual symbols of holiness rather than purely as conveyors of written information. The process of writing and the forms in which sacred texts appear have extreme ritual significance in Hebrew religious tradition as well. The enrichment and embellishment of sacred texts in Hebrew traditions as manifest in the intriguing form of micrographic writing is discussed in this section. This section concludes with a short discussion of the spiritual aspects of Chinese and Japanese calligraphy and several modern western artists (such as Brice Marden and Mark Tobey) who were deeply inspired by these forms and practices.

Because the presentation and association of images and texts is not restricted to two-dimensional media, Chapter Six, "Monumental and Moving Words," considers the relationship of words and visual texts to the physically three-dimensional arts such as sculpture and environmental art. The first section ("Monumental Words") concentrates on examples of three-dimensional illusionism—where words and texts (albeit rendered on flat surfaces) appear to have a monumental presence due either to their placement, scale, or clever and careful perspectival rendering. In these examples, ranging from Renaissance manuscripts to modern art, words and texts appear to be physically solid and contribute substantially to the often dramatic spatial illusionism of the works. The second section of this chapter, "Three-Dimensional Words," focuses upon the actual construction of three-dimensional texts and letters in sculptural forms, both large and smaller scale. In these cases, the words and texts often have a dramatic and substantial physical presence—whether as outdoor public monuments (such as represented by the works of Claes Oldenburg and Cossje van Bruggen) or installations involving "found" words derived from discarded commercial signage sources (such as by Jack Pierson). The final section of this chapter ("Moving Words") considers works of art, primarily large scale and contemporary, in which words and texts are presented as forms that appear, disappear, change shape, and fluctuate in ways that can, quite ironically, challenge any sense of textual solidity or authority. The large scale technological-based works by Jenny Holzer are especially considered here.

Although pictures and words, the visual and verbal modes of representation and perception, do differ significantly, the various word/image combinations represented by the examples considered throughout this study demonstrate the often very lively and always thought-provoking interplay between the visual and written modes of human communication. If a picture is worth a thousand words, then surely, words in pictures and words as pictures are fully deserving of our attention.

ONE

Pictures in Words/Words in Pictures: Working Together

Word/picture combinations—in which the images and writing work closely together to provide the same message—are among the most common forms of text/picture relationships throughout the history of art. This chapter discusses word/picture combinations in which texts and images are coordinated in mutually elucidating manners and in which written language and visual imagery are utilized in conjunction with each other to clarify or contribute additional information.

The possibilities for these mutually elucidating text/picture combinations are numerous and varied, ranging from decorated or illustrated letters in medieval manuscripts to explanatory captions, labels, and indications of spoken dialogue frequently found in examples from ancient to modern art, as well as works of art which include inscribed texts that directly address the viewer, offering information on how the viewers should understand and experience the work of art. All of these instances of words-in-art represent the coordination of the visual and the verbal to convey mutually informative messages and allow for the reader/viewer to glean information based on artful combinations of pictures and words.

Pictures in Words

The use of alphabet letters as vehicles for—or containers of—imagery certainly represents an extremely close combination of text and image. The pictorial embellishment of alphabetic letters has a very lengthy history indeed, with many marvelous examples ranging from the medieval to the modern period.[1] However, the decoration, enlargement, and use of letter forms for pictorial purposes may perhaps best be seen in the many intriguing word/picture combinations found in medieval and early Renaissance illustrated manuscripts. From approximately the eighth through the fifteenth centuries, this period certainly stands out as a time in which words and pictures had an especially close relationship. Medieval illuminated manuscripts, in all their variant forms, often exhibit extremely creative and uniquely close associations of words and images. Although it is clear that both text and pictures will necessarily play important roles in illustrated books generally, the relationship of texts and images was explored in an enormous variety of creative formats in medieval manuscripts. Apart from the illustrations (or miniatures) that may appear in medieval manuscripts as framed or unframed half-page, full-page or marginal scenes separated from but contributing to the texts, words may be constructed of pictures, pictures may include words, letters may function as letters as well as pictures, and pictures may be created of words.

Many terms have been developed by art historians to describe the different categories of text/picture relationships in medieval manuscripts generally.[2] Some highly specialized terminology has also been developed to define specific types of decorated letters within particular schools or regions or periods.[3] In widest terms, a useful distinction can be made between the "decoration" and "illustration" of medieval texts. Although these categories are by no means watertight, in the former group would fall such types of text decoration as enlarged letters that are constructed of "anthropomorphic," "zoomorphic," "zooanthropomorphic," "gymnastic," and "inhabited" letters, while the latter category would include "historiated" initials with illustrations of direct textual relevance.[4] In other words, the examples of medieval manuscript adornment where letters are constructed of clambering and intertwining beasts and human figures, of foliage filled with patterns, dragons, biting dogs, snakes, intertwined birds, and other such forms are often classified as "decorated"—due to the fact that the images lack direct or obvious textual relevance—whereas the enlarged initial letters with textually-relevant images or narrative stories depicted within them may be classified as "illustrated" or "historiated."

Both decorated and historiated letters are the most prevalent forms of medieval manuscript enrichment and are especially characteristic of manuscripts produced during the Romanesque and Gothic periods. Both formats seem to have developed gradually. Investigating exactly where and when these forms were first invented has provided copious material for scholarly discussion. Simple decorated letters with added flourishes or infilling designs can be found in late antique manuscripts as early as the fourth century, and early examples of illustrated letters containing scenes relevant to the text have been identified in early eighth-century manuscripts.[5]

The broad classification of letters as either decorated or historiated is a very traditional distinction, but by no means the only or clearest way to describe and categorize the varieties of forms. Scholars such as Carl Nordenfalk and Jonathan Alexander have also developed other sets of terminological distinctions for describing the formats of letters in medieval manuscripts. Nordenfalk used the terms "filling," "adding," and "substitution" to describe different treatments of letters.[6] "Filling" refers to cases where the widened outlines of a letter are filled in with decorative designs or color patterns. In these instances, the letter maintains its basic shape and the designs do not project beyond the confines of the letter itself. "Adding" refers to cases where various design elements such as scrolls, flourishes, and even recognizable images project from the letter or twine around and within the letter. Depending upon the extent and complexity of these added elements, it may be more or less challenging

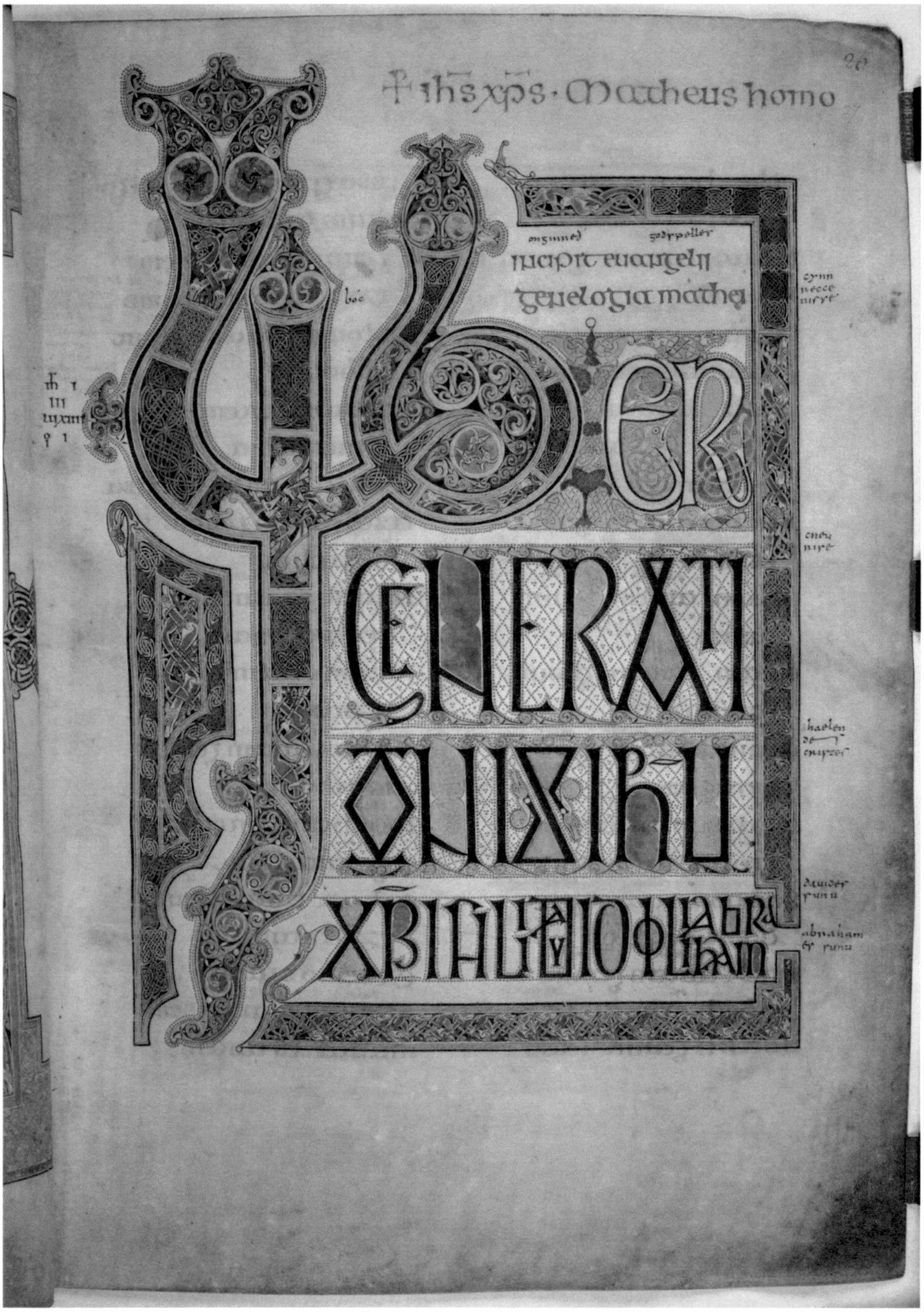

1. The Lindisfarne Gospels, ca. 700. Incipit page to St. Matthew's Gospel. London, British Library MS Cotton Nero D. IV, folio 27 (© British Library Board/Robana/Art Resource, New York).

for viewers to determine the underlying structure of the letter. Finally, Nordenfalk used the term "substitution" to refer to cases where the letter itself is actually made up of figures or decorative forms.

Jonathan Alexander developed yet another way of categorizing the many creative design possibilities explored by medieval manuscript artists. He made a distinction between what he termed "classical" and "anticlassical" formats.[7] In the former case, the clarity and legibility of the letter form remains critical. Decorative or figural additions do not overwhelm the fundamental readability of the letter. In contrast, according to Alexander, the "anticlassical" (medieval) tendency is to sacrifice the legibility of the letter form in favor of complex patterns, decoration, and symbolism. In these cases, it is often challenging for a viewer to make out exactly what letter is being represented.

We can explore the usefulness of some of this scholarly terminology by studying some specific examples. Both the Lindisfarne Gospels (London, British Library Cotton MS Nero D.iv) and the Drogo Sacramentary (Paris, Bibliothèque Nationale, MS Latin 9428) are extremely renowned and well-studied examples of beautifully illustrated and decorated manuscripts of the late seventh to early eighth centuries. The Lindisfarne Gospels is a cherished exemplar of Hiberno-Saxon art, and the Drogo Sacramentary, a Carolingian manuscript, represents a very early example of the use of historiated letters.[8]

The opening page (folio 27) to the Gospel of Saint Matthew in the Lindisfarne Gospels is a dazzling display of letters, colors, and patterns (illus. 1). Each one of the four gospels in this manuscript has a similarly lavish opening page. The manuscript also has a series of author portraits prefacing each gospel, full-page ornamental pages with cross motifs set in deeply patterned backgrounds, several other prefatory pages with lavishly decorated and enlarged texts, and a plethora of decorated initial letters throughout the entire text of the manuscript. The Matthew incipit (opening) page is a remarkable and complex example of the decorative vocabulary of interlace patterns, geometric devices, and bird and animal forms such as can be found in Celtic and Anglo-Saxon art generally, but is here brought to an extreme level of sophistication and complexity. Texts and images are combined here in a very closely knit relationship.

The three enlarged letters of the first word ("Liber") appear in grand scale on the left side of the page. These enlarged letters overlap each other in a sinuous pattern. Each letter is created of panels of sharply delineated interlace patterns interspersed with panels of interlace created of the abstracted bodies of animals and birds. Sections within the enlarged letter forms also include roundels with swirling patterns of spiral and comma shapes, elongated ovals, and trumpetlike shapes. Some of this decorative vocabulary derives from ancient Celtic art.[9] These patterns are also found on the framing panels that create a partial enclosure for this impressive composition. Beyond the opening letters of the word ("Liber") that expand to fill the top left of the page, the text continues on four additional lines of diminishing size. The lines, in full, read: "Liber generationis ih(es)u (christi) filii david filii abraham" (The book of the generation of Jesus Christ, the son of David, the son of Abraham). Many of these crisp and angular letters are infilled with colored panels, several terminate in or are enriched with bird or animal heads, all of the letters are additionally encircled with outlines of tiny red dots, and the two central lines of letters appear against a background of red dots arranged in a diapered pattern. Other nondecorated sections of script that appear on the page and in the margins further specify the subject matter of the text as "The Gospel of Matthew." The small marginal annotations are an Anglo-Saxon translation of the Latin, added later, in the tenth century. The Lindisfarne Gospels is traditionally dated to the late seventh century and was produced at the island monastery of Lindisfarne in northern England.

The extremely elaborate treatment of the letter forms in the Lindisfarne Gospels represents one of the highest achievements in medieval letter decoration.[10] The care and attention to detail shown in this work is truly remarkable. Each carefully crafted letter of even this one page of holy text, and especially the three opening letters on the page, is treated with meticulous attention. The letters have become frames for a display of sophisticated and intricate patterns, designs, and forms. The letters are full of movement and vivacity, including life forms such as birds and animals. The patterns serve to decorate and enrich the letters. The designs contribute to and demonstrate the textual significance of

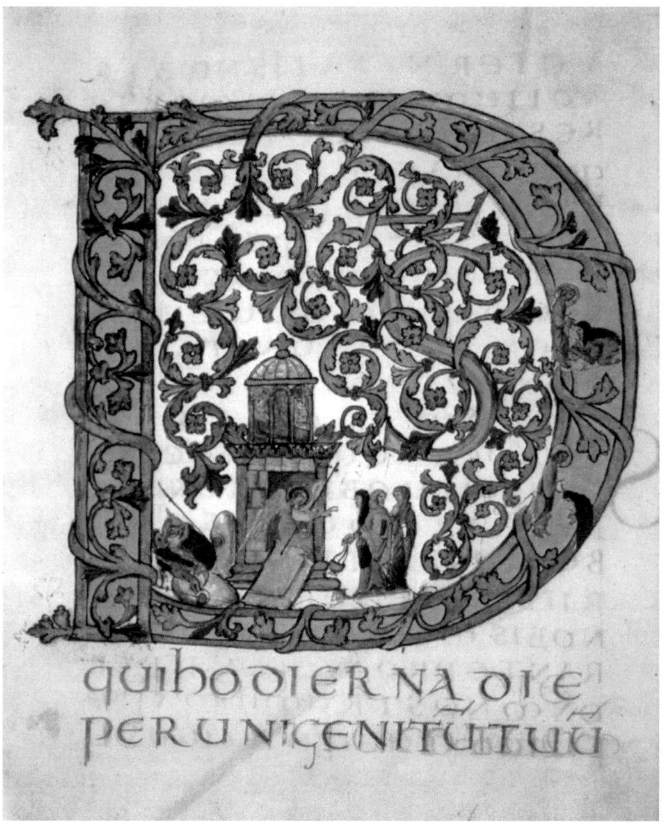

2. The Drogo Sacramentary, ca. 845–55. Large initial D with the Holy Women at the Tomb. Paris, Bibliothèque Nationale de France (BnF), MS Latin 9428, folio 58 (Scala/White Images/Art Resource, New York).

the letters but do not serve in any way to actually illustrate the topics contained in the texts.

In contrast, the enlarged initial letter "D" found on folio 58 of the slightly later Carolingian Drogo Sacramentary shows a different approach to letter decoration (illus. 2). This liturgical manuscript was created ca. 840–50 for a son of Charlemagne, Drogo, who served as Bishop of Metz from 844. It contains the prayers recited by the priest during the celebration of Mass.[11] In many instances in this manuscript, the opening letters and words of these liturgical sections are enriched with enlarged decorated letters, such as the "D" initial for the prayers on Easter Sunday. The letter itself is made up of panels enriched with flowing golden vine scrolls that twist and twine sinuously around the green panels of the letter shape. These flowing scrolls spill into and fill up the internal space of the letter as well. The letter "S" and a horizontal abbreviation mark also appear within the inside space of the letter; these are similarly entwined in golden scrolls. These two letters represent the word "DS" ("Deus," God) and the text, written in gold, continues below the enlarged letters. Of signal importance, however, is the presence of small figural narrative scenes both within the letter and within the bow of the letter. Enframed within the lower section of the letter is an illustration of the Three Marys visiting the empty tomb of Jesus (Mark 16:1–7.) The tomb itself is represented as a tall, narrow, domed architectural structure. A cross-bearing angel appears at the opened entrance to the tomb gesturing towards the three women on the right side. The sleeping soldiers appear to the left of the tomb. Additionally, two small figural vignettes appear in the curved bow of the letter "D." These illustrate related scenes derived from the gospels of Mark and Matthew: Christ and Mary Magdalene, and Christ worshipped by the two Marys. Clearly, all of these figural scenes serve to narrate episodes directly relevant to the Easter Sunday services, thus their presence relates intimately to the subject matter of the text and liturgy. There are a significant number of other historiated initials in the Drogo Sacramentary making this manuscript a rare and early instance of the developed employment of textually relevant narrative scenes within enlarged letters.

The textual relevance of motifs and scenes included in or around a letter is what differentiates a decorated letter from an historiated letter. Historiated letters contribute pictorial information to visualize the text, whereas decorated letters enrich the text but generally do not provide complementary pictorial or narrative information.

This basic distinction (decorated versus historiated) is useful, however, it also requires extremely careful scrutiny of both text and pictures to determine whether a letter should be described as purely decorative or as an example of text illustration.[12] There are many instances in medieval manuscript illustration where letters are created of, or filled with, forms, figures, scenes, and episodes that might not immediately appear to be textually relevant but actually can be connected in some general or more specific ways with the textual content, providing, for instance a "textually related allegory."[13] Unraveling the possible meanings of the pictorial subjects in these instances has provided much lively fodder for scholarly discussion indeed.

For example, the famous scenes of monastic life and illustrations of combating humans and animals that appear in the early twelfth-century *Moralia in Job* manuscripts from Cîteaux (Dijon, Bibliothèque Municipale MSS 170–173) have been subject to much scrutiny, especially by scholars eager to find specific textual connections and meanings in these remarkable scenes.[14] The interpretative challenge here (and in many other instances as well) seems to be that the illustrated initials are not so much directly literal "illustrations" of Saint Gregory's lengthy and complex commentary on the biblical book of Job, but rather may be seen as "contemporary expressions of concerns discussed in the text and made in response to—rather than in illustration of—its literality or sense."[15] Thus, the numerous initials showing scenes of struggle and/or violent combat between human figures and threatening beasts (especially dragons) may, in some cases, directly reflect textual references to dragons as symbols of evil, or may serve as more general reflections of the themes of spiritual struggle against evil and temptations, or the trials and triumphs of the good over the forces of evil.

The several other initials in these manuscripts that depict scenes of monastic life—monks splitting a log, harvesting grain, folding cloth, felling a tree, and so forth—have long impressed modern viewers by their clever and charming compositions. These seem clearly to be illustrations of daily life and monastic agricultural labors, including what seem to be touches of whimsy and humor as well. For example, the enlarged initial "I" that appears on folio 41 in the third of these volumes (Dijon, Bibliothèque Municipale MS 173) is created of a huge leafy tree that extends the entire length of the left side of the page (illus. 3). It functions as the opening letter for the text section (Book 21) and also as a vehicle for pictorial vignettes. Two figures are vigorously and busily at work chopping away at the tree. One man has climbed up to the top of the tree and is cutting branches, while the other figure (clearly a monastic, due to his robe and tonsure) is at work chopping down the tree at the base. The upper figure is obviously in a somewhat precarious position should the tree be felled while he is still at work in the upper branches.

Modern viewers of this image might find the apparent obliviousness of each of the two hardworking figures to the labors of the other to be rather amusing. Surely the monk who is chopping down the tree should be aware that someone else is at work cutting away at the upper branches, and surely the figure perched up in the tree should be aware that the tree is being felled. It might be possible to read any number of meanings into this pictorial story and indeed into many other of the illustrations of monastic life that appear in these particular manuscripts, but, as has been pointed out, the section of the text that this initial introduces does not concern "forestry."[16] Rather, Book 21 of Gregory's *Moralia* is concerned with the avoidance of temptation and the importance of anticipating sources of temptation. The monk at the bottom, thusly, may be seen as cutting away at the base of the tree of temptation, whereas the layperson (poised up in the tree's branches) is not as effective at so doing.[17] This is decidedly not a literal illustration of the text section but might be seen as capturing the sense and meaning of the text via a creative pictorial interpretation.

It is important to remember that "as readers in a long-established print culture, we tend to see the pictorial designs in medieval manuscript pages either as 'decorative' or as illustrations of the literal sense of the words."[18] This distinction between decoration and illustration can not always be neatly applied. For example, the colorful letters constructed of fish and birds in several Merovingian religious manuscripts are not simply decorative but are imbued with important Christian symbolism via the choice of the creatures used to construct the letters. Both fish—as symbols for Christ—and birds—as symbols for heaven/paradise—feature frequently in Christian art. Thus, although the bird and fish motifs may not directly tell a specific story as narrated in the text, their choice is far from arbitrary. They add important symbolic dimensions when chosen to enrich sacred Christian texts.

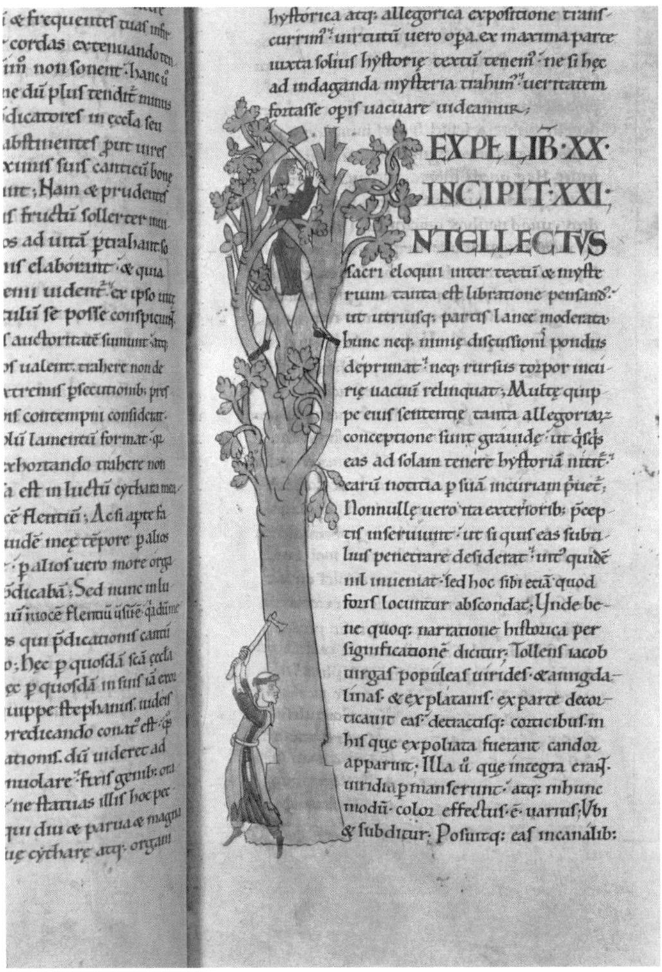

3. St. Gregory's Moralia in Job, early 12th century. Tree cutting scene. Dijon, France, Bibliothèque Municipale MS 173, folio 41 (Snark/Art Resource, New York).

Purposeful symbolism may also be ascribed to the letters found in medieval manuscripts that are created of flowing, vegetal, and floral scroll forms that appear to be moving, growing and exhibiting a "natural, presence-bearing trace."[19] Letters that are created of vegetation—whether stylized or more naturalistic—make specific reference to the world of nature in a way that geometric patterns or abstract designs do not. The use of motifs from the natural world in the embellishment of medieval letters may be far from purely ornamental but may serve to give the letter forms a sense of life and physical presence as well. Perhaps this represents "an attempt to compensate for the dissatisfying lack of presence perceived in ordinary alphabetic writing by integrating (or reintegrating) pictorial design into alphabetic inscription."[20] Although there may be no direct textual purpose or relevance of the vegetal forms frequently used to create elaborated letters in medieval manuscripts, the sense of life and physicality implied by these growing forms may serve to give life to the letters and to the text. To describe these letter forms as purely ornamental—by implication, meaningless—may miss the potent level of symbolic meaning these life-filled forms carry. As well, the dense vegetation that frequently entwines figures and animals in inhabited initials might also be interpreted as "the forces of nature" enmeshing "frail humanity striving to free themselves from the world of sensual temptation that besets their bodily existence."[21] Again, the possible text-image relationships are multitudinous.

Words in Pictures in Words

Continuing the discussion, for now, of medieval manuscripts and their use of letters as containers for—or vehicles of—pictorial imagery, these text/image relationships in medieval manuscripts are often further enhanced and complicated by the inclusion of additional texts contained within the letter forms. In these cases, the enlarged initials function not only as important textual components, as frames for pictorial imagery, but as containers for additional texts as well. These additional texts may include captions or labels identifying the figures or scenes depicted within the letter, or other texts which contribute to the pictorial images or themes contained within the letter. Examples of these formats range from the relatively straightforward (for instance, when the names of figures depicted within the letter are inscribed next to them) to far more complex examples when longer texts are included, such as indications of dialogue or other textual excerpts from a variety of sources.

Particularly intriguing examples of such text-within-image-within-text combinations appear especially in later Gothic manuscript illumination. The extremely lavishly illuminated early fourteenth-century English Tickhill Psalter (New York Public Library Spencer Collection MS 26) can serve here as an excellent example of this textual/pictorial complexity.[22] The manuscript is enriched with a remarkable series of nearly full-page historiated initials each containing numerous scenes, and, in many cases, additional texts as well. For example, on folio 26v, the enlarged letter "D" has expanded to occupy a major portion of the page and is filled with a series of narrative scenes from the lives of David and Solomon as well as small sections of text (illus. 4). The characters in all four of the pictorial vignettes included in the enlarged letter, as well as in the additional marginal scenes below, are identified by inscriptions on banners above their heads: Jonathon, David, Saul, etc. Portions of their conversations also appear on speech scrolls that issue from their mouths or that they hold in their hands. These elegantly curling speech scrolls and the captions identifying the figures serve nicely to add further written narrative elements and information to the pictures that are included in the margins and inside the enlarged historiated letter. The curling speech scrolls and banners mirror the elegant linear patterns and vegetal scrolls that surround and create the enlarged letter so that the enlarged letter, the frames of the pictorial vignettes within the letter, the scrolling forms that extend from the letter, and the text scrolls themselves are all united in a flowing and complex interplay of text and image.

The informative writing (captions and speech scrolls) found on this page of the Tickhill Psalter may also more precisely be described as representing two different sorts of additional textual information. The inscriptions floating on banners above the heads of the figures serve to identify the characters, whereas the curling speech scrolls indicate fragments of dialogue between the figures represented. These statements are actually quotes extracted from the scriptural accounts of the lives of Saul, David, and Solomon, not texts from Psalm 26 which this page introduces in the psalter manuscript. So, in this case, texts have been carefully excerpted from other sources (biblical books and

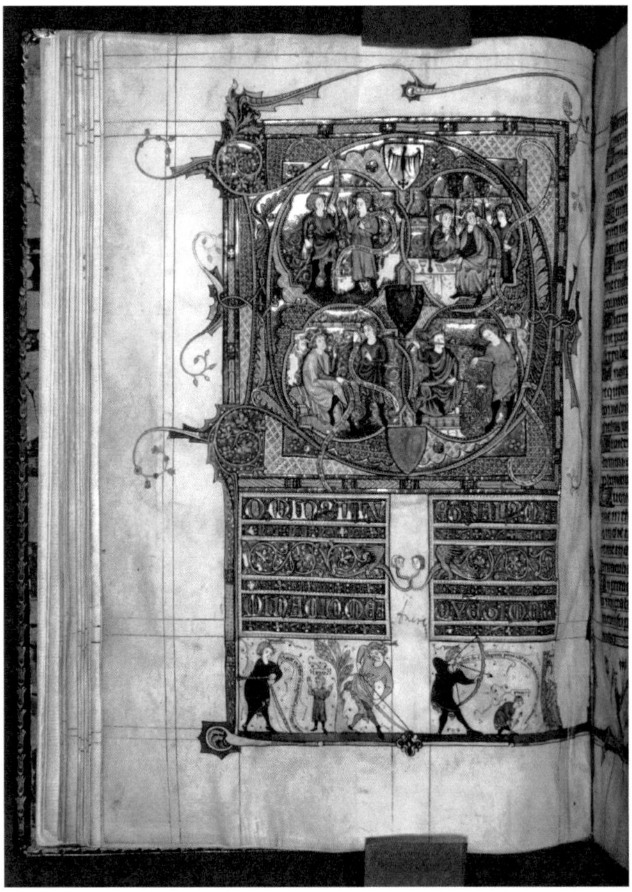

4. The Tickhill Psalter, ca. 1310. Full-page initial D of Psalm 26. The New York Public Library Spencer MS 26, folio 26v (Spencer Collection, The New York Public Library, Astor, Lenox and Tilden Foundations).

commentaries) and appropriately inserted here to represent portions of dialogue between the characters in the illustration.

Such words-in-pictures, labels, speech scrolls and other types of inscriptions occur frequently in medieval art in all media.[23] The customarily didactic and inspirational purposes of medieval art make it very much an art of the text, often quite literally. Texts abound in medieval art which has been described as "an art in which the bond with language determines some pictorial features... Founded on texts, the image admits the written word as a concrete component free to rotate in the two dimensions of the picture plane."[24]

Copious other examples could be cited of illuminated letters in medieval manuscripts that simultaneously serve as text elements and containers for pictures and additional words (captions, inscriptions, and speech scrolls). The complexity of some of these forms is truly remarkable. The viewer often receives the impression of a whole microcosm of scenes and texts enclosed within a macrocosmic letter. No wonder it has often been pointed out that "nowhere was the freedom of formal invention more striking than in the development of illuminated letters."[25]

Words in Pictures

In addition to the manuscript forms cited above, words in medieval art may also range from, for example, the basic and abbreviated Latin "running commentary" identifying people and events in The Bayeux Tapestry's ca. 1080 pictorial narration of the Norman Conquest of England (illus. 5) to the sophisticated and complex inscriptions elucidating the typological programs found on the enamels of the late twelfth-century Klosterneuburg Altarpiece of Nicholas of Verdun (illus. 6).

The Bayeux Tapestry, one of the most well-studied monuments of medieval art, consists of multiple strips of linen sewn together to form a 230-foot long, 18-inch high cloth panel onto which was embroidered, with colored wool threads, a detailed pictorial account of the events leading up to the Norman Conquest of England concluding with the Battle of Hastings.[26] It is a long story, with numerous episodes and hundreds of figures depicted. The story unfolds sequentially and clearly with the key players (such as William and Harold) repeated numerous times in continuous narrative format. An embroidered inscription runs, irregularly, primarily along the top of the central section, in close proximity to the events described, and is "presented for the most part in short declarative sentences or demonstrative affirmations."[27] The letters are about an inch high, thus quite legible, and the Latin is fairly simple. The inscriptions provide a very basic summary of the main events, such as: Here Harold Sailed the Sea; Here William came to Bayeux where Harold took an oath to Duke William; Here Duke Harold returned to English soil; Here sits Harold, King of the English; Here the soldiers went out from Hastings and came to battle

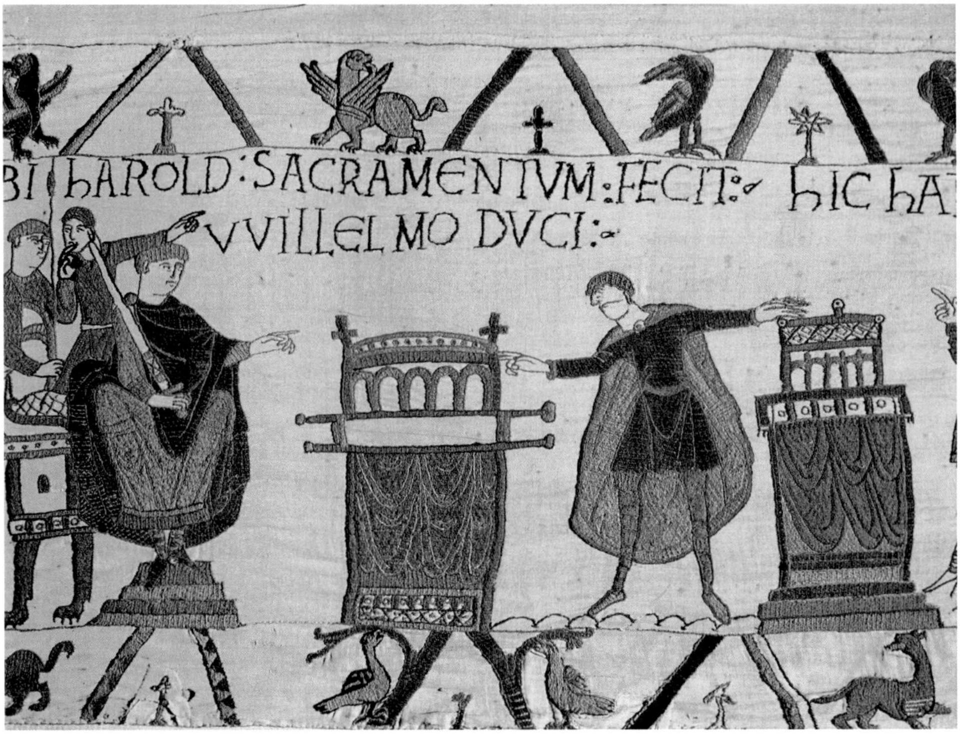

5. The Bayeux Tapestry, late 11th century. Detail: Harold swears fealty to William, Duke of Normandy. Musée de la Tapisserie, Bayeux, France (Erich Lessing/Art Resource, New York).

against King Harold; Here English and French fell together in battle; Here King Harold was killed.

Assuredly, the audience for whom the tapestry was initially created would have been well familiar with the dramatic events and the key players, thus the inscriptions serve to reinforce the visual images, providing a "stripped down" version of the visual narrative.[28] The somewhat irregular placement of the inscriptions has led some scholars to the suggestion that "although basically contemporary with the main work" they may have been "an after-thought, added to strengthen or clarify the visual narrative."[29] Others believe that the inscriptions were "an original and integral part of the tapestry's design."[30] In any case, the inscriptions certainly work in tandem with the imagery, effectively accomplishing, in a total of about 378 words (many of them the repeated names of the key figures) a much-abbreviated written summary of the far more detailed pictorial narrative. The inscriptions, in other words, do not describe or comment upon all of the many scenes shown in the embroidery but provide just enough information for viewers/readers to follow the basic story line.

For medieval audience members who were literate in Latin, the brief inscriptions would have been helpful supplements to the visual narrative, whereas for other medieval viewers who were not versed in Latin (presumably the majority) the presence of the inscriptions might have contributed to the general sense of the work's importance, but were not really required in order to follow the visual narrative. As with many other examples of medieval monumental art enriched with inscriptions (discussed later in this chapter), it is generally thought that the writing was indeed legible to some audience members, and those people who were able to read the texts may have assisted those who could not by reading the descriptions aloud. In the case of the Bayeux Tapestry, a dramatic account of an event of great political significance for both Normans and Anglo-Saxons, the work doubtless served as a vehicle for telling and retelling the story. Thus, both the texts and pictures surely provided the basis for oral performance in which "the reader or interlocutor would have been allowed, even encouraged, to improvise in public, stimulated by the vivid pictures, by his memory, and by the audience's enthusiasm."[31]

Although the specific setting in which the Bayeux Tapestry was originally displayed (or the location for which it was originally intended) remains tantalizingly unknown, a full viewing of a work of this monumental size involves a significant time commitment on the part of the audience, whether in reading or translating the inscriptions, viewing the images, or hearing and discussing the story. So in that sense, the words and the pictures were here designed to work together, each providing contributing components in the visual/written/oral narration. While some of the tapestry's inscriptions remain perplexing (such as the labeling of some figures who play only very brief roles in the pictorial narrative but whose significance may well have been understood by the medieval audience), for the most part the inscriptions are short, clear, and simple descriptions of the visual narrative.

There are far more images than words on the Bayeux Tapestry. Other medieval works of art are enriched with a far greater number of texts—texts that are also designed to increase understanding of the visual materials presented. Among such examples of text-dense medieval art, the late twelfth-century Klosterneuburg Altarpiece certainly stands out.[32]

The Klosterneuburg Altarpiece took its present form in the 1330s when it was remodeled from its original shape as a pulpit. Designed for the Augustinian Canons of Klosterneuburg abbey by the eminent metalworker, Nicholas of Verdun, in the late twelfth century, this remarkable work of art consists of multiple panels of enamel plaques arranged in three horizontal registers according to a complex typological scheme of textual and visual connections between events in the life of Christ (middle register, labeled *sub gracia*), and events from the Old Testament/Hebrew scriptures before (top register, labeled *ante legem*) and after (bottom register, labeled *sub lege*) the revelation of the law to the prophet Moses. Inscriptions on each of the plaques identify the scenes and their significance; further inscriptions tell the name of the artist, date of completion, and the name of the patron who supervised the fourteenth-century remodeling. Although an interest in the textual and pictorial paralleling of events and symbols from the Hebrew and Christian scriptures had long featured in previous medieval Christian art and theological writings, the Klosterneuburg Altarpiece is by far "the most extensive typological programme to have survived from the twelfth century."[33] The choice of texts and scenes is presumed to have been directed by a learned patron/supervisor from among the Klosterneuburg Augustinians who was well versed in contemporary typological writings. The audience for whom this work was intended would have been literate in Latin and doubtless well familiar with the biblical and liturgical foundations and sources for many of the inscriptions.

Although the theological complexity of the densely inscription-laden Klosterneuburg Altarpiece differs significantly from the Bayeux Tapestry with its succinct inscriptions describing the basic episodes shown in the pictorial narrative, in both cases the words included in the pictures are designed to explain and enhance the meaning of the visual presentation, just as historiated letters, discussed above, visually contribute to the texts they illustrate and accompany. Words in art often function this way—to give more information, to assist the viewer with reading the visual story, to identify what is shown, and sometimes to conjure up additional levels of meaning. These are the type of inscriptions in art that scholars such as Mieczyslaw Wallis (see

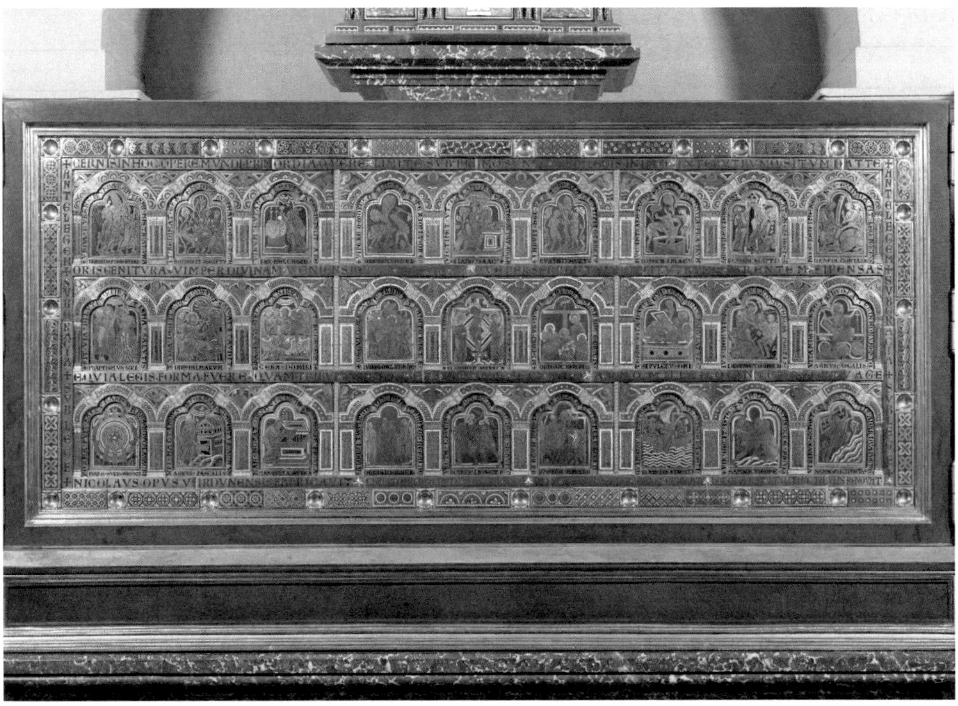

6. Nicholas of Verdun, the Klosterneuburg Altarpiece, ca. 1180. Sammlungen des Stiftes, Klosterneuburg, Austria (Erich Lessing/Art Resource, New York).

introduction) termed "information-conveying inscriptions."[34] Such inscriptions may serve to succinctly identify the figures or scenes depicted and/or may provide additional adjectives and explanations emphasizing certain aspects of the figures, scenes, or events pictorially narrated.

Further examples could include the labels identifying authors (such as the Four Evangelists) that appear often in medieval manuscripts and other media, frequently in conjunction with the traditional pictorial symbols (man/Matthew, lion/Mark, ox/Luke, and eagle/John) used to identify these figures. The fragments of text that frequently are shown on open books of these same and other authors may also serve as identifiers. When the texts are legible, the opening words of an Evangelist's gospel, for example, the texts can also serve to identify the figure in question.

Although the art of the Middle Ages may be especially "wordy," written texts designed to increase pictorial legibility appear in art of many time periods. Postmedieval art is also replete with examples of texts-in-pictures; Renaissance paintings especially often have inscriptions "strewn lavishly over [their] surfaces."[35] Titles or other texts identifying the subject matter often occur in Renaissance art works. For example, the classically styled Latin inscriptions on the painted tomb monument in Paolo Uccello's 1436 fresco of *Sir John Hawkwood* in Florence's Basilica di Santa Maria del Fiore cathedral identify the subject as an important English military figure active in the service of Florence in the late fourteenth century (illus. 7).[36]

One of Uccello's earliest dated and authenticated works, the fresco depicts the *condottiero* (soldier of fortune, mercenary) John Hawkwood, holding a baton, astride a parade horse posed atop a cenotaph or tomb monument supported by a study pedestal. The work is designed to look as if it were a bronze (or painted marble) statue supported on a substantial base. Indeed, the fresco is a painted substitute for a monumental sculptured tomb that Hawkwood had been promised before his death in 1394.[37] The original commission appears to have been for a tomb monument containing sculptural relief with painted elements, but by the time Uccello was called to recreate this work, a fresco in imitation of sculpture was desired by the commissioners. Uccello's fresco is primarily painted in *terra verde* (literally, green earth) on a deep red background and definitely gives the appearance of a monumental work in sculpture.

Uccello's lifelong fascination with perspective and *trompe l'oeil* illusionism are extremely well demonstrated here as well as his use of multiple perspectival viewpoints. The classically styled Latin inscription on the cenotaph identifies the subject as *John Hawkwood, British knight, most prudent leader of his age and most expert in the art of war*. The wording of the inscription is taken from the ancient classical eulogy for the Roman general Quintius Fabius Maximus (third century BCE), a literary reference well known to Renaissance humanist-scholars and here adeptly borrowed for a contemporary, classically inspired composition.[38]

Uccello's fresco also includes an inscription, lower down on the pedestal, identifying himself as the artist: *Pavli Vgielli Opvs*.[39] Although inscriptions naming artists appear frequently in Renaissance and later art, of course, there are plenty of examples of pre-Renaissance work with artists' "signatures" as well. Uccello's signature on the Hawkwood fresco is designed to look as if it is carved into the illusionistic pedestal supporting the monumental *trompe l'oeil* equestrian statue. The classical style lettering here reflects the Renaissance revival of ancient forms generally, and numerous other Renaissance paintings include depictions of antique-looking sculpture and architectural fragments with inscriptions emulating or copying classical writing styles.[40]

The interest in classical palaeography was, after all, a hallmark of Renaissance humanistic studies and this interest is well demonstrated in copious other examples of art works from the period that include "antique" inscriptions as pictorial elements designed to work within the context of the scenes depicted. Domenico Ghirlandaio's 1485 *Nativity and Adoration of the Shepherds* altarpiece (Florence, Santa Trinità, Sassetti Chapel) is yet another fine example of a Renaissance painting filled with antique references ranging from the triumphal arch shown in the background—which includes an inscription of Pompey the Great—to the classical sarcophagus in the foreground bearing an inscription referring to an ancient Roman auger (diviner) named Fulvio (illus. 8). Although fully convincing in their classical epigraphy, these inscriptions are actually Renaissance inventions of the eminent fifteenth-century Florentine humanist, Bartolomeo Fonzio (or Bartolomaeus Fontius) who was a lifelong friend of Francesco Sassetti (the patron of the chapel). Both Sassetti and Fonzio, as many other well-

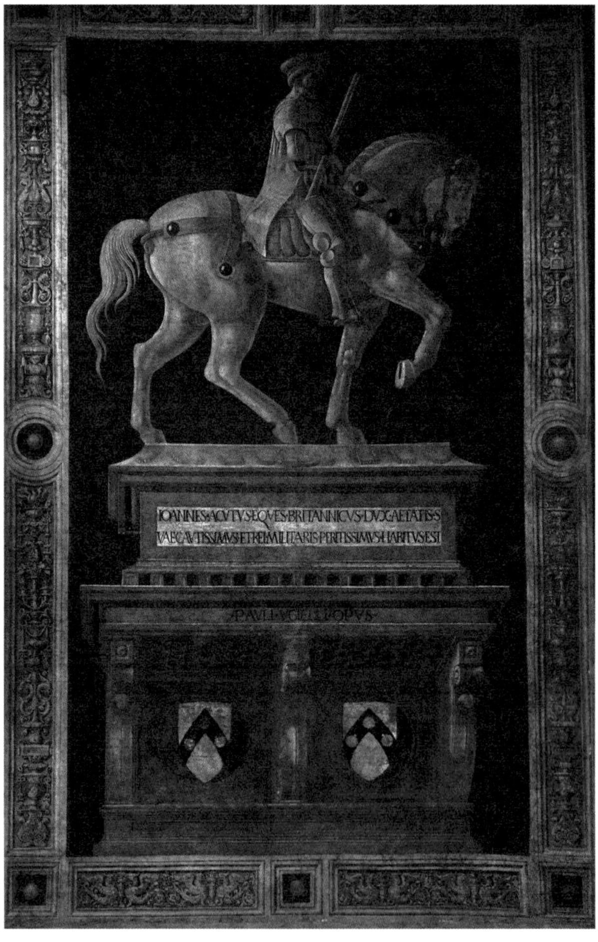

7. Paolo Uccello, *Sir John Hawkwood*, 1436. Florence, Italy, Duomo (Alfredo Dagli Orti/The Art Archive at Art Resource, New York).

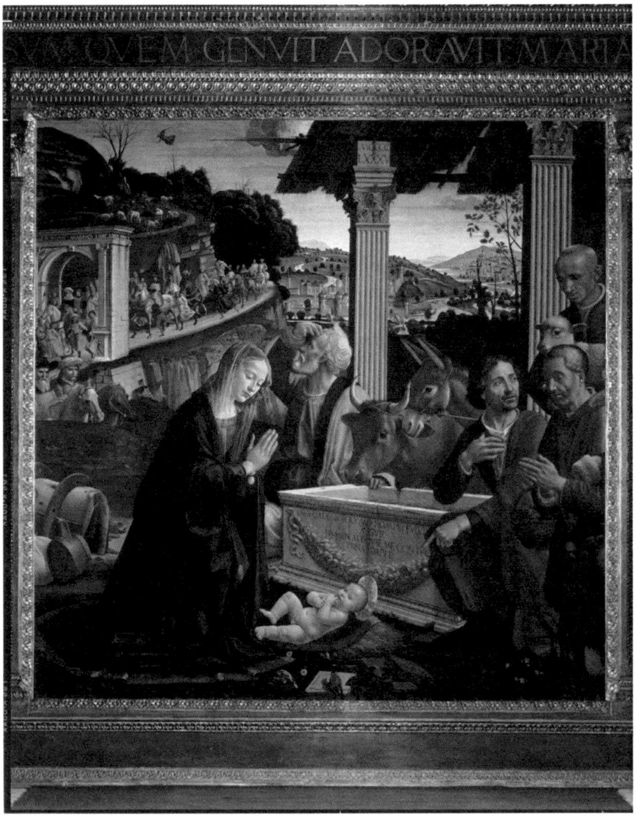

8. Domenico Ghirlandaio, *Adoration of the Shepherds*, ca. 1482–85. Florence, Italy, Santa Trinità (Scala/Art Resource, New York).

educated Italians of the time, were deeply interested in all things antique: numismatics, inscriptions, and classical archaeological sites. The classical-style inscriptions invented by Fonzio for this Christian altarpiece also bespeak a larger humanistic interest in correlating ancient and Christian history and themes. The inscription on the triumphal arch in the background (under which the procession of the Magi passes) references the Jewish high priest Hircanus and the Roman general Pompey who conquered Jerusalem, "the supposition being that … Hircanus erected the monument in gratitude to Pompey, who after the conquest reinstated him in office."[41] The inscription on the sarcophagus, placed behind the infant Jesus in the foreground of the painting, conveys "the message that the sarcophagus originally held the bones of a certain auger, Fulvio, who died during Pompey's siege of Jerusalem and predicted that his tomb would eventually serve a new deity."[42] Thus, "if the first inscription on the picture indicated the triumph of paganism over Judaism, the second signifies the victory of Christianity over the heathen world."[43] Although extremely erudite in their invention and references, these inscriptions serve to bring a great depth of meaning to "the full content of the miracle of the Nativity as Sassetti and Fontius conceived it."[44] Classical and Christian references are here mingled in typically Renaissance fashion and the classical-style inscriptions lend a scholarly aura of antiquity to the work.

Ghirlandaio's panel also includes an inscription identifying the subject matter (on the frame) and the date of 1485, which is "carved" in Roman numerals above one of the Corinthian-style piers supporting the "manger" in this Nativity scene. This bit of numeral information, although meant to appear as an internal element in the scene, really functions (like an artist's signature) to provide imposed or external information about the piece.[45] In other words, unlike the classical-style inscriptions (on the triumphal arch and sarcophagus depicted in the panel) that work within the painting as internal pictorial elements, the 1485 date inscription functions as an external element providing a contemporary piece of information—specifying the late fifteenth-century date for the work.

All in all, these types of inscriptions (identifying artist or date or subject matter or contributing additional critical information or references) function in much the same way as the labels and captions previously discussed in medieval art. These inscriptions serve to provide information in written form about the visual depictions. The additional information provided by the speech scroll and text scroll forms noted in medieval art can be seen in numerous postmedieval examples as well. Angels, prophets, patriarchs, and various holy figures holding scrolls containing, for example, biblical quotes are frequent in both medieval and Renaissance art. A variety of appropriate written texts may be included. In some cases, these inscriptions may be intended to be understood as statements made by the figure portrayed in the scene—either texts addressed to other figures in the composition—or to the audience viewing the image. This type of presentation of texts from various sources within paintings or other works of art serves to amplify the "reading" of the visual narrative by providing written information relevant to the visual images.

Cartouches, banderoles, inscriptions, speech scrolls, and variations on these themes occur throughout the history of art in many diverse manifestations. Jacques-Louis David's famous 1793 painted tribute to the French revolutionary journalist, Jean-Paul Marat (*Death of Marat*, or *Marat à son Dernier Soupir*—"Marat Breathing his Last Breath"—as David himself described the painting) includes the artist's signature, the date (*l'an deux*), and the inscription "à Marat" on the wooden box in the foreground of this murder scene (illus. 9).[46] "An ex-voto, the painting offers itself to the dead man, to his memory. In so doing, however, the painting calls attention to itself as though making sure we understand it devotes itself to the task of taking us to Marat. It says, 'this is a painting '*à* Marat,' 'for,' 'to' or 'toward' Marat, on the way to him, a painting that makes us see Marat and thereby gives Marat the gift of being seen."[47] The brevity of the inscriptions here accords with and contributes to the gravity of the tragic scene depicted in this work. In addition, Marat is shown still grasping the letter of introduction from his murderess, Charlotte Corday. Most of the text of this letter is legible, including the date, and these details serve to add further written contextual information to the dramatic scene. Further written information appears on the partly legible text of the letter Marat was composing and the partly folded *assignat* (a piece of Revolutionary-era paper money) that are positioned on the wooden box.[48] The letter and *assignat* were intended to be sent to a widowed mother of five children whose husband had died "defending his country."[49]

David accepted the commission to produce this work the day after the murder

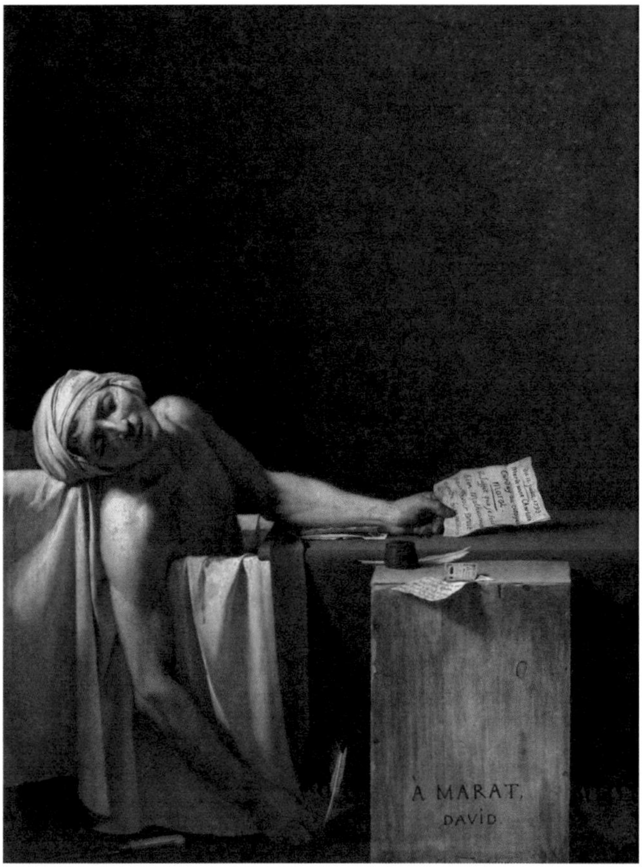

9. Jacques Louis David, *The Death of Marat*, 1793. Brussels, Belgium, Musée Royal des Beaux Arts (The Art Archive at Art Resource, New York).

took place and also orchestrated the elaborate funerary arrangements for Marat including the public viewing of the body (posed as in the painting) and the grand procession before Marat's entombment. Marat was so widely admired and hailed as a Revolutionary hero that several copies of this iconic work were subsequently commissioned from David himself and his pupils. One of these versions does not include any inscriptions on the wooden box in the foreground of the painting whereas others (such as the Louvre copy) include a more lengthy inscription: *N'ayant pu me corrompre ils m'ont assassiné* (Unable to corrupt me, they murdered me). In this case, the inscription functions not only as a dedication to Marat but also as a sort of posthumous statement from the murdered figure himself.

In a far more colorful and cheerful manner, the twentieth-century French artist Fernand Léger expressed his deep admiration for Jacques-Louis David by including an inscription in his 1948–49 painting *Les Loisirs* (Paris: Musée National d'Art Moderne, Centre Georges Pompidou) (illus. 10, in color insert). The reclining female figure in the foreground of this work holds a scroll/newspaper inscribed: *Hommage à Louis David.* Although Léger produced several versions of this image, the inscription included in the 1948–49 piece specifically contributes additional information conveyed from the artist to the viewer that adds to the visual "reading" of the work, especially for visually literate viewers able to make the connection to David's oeuvre. Indeed, the reclining woman in the foreground of this colorful painting of people enjoying peaceful and pleasurable leisure time is posed very much like the figure of

Marat in David's earlier work and has been described as "Léger's complicitous wink at David."[50] This work functions as Léger's tribute to David as David's painting was a tribute to Marat. Léger often spoke of his deep regard for David's directness and "spareness." In this work, he "rendered a tribute to David ... as the Revolution's bard, the poet of the Empire ... [and to] the clarity and architectural structure of his work."[51]

Informative inscriptions of this sort, by making reference to and conjuring up associations with past art, might be said to offer "viewing directions" to the audience. The reference to "Louis David" in this piece inspires a quite different "reading" than would be the case if the inscription were not included (as is the case with Léger's inscriptionless versions of the image).[52]

Talking Art

Indeed, many levels of complexity may be noted in inscriptions included in artworks that offer such "viewing directions" to the audience. The inscriptions that abound in medieval architectural sculpture, for example on church portals, often "speak" directly to viewers about the content of the images shown and how they are to be understood.[53] For instance, observers of the early twelfth-century tympanum

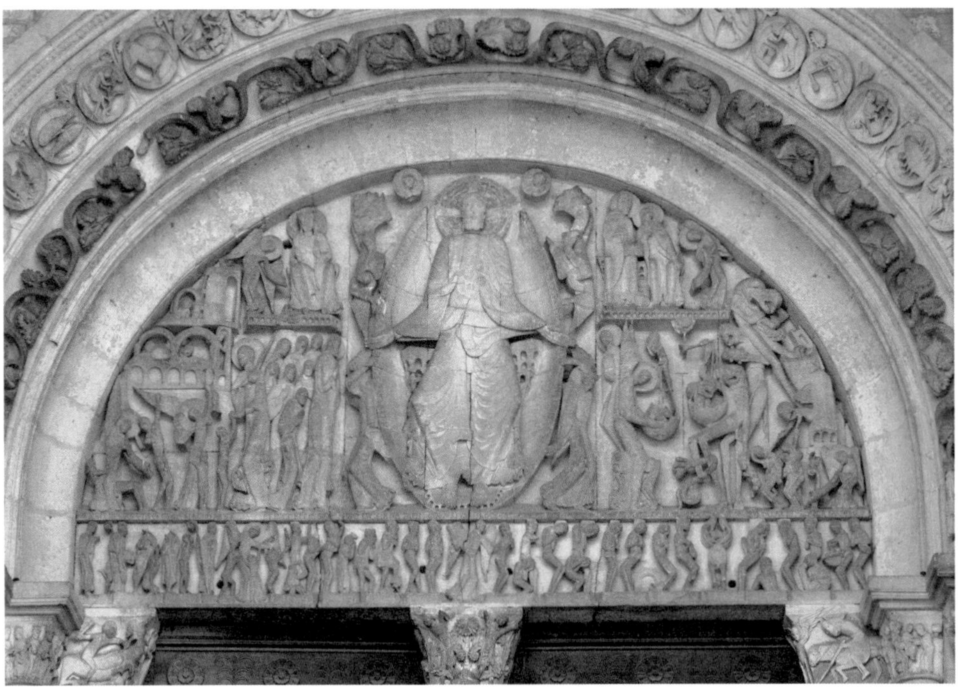

11. Last Judgment tympanum, ca. 1130. Cathedral of Saint Lazare, Autun, France (Scala/Art Resource, New York).

on the church of Saint Lazare at Autun in France are directed, quite clearly, how to read this admonishing vision in sculpture (illus. 11). The work includes numerous Latin inscriptions carved around the mandorla (body halo) of Christ and along the lintel. The inscription surrounding Christ reads: "I alone arrange all things and crown the deserving. Punishment, with me as judge, holds in check those whom vice stimulates."[54] The inscription below the feet of Christ (in addition to the famous "signature" of Gislebertus[55]) describes the rewards of the pious and the horrendous torments awaiting the sinful at the Last Judgment: "Here let fear strike those whom earthly error binds for their fate is shown by the horror of these figures"[56]—or—alternately translated: "May this terror terrify those whom earthly error binds, for the horror of these images here in this manner truly depicts what will be."[57]

These types of images and inscriptions on church doorways are quite characteristic of the twelfth-century Romanesque period, and numerous other examples could be cited here of inscribed portals that address the viewer in the voice of God or The Church.[58] The inscriptions speak directly to the viewer, and although "it is difficult to gauge the effect of these words in stone on a medieval audience ... the allegorization of the church invested the portal with a numinous quality that would have given its 'voice' a reality unlike that which any modern viewer is likely to experience."[59]

A great deal of scholarship has been devoted to issues of medieval literacy and the degree to which inscriptions such as appear so frequently in medieval art were actually accessible/legible to their contemporary audiences.[60] At the risk of generalizing across the medieval centuries, it does seem safe to assume that certainly some literate people were able to understand and read the inscriptions, whereas others may have relied on the literate "for access to written transmission."[61] The situation is really not so vastly different from the present day when the ability to read medieval Latin is beyond the grasp of many (otherwise "literate") people. Modern-day viewers of the medieval Latin inscriptions, if they are interested in the written messages conveyed, need to have the inscriptions translated to them as well. We imagine that this translation process took place orally during the medieval period with people talking together in front of the sculpture, whereas audiences today may be more likely to consult their tourist guidebooks or electronic devices to discover the meanings of the inscriptions. Modern viewers/readers, however, may certainly not have the same sense as did the medieval audience of the "special potency and prestige"[62] of Latin writing. The visual displays of literacy seen in medieval art were certainly designed to impress both literate, semiliterate and illiterate alike.[63] Indeed, the "prominence and prevalence [of inscriptions] suggest an evocative and persuasive power equal to that of the images themselves, yet curiously for an audience which seems to have been largely illiterate."[64] In some senses it might be said that "the very presence of language served to authenticate" the visual imagery.[65]

Whether the inscriptions were legible to a majority or (more likely) minority of viewers, it should be noted that the language chosen at Autun, for example, provides "viewing directions" for the audience in just as clear, direct, and dramatic a fashion as the visual narrative images of the tympanum sculpture. As in many other examples of sculptured portals with inscriptions, if the medieval audience "needed help with some of the visual details and perhaps with the Latin of the verses, they would surely have had little difficulty in comprehending ... [the] message. It seems designed to be accessible."[66]

Clarity and directness of pictorial imagery and written inscriptions also characterize the works of the twentieth-century religious/visionary artist, the Reverend Howard Finster (1916–2001).[67] Finster's works, in a variety of both two- and three-dimensional media, are often more than liberally enriched with written texts, labels, and captions identifying the images, quotes from the Bible, and statements by the artist to the viewers. Finster was a self-taught artist and Baptist preacher from Georgia, and his artistic output was prodigious and often prodigiously text laden. For example, his 1980 piece *VISION OF A GREAT GULF ON PLANET HELL* depicts a terrifying apocalyptic scene in which myriads of small human figures are tumbling into a great chasm filled with menacing serpents and other frightening demonic forms (illus. 12, in color insert). The title of the work is written in enlarged capital letters in white across the top of the piece; additional texts written in white, black, and yellow abound in the densely packed composition. The texts warn the viewers that there is "no food in hell," "no way out," "no weapons to fight with," "clocks are useless here," "the sun never shines here only firelight and darkness," and "when you climb to top of hell its just going down again." This fiery sermon in images and writing also includes the admonition, "if you make it to hell you can say Howard told you about it on earth." Biblical quotes, angels, demons, apocalyptic imagery, and written commentary by the artist run rampant through the majority of Finster's works, and although the textual excesses may, at times, overwhelm the viewer, the artist's combinations of words and pictures are ultimately designed to convey highly specific—loud and clear—messages to the audience.[68]

The "voice" of the artist comes through clearly in many of the examples noted above: David's admiration for Marat, Léger's admiration for David, and the visionary fervor of the Reverend Howard Finster. As we have seen previously, sometimes artists include other "voices" in their works via speech scrolls, indication of spoken dialogue, and inscribed quotes, such as the voice of God speaking through the church portal at Autun. Other intriguing examples include the cross itself which "speaks" in runic inscriptions on the early eighth-century Ruthwell Cross (illus. 13); the runic inscriptions on the Franks Casket that talk to each other—asking and answering riddles (illus. 14), and the voice of death that speaks out in the Latin inscription on the tomb depicted in Nicolas Poussin's *Et in Arcadia Ego*, ca. 1640 (illus. 15).

The Ruthwell Cross, "undoubtedly the most important sculptural survival from Anglo-Saxon Britain and arguably from early medieval Europe,"[69] stands over seventeen feet high and is carved with figural narrative scenes, interlaced vine scrolls,

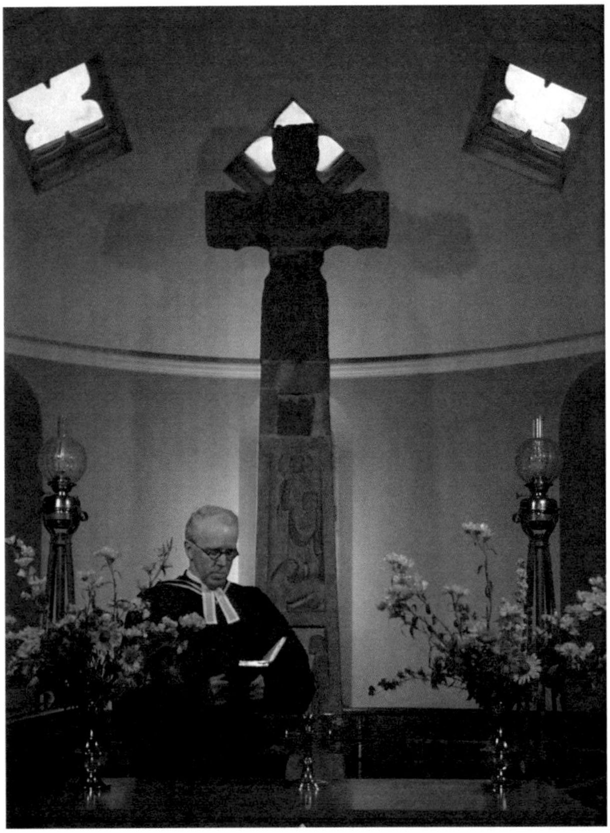

13. The Ruthwell Cross, early 8th century. Ruthwell, Dumfriesshire, Scotland, Great Britain (NGS Image Collection/The Art Archive at Art Resource, New York).

and inscriptions in both Latin and runic lettering. An enormous amount of scholarship has been devoted to this monument and a number of different theories have been proposed as to the identification and symbolism of the sculptured scenes as well as the overall cultural/historical significance of this work.[70] For our purposes, the runic inscriptions are of greatest interest. Although runes are widely found on carved stones and in many other media from medieval northern Europe especially,[71] the Ruthwell runes significantly preserve several verses from the important Anglo-Saxon poem *The Dream of the Rood*, in which the cross upon which Jesus was crucified speaks and recounts the events of the crucifixion. The Ruthwell runes appear to predate extant manuscript copies of the poem. The earliest manuscript version is from the late tenth century, although the dates of and the relationship between the Ruthwell runes and early manuscript versions of the poem is a matter of some scholarly debate.[72] The poem itself is much longer than the several lines found on the Ruthwell Cross and is phrased in the form of a mystical dream vision in which the speaking cross appears to the poem's narrator. The inscriptions on the Ruthwell Cross represent several passages of this first-person speech of the cross, including the lines:

> I raised up the powerful king, the lord of heaven.
> I dared not bend.
> Men mocked us both together. I was drenched with blood…
> I beheld it all. I was painfully afflicted with sorrows.[73]

The speech inscribed on the Ruthwell cross thus creates an extremely powerful impression of a "speaking" work of art whose "voice" directs viewers to adopt a pious and emotional response.

The Ruthwell Cross could also be described as a multilingual monument as it preserves numerous Latin inscriptions as well. The issues of legibility and audience literacy naturally arise again here, but we can only assume that if the texts were not accessible to (or even intended for) a general public, "prominent or important inscriptions would sometimes be read or interpreted by those who could read to those who could not. ...such inscriptions need not be thought of as addressing only the very restricted numbers of people capable of reading."[74] Indeed, imagining that the inscriptions on the Ruthwell Cross were read aloud to an audience quite reinforces the ongoing "speech act" of this important monument.[75]

Another intriguing example of a multilingual and speaking art work from the early medieval period is the Franks Casket.[76] This is a small box (approximately nine by seven by five inches) made of whalebone, richly and densely carved with low-relief scenes and inscriptions—primarily in runic but with some Old English and Latin phrases as well. It is generally thought to be an Anglo-Saxon Northumbrian work of the early eighth century; it may perhaps have been produced in a monastic context for a secular or royal patron and might have been designed to hold an important small manuscript. The majority of the panels are displayed in the British Museum

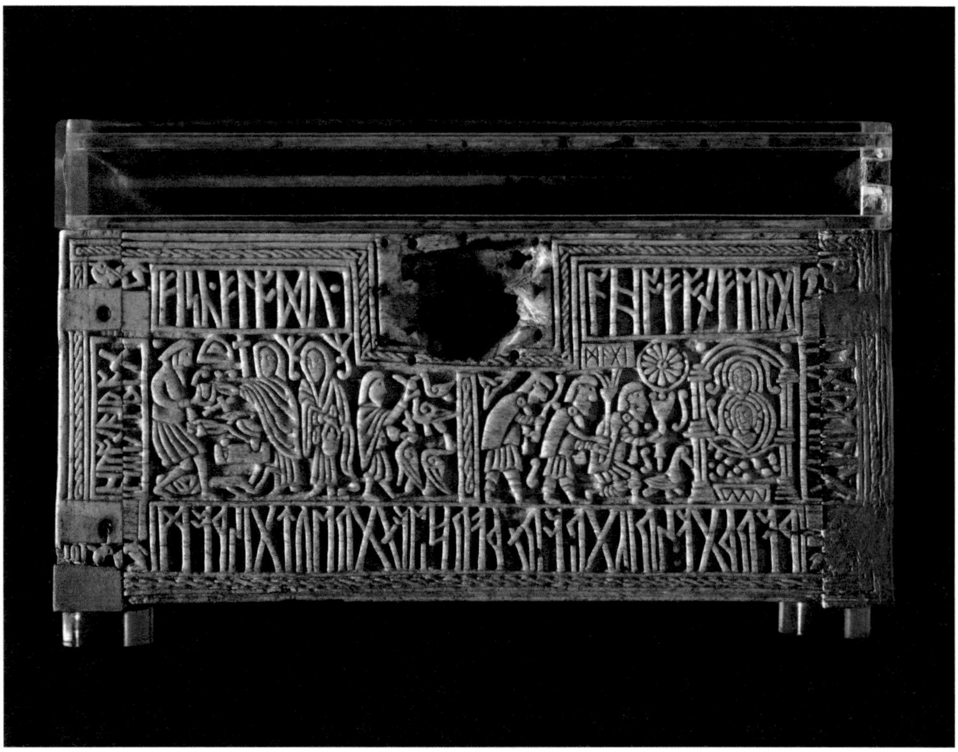

14. The Franks (Auzon) Casket, ca. 700. London, British Museum (© The Trustees of the British Museum/Art Resource, New York).

whereas the right side panel, which became detached in the nineteenth century, is now in the Bargello Museum in Florence.

Much scholarship has been devoted to the identification of the scenes as well as the inscriptions. The pictorial subjects include at least one Christian scene (the Adoration of the Magi), episodes from Roman history and mythology (such as Romulus and Remus), and episodes from Germanic legends (such as the Legend of Weland the Smith). The thematic juxtapositions of these scenes drawn from Roman, Christian, and Germanic sources is doubtless far from random, although scholarly opinions continue to diverge about the identification of some of the scenes as well as the overall iconographic program of the work. The inscriptions and captions (some of which read in retrograde—from right to left—as well as left to right; others are upside down) are in combinations of Latin, Old English, and runic (the latter especially subject to diverse translations). The inscriptions primarily serve to identify or describe the scenes shown, such as the Magi, Romulus and Remus, and so on. In contrast to these descriptive texts, the runic inscription on the front of the casket poses and answers a riddle about the material used to create the object. Translations vary:

> The flood lifted up the fish on to the cliff bank;
> The whale became sad, when he swam on the shingle.
> Whale's bone.[77]
> —or—
> The fish beat up the seas on to the mountainous cliff;
> The king of terror became sad when he swam on the shingle.
> Whale's bone.[78]
> —or—
> The sea cast up the fish onto the mountainous high beach;
> The king of terror became sad when he swam on the shingle.
> Whale's bone.[79]

This self-referential "riddling explanation"[80]—spoken by the work of art itself—states that the material used for creating the casket was bone from a beached whale. Riddles were very popular in Anglo-Saxon culture as aspects "of a very long—and very lively—oral tradition."[81] Indeed, the complex messages contained in this artwork may be understood to have many levels of symbolism. The clever riddle—asked and answered—on the front of the casket "suggests that the casket itself is a riddle, to be read at more than its face value."[82]

Nicolas Poussin's *Et in Arcadia Ego* might also be termed a "speaking" work of art due to the inscription that provides the title as well as the pictorial/symbolic focus for the painting. Although the precise meaning and translation of this inscription has been much discussed, the group of classically garbed figures gathered about the tomb in this bucolic landscape setting are musing upon the words clearly inscribed on the tomb: *Et in Arcadia Ego*.[83] "Ego" represents a voice speaking—not only to the viewers of the painting—but also to the viewers who are depicted within the scene itself. Are these the words of the deceased former inhabitant of

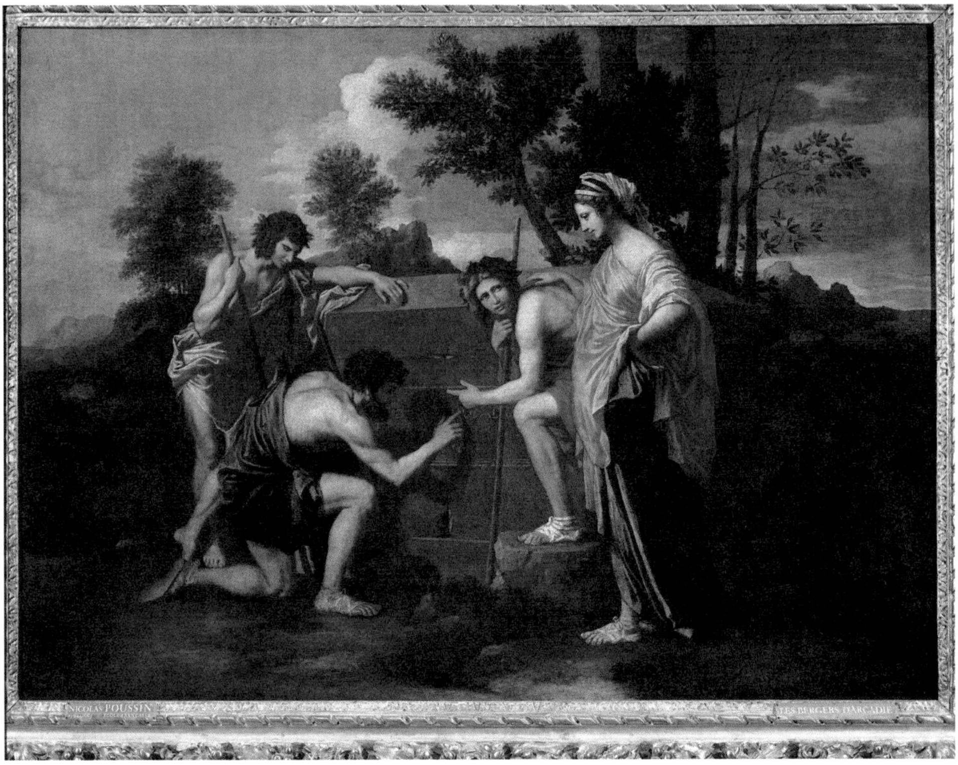

15. Nicolas Poussin, *Et in Arcadia Ego*, ca. 1640. Paris, France, Musée du Louvre (Gianni Daglo Orti/The Art Archive at Art Resource, New York).

Arcadia, or the words of death who too is present in Arcadia? "The fact that ego's name has disappeared makes ego a kind of 'floating signifier' waiting for its fulfillment by our reading."[84] Viewers of the picture muse upon the musings of these silent figures who have encountered a quiet but very potent "voice" speaking from the tomb.

In contrast, extremely loud "voices" come through in many examples of twentieth-century art, perhaps especially in the Pop art paintings of Roy Lichtenstein and notably in his dialogue and text-filled "comic strip" images of the 1960s. In these bold and bright canvases, Lichtenstein reproduced and replicated details from comic strips, including the speech bubbles, thought bubbles, and sound effects typical of the medium. *WHAAM!* is the title and also some of the text in a famous example from 1963 where the thoughts of the fighter pilot engaged in combat ("I pressed the fire control... And ahead of me rockets blazed through the sky...") are also included/written out in the picture (illus. 16). Although Lichtenstein did not rely exclusively upon the speech/thought bubble or balloon form to enclose the texts in his works, this highly effective device was developed in cartoon and satirical art in the nineteenth

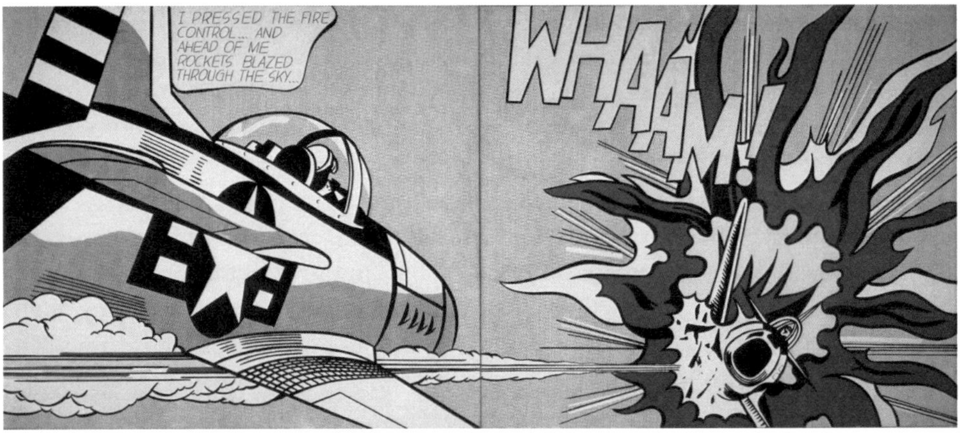

16. Roy Lichtenstein, *Whaam!*, 1963. London, Tate Gallery (Tate, London/Art Resource, New York. Image © Estate of Roy Lichtenstein).

century, ultimately replacing the speech scroll, banner, legend, and caption forms as a more effective way of conveying speech and thoughts of figures.[85]

"Words in speech balloons are intended to be heard by readers who know the language in which they are written."[86] The texts included in Lichtenstein's "comic strip" works carry a major portion of the messages of these visual images. The written thoughts and words of dialogue are required; they are inherent in the originals that Lichtenstein transforms. Although it has been said about these works that "he makes of a confusing narrative sequence a clear well-knit design in which the 'story' is so blatant that it can be instantly appreciated for its humour, or horror, and as instantly dismissed,"[87] it should be noted that the succession of images in the comic strip, in which sequential frames function to tell a story,[88] is quite negated by Lichtenstein's enlargement of selected vignettes. The words and images may indeed be reduced to essentials and thus encapsulate a larger "story," but we retain the sense that they are only extracts or excerpts. "Because we interpret a comic by gathering together the successive scenes, it takes a certain self-conscious effort to linger on a single panel, treating it as if it were a self-sufficient picture. Isolate segments, and they become highly ambiguous."[89] Out of context, only a portion of the story is told in spite of the clarity of the text and image. So while the texts in Lichtenstein's work certainly contribute information to the scenes depicted, they are only part of the story.

Summing Up

The majority of examples of text/picture combinations discussed above show words and images functioning in mutually informative manners. The primary function of the captions, labels, speech scrolls, signatures, and so on noted in these examples is to provide information to the viewer of the images. We understand that the words and texts included in these examples are placed there primarily to enhance and contribute to the viewer's understanding of the pictorial subject matter. Such labels, captions, and inscriptions may serve to identify the subject matter of the scene, to identify the artist, or otherwise increase the viewer's understanding of the images by providing texts that guide in interpreting the work.

Whether or not these inscriptions are read as "external" or "internal" compositional elements (whether they are imposed on or inherent to the pictorial illusion of the images) are concerns that ultimately matter less here than the overriding intention of these words-as-information. Similarly, although the issues concerning legibility of these inscriptions (whether or not the language in which the inscriptions are written is or was accessible to great numbers of viewers amongst modern or past audiences) provide extremely worthwhile questions indeed, it does seem clear, in the cases noted above, that the inscriptions were designed with an audience in mind and that at least some members of the audience were meant to read and to understand the texts.

In other words, the texts found in these examples are not primarily designed to confuse or puzzle viewers. The captions and labels provide identifications of the figures and scenes. The speech scrolls are meant to represent spoken dialogue between the figures. The prayers and invocations inscribed on these examples are meant to inspire or reflect pious attitudes. The texts, in that sense, are not deliberately cryptic or mystifying. If many of the medieval pilgrims to Autun, for example, could not read the inscriptions on the tympanum, the fact still remains that the inscriptions were designed to contribute to the meaning and symbolism of the imagery, not to negate or contradict the pictorial subjects.

This relatively straightforward and informative function of words in pictures, however, represents only one type of extremely common and widespread text/image relationship. Not all text/image combinations are of this genre. In the following chapters we will see how words and pictures may function in much less mutually elucidating roles. The snippets of text included in the "comic strip" works of Roy Lichtenstein, that provide a sense of partial narrative only, are an excellent introduction to the exploration of text/image relationships of a less straightforward and more complex nature.

Two

Word/Picture Puzzles

In the examples covered in the preceding chapter we have seen how words and pictures have often been combined in mutually informative ways. In those cases, the words and images may be said to work together towards the same aim of conveying a subject, theme, or idea. Written insertions in works of art, such as captions, labels, inscriptions, and portions of dialogue may serve to identify the subject matter, increase or contribute to the pictorial information, or guide the viewer in understanding and interpreting the work of art. Inscriptions on works of art may directly address the viewer via offering written texts that assist in the reading of the pictorial images. Captions and labels can assist the viewer with identifying the figures and subjects. Indications of spoken dialogue between figures depicted in the work of art can add critical levels of meaning to the overall subject matter of the piece.

Not all texts that appear in pictures necessarily function in these relatively straightforward and informative ways. Many other text/picture combinations are far more puzzling. Rather than functioning in purely informational roles, texts in artworks can also convey a variety of mixed messages to viewers/readers. Audiences may be puzzled, for example, by attempting to understand where, exactly, texts/inscriptions are meant to be perceived in relationship or location to the pictorial subject matter. Some texts, although otherwise quite clear and legible, may appear to be appended to, or suspended on pictures in unclear spatial relationships to the primary subject matter. Texts that are fragmentary, incomplete, or otherwise cryptic may also puzzle the audience by their lack of legibility. In these cases of "mixed messages" and "hidden texts," the written/visual combinations move substantially away from the basic and informative mode into more deliberately challenging realms.

Mixed Messages

One of the most intriguing and often quite visually puzzling text/image relationships is represented by the device known as the *cartellino*.[1] These are illusionistically rendered little pieces of paper, usually bearing artists' signatures and sometimes dates and other written information, that appear to be affixed to paintings or to objects depicted in paintings. They represent a specific type of *trompe l'oeil* illusionism that challenges the viewer's perceptions of the spatial relationships represented by and within the work of art. In many cases, the viewer may be initially unsure whether or not they are painted or actually stuck on to the painting.[2] Although these clever devices often have an explanatory function, providing written information about the artist or date of the work, their presence adds an element of ambiguity via the convincing illusionism with which they are rendered. They are not simply labels or identifying captions written *on* works of art, but appear to be fully realistic and independent pieces of inscribed paper affixed *to*, or located somewhere *within*, the artwork.

Cartellini appear frequently and especially in northern Italian Renaissance painting, and are especially but by no means exclusively associated with the works of Jacopo and Giovanni Bellini and related "Bellini school/workshop" productions.[3] An excellent specimen of a *cartellino* can be seen, for example, in Giovanni Bellini's *Madonna of the Pear* (or *Morelli Madonna*) ca. 1488 (illus. 17). Typical of so many Bellini-style devotional images, the work features a half-length Madonna tenderly holding the infant Jesus. They are depicted in front of an extensive and calm landscape which is partially obscured by a curtain (or cloth of honor) hanging directly in back of the Madonna. A marble parapet appears in the lower front of the scene; these are also very typical of Bellini school and related works.[4] The parapet creates a spatial and psychological division between the spectator and the holy figures, a divide between the realms of the viewer of the scene and the sacred figures depicted within it. Bellini's *cartellino* appears directly on the center front of the parapet. This small piece of white paper attracts the viewer's eye. It is very carefully rendered and appears to have been folded,

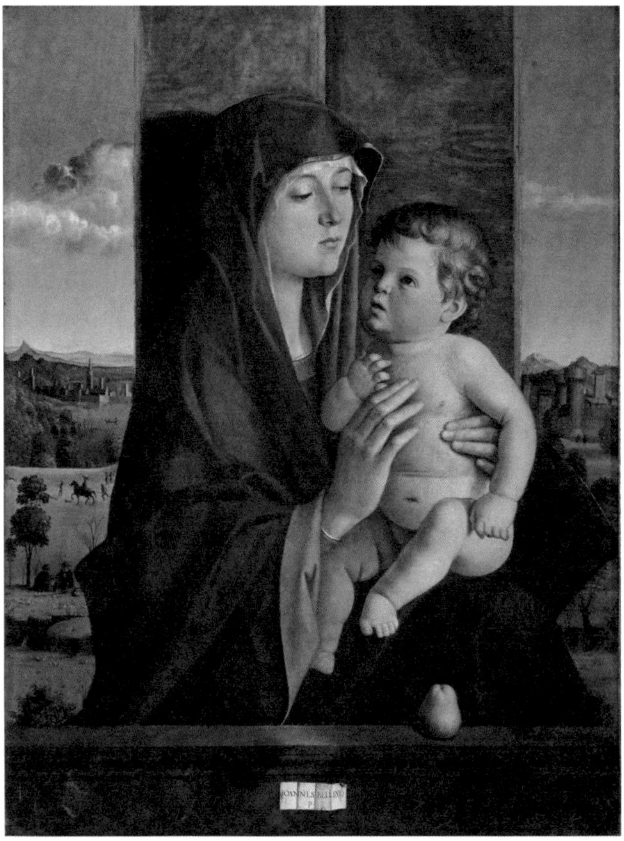

17. Giovanni Bellini, *Madonna of the Pear (Morelli Madonna)*, ca. 1488. Bergamo, Italy, Accademia Carrara (Scala/Art Resource, New York).

unfolded, and then affixed somehow to the front of the parapet, or to the surface of the painting itself. One corner of the paper is still bent, casting a slight shadow, but the artist's name is clearly legible, rendered in bold capital letters. The viewer of the painting receives the very strong impression that the *cartellino* is, as it were, a removeable element. One could imagine reaching into the picture and plucking it out, folding it up again, and carrying it away. Indeed, the transitory sense conveyed by the *cartellino* is one of the defining characteristics of the genre. "The *cartellino* suggests that it is somehow unexpected if not extraneous—contingent on the artist's apparently having decided 'at the last minute' to place it in or within his image."[5] Like a "calling card,"[6] advertisement, or studio label, the *cartellino* announces the authorship of the painting in a form that appears to be both fixed and ephemeral, deliberate and spontaneous, internal and imposed at the same time.

Such is also the case with the illusionistically rendered little strip of once-folded paper that appears to be fixed to the painting's surface or to the cloth depicted in the front of Carlo Crivelli's *Madonna and Child* panel (the *Lenti Madonna*) from the late 1470s or 1480 (illus. 18).[7] This exquisite and highly detailed painting more than well demonstrates the artist's skills with pictorial illusionism, his love for rich textures and patterns, and his frequent use of fruit and vegetable symbolism. The pinkish moiré silk cloth hanging in back of Mary, which sets her off from the gently wooded landscape, appears to be tied to the back of the frame, or to something else unseen behind the frame, with red laces. Mary stands behind a classical, and partly cracked, marble parapet upon which she carefully balances the infant Jesus. He is seated on a costly cushion, atop the yellow moiré silk cloth that

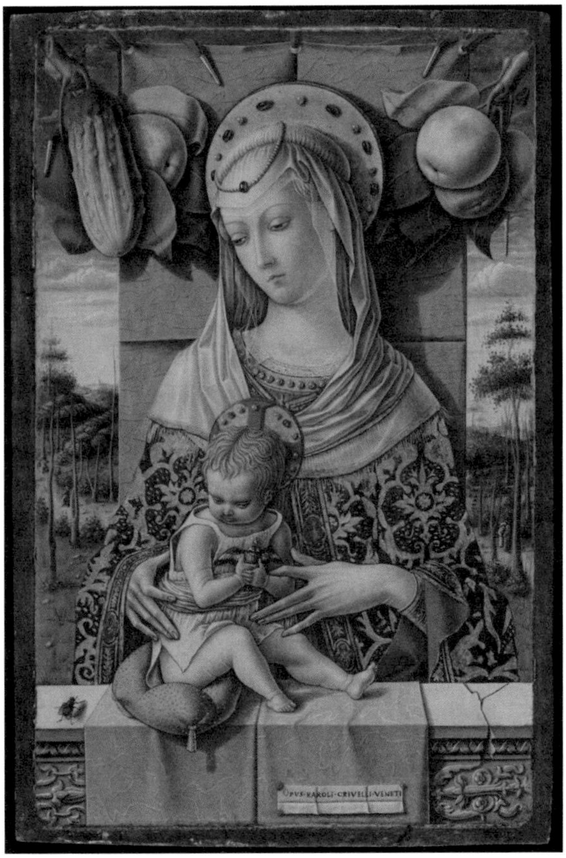

18. Carlo Crivelli, *Madonna and Child*, ca. 1480. New York, The Metropolitan Museum of Art (© The Metropolitan Museum of Art; image source: Art Resource, New York).

descends below the lower edge of the picture. The *cartellino* in the foreground is inscribed: OPVS.KAROLI.CRIVELLI.VENETI, specifying his authorship of the piece as well as his origins in Venice. This inscribed paper strip appears to be fastened to the foreground cloth with bits of red sealing wax visible at three of its corners, and it casts a shadow onto the cloth, further enhancing the sense of three-dimensional illusionism. Although the *cartellino* appears to be anchored to the cloth depicted in the painting, it might simultaneously also be perceived as being fixed to the surface of the painting, quite a bit closer to the viewer's space than any of the other pictorial elements depicted. A similar sense of spatial ambiguity is also represented by the additional *trompe l'oeil* detail of the rather large fly that is perched on and casts a shadow onto the left side of the parapet. Perhaps even more so than the *cartellino*, this much-discussed intrusive insect appears to have momentarily landed on the painting's surface and could fly away or be brushed away by viewers.[8]

The sense of independence and potential portability conveyed by the *cartellino* form fundamentally signals its difference from closely related artistic devices such as scrolls, banderoles, banners, cartouches, tablets, and shields. Unlike these frequently inscribed devices that also appear very often in medieval and Renaissance paintings, the *cartellino* form is distinguished by its seemingly casual appearance, its ambiguous position in or on the painting, and its important, signature-bearing role. However, it should be noted that "no law requires that a *cartellino* bear a signature. The fictive paper might just as well carry the name of the subject or any other information."[9]

Indeed, this is the case with the early sixteenth-century painting by Vittore Carpaccio titled *Portrait of a Knight*, or *Young Knight in a Landscape* (illus. 19). This has been described as the earliest full-length portrait in western painting, although the exact identity of the figure shown remains a topic of scholarly discussion.[10] It is, in any case, a complex composition including the central figure of the armored young knight drawing his sword, another knight—or the knight's squire—on horseback in the background, a depiction of a walled city, other architectural details and fortifications, and birds, animals, and landscape elements including trees, foliage, and identifiable flowers. The painting is clearly filled with symbolism, as only to be expected from its date.

Most significant for our present purposes is the fact that the painting contains two *cartellini*. One of these appears to be attached to a remaining branch from a chopped-down tree depicted in the lower right of the scene, and the other appears propped up in the foliage shown on the lower left of the composition. The first *cartellino* bears the artist's name: VICTOR CARPATHIVS and the date M.D.X (1510). The other *cartellino* bears the motto: MALO MORI QUAM FOEDARE ("I would rather die than be dishonored"). Efforts, of course, have been made to connect this motto with various historical figures, families, or knightly orders of the Renaissance period, such as the Order of the Ermine founded in the mid-fifteenth century by

King Ferdinand of Naples.[11] An ermine creeping through the foliage beneath the motto-bearing *cartellino* should be noted.

Conceptually but not so much visually akin to the *cartellini* discussed above in works by Bellini and Crivelli, these bits of paper in Carpaccio's painting appear to be improbably tucked into the landscape elements, hanging in a tree, or semi-buried in foliage. The very unlikeliness of their presence causes a sense of spatial disjuncture and ambiguity. While they are very carefully and cleverly integrated into the scene, they also appear alien, intrusive, and realistically improbable. However, to remove or pluck them from the composition would cause meaningful information to be lost.

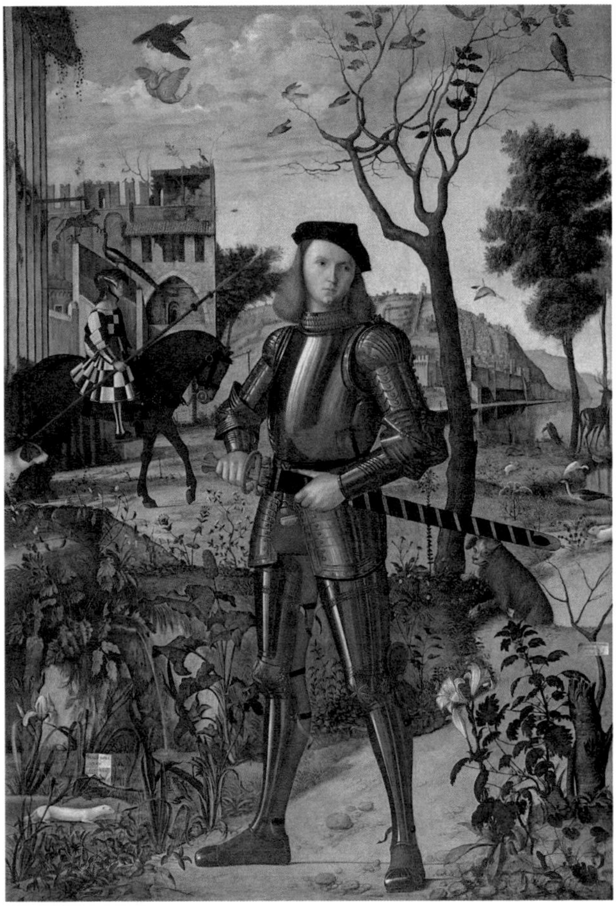

19. Vittore Carpaccio, *Young Knight in a Landscape*, ca. 1510. Madrid, Spain, Museo Thyssen-Bornemisza (Museum Thyssen-Bornemisza/Scala/Art Resource, New York).

Cartellini, in all their variant formats, represent rather uniquely puzzling instances of text/image relationships in the history of art. Naturally, scholars have been interested not only in coining a clear definition of *cartellini* but also in tracing the origins and first appearances of the form. Fra Filippo Lippi's 1437 *Tarquinia Madonna* has frequently been cited as the earliest appearance of a *cartellino* in Italian Renaissance art (illus. 20). But there is some scholarly disagreement about the appropriate terminology to be employed in describing the date-bearing element that appears on the base of the Madonna's throne in this painting. Although Millard Meiss described it as a *cartellino*,[12] later scholars (such as Jeffrey Ruda[13] and Rona Goffen[14]) have preferred to use the term "scroll" or "cartouche." The element in question is indeed a little scrolling form, partially unrolled, placed on the ledge at the base of the throne. It bears the date 1437, and although this pliable little scroll does not include the artist's name, we have seen already that *cartellini* do not always include signatures. One could perhaps imagine that one could reach into the painting, pluck this little scroll out of the composition, reroll it, and take it away. Certainly, the scroll in this painting draws the viewer's eyes just as much as any similarly placed *cartellino*; it appears to function both as an internal as well as an imposed element in the composition. However, the scroll form is definitely different from the flatter folded/unfolded fictive paper devices most customarily classified as *cartellini*, those that puzzle and challenge viewers by their simultaneous realism and by their ambiguous relationship to the pictorial spaces otherwise realistically represented in works of art.

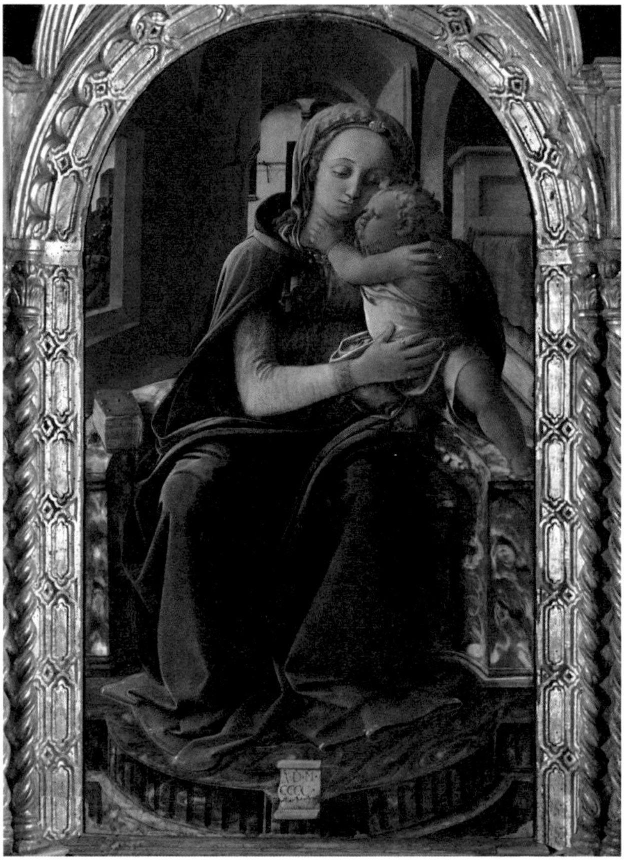

20. Fra Filippo Lippi, *Tarquinia Madonna*, 1437. Rome, Italy, Galleria Nazionale d'Arte Antica (Scala/Ministero per i Beni e le Attività culturali/Art Resource, New York).

In this case, the cartouche/scroll in Lippi's painting is set back into the pictorial space and, one could argue, appears to be more incorporated into the scene than, for example, Bellini's or Crivelli's *cartellino*/parapet combinations or even Carpaccio's *cartellini* hanging on landscape elements or buried in foliage. Indeed, Lippi's *Tarquinia Madonna* has been cut down on all sides, so the original effect and sense of depth in the painting has been somewhat lost. Originally the cartouche/scroll might have seemed even further out of reach of the spectator. "Lippi's paper seems rather something between a *cartellino on* the painting and a scroll *within*, attached to the base of the Madonna's throne and as much a part of her represented world as any other element in the picture."[15] The scroll/cartouche in Lippi's work differs from the previously described *cartellini* in that it appears to be somewhat more within the visual space of the composition rather than a textual element that appears added to the scene, an element

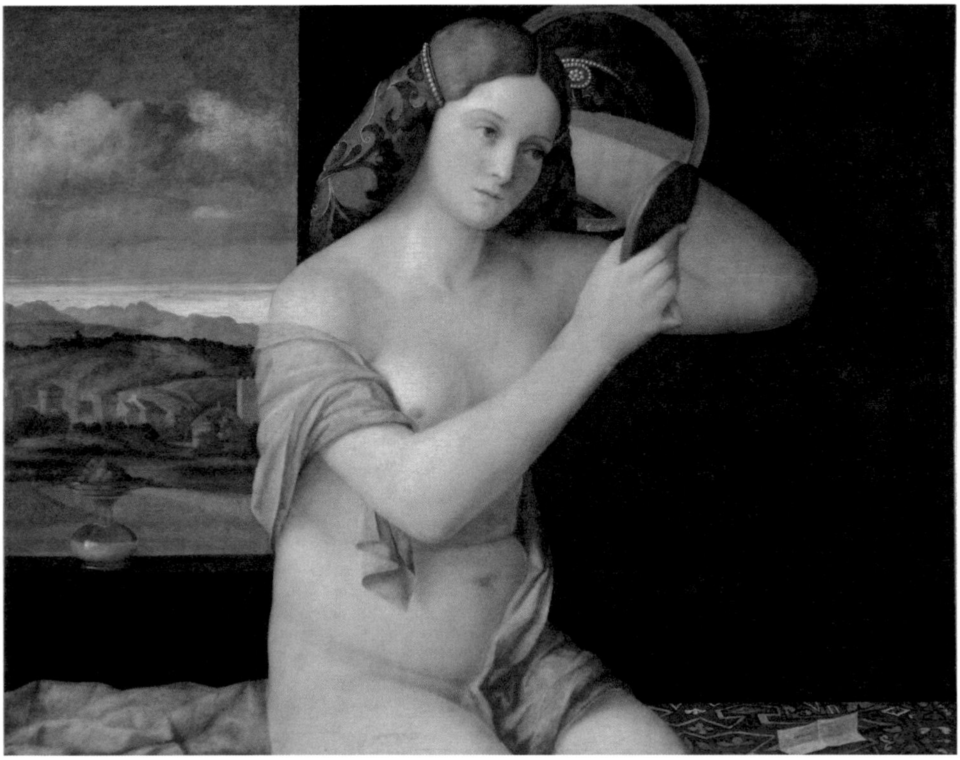

21. Giovanni Bellini, *Woman with a Mirror*, 1515. Vienna, Austria, Kunsthistorisches Museum (Nimatallah/Art Resource, New York).

that might be perceived as belonging more to the viewer's space than the painting's pictorial space. Indeed, the visual trickery of the *cartellino* form is essentially characterized by just this very perceptual disjuncture. *Cartellini* puzzle and attract viewers by their appearance of realism as well as their oddness. They may function simultaneously as believable elements in a scene, but also draw attention to other levels of reality.[16]

For example, Giovanni Bellini's 1515 *Nude with Mirror* contains a seemingly casually placed slip of paper/*cartellino* positioned on the bench next to the seated woman (illus. 21). The unfolded piece of paper bears the artist's handwritten signature in cursive (versus printed) script and the date.[17] The woman is shown in three-quarter length, posed against a dark background and a window that admits a view of a peaceful landscape scene. She is partially draped in a red cloth and is admiring her reflection and her pearl-studded brocade headdress in a small mirror that she holds in her right hand. This slip of paper placed on the carpet-covered bench next to the seated woman could easily be perceived by the viewer as something along the lines of a note or short letter that the woman in the picture has read, set aside, and is thinking about as she continues to arrange her hair. However, the texts inscribed on the unfolded piece of paper do not contribute more specific iconographic information to the scene or aid in the identity of the figure shown. The little piece of paper is not, for example, the summons from King David to Bathsheba, or the dying words of Lucretia as found in a somewhat similar placement in Lorenzo Lotto's ca. 1530 *Lucretia*,[18] but rather the signature of Bellini and the date of the painting. Although this piece of unfolded paper "has become an integral part of the composition—not merely a label applied to or 'incised' on the surface,"[19] it still presents a visual puzzle for the viewer. It functions as a believable element in the scene but also presents textual information that appears to have no immediately obvious connection to the painting's subject matter. It appears to be a *cartellini* that has migrated into the picture from its "conventional location."[20] Although appearing to be an internal element and integral to the scene depicted, it simply contains written information that serves to establish the authorship and date of the piece. It thus provides the viewer with a mixed message about the text/image relationships in the work, drawing attention to itself and its puzzling presence.

The *cartellini* form, even as briefly analyzed in the few samples here, serves as an excellent example of one type of word/picture puzzle, where the texts depicted in works of art may indeed be quite informative but also challenge viewer's perceptions of the spatial relationships within the work of art. *Cartellini* represent a distinct category of *trompe l'oeil* illusionism, bringing texts into relationship with imagery in a perceptually puzzling format. Other types of word/pictures puzzles can also create mixed messages for viewers, especially when the texts and their meanings are partially hidden.

Hidden Texts

Works of art that include snippets and fragments of text, such as collages that combine painted words and images with clippings from advertisements, newspapers, magazines, and various other ephemera, are especially apt examples where the included writings generally do not have a purely explanatory function, where the texts themselves are often literally hidden or where their meaning is hidden. Instead of functioning as elements of informative textual clarity in a visual scene, texts may serve to challenge and direct the viewers' attention to different artistic agendas and goals.

For example, any number of early modern collage works could be cited here, such as Pablo Picasso's 1913 collage *Guitar*, which consists of cut and pasted paper and other shapes created of charcoal, ink and chalk (illus. 22, in color insert).[21] The collage form, as developed by Picasso and his colleague Georges Braque around 1912, represented a revolutionary new way of working with texts and images.[22] In their further cubistic explorations of the flattening and splintering of pictorial subject matter into planes and facets and shapes seen from multiple points of view, both Picasso and Braque began to use fragments of printed materials—such as newspapers, magazines, musical scores, wallpaper, playing cards, and advertising labels—incorporating these nontraditional elements from the everyday world into their cut-and-pasted works, or *papiers collés*. Between 1912 and 1914 Picasso created a great many collages with traditional still life elements, such as tableware, bottles, and musical instruments, rendered in the semi-abstracted cubist style.[23]

The motif of the guitar was especially prominent in his early collages as well as in his three-dimensional paper constructions of these years, perhaps due to its traditional association with his Spanish cultural heritage and popular music "as an alternative to incipient, industrialized mass culture and to the traditions of fine art."[24] The particular example illustrated here was created when Picasso was staying in the town of Céret, in southern France, in close proximity to the Spanish border. The composition is one of several he created with the motif of an upright guitar, perhaps to be understood as either hanging on a wall or placed atop a table. The body of the guitar itself is broken into two curving parts with the neck indicated by vertical shapes ascending on the left of the collage. Fragments of a printed page from a Spanish publication are pasted on the lower left section of the composition and one round newsprint clipping indicates the central hole of the guitar. The collage also is enlivened by further curvilinear and geometric lines and markings, plus sections of printed wallpaper, one of which is cut in a shape representing one half of the guitar.

The clipped pieces of printed material Picasso used here are semi-legible and certainly can be partially read by viewers, but this does not seem to be the primary motivation for their inclusion. The printed texts here do not convey additional written information about the work; they do not provide clues as to the subject matter or the meaning of the work, but rather serve primarily to draw attention to the materials used to create the piece and thus to the revolutionary approach to image- and object-making represented by such compositions. Scholars, however, do remain somewhat divided about the choice of printed texts used by Picasso in his collage works of this period especially.[25] Some have emphatically identified specific sociopolitical messages and reflections of Picasso's own political sentiments and concerns during these years,[26] whereas others have argued that "to focus exclusively on 'reading' the newspaper cutouts, as though the text itself always matters, distracts attention from their differential function within Picasso's overall compositions."[27] In other words, these collages continue to puzzle with their potentially mixed messages and hidden texts. Every element in a collage "has a dual function: it refers to an external reality even as its compositional thrust is to undercut the very referentiality it seems to assert."[28]

It has been said that the "main point" of such collage works that include texts "is that we do not attend to the words but to the form."[29] So, the letters and the words here largely do not seem to function as conveyors of explanatory information, at least in the same sense as labels, captions, or identifying inscriptions as noted in the examples previously discussed in chapter 1. Rather, the texts convey different messages to the viewers about the materials used to create the piece and the compositional aims of the artist, if not also serving as reflections of contemporary society due to their origins in current popular media. In general, the collage form "layers into a work of art several levels of meaning: the original identity of the fragment or object and all of the history it brings with it; the new meaning it gains in association with other objects or elements; and the meaning it acquires as a result of its metamorphosis into a new entity."[30] In Picasso's own words:

> If a piece of newspaper can become a bottle, that gives us something to think about in connection with both newspapers and bottles, too. This displaced object has entered a universe for which it was not made and where it retains, in a measure, its strangeness. And this strangeness was what we wanted people to think about because we were quite aware that our world was becoming very strange and not exactly reassuring.[31]

The use of texts and elements of lettering is, of course, characteristic of a great number of early twentieth-century artists and movements in addition to Cubism. The Futurists, Dadaists, and Surrealists alike eagerly explored text/image combinations of a revolutionary and nontraditional nature.[32] The messages contained in these frequently text-laden works, whether social/political or philosophic/aesthetic, are often conveyed not via the use of clearly legible texts but via the fact that the texts are often fragmented, illegible, and obscure.

Another, especially well-known and well-studied example is the 1914 collage by the Italian Futurist artist, Carlo Carrà, titled *Patriotic Celebration (Free-Word Painting)* (illus. 23, in color insert). This is an excellent instance of the evocative (versus fundamentally explanatory) use of texts in art. The pasted and written bits of texts in this work create a dense overlay in a rotating and splintering composition designed to evoke "a large crowd in an urban setting," however, "the exact nature of this gathering has been vigorously disputed."[33] It has been described as representing "the sounds of the street and the noises of a nation preparing to go to war,"[34] a general image of "civic tumult,"[35] and a representation of an energetic and exuberant crowd gathering in the city of Milan for the celebration of a specific national holiday (the Festa dello Statuto) in 1914.[36] Many of the texts can be read and many of the words are recognizable, although seemingly nonsensical words, strange text fragments, and texts representing sounds (onomatopoeia) run rampant through this piece as well. "The collage thus challenges us to read the signs and decode the symbols, to take the scrambled clues and put them into a more orderly sequence."[37]

The composition, in spite of its initially chaotic and cacophonous appearance, is quite carefully structured in a wheel-like, circular form, with spokes of collaged texts revolving around and rotating from the center.[38] The noise of a siren slices through the composition diagonally and is indicated by the repeated words "siren" interspersed with the letters HUHUHUHUH representing the sound. Other sounds, such as "traaak tatatraak," "bree," "cric crac," "croc," and "trrrrrr" evoke the noises of cars and other vehicles on the streets of this busy modern city. Note the words "Strada" and "città moderne" at the top of the composition and the word "Piazza" on the upper right. The phrase "ECHI" is repeated several times throughout the piece, representing the reverberating sounds captured in this dynamic display. The words on the upper left ("sole scroto sbadiglio" and "sole bruciaticcio") evoke the heat of the burning sun shining down on this outdoor event. Carrà placed the words "aviatore" (aviator) and "Italia" with additional phrases referring to a record-breaking aerial performance at the center of the composition, thus inviting "the viewer to assume the daring vantage point of the aviator at the fulcrum of [the] whirring propellers."[39] Perhaps viewers are meant to perceive this work as a birds-eye view, looking down on the patriotic festival in Milan from the perspective of the aviator. Indeed, it has been pointed out that the composition's overall structure bears some significant similarity to the street plan of Milan.[40]

Carrà's collage was published in the short-lived Florentine avant-garde literary magazine, *Lacerba*, that prominently featured many Futurist works in preceding and subsequent issues. Several of the other phrases contained in Carrà's collage are snippets from previous poems, or picture-poems, published in *Lacerba*, as well as slogans from contemporary advertising imagery. These include TOT (a popular brand of antacid), in the upper right of the composition and Odol (a popular brand of oral care products, such as toothpaste and mouthwash), in the lower left of the composition. The pasted and written texts in this work are included not so much because of their inherent or individual textual content but rather in order to give a general sense of the dynamic scene that the artist wished to convey.

Filippo Marinetti, the Italian founder of the Futurist movement, inspired the creation of works such as these with his ideas of "free words" (*parole in libertà*) as forms of revolutionary expression.[41] Many Futurist works make use of expressive typography, nontraditional layouts, and specialized symbols that were designed to communicate ideas efficiently and quickly. The reproduction of sounds and the use of divergent typefaces generally characterize these complex "free word" creations by the Futurists. Futurist artists and writers frequently separated words and texts from their traditional meanings and syntax; "words were organized like images in painting and became part of the formal and symbolic meaning" of the pieces.[42] The power of these words is not so much based on textual legibility but rather on the sense of the imagery that the words evoke. The "word-image conundrums" of many Dadaist and Surrealist works also serve to conjure up additional, and often obscure, levels of meaning.[43] Viewers are required to suspend their old-fashioned and traditional expectations that words and texts in artworks are designed to be read and understood; rather they are asked to look at/read/see these text fragments as important design elements that may evoke any number of mixed messages.

Precedents for the sort of mixed messages conveyed by the letters and text fragments in early modern collage works can be found in many examples of earlier art as well. A number of American painters of the nineteenth and early twentieth century, notably William Michael Harnett (1846–1982), John F. Peto (1854–1907), and John Haberle (1856–1933), specialized in incredibly masterful *trompe l'oeil* images, often including illusionistic depictions of inscribed bits of paper such as money, envelopes, letters, newspaper clippings, and so on.[44] These are not collage works using actual fragments of texts, but rather include carefully rendered replications of textual bits and pieces. Depicted with painstaking realism, many of the visible texts in these pictures are often quite legible to viewers, although the impression of textual clarity is generally belied by the fragmentary nature of the texts displayed. Worn and torn labels, folded and overlapping pieces of correspondence, envelopes, business cards, and other scraps of paper create a sense of partially hidden information, partially obscured clues as to the meanings of the works.

The envelope printed with the notice reading "Important Information Inside" that appears in several of John F. Peto's "letter rack" or "office board" paintings certainly captures this ambiance of obscured textual information. Peto created over a dozen such paintings, several of which include this particular motif.[45] One of these is titled *Old Souvenirs* and is dated to 1881–1901 (illus. 24). In all cases of his use of this motif, the inscription is completely legible to the viewer but the nature of the "Important Information" contained in the letter remains completely mysterious and very puzzling. The viewer is not privy to the information "inside" the envelope and really cannot make any convincing guesses about the "important" contents by reading any of

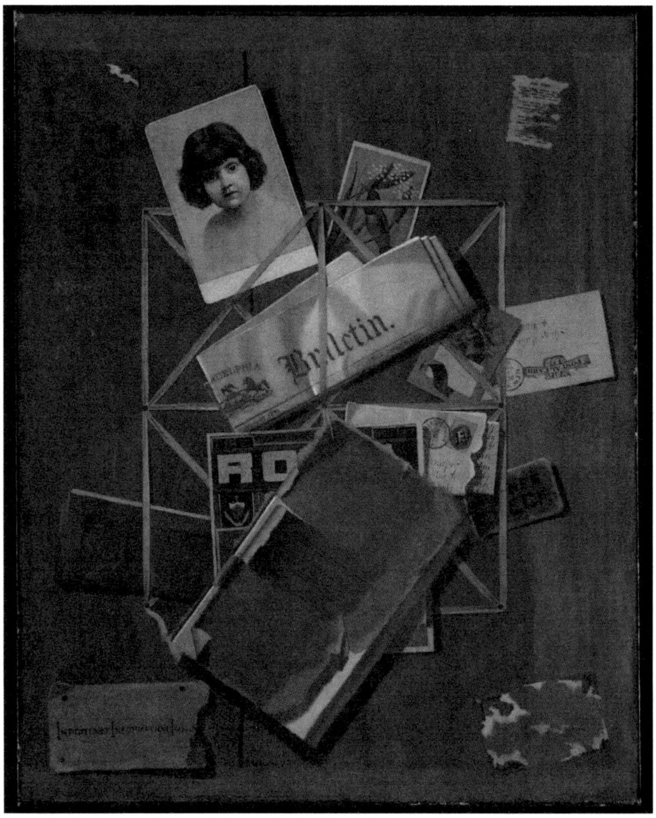

24. John Peto, *Old Souvenirs*, ca. 1881–1901. New York, The Metropolitan Museum of Art (© The Metropolitan Museum of Art; Image source: Art Resource, New York).

the other labels or inscriptions in these works by Peto or by trying to correlate the fragmentary texts with the other visual materials depicted in these works. Naturally, the tantalizing and fragmentary nature of the written materials contained in similar works by Harnett and Haberle as well have inspired decades of scholarly debate and attempts at decipherment. References to events in the lives of these artists, the biographies of their patrons, contemporary political and social events, and various other narratives have been identified in these complex pictures.[46]

The text/image combinations in these works definitely create puzzles for the viewing audience.[47] The audience wants to know more, and the search for meanings (narratives, symbols, literary references, references to contemporary events, and so on) seems particularly appropriate and certainly especially engaging when even fragments of written texts are included in the visual arts. Words are generally understood as conveyors of information, after all, and words in pictures become especially puzzling when their choices, placements, and messages are not quite clear or obvious. When written texts are used as still partially legible design elements, or when written texts appear to perhaps still have some messages to convey, the viewer senses some hidden meanings in these puzzles and the process of decipherment may present some unavoidably enticing challenges. The texts seem to be "not banal accessories displaced from the principal scene of actions, they are rather the ghosts that haunt the emptiness of the stage."[48]

The history of art is replete with examples of *trompe l'oeil* texts and there are many earlier precedents for the "letter rack" form as noted in the nineteenth-century American examples.[49] A plethora of examples could easily be cited, such as the Renaissance-era works by the Neapolitan artist Niccolò Colantonio (or Colantino), *Saint Jerome in his Study*, 1445–50 (illus. 25), and the eminent German painter Hans Holbein's 1532 *Portrait of Georg Gisze of Danzig* (illus. 26).

Colantonio's work depicts the scholarly Saint Jerome (ca. 342–420) seated in his study, carefully extracting a thorn from the paw of a lion. This is one of the most popular legends in the life of this church father, although this episode is more customarily depicted as having taken place outdoors rather than in an interior space.[50] This panel is likely to have originally been a section of a larger altarpiece designed for a chapel in the Franciscan church of San Lorenzo in Naples.[51] As befits the great scholar and translator of the Bible from Greek and Hebrew sources into Latin, Jerome's study is depicted as replete with bookshelves, manuscripts, scrolls, and writing materials. Saint Jerome is a very popular subject in Christian art and, especially from the fourteenth century onwards, is often presented as a studious scholar and writer, with the setting and materials frequently updated by artists to reflect their own time periods.[52] Here he is presented with "the books and furniture of traditional scholarship in the mid-fifteenth century."[53] All of these elements are meticulously detailed, doubtless reflecting the influence of early fifteenth-century Northern masters of extreme realism, such as the Flemish artist Jan van Eyck. One can see an inkwell, hourglass,

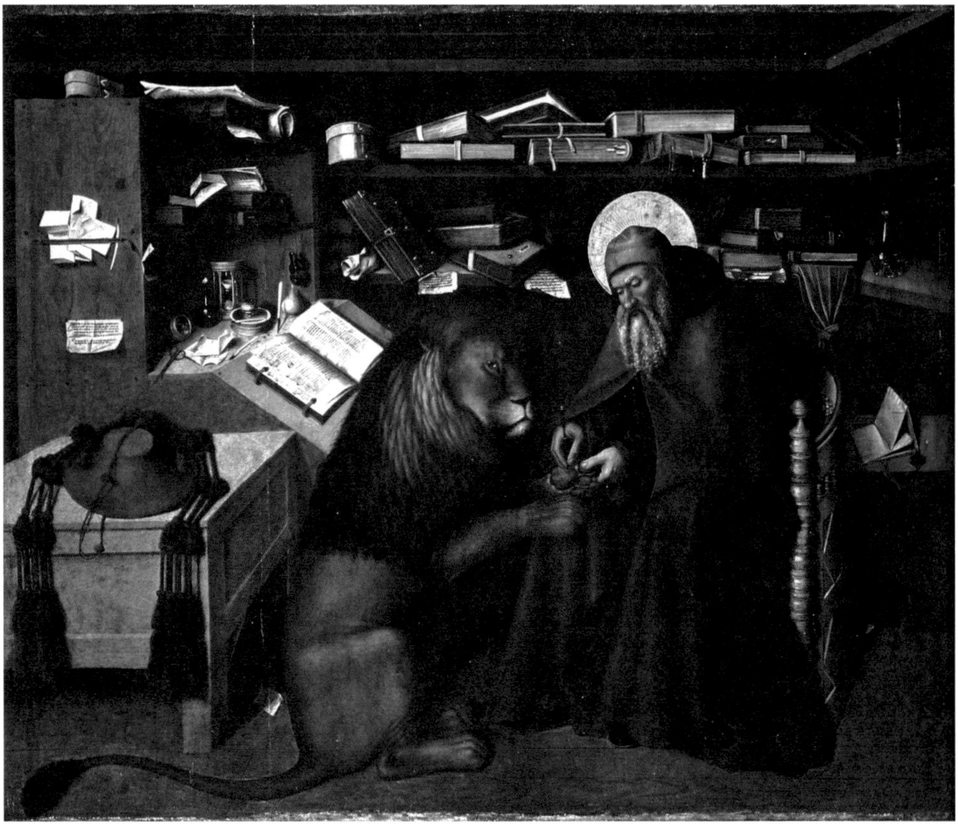

25. Niccolò Colantonio, *Saint Jerome in his Study*, 1445–50. Naples, Italy, San Giorgio Schiavoni (The Art Archive at Art Resource, New York).

sand shaker, pens, scissors, and a magnifying glass on the lower shelf of the saint's desk. The bookshelves are cluttered with various manuscripts—some with sturdy clasps—plus scrolls, oval shaped boxes, a candlestick, and several stoppered glass carafes. On the bench to the right of the saint is a partially unfolded document with a papal seal (*bulla*) attached to it bearing the images of Saints Peter and Paul. Many little scraps of paper appear strewn around the floor of this interior space. A little mouse, under the bench on the right side, is busily chewing away at one of these scraps, perhaps "a reference to the oblivion that results when records are destroyed."[54] A piece of paper is attached to the outward-facing edge of the panel forming the left upright side of the saint's desk. This *cartellino*-like device appears to be attached to the surface of this piece of furniture with dabs of wax at its four corners, although one corner is pulling up and casts a shadow onto the surface beneath it. This particular element was especially noted and admired in early descriptions of the painting, such as that written by the Neapolitan scholar and art historian, Pietro Summonte, in the early sixteenth century, who described it as being "painted with great interest in the imitation of precious things."[55] The writing on this document is illegible, like the similarly placed element in Antonello da Messina's later version of *Saint Jerome in his Study* (1475) which was partially inspired by Colantonio's work.[56] Immediately above this partially detached paper, the artist depicted a dark red ribbon tacked to the upper area of this side of the desk. This band or ribbon supports several folded documents and a quill pen. Another document, tacked to the front side of this area, is depicted curling outwards towards the saint. All told, the elements of text fragments throughout this painting and especially the ribbon holding up the folded documents, bear a remarkable similarity to the larger "letter rack" examples noted previously.[57]

Hans Holbein's *Portrait of Georg Gisze of Danzig* presents yet another fine example of a "letter rack" motif contained within a larger composition. Not a portrait of a saintly scholar surrounded by manuscripts and documents, rather, this panel depicts the young merchant in his London office which is filled with various objects reflective of his collecting enthusiasms and paperwork related to his business as a prominent German merchant in early sixteenth-century London. In addition to the letter he is holding, addressed to him by one of his brothers, several of the documents secured by bands on the office wall also bear some legible inscriptions in the overlapping displays. These letters primarily represent business correspondence from a number of his German colleagues and include symbols, known as merchant marks, which served to verify their authenticity. Gisze's personal motto ("No joy without sorrow") is inscribed on the back wall under the shelf. One piece of paper affixed to the upper portion of the back wall tells us about the sitter: "The picture of Georg that you see records his features, such lively eyes, such cheeks has he, such is his face. In the years of his age thirty-four. In the year of the Lord

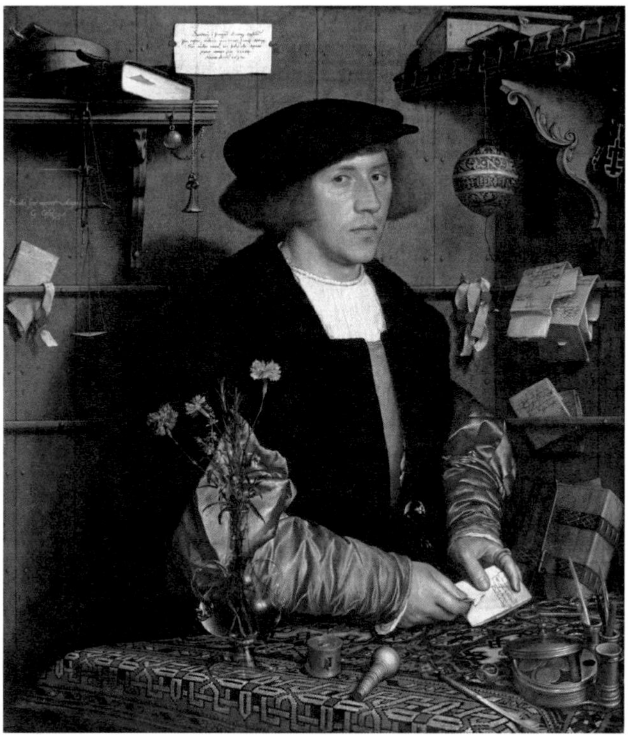

26. Hans Holbein the Younger, *Portrait of Georg Gisze*, 1532. Gemaeldegalerie, Staatliche Museen, Berlin, Germany (bpk, Berlin/Staatliche Museen/Art Resource, New York).

1532."[58] As has been pointed out, the display of paperwork here "anticipated that eye-catching genre [of] artists such as William Harnett."[59]

Larger still life displays of paperwork and textual tidbits can be seen in the works of several seventeenth- and eighteenth-century Flemish and Dutch artists who specialized in the genre, such as Cornelius Gysbrechts, Franciscus Gysbrechts, Wallerant (or Wallerand) Vaillant and Evert (or Edward) Collier (or Colyer). Cornelius Gysbrechts produced a number of remarkably complex *trompe l'oeil* compositions including "letter racks" and is described as "having brought this genre to a pinnacle."[60] His 1668 painting, *Letter Rack*, is an excellent example of his work (illus. 27).[61] This densely packed composition absolutely overflows with illusionistic papers, letters, documents, prints, seals, sheet music, and writing implements. Some of the texts are legible but many are obscured by other overlapping materials. Some of the letters and documents are folded; others are partially open and reveal bits of text fragments. The sense of hidden information in this intriguing composition is also amplified by the black curtain positioned diagonally on the right side of the painting. The curtain appears to be drawn back, revealing only a portion of this letter rack. Additional documents behind the curtain project upwards at the top of the composition. Many of the texts that are visible are obscured by the dense overlapping; the viewer senses that many more texts remain hidden behind the curtain. His works do seem "oddly prophetic of American interpretations of the same theme over two hundred years later."[62]

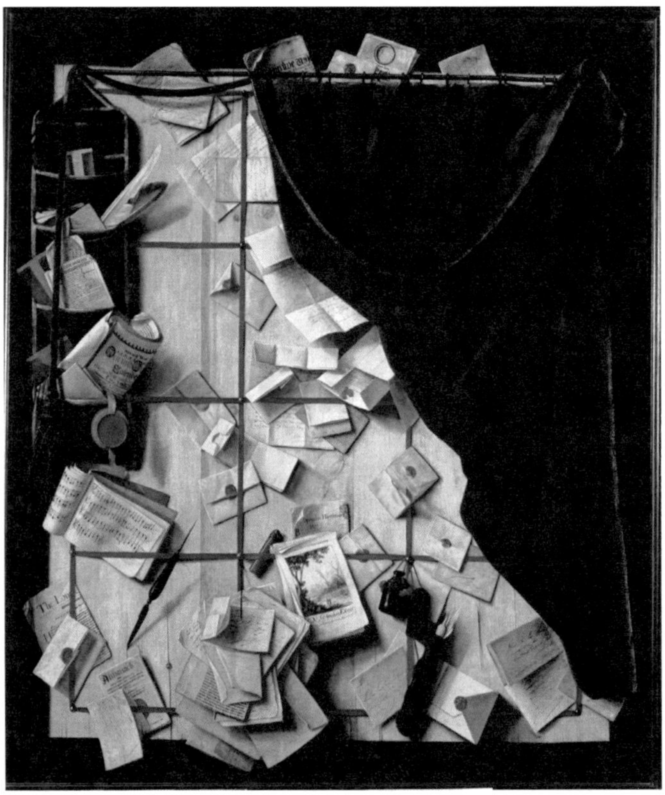

27. Cornelius Gysbrechts, *A Letter Rack*, 1668. Copenhagen, Denmark, Statens Museum for Kunst (Erich Lessing/Art Resource, New York).

The same could certainly be said for the 1658 *Letters with Quill and Penknife* "letter rack" composition by Wallerant Vaillant (illus. 28). Although not a specialist in this genre (Vaillant was primarily a portraitist and engraver), Vaillant created in this unique work with its seemingly haphazard display of folded documents another remarkable precursor to the works of Harnett, Haberle and Peto centuries later.[63] Vaillant's composition presents a close-up view of a wooden wall with carefully simulated graining. The date appears to be written in chalk at the top of the composition. Strips of red ribbon appear to be tacked to this wall and support a number of folded letters, some showing dabs of sealing wax. A quill pen and a penknife are also tucked behind the ribbons. The shadows cast by the ribbons, documents, and writing materials create a masterful *trompe l'oeil* effect. Some of the texts on the folded letters are legible; the crumpled document on the lower left bears his signature: "Wallerand Vaillant fecit." Other texts in the display are illegible, such as the writing inside the folded letters which is indicated by ink showing through to the other side. The viewer can see these texts but not read them.

As a general category within the genre of *trompe l'oeil* art, these paintings depicting letter racks, writing materials, and bits of ephemera are often referred to as *quod libet* pieces, loosely translated as "something popular," or "what you will" or "what pleases."[64] This is a term borrowed from styles of musical compositions that combine different melodies in a pleasant, light, and entertaining manner. Although *quod libet* paintings may give the impression of random arrangements of ephemera (or "papyromania"[65]), it is wise to remember that "the grouping of particular objects, carefully and meaningfully chosen to reflect facets of a personality … or to suggest, to symbolize, certain beliefs and attitudes, turns *quod libet* or letter-rack subjects into literal portraits, professions of faith, or political protests. Although we may miss many of the allusions, we can be certain that nothing was left to chance in these pictorial acrostics."[66] The very fact, however, that many of the texts,

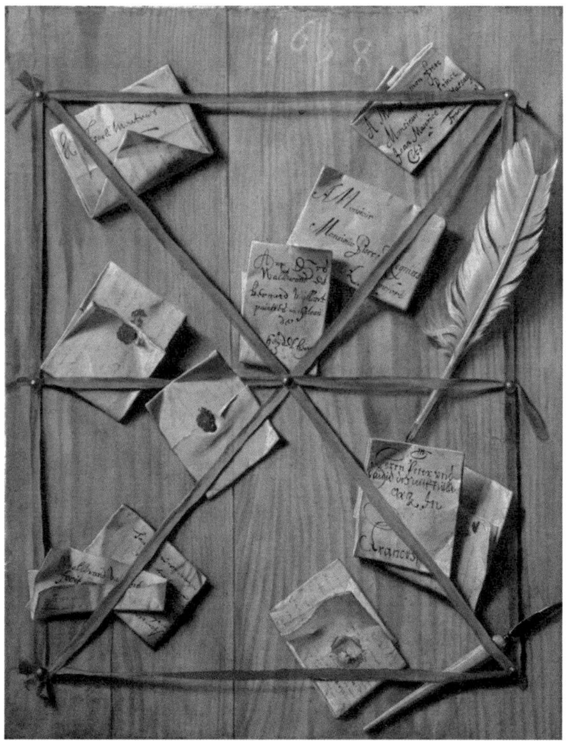

28. Wallerant Vaillant, *Letters with Quill and Penknife*, 1658. Gemaeldegalerie Alte Meister, Staaliche Kunstsammlungen, Dresden, Germany (bpk, Berlin/Gemaeldegalerie Alte Meister, Staaliche Kunstsammlungen, Dresden/Hans-Peter Klut/Art Resource, New York).

although carefully selected, remain hidden, overlapped, obscured, and illegible creates a puzzling sense of mixed and partially concealed messages in these compositions.

The analysis and decipherment of puzzling words in pictures can be especially rewarding when artists who use words in their artworks have also written about their reasons for so doing. For example, the early twentieth-century American painter, Stuart Davis (1894–1964) produced not only many word-filled paintings throughout his career but also copious notebooks, papers, and other writings discussing his art theories.[67] Davis was extremely interested in the relationship of written language and visual imagery; words, letters, and letter-like shapes appear in his paintings throughout the many decades of his artistic career. His early works from the first decades of the twentieth century often include fragments of text: signs on shop fronts, advertisements, store entrances, and so on. While these elements of lettering are often cut off by the frames or are otherwise incompletely rendered, the viewer easily recognizes these letters and words as contributing to the reality of these urban or rural scenes. Even as fragments, these words make clear pictorial sense in his early scenes; they contribute written information to the visual depiction and can be read as believable or realistic elements in the scenes depicted.

As Davis's career progressed, however, his use of words and texts became increasingly more abstract and cryptic. By the 1940s and 1950s, his works were rendered in a bold, colorful, abstract style—frequently including suggestions and bits of text—the significance of which is rarely as immediately clear as in his earlier more realistic works. These latter words require more detailed decoding; they are filled with optical puns and fragments of texts, and often have clever alliterative titles, such as *Rapt at Rappaports, Engrossed at Grossingers, Owh! In San Pao*, and so on. Titles were very important for Davis and his visual/verbal plays on words are a special hallmark of his mature style. In all of these works there is more to be seen, read, and understood than immediately meets the eye, and the beholder is required to investigate further in order to understand the full stories behind these pieces. Indeed, the words and phrases included in these works by Davis not only often function as compositional elements but provide critical themes, symbols, and references. Statements made by the artist, as well as the copious written notes and art theory sketches he created throughout his career, provide researchers with some clues as to the choice and meaning of these words and phrases. An understanding of Davis's own theories about art and his interest in "the manufacture of the Word-Shape"[68] are critical to the decipherment of these pieces. Davis once said, "The artist sees and feels not only shapes but words as well. We see words everywhere in modern life; we're bombarded by them. But physically words are also shapes. You don't want banal boring words any more than you want banal boring shapes or a banal boring life."[69]

Works such as *Semé* from 1953 are dense with references and symbols drawn from Davis's unique pictorial and visual vocabularies (illus. 29). The title *Semé* means "sown," or, according to Davis, "strewn, lots of *things*."[70] This bold and colorful composition is indeed filled with many things: many shapes, words, and letters rendered in the artist's typically hard-edged style of the 1950s. The vivid colors and lively overlapping shapes create a quite energetic effect. The large "X" and "O" shapes, and the word "any" that appears in the lower right of the canvas, are motifs that occur frequently in Davis's work. "Any" stands for his idea that an "artist is free to use any subject matter."[71] Davis said, "In this painting ANY means any subject matter is equal in art, from the most insignificant to one of relative importance. What is significant in subject matter is what is spontaneously given."[72] The "X" and "O" shapes as well as the "S" squiggles are elements of what Davis termed his "Alphabet Syntax"; he sometimes used the "X" to refer to "external" forces on or in compositions.[73] His signature appears in bold script at the upper right of the picture, and the word "EYDEAS" is written in the lower left. Defining this latter as a clever fusion of the words eye and idea, Davis stated, "The Analogy content of this word consists of EYE and Ideas, a casual and unimportant combination (although made into a valid structural element in the painting.)"[74] "Script in writing, the free sequence of written letters is the equivalent of the visualization and drawing of a shape," Davis wrote in 1952[75]; so for Davis, visual art and written language were parallel systems of expression to be used in the manufacture of the Word-Shape. These ideas are naturally very akin to the Dada and Surrealist "word-image" concepts.[76]

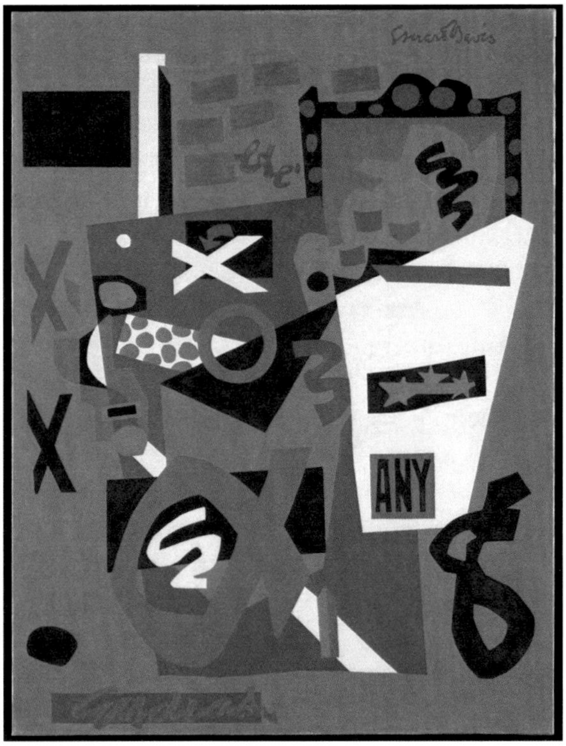

29. Stuart Davis, *Semé*, 1953. New York, The Metropolitan Museum of Art (Art © Estate of Stuart Davis/Licensed by VAGA, New York, New York; Image © The Metropolitan Museum of Art; Image source: Art Resource, New York).

Again, both Davis's word-filled paintings and his drawing-filled writings on art require decipherment. Even the most diligent researchers, however, may remain quite puzzled about the specific meanings of the words and letters that Davis chose to put in his paintings and drawings. This is largely because, even in his own descriptions of his works, Davis was not always "consistent about his homespun definitions and their meanings evolved over time."[77] Hence, while many of the words and phrases included by Davis in his paintings and drawings are often quite legible, in "Davis's elaborate, self-defined word-system, the same concept can be signified by different terms, and equally, the same word (or sign) can have different signifiers, depending on its context."[78] Many of Davis's more cryptic words and statements thus involve many levels of meaning that require and may also reward (if not tax) the patience of viewers/readers willing to engage with his often puzzling visual/written systems of expression.

The intellectual pleasure that a viewer may gain from deciphering the sophisticated word/picture puzzles of Stuart Davis can be experienced in the works of numerous other modern artists as well. The "Metaphysical Funk Monk,"[79] California-based William T. Wiley (b. 1937) is another excellent example of an artist whose works rely upon an extremely close and intimate entwinement of words and images.[80] When asked in a 1979 interview what type of art he does, Wiley ended his list (abstract and representational paintings, watercolors, landscapes, sculpture) with the wry understatement: "Yeah—and some writing too."[81]

A majority of Wiley's works, from the 1960s to the present day, involve dense overlays of written texts and images. Words and phrases surround and appear to flicker through his pieces; not all is evident at first glance. Not unlike Stuart Davis's use of alliteration and complex phrase fragments, Wiley is a true master of verbal tricks, visual and verbal puns, and wording that shifts through and maintains various levels of possible interpretation. Titles of his works thus include such constructs as: *Art Official Birth Plan*, *Lord Half Mercy*, *Only the Brave Sea*, *Eye Sword*, *X Stream Art*, *How to Chart a Coarse*, *Wizdumb Bridge*, *Where the Scare Grows*, *Putting the Heart Before the Course*, and so on. His works are filled with personal symbols and characters including Rim Rat (Rembrandt), Ray Done (Redon), and Sir Rot (Seurat). Indeed, references to the history of art provide a substantial theme in Wiley's work,[82] intermingled also with his many other interests, especially Zen Buddhism.

The complexity of Wiley's visual/written style is well illustrated in his 1971 watercolor *Hide as a State of Mind* (illus. 30). The words of the title appear in the center of the "hide" (Wiley had previously acquired an animal skin that inspired several pieces) that is roughly shaped like a map of the United States. The right section of the hide/map is largely uncolored and the words "Polarized D.K." can be read across this area. A black and white surveyor's rod or measuring stick—a ubiquitous symbol for Wiley—creates the barrier between this section of the composition and the more colorful areas to the left. The rod bears the legend: "Who Shows the Class." Viewers familiar with cartographic conventions may recognize that the position of the surveyor's rod is along the polar declination, hence partially explaining the "Polarized D.K." inscription. The phrase: "God only knows what we were expecting" is written in the lower right corner of the piece and is partially obscured by a back view of one of Wiley's traditional characters, Mr. Unatural. A small boat bearing the figure eight/infinity symbol (another of Wiley's favorites) sails through the bottom of the

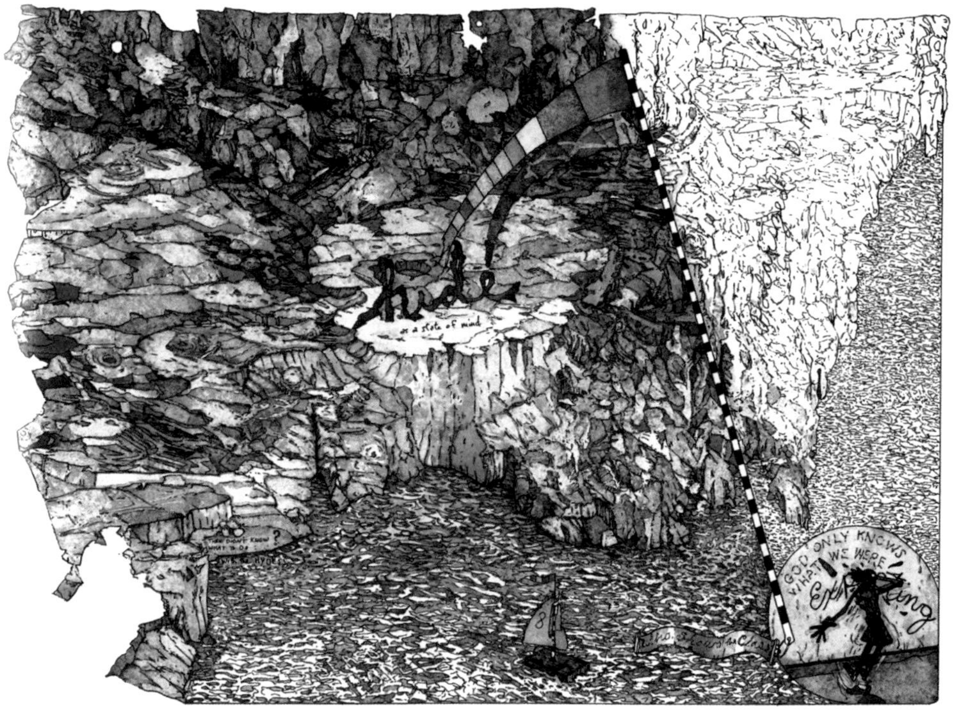

30. William T. Wiley, *Hide as a State of Mind*, 1971 (courtesy Wanda Hansen).

picture. "They didn't know what to do with the hydes" is another phrase embedded in the lower section of this work. The phrases, puns, and riddles found throughout Wiley's works often function, as has been pointed out, like Zen koans—inspiring creative thought but also serving as a reminder that "the intellect too has its limitations."[83] In many cases, the written statements in Wiley's works, "though capable of some intuitive interpretation, cannot be fully explained in relation to the visual image. Rather [they] act as a stimulus to contemplation."[84]

Wiley's 1975 watercolor *Pure Chance* includes the infinity symbol, dunce cap (symbol of the Wizdumb of Mr. Unatural), and various phrases—"precious little time," "whyyourjustakid"—inscribed on a representation of an old-fashioned school slate board complete with wooden frame (illus. 31). The sense of time passing and metamorphosis is captured by the impression of many previous erasures on the slate board itself as well as by the graffiti-like doodles and phrases written on the wooden frame depicted. One of these reads: "Tromp 'Lowell' High"—an obvious pun to those-in-the-know that combines references to Lowell High School in San Francisco with the phrase *trompe l'oeil*, of which this piece is a wonderful example, of course. Another inscription on the slate tells the viewer: "If you get too serious you have to leave."

Wiley's works, although visually very dissimilar to those of Stuart Davis, are

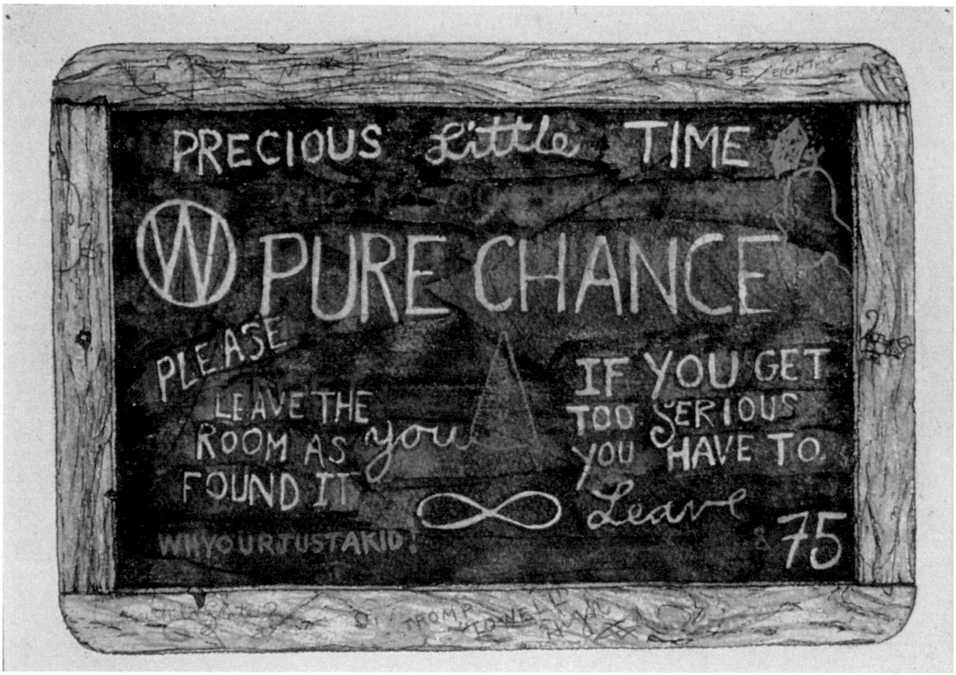

31. William T. Wiley, *Pure Chance*, 1975 (courtesy Wanda Hansen).

also founded upon often complex personal symbols and sophisticated references. His works, frequently in a lighthearted and witty manner, engage the viewer to consider solving (or at least contemplating) the word/picture puzzles. The embedded texts, layers of writing, and erasure found in many of Wiley's works challenge the viewer by their visual as well as textual elusiveness. Not seen fully at first, snippets of words and phrases come into focus only after, in some cases, prolonged scrutiny of Wiley's works. Viewing these works becomes a process of discovery for the observer whose level of appreciation for and apprehension of these works is based upon a willingness to perceive the texts and symbols as they emerge.

Works of art that include elusive or hidden texts actually have a very long history and appear in a great variety of formats, time periods and cultural contexts. Within the broad category of *carmen figuratum* ("word pictures" or "figured songs") the grid text or pattern poem is especially relevant here.[85] Examples of grid texts, anagrams, and acrostics have been traced back to ancient Egypt and classical Greece. Popular with the ancient Romans as well, the form was notably employed in the early fourth century CE by the court poet, Publilius Optatianus Porfyrius, who addressed and presented his productions most favorably to the emperor Constantine the Great in 325. The labyrinthine complexity and rigorous sophistication (if not "neurotic virtuosity"[86]) of the grid poems of Porfyrius earned him lasting renown, and his works were much copied and imitated in later centuries.

A grid poem of Porfyrius typically looks "like a highly sophisticated mosaic of letters."[87] The total area of the page is completely filled with letters that spell out the words of a carefully structured poem. Additionally, certain letters within this grid are picked out, usually by a change of color or by outlines drawn around them, and these selected letters create shapes (for example: crosses, geometric patterns, tree-like forms, chevrons, other letters, and so on) while simultaneously providing other texts ("intexts" or: *versus intexti*) that can also be read.[88] Thus the grid-letters-words of the base text have dual functions; they can be read across the page and also serve to create the "intexts."

The grid poem form of Porfyrius provided inspiration for numerous other writers during the early medieval period. In the sixth and seventh centuries, authors such as Venantius Fortunatus and Ansbert of Rouen created grid poems with embedded cross shapes. Many other significant and influential writers of the medieval period experimented with the form as well, but the supreme master of the form in the medieval period was, without doubt, Hrabanus (or Rabanus) Maurus (ca. 780–856). Abbot of Fulda and then archbishop of Mainz, Maurus was a highly influential figure and author of many works. For our purposes, his treatise containing poems in praise of the holy cross (*De laudibus sanctae crucis*, ca. 813–14) is extremely significant in the further development of the grid poem into a more image-filled genre, or "intertextual imago-poem."[89] The treatise, ultimately addressed and dedicated to Louis the Pious (a son and heir of Charlemagne) contains twenty-eight grid poems with variously developed patterns of pictures within them.[90] The "increased use of pictorial techniques"[91] and detailed imagery are especially notable in Maurus's work.

Appropriate for the theme of the treatise, the majority of poems/diagrams display cruciform patterns. Others include images, such as the symbols of the evangelists, depictions of angels, the crucified Christ, a portrait of Maurus himself kneeling before the cross, and a dedication page containing the figure of Louis the Pious which Maurus originally created sometime in the 820s or 830s for the copy of the manuscript he dedicated to the emperor (illus. 32).[92] This ambitious composition presents a full-length image of Louis the Pious, haloed and garbed in the style of an ancient Roman soldier, holding a shield and a cross-staff. The image is superimposed on a textual grid of fifty-one lines of Latin verse; each line has thirty-seven letters. This base poem offers prayers to Christ, copious praises for the emperor, and Maurus's dedication. The outlines and colored figure of the emperor, his halo, cross-staff and shield "privilege certain letters in the grid which are to be read a second time, now in the directions demanded by the pictorial forms."[93] Within the yellow outline of the halo, for example, the phrase "You Christ crown Louis" can be read in a clockwise direction starting from the lower left section.[94] The tall red cross-staff contains the phrase: "On the cross, Christ, your victory and true salvation, you rule all things properly."[95] This phrase largely reads vertically from the top of the staff down to its base, with the exception of the cross bar. The emperor's shield encircles and contains phrases referencing the "shield of faith" that protects the emperor who relies on God's gifts, and the figure of the emperor and his garments contain further praises for Christ and the power of the Christian ruler. These phrases are read from left to right beginning from the emperor's head, through his right hand and elbow, across his body, then down his left foot and finally his right foot.

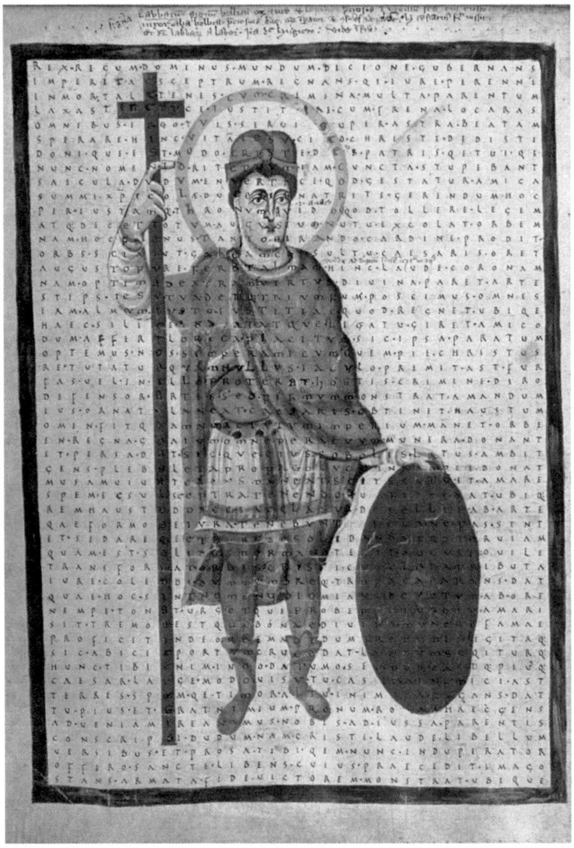

32. Hrabanus Maurus, *De laudibus sanctae crucis*, ca. 826. Full-page image of Louis the Pious. Oesterreichische Nationalbibliothek, Vienna, Austria (bpk, Berlin/Oesterreichische Nationalbibliothek, Vienna, Austria/Art Resource, New York).

This is altogether an extremely intricate linkage of imagery with text, or rather, two textual layers with shared themes. Elsewhere in the manuscript, Maurus created diagrams spelling out, in Greek cross format, the words CRUX SALVUS (Diagram III) and cruciform patterns of symmetrical floral motifs in which the flower petals spell out the names of the seven gifts of the Holy Spirit (Diagram XVI). In another poem/diagram, the symbols of the four evangelists are laid out in a cruciform pattern with the Lamb of God forming the center of the diagram (Diagram XV). The base text explicates the themes of the images, and the images themselves contain words that further reinforce their significance in the pictorial/written schema. The effect of these diagrams is altogether stunning, and the continued popularity of this work is more than well evidenced by the plethora of copies which continued to be produced up to the sixteenth century.[96]

The figured diagrams of Hrabanus Maurus show words and images functioning together on a variety of different levels, and Maurus's own accompanying commentaries or glosses on the diagrams are critical to an understanding of especially some of the most abstract among them. The four circles of Diagram VII, for example, we understand from Maurus's explanation, signify not only "the four seasons, four elements, the four parts of the world, and the four quadrants of the natural day" but are also described as " 'wheels'—because the whole machine of the world is temporal ... and variable and mutable."[97] Meaning is often found, as well, in the number of letters included in the intexts or in the numbers signified by certain letters of the alphabet. These concepts are explained by Maurus in his accompanying descriptions of the poems—his *declaratio figurae*—in which he "worked to bridge the distance between word and image. Practically speaking, the two modes of expression worked together. Understanding came from correlating verbal and visual information."[98] As with the earlier works of Porfyrius, the meanings are "revealed to anyone who is willing to see the design in the text, the picture present in the letters,"[99] while simultaneously reading the base texts and the intertexts. There is no doubt at all that Maurus "intended [his] poems to require time-consuming decipherment" and that "he was concerned with the spiritual benefit [his readers] might derive from contemplating his works."[100] Readers of these pieces embark on a process of discovery, guided by Maurus through increasingly deeper levels of understanding, gradually unearthing the hidden texts and messages contained in these ingenious word/picture puzzles.

The words, phrases, and texts embedded in the figured poems of Hrabanus Maurus, as well as in the works of twentieth-century artists such as Stuart Davis and William T. Wiley, create challenging and engaging puzzles for viewers to decipher. The use of words in these pictures—or pictures in these words—is complex and rarely as immediately understandable as the more straightforward forms of explanatory captions, labels, or speech scrolls discussed in the previous chapter. Apprehension and interpretation of these more complex word/picture puzzles depends on the viewer's patience and ability to uncover the relationships between the words and the images. The assumption, however, is that the words and the images do indeed have a relationship of some sort, that they are combined for some specific reasons, no matter how arcane or flexibly interpreted these meanings may be. Hrabanus Maurus certainly explained his reasons for combining words and images in his quite typically complex medieval fashion. Stuart Davis's notes and theory papers, although often quite cryptic, also provide helpful clues about his intentions and theories. The lengthy titles and copious inscriptions included in Wiley's works certainly provide stories and ideas for the viewer to consider when contemplating his pieces. And, although the use of words (as storytelling devices or simply as elements of pictorial realism) in the works of the American *trompe l'oeil* masters discussed above has inspired continuing art historical debate, these word-filled pictures as well certainly inspire the viewer to, at least, imagine that "important information" may be hidden in many of these works. Again, a relationship between the words and images is assumed, even if the specific nature of the relationship is not immediately evident in all cases. The next chapter will discuss word/picture puzzles in which texts and images often appear to be working against each other, or at crossed purposes.

THREE

Picture/Word Puzzles

In the examples of text/image puzzles discussed in the preceding chapter, the viewer senses that a relationship between the combined words and pictures is implied, even if it is not immediately obvious. Unlike the relatively straightforward and informational roles played by texts in art, such as captions and labels, that serve to identify the pictorial subject matter or contribute information about the artistic authorship, puzzling combinations of words and pictures may conjure up mixed messages for audiences or may involve hidden texts. Viewers faced with these text/image puzzles may need additional information in order to decipher the texts and understand their relationship to the pictorial imagery shown in the work of art. Even so, in the selected examples covered in the preceding chapter, the words and pictures do indeed have some shared relationship to each other, albeit this relationship may be rather confusing at first, or even continue to be quite mystifying.

Visual puzzles, such as presented by the inscribed *cartellino* form, may challenge viewers' spatial perceptions about where, exactly, these texts exist. Are they meant to be "on" or "in" the work of art? Nevertheless, *cartellini* play an important role in providing written information about the artwork, primarily in the form of offering data about the work's authorship and date. Other visual puzzles, such as the hidden and overlapping texts found in any number of *trompe l'oeil* "letter rack" compositions and related examples, generally serve to imply at least some sort of narrative about the owner of the documents if not also evoke the issues and concerns of the time period represented by the collections of masterfully painted ephemera. The seeming whimsicality, spontaneity, and apparent randomness of these compositions leads viewers to search for messages in them largely because they are so extremely meticulously painted and often contain legible writing. The cut-and-pasted text/image compositions of the early modern collage form similarly have inspired a great deal of discussion about the selection processes used by artists such as Picasso and Braque. Do their selected textual fragments have specific meanings? Do they comment on or reflect sociopolitical issues of the early twentieth century? Or were these text fragments selected simply because they were drawn from nontraditional sources in the contemporary print media as the Cubists and Futurists challenged traditional ideas of art-making, literary forms, and materials? In any case, the snipped texts used in collage compositions are indeed closely related to the aims of the artists who selected and employed them, if not due to their specific textual content then at least due to the forms and materials they represent. The development of highly personal and often cryptic written/visual vocabulary systems by artists such as Davis and Wiley also serve to create notable word/picture puzzles for audiences willing to engage with their decipherment, to find out exactly why the artists used these texts and references. Again, a relationship between the words, pictures, phrases, subtexts, and intertexts can eventually be seen, if not fully grasped. Similarly, the words outlined in Hrabanus Maurus's figured diagrams are there for an important purpose; they have specific associations, functions, and meanings within their pictorial contexts.

There are, however, other examples of picture/word puzzles where the level of association between the texts and the images is even less clear, if not deliberately contradictory and quite purposefully cryptic or enigmatic. In these cases, the words and pictures may appear to be functioning on two quite different levels, making reference to conflicting or differing modes in visual and verbal forms of expression, or simply providing enigmas unlikely to be solved. In these cases, the words and pictures may appear to be working at "crossed purposes" to one another or to be otherwise deliberately enigmatic.

Crossed Purposes

In contrast to the more clearly "associative" use of words and images, other influential artists of the twentieth century, such as the Belgian Surrealist painter, René Magritte (1898–1967), deliberately turned the tables in quite the opposite direction. Well known for his meticulously rendered but improbable dreamlike imagery, he also devoted a great deal of his career to exploring the relationship of written words and visual imagery. While living in Paris in the late 1920s, Magritte produced a remarkable series of "word-pictures" or "script paintings,"[1] initially developing, during these years, themes that would continue to appear in his works periodically and consistently throughout the rest of his prolific career.[2] These highly influential works represent an extremely important contribution to the discourse between words and images by their perceptually intriguing and philosophically challenging nature.

Magritte's "word-pictures" may be categorized into several different types: written words combined with recognizable images, written words combined with abstract forms, and written words accompanied by both recognizable and abstract forms.[3] The overriding theme in all of these works, however, is "representational and verbal contradiction."[4] Magritte was extremely interested in the relationship of words and images, between "linguistic and pictorial systems of representation."[5] He developed these ideas also in an influential illustrated essay titled: "Les Mots and les Images" ("Words and Images") which was first published in the journal *La Révolution Surréaliste* in late 1929. In this essay, as in his "word-pictures," Magritte explored the ambiguous nature of written words/language and pictorial imagery, challenging the readers/viewers of his works with paradoxical combinations of images and writing. "His pictures served as puzzles in which the relationship between an object's appearance and an object's poetic or psychological significance was examined. When he introduced ordinary language into these paintings, he speculated on how it obscures thought, how it makes reference to other realities, how it arbitrarily conjures up visual images."[6]

In a number of these works, for example *La Clef des Songes* (*The Interpretion of Dreams*, 1930), recognizable objects are depicted but with largely "incorrect" labels; a shoe is labeled "*la lune*," a hat is labeled "*la neige*," and so forth (illus. 33, in color insert). Magritte did several variations on this, in English as well as French versions, and some of these include at most one "correct" match of image and name. A sponge is labeled "*l'éponge*," a suitcase is labeled "the valise." All told, these compositions have the appearance and "deadpan presentation, style and writing of a school blackboard or a page from a child's primer."[7] The extremely neat and clear cursive writing as well as the simple, generic character of the easily recognizable images depicted make these works appear to be illustrated lessons in vocabulary acquisition. However, the fundamental lesson conveyed here is "the failure of words and images to cooperate."[8] These pictorial puzzles also often challenge the viewer to imagine that the texts/labels are simply misplaced, that if the captions were moved to their correct locations under the appropriate images, all would be clear and sensible. In the vast majority of cases, however, none of the labels can be matched with any of the images, thus furthering the sense of mystification and disassociation between pictures and words.

In other works of this period, Magritte provided written names to completely nondescript shapes. For example, *L'Espoir Rapide* (*Swift Hope*) of 1927 includes an arrangement of dark abstract forms with labels in French naming them as pictorial elements: cloud, horse, village on the horizon, tree, and so on (illus. 34, in color insert). Clearly this is absurd because no recognizable images can be seen, just abstract shapes. However, the labels can also serve to inspire the viewer to imagine that the named elements are indeed "there" in some paradoxical way. What Magritte has done here is to use written language, rather than images, to describe what could be a readily imaginable landscape scene. "Any shape whatever may replace the image of an object," Magritte wrote in his 1929 essay mentioned above, and "an object never performs the same function as its name or image."[9]

Among the approximately three dozen "word-pictures" that Magritte produced in the late 1920s, his iconic image of a pipe bearing the inscription: "*Ceci n'est pas une pipe*" (*The Treason of Images*, 1929) is doubtless one of the most well known and frequently reproduced (illus. 35, in color insert). This work "launched one of the most philosophically significant and intellectually difficult of Magritte's themes. Here, he is dealing with the kind of errors which arise from the arbitrary structure of language and thus lead to philosophical misunderstanding."[10] Magritte created several variations on this image as well, using it in numerous later compositions, as well as in many other works exploring the same theme of label/image. The inscription: "*Ceci n'est pas une pipe*" represents an important visual/verbal paradox. The viewer, by being told "This is not a pipe" is reminded that the image of the pipe, no matter how much it looks like a recognizable representation of a pipe, is not a real pipe but just a picture of one. It could just as well be labeled differently also. Magritte wrote, "Everything tends to make one think that there is little connection between an object and that which represents it."[11] Objects as well as concepts may be represented by both written and pictorial signs. Magritte explored the arbitrary nature of these signs in his "word-pictures" especially, although his interest in the general issues of reality, illusion, and perception are themes recurrent throughout his work.

It should also be noted that Magritte's titles for his works are frequently strange and paradoxical as well. Wishing to avoid descriptive titles, or the implication that an image or object can be translated into or described in words, he preferred what he called "poetic titles" that "surprise and enchant" the viewer.[12] Hence, even the titles of Magritte's "word-pictures" do not contain any of the words depicted in the paintings, nor indeed make reference or give names to any of the images represented in the pictures. Although nonreferential or abstract titles had already become common in early modern art, Magritte's titles, especially, represent his ongoing interest in separating words and images and names and objects, disrupting traditional meanings and conventions, and inspiring the viewer of his pieces to consider "the vagueness and ambiguity of language"[13]—both written and pictorial.

Magritte "disliked being called an artist, preferring to be considered a thinker who communicated by means of paint."[14] He was extremely interested in philosophy and he read widely, although he developed his own ideas on word/image relationships long before the publications, for example, of the major twentieth-century linguistic philosopher Michel Foucault (1926–1984). Magritte deeply admired Foucault's 1966 work titled *Les Mots et les Choses* (*The Order of Things*, or *Words and Things*) and Magritte and Foucault corresponded for a period before Magritte's death in 1967.[15] In 1968 Foucault produced a long essay titled "Ceci n'est pas une pipe" (revised and expanded in 1973)[16] "in which he analyzed Magritte's mental processes [concentrating on] Magritte's methods of including words and an 'image' of an object."[17] It has often been pointed out that Magritte's image/word investigations also bear a remarkable similarity to the linguistic theories developed by Ludwig Wittgenstein (1889–1951) and Ferdinand de Saussure (1857–1913). "Like Wittgenstein, Magritte was concerned with the way in which logic could be used to break the tyranny of words and reveal the confusions which originate in the very forms of our language."[18] Although it does not appear that Magritte was directly familiar with these authors, their writings were certainly extremely influential on many other twentieth-century artists and art movements.[19]

Magritte's own influence cannot be underestimated as well, and his persistent themes—of name/image/object displacement—have been taken up in various ways by a great number of other twentieth-century artists and continue to be influential today.[20] For example, the important American artist Jasper Johns (b. 1930) began creating, in the late 1950s, works that included stenciled letters spelling out the names of colors with, however, the majority of "names" rendered in "incorrect" colors. Johns, an admirer and collector of Magritte's work, had seen the major 1954 exhibition of Magritte's paintings at the Sidney Janis Gallery in New York, and the catalogue for this exhibition included an English translation of Magritte's essay "Les Mots et les Images." This exhibition, along with several others during these years, furthered the reputation that Magritte was already gaining in American as well as international art circles.

The influence of Magritte's verbal/visual contradictions may be seen, for example, in Johns' brilliantly colored oil painting *False Start* (1959) which consists of splashes of colors and stenciled names of colors (illus. 36). The word "white" is written in red on a yellow background; "orange" is written in white on a red background, and so on. Some of the names and colors match; many do not. The stenciled names of the colors "bring the concept of verbal language into the context of the work of art ... and refer specifically to color as an essential aspect of painting."[21] However, the color names and the colors with which the names are written as well as the actual painted sections of color upon which these color names are stenciled generally do not coordinate. As in Magritte's juxtapositions of labels and images, the viewer is faced with puzzling perceptual contradictions concerning the relationship between what is seen and what is read. A companion piece also from 1959, *Jubilee*, uses the same format, including the stenciled names of several different colors, but the words, in this case, are rendered primarily in the tones of white, gray, and black used for the whole composition. "Among the color words are the literally true words 'Gray' and 'Black.' Do the color words as we look at them, make the painting occur inside the viewer's mind? Or do these words stand for the failure of words, their powerlessness in the face of paint [?]"[22]

The sense of disorientation produced by these mislabeled colors has been discussed extensively, and as has been pointed out, "much critical commentary has been devoted to the contradictions inherent in this mislabeling. The commentary itself is paradoxical; nearly everyone begins by saying the device is uninteresting, and then discusses it at length."[23] The perceptual effects of mislabeled colors have also been studied for decades by psychologists as the "Stroop Effect," referring to J. Ridley Stroop's 1935 doctoral thesis and other publications on the subject.[24] The Stroop Effect demonstrates the mental challenge that people have in correctly naming colors when they are presented with lists of color words that are printed in incompatible colors. If the word "yellow" is printed in blue ink, people have much greater difficulty in naming the color as blue than if they are asked to "say 'yellow' in response to the word 'yellow' printed in blue ink."[25]

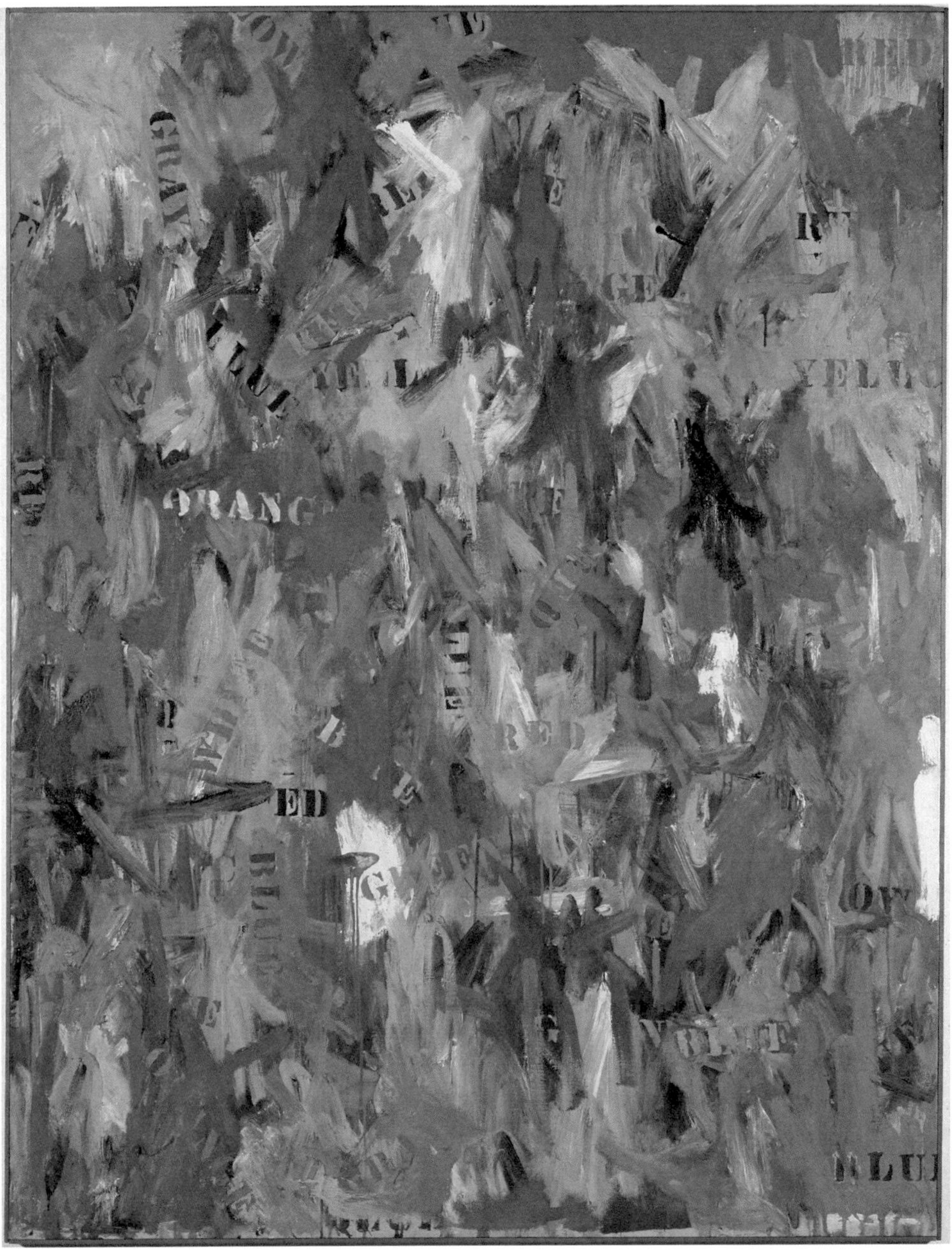

36. Jasper Johns, *False Start*, 1959. Private collection (Art © Jasper Johns/Licensed by VAGA, New York, New York; Erich Lessing/Art Resource, New York).

In any event, Johns, who has been called "a grammarian of pictures,"[26] produced numerous other variations on these themes of paradoxical labeling throughout his career both in painting and in mixed media/collage pieces. In many of his works, "Johns concentrates on how words function in our perception of reality."[27] He often used labels to evoke unspecific things as well as to draw attention to actual three-dimensional objects included in his works. Johns was deeply interested in the writings of Ludwig Wittgenstein and his philosophical investigations of the relationship of spoken and written language to our perceptions of the world.[28]

Shifting relationships between labels/names and images/objects were also explored during this period by Johns' contemporary East Coast artist, Larry Rivers (1923–2002). In the early 1960s, Rivers produced a whole series of labeled pieces both in painting and sculpture. Ultimately inspired by a labeled diagram in a French language textbook he was using for his studies at the Alliance Française in Paris in 1961, Rivers' "Vocabulary Lessons/Parts of the Body" creations from these years indicate, often by stenciled letters, the names for various body parts with lines pointing to these areas on a painted or sculptural image of a human figure. Whether the labels are in French or English (or Italian or Polish), the word/image correlation is intriguingly explored in examples such as *Parts of the Face: French Vocabulary Lesson* of 1961 (illus. 37). In this example, the composition consists of a somewhat sketchily rendered human face surrounded by a series of stenciled French words indicating *oeil*, *nez*, and so on. Viewers who are fluent in the French language can easily determine that these labels are indeed the correct vocabulary words for the various facial parts while viewers who do not read French may or may not assume that the words are correct. Viewers naturally also mentally translate these perhaps unfamiliar vocabulary words into their own language. Different words can be used to mean the same thing, or, as per Magritte, "an object is not so possessed of its name that one cannot find for it another which suits it better."[29] In other examples of Rivers' work in this genre, the viewer can read some but not all of the labels clearly, or can clearly see portions but not the whole of the human figure indicated. In these cases, "this dichotomy alludes to the incompleteness of experience and the desire for clarification that it engenders."[30]

Rivers' labeled pieces function like "bilingual rebuses"[31]; in most cases they seem to use words and images to reinforce rather than to contradict each other. In this sense, these works pose a contrast to the deliberate "mislabeling" of objects and colors by artists such as Magritte and Johns. Even so, the exploration of language and vocabulary words in various written/spoken languages that may or may not be familiar to the viewer represent a level of complexity that challenges viewers in their perceptions of the general meaning and function of labels/terms/words/images. It should be noted that Rivers was also involved in several collaborative projects with contemporary poets and authors, and an interest in image/word relationships as "two different methods, visual and lingual, of transmitting"[32] messages is a recurrent theme throughout Rivers' work.

The mental challenges posed by the various word/picture and picture/word puzzles discussed here and in the preceding chapter represent complex and sometimes contradictory manipulations of texts and images. From even this small sampling, it is evident that the creation of puzzling word/image combinations takes on a variety

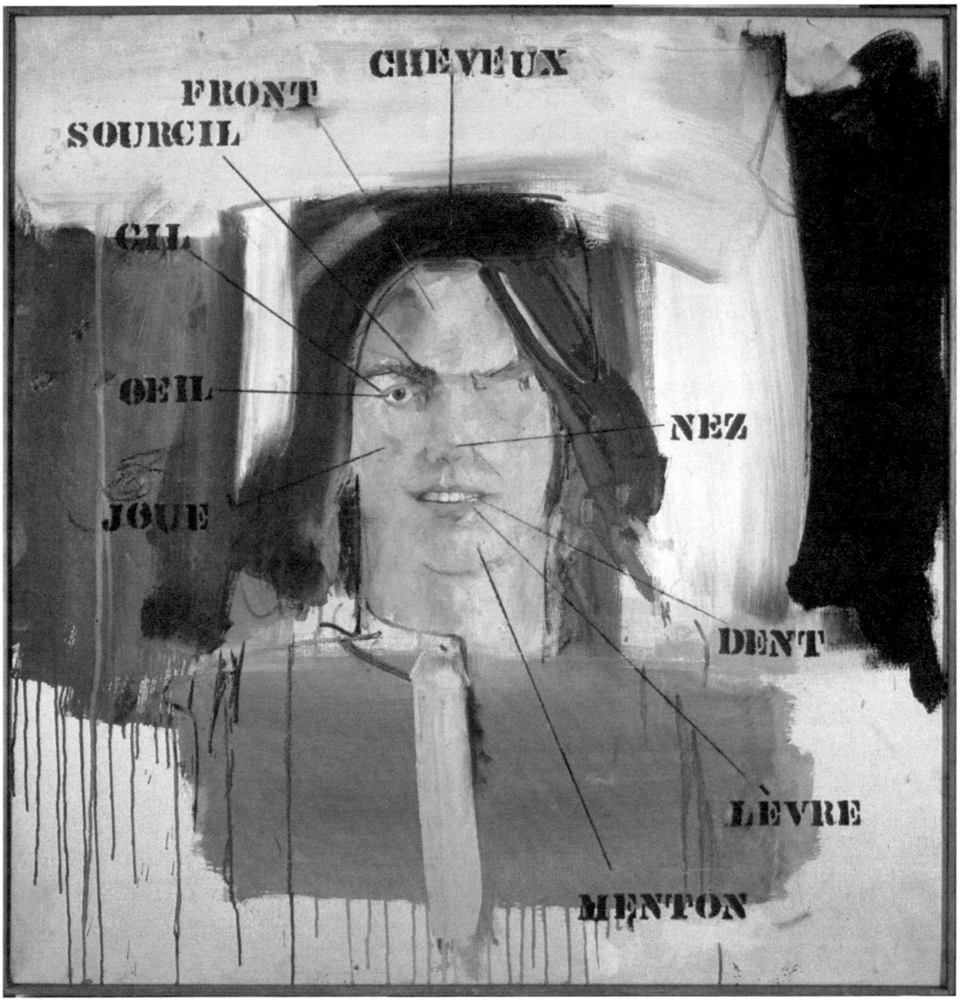

37. Larry Rivers, *Parts of the Face: French Vocabulary Lesson*, 1961. Tate Gallery, London (Art © Estate of Larry Rivers/Licensed by VAGA, New York, New York; Tate, London/Art Resource, New York).

of forms and can be noted in examples ranging widely from ancient to modern art. Texts and words may be hidden in images that in turn may be created of texts and words, such as the intertextual image-poem productions of the late Roman author Porfyrius and the medieval writer Hrabanus Maurus. These complicated productions require very careful and patient study on the part of the viewer in order to unravel their hidden meanings. Similarly, viewers of the word-filled works by twentieth-century artists such as Stuart Davis and William T. Wiley need to engage in a process of decipherment as well as discernment of the artists' own verbal/pictorial vocabularies in order to grasp the mixed and often shifting messages encrypted in these works. Often puzzling, these works raise questions and may be subject to multiple interpretations. The texts included in the dramatically realistic productions of the late nineteenth- and early twentieth-century American *trompe l'oeil* masters of the "letter rack" genre function as elements of realism but often maintain rather unclear "associative relevance to the subject of the picture,"[33] and the deliberately paradoxical use of words in paintings by artists such as Magritte are excellent examples of words and images being combined in contradictory fashions to raise questions about the fundamental natures of visual imagery and written language. Although Magritte's iconic image of a pipe (labeled as "not" a pipe) or Jasper Johns' painting of the word RED (rendered in blue) may inspire many questions and philosophical musings for viewers, the challenges and puzzles posed by such pieces pale in comparison to many, as yet unsolved, mysterious and completely enigmatic word/picture combinations.

Enigmas

Letters, or letter-like shapes, that cannot be deciphered or whose presence cannot convincingly be explained in works of art represents yet another highly intriguing variation on the theme of puzzling picture/word combinations. Inexplicable letters, pseudoscripts and script-like elements that make reference to no known writing systems can be found in the visual arts of many different periods. Some of these enigmas may indeed represent mysteries simply waiting to be solved by careful researchers; others may represent the astute attempts of artists to mimic writing systems with which they are fundamentally unfamiliar; whilst others represent the highly personal creations of artists in developing symbolic writing-like marks that are not, however, really meant to be read in a conventional sense. All told, these enigmas present yet another fascinating facet of words in art.

There are several instances, in late medieval manuscript art especially, of the apparently random use of letters in pictures. Scattered or geometrically configured letters appear in the border designs of several late medieval prayer books, of which the Soane Hours (London, Sir John Soane's Museum MS 4) may serve as an excellent preliminary example.[34] Produced in Flanders, ca. 1512, this manuscript is closely related to a number of others of the Ghent/Bruges school in its detailed iconography, masterfully naturalistic painting style, and decorated borders enriched with architectural/sculptural forms, identifiable flowers and insects, pilgrims' badges, and other devotional objects. Included in the repertoire of border decoration in this manuscript are several pages in which letters are found.[35] Folio 31v, for example, contains a scene illustrating the Dream of Pharaoh which is surrounded by a border of colorful letter-filled lozenges (illus. 38). Attempts to read these letters as words in any pattern (either vertical, horizontal, or diagonal) have proved fruitless for researchers. The letters simply do not appear to make any sense at all in forming words or phrases or even

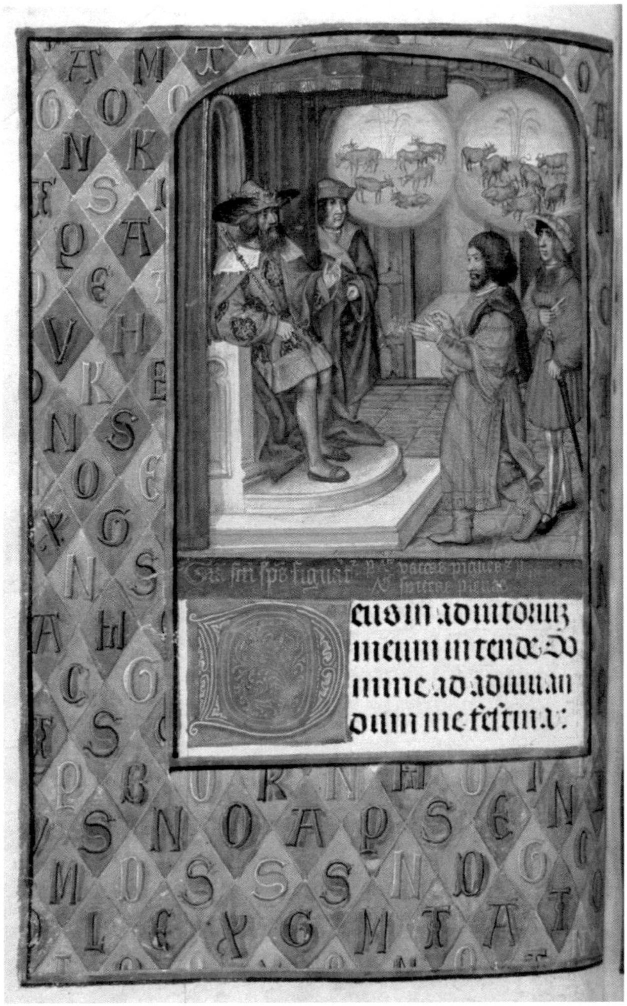

38. The Soane Hours, ca. 1512. London, Sir John Soane's Museum MS 4, folio 31v (courtesy Trustees of Sir John Soane's Museum).

abbreviations. The same can be said of the inscriptions found on the border of folio 103 of the same manuscript. Here, accompanying an illustration of the Pietà, enlarged leafy letters spell out: "NAVI-KMANSIAV-MESKAI"—an inscription which remains puzzlingly indecipherable.[36] On the other hand, a similarly leafy inscription on the border of folio 116v of the Soane Hours clearly reads: "ORA PRO NOBIS KATHE"—an appropriate invocation to Saint Catherine whose attempted torture on a wheel fitted with iron spikes is illustrated in the main scene on the page. The fact that this inscription can be read, and that it clearly relates to the subject matter of the scene illustrated, makes the puzzling inscription and random letters on the other two pages mentioned seem ever more perplexing.

The Saint Catherine illustration in the Soane Hours is one of several that appear to have been copied from an earlier manuscript of the late 1480s produced in the workshop of the renowned Flemish painter, Simon Marmion, the Huth Hours (London, British Library MS Add. 38126).[37] This manuscript includes the Saint Catherine scene, but without the inscribed border. Elsewhere in the Huth Hours, however, the letter-filled lozenge type of border may also be found. On folio 228, facing an illustration of Saint Jerome in penitence, a red and blue diamond-patterned border contains letters rendered in gold and white (illus. 39). These letters have a remarkably three-dimensional quality, appearing to be floating slightly above the page and thus casting shadows on the surface below them. This same illusionistic effect appears on folio 31v in the Soane Hours as well, but the letters used in the lozenge-borders of the two manuscripts are not the same letters. Although the letters on this page in the Huth Hours also are "seemingly set at random," they may in fact be "a reference to the text opening they decorate."[38] In other words, the P, S, A and H, E, R, O may refer to the *Psalterium Iheronimi*, as has been suggested[39]; however, the remainder of the many other letters included in this border remains undeciphered.

The use of illusionistically presented letters as border devices in these late medieval manuscripts may ultimately be derived from the many innovations of the highly influential artist, active probably in Ghent between 1475 and 1485, known as "The Master of Mary of Burgundy."[40] In a prayer book (Oxford, Bodleian Library MS Douce 219–220[41]) produced for Engelbert of Nassau, a lieutenant to the Burgundian duke Charles the Bold, these illusionistic letter forms can be seen notably on folios 33 and 190v. Although the repeated letter "e," written in alternating gold and silver, that appears in the alternating white and blue squares in the border of folio 33 doubtless stands for Engelbert, the leafy gold letters that are depicted as if suspended with a leafy golden grill against a blue ground on folio 190v again appear to be random selections (illus. 40).

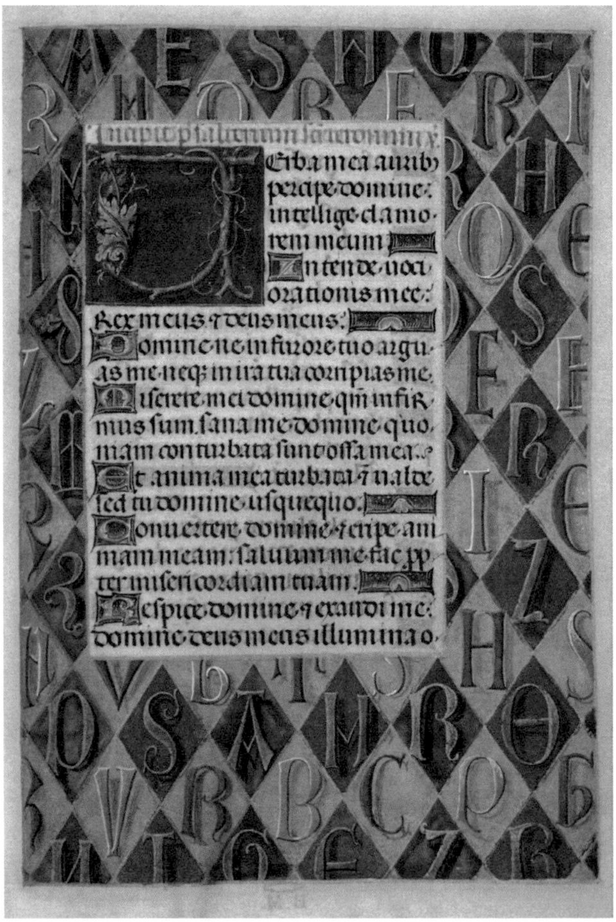

39. **The Huth Hours, 1480s. London, British Library MS Add. 38126, folio 228 (© The British Library Board).**

A charming series of additional uses of the letter "e" in this manuscript occurs in the "tournament sequence" in the middle of the book. Several scenes illustrate a unicorn sporting a blue blanket enlivened with golden "e"s, and in one especially delightful scene on folio 96v, a lady appears to be taking "e"s from a basket at her feet and sewing them onto the trappings of the unicorn. The many "e"s in the Hours of Engelbert of Nassau surely refer to Engelbert, as is the case with the initials identifying other owners of medieval prayer books and other works of art. There are, however, other examples of letters that may serve to signify the initials of as-yet-unidentified owners of medieval manuscripts and other unidentified texts encrypted, especially in the borders of these late medieval manuscripts, that remain highly puzzling.

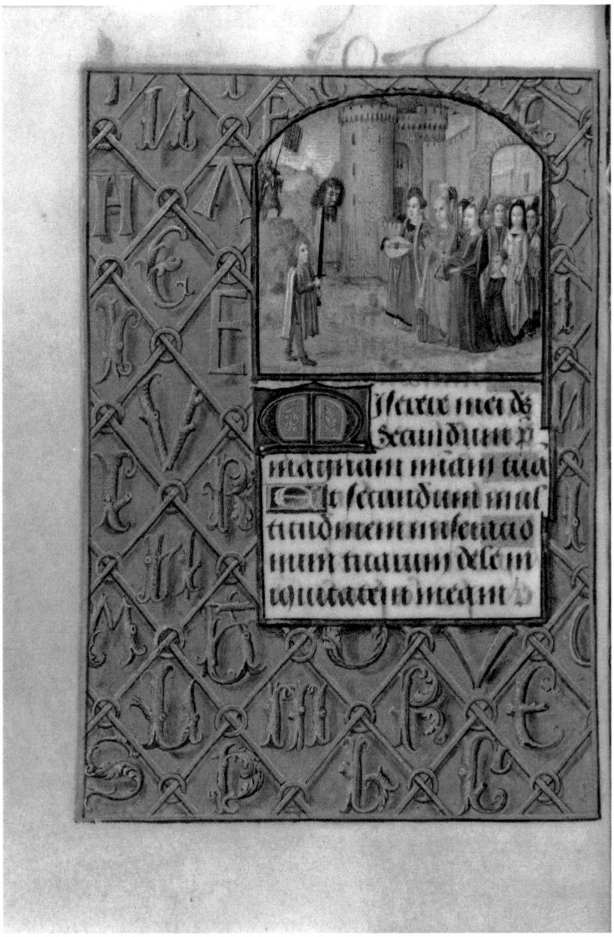

40. The Hours of Engelbert of Nassau, 1475–85. Oxford, Bodleian Library MS Douce 219–220, folio 190v (The Bodleian Libraries, The University of Oxford).

Another delightful but very puzzling example of seemingly random and strewn letters can be seen on folio 135 of the prayer book produced for Marguerite d'Orleans around 1426 (Paris, Bibliothèque Nationale MS Lat. 1156B) (illus. 41).[42] The main miniature on this page depicts the scenes of Jesus before Pilate and Pilate washing his hands, while the golden border is decorated with floral roundels and copious little letters placed at all angles. Two men and a woman appear to be busily at work trying to sweep up and collect these disorderly letters and place them tidily away in little golden baskets. Again, attempts at discerning any words in these letters have proven quite fruitless. The letters do not seem to make any sense at all and appear simply to be rather whimsical design elements in need of tidying up. This alphabetic chaos defies explanation, although it has, interestingly, been suggested that the confusion of the strewn letters may symbolically reflect the confused processes in the trials and sentencing of Jesus.[43]

Amongst the most highly enigmatic and puzzling examples of cryptic letters in medieval books are those to be found in a couple of manuscripts produced for Jean Lallement the Younger (d. 1548), major of Bourges in the early sixteenth century. Jean the Younger, from an eminent, wealthy, intellectual, and evidently very pious family, commissioned several prayer books in the first quarter of the sixteenth century, two of which are especially intriguing for their use of cryptic letters in conjunction with emblematic devices. Baltimore, Walters Art Museum MS W. 446 (ca. 1524) and Washington, DC, Library of Congress, Rosenwald MS 11/12 (ca. 1506) share, with some divergences in scale and scope, distinctively innovative motifs including several illustrations of a letter-strewn torn curtain through which additional scenes and other objects may be glimpsed.[44] For example, folio 37v of the diminutive Walters manuscript shows a dark curtain suspended in several looping folds from the illusionistically rendered wooden frame or window that serves as the border for this page (illus. 42).

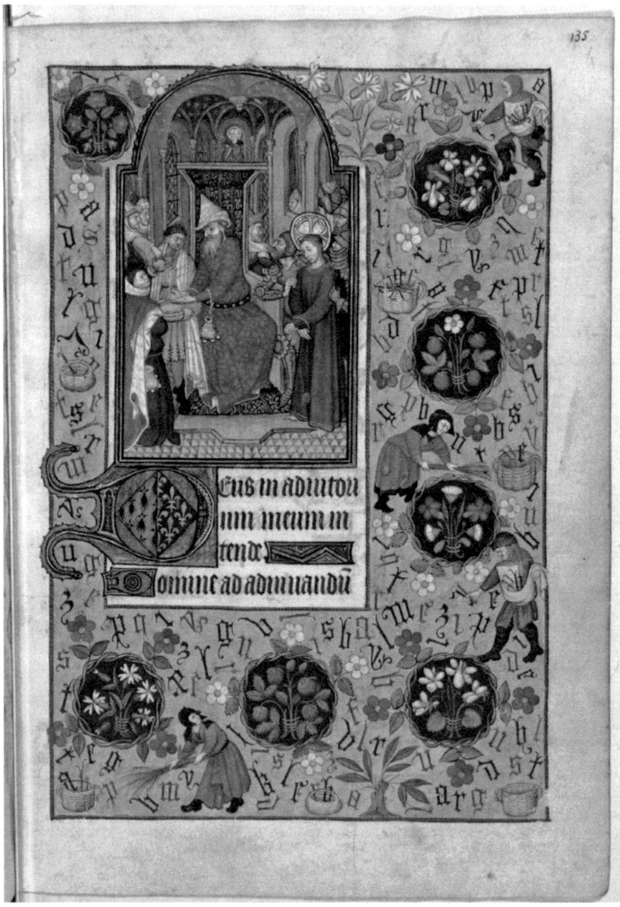

41. The Hours of Marguerite d'Orleans, ca. 1426. Paris, Bibliothèque Nationale MS Lat, 1156B, folio 135 (Bibliothèque Nationale de France).

The reverse side of the curtain is rendered in alternating red and white diagonal stripes, clearly seen via the curling lower left side of the curtain as well as by the tears in the center of the fabric that reveal irregular and hanging shreds of the back side of the drapery unfolding onto the front of the curtain. Through the jagged tear, the viewer can see a folded gray-brown hair shirt, a reference to Saint John the Baptist, the namesake of the owner of the manuscript, and a reference perhaps also to the owner's own penitential practices. The hair shirt is placed against the same blue background that can be glimpsed around the edges

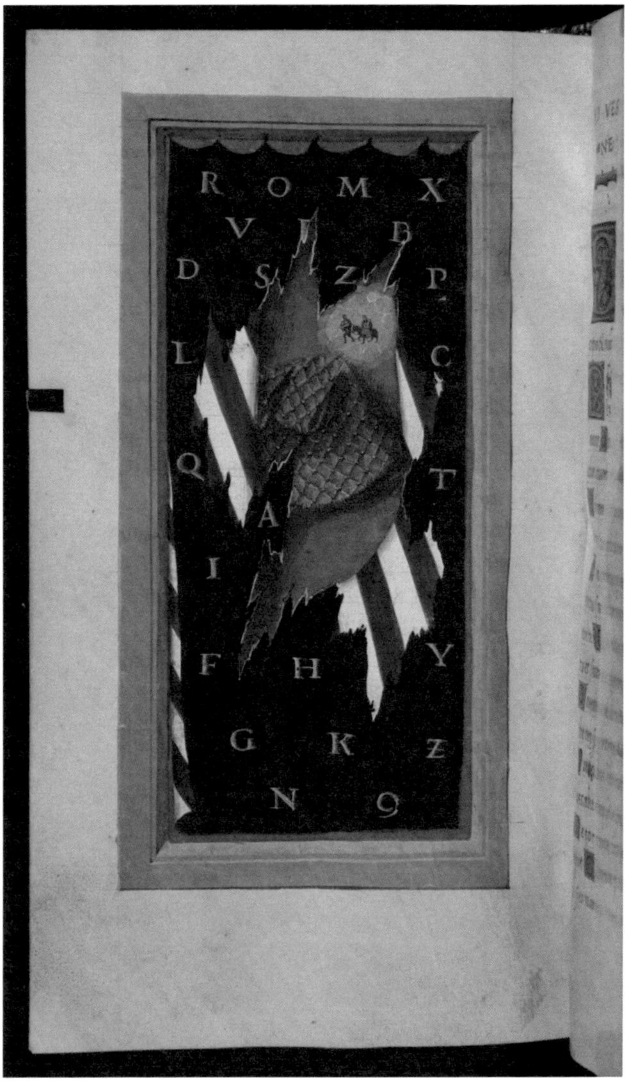

42. The Hours of Jean Lallement, ca. 1524. Baltimore, Maryland, Walters Art Museum MS W. 446, folio 37v (courtesy Walters Art Museum).

of the curtain. A tiny figural scene appears to the upper right of the hair shirt: the flight of the Holy Family to Egypt, with Joseph leading a donkey bearing Mary and the infant Jesus. This little scene seems to appear in a radiating burst of bright yellow light with cloud-like forms surrounding it. The marginalization and tiny scale of this traditional iconography is notable in itself,[45] in addition to the highly unusual torn curtain motif that appears on numerous other folios of the manuscript, similarly admitting glimpses onto other scenes of biblical figures, angels with sealed books, and so on. A series of twenty-four capital letters is written in gold across the curtain on this page, beginning with ROMX and concluding with the cipher 9 at lower right, possibly an abbreviation for another word. Other folios include similar letter and cipher forms. The tear in the curtain obviously gives the impression that other letters, once legible, might be partially obscured by the jagged fabric. In any case, efforts to read these letters as words or phrases in any manner have proven quite elusive. Much careful scholarship has been devoted to unraveling the mysteries of these letter combinations and a variety of potential explanations have been offered, including alchemical formulae, anagrams, references to artist's initials, correlations with especially significant dates and events in the life of the patron and his family, and coded suggestions for the composition of prayers.[46] "The letter-strewn backgrounds form an insistent and persistent enigma with the series of ciphers composing some kind of hidden message."[47] It seems generally agreed that these letters and their repeated combinations are not simply random selections, but "the code in the cod[ices] remains elusive."[48] Our inability to decipher the messages here does not, of course, mean that no messages were intended. But again, it is difficult to make a confident assessment about the level of legibility of these letter combinations and the degree to which they contained meaning for even a limited audience in the early sixteenth century.

Cryptic combinations of letters, as well as letters that are not really letters at all, actually appear with some regularity in many periods in the history of art. This is especially the case where artists have attempted, with varying degrees of success or confusion, to copy letters and words in writing systems with they are unfamiliar, or to make or invent graphic markings that appear to replicate writing systems but really do not. The general term for these is "pseudoscripts."[49] They are meant to appear as if they are indeed realistic and *bona fide* writing drawn from specific foreign sources, but upon further analysis always reveal their inherent illegibility. Pseudo-inscriptions (pseudo-Arabic, pseudo-Hebrew, pseudo-Asian) appear quite often in medieval and Renaissance art of both Italy and northern Europe.[50] Written documents in foreign languages and scripts, as well as various forms of luxury goods, such as textiles, metalware, and so on that were enriched with inscriptions in foreign languages, were avidly traded, gifted, and collected in the medieval and Renaissance period in Europe.[51] Documents and luxury goods from Mongolia and especially the Islamic world brought awareness, if not actual "reading knowledge" of these foreign writing systems to late-medieval and Renaissance Europe. The arts of medieval Islamic Spain, of course, also served as important design sources. Many European artists, intrigued with these foreign scripts but unable to read them, created highly clever and creative variations on them and often used them to lend an aura of authenticity to their paintings of biblical subjects especially. Paintings by early Renaissance artists such as Cimabue, Duccio, Bernardo Daddi, Simone Martini, Giotto, and many others exhibit various types of "oriental" scripts.[52] Variations on these forms may readily be seen in many works by later Renaissance artists, such as Fra Angelico and Andrea Mantegna. There are actually hundreds of examples of the use of Asian- or Arabic-inspired scripts in Italian painting from the late thirteenth to the early sixteenth century.

These scripts often, although not exclusively, appear in the forms of bands or borders on garments worn by the biblical figures in these Renaissance works and especially those garments worn by the Virgin Mary, doubtless reflecting the honorific and luxury textiles from the Islamic world with which Europeans were becoming increasingly familiar.[53] The Arabic-inscribed band motif (or *tirāz*)[54] on textiles from the Islamic world has a lengthy history and distribution from the eighth to the fourteenth century, from Egypt to Persia and Sicily. Used as a symbol of political power, wealth, authority, and royalty, *tirāz* inscriptions appear primarily but not exclusively on luxury garments created for religious or courtly use. The inscriptions are often highly formulaic, including standard, significant Muslim prayers, the insignia or name of the ruler under whose patronage the fabric was produced, the name of the workshop, and the place of manufacture and the date. Depending upon the time period and production context, these inscriptions were embroidered, painted, or woven into the cloth. These textiles ultimately provided the inspiration for the woven cloths with repeating Arabic calligraphic motifs that continued to be produced in both the Muslim and Christian worlds up to ca. 1500, as well as those textiles produced in non–Muslim workshops that generally display "non-semantic calligraphic motifs."[55]

When depicted in early and later Renaissance paintings, "the Arabic-inscribed border moved from the actual world of politics to the imagined world of art."[56] The inscriptions on the textiles depicted in works by western European artists are imitative and evocative of Arabic calligraphy, rather than strict replications. Although in some cases, actual Arabic letter forms appear, they do not have any meaning. Indeed, many of these "fantastic oriental characters cannot be identified with any actual oriental language,"[57] whereas others of these letter and character forms are clearly, although rather loosely, based on specific scripts such as Arabic Thuluth, Kufic or Naskhī, and Mongolian 'Phags-pa.[58]

For example, the garment of Jesus held by the Roman soldiers as well as the robes worn by these soldiers depicted in the Crucifixion scene by Giotto in the Arena Chapel in Padua, ca. 1304–13 demonstrate Giotto's obvious awareness and inventive replication of "Oriental" scripts (illus. 43). These garments are enriched with bands of lettering around cuffs, hems, and necklines and in vertical and horizontal strips on the robe of Jesus. The letters are arranged in distinctively blocky configurations with a mixture of geometric and curvilinear forms. All told, these inscriptions bear a significant resemblance to the Mongolian 'Phags-pa style of writing, a script that the great Mongolian ruler, Kublai Khan, ordered to be created and used on official documents in the mid-thirteenth century.[59] Missionaries, travelers, and envoys to Asia in the thirteenth and fourteenth centuries brought back documents, silks, souvenirs and paper money containing this form of writing, and "it is very likely that [Giotto] was attracted by the mysterious shape of these letters and may have copied or adapted their general properties."[60]

In other words, the western awareness of and appreciation for these foreign styles of writing generally resulted less in exact replication of the writing forms but rather in the primarily ornamental use of certain elements of these scripts as design motifs.[61] Generally speaking, these artists "had no idea of the meaning of the oriental characters. The designs give the impression of oriental characters but are not exact enough to be read as such."[62] These inscriptions seem primarily designed to lend an ambiance of exoticism as well as to "give an authentic oriental air to biblical scenes."[63] In particular, the use of pseudo–Arabic inscriptions[64] on western medieval and

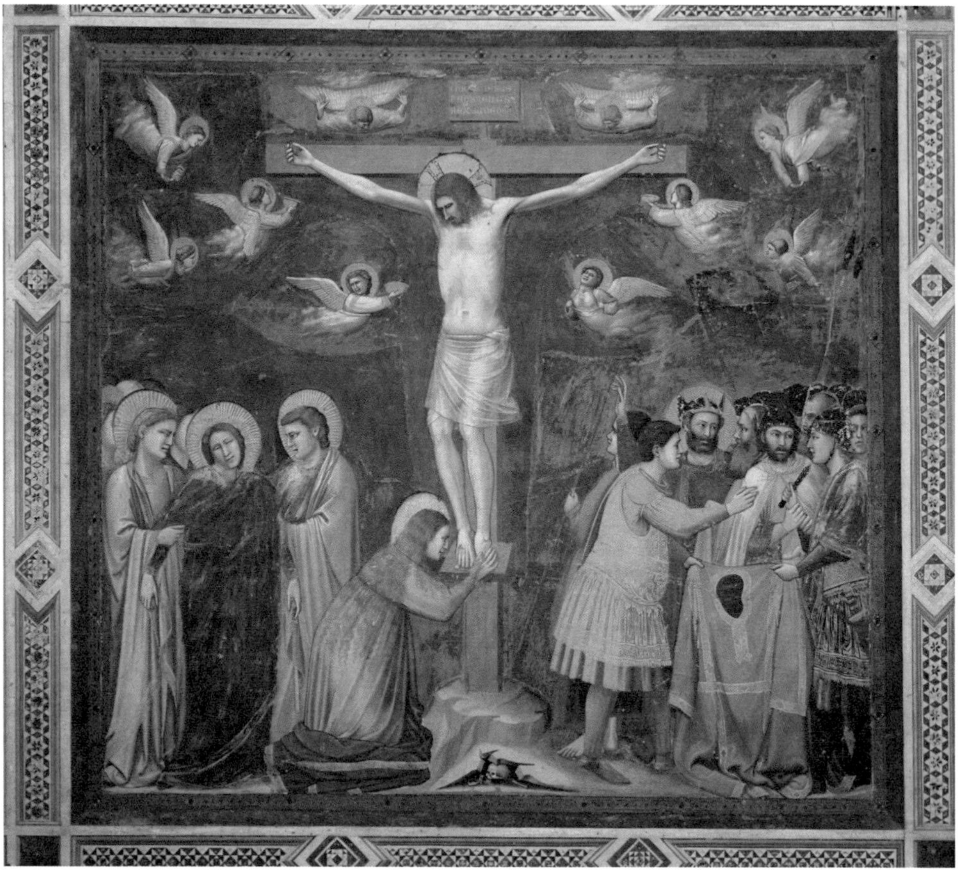

43. Giotto di Bondone, *Crucifixion*, ca. 1304–13, Padua, Italy, Scrovegni Chapel (Alfredo Dagli Orti/The Art Archive at Art Resource, New York).

Renaissance paintings depicting biblical figures rather boldly reflects the western misunderstanding of the use and development of Arabic as a dominantly Islamic script. In other words, the pseudo-Arabic script styles that western medieval and Renaissance artists often use in their depictions of biblical subjects are far from accurate. The garments worn by the figures as well as the other textiles and objects depicted in their paintings would not have used the Arabic script styles that these artists imitated because these were not the writing forms that had developed during the eras in which their biblical scenes are placed. The robes of Jesus or the hems and edges of the garments worn by Mary would obviously not have been enriched with Arabic script based on the Islamic examples available to western European artists of the late medieval and Renaissance periods. Although they correctly associated Arabic script as "Eastern" and "realized that it had a highly honored status in the region where Christianity was born," their "confusion between the Eastern past and present" resulted in their use of current styles of Arabic script for scenes set in the biblical past.[65]

> Although Arabic writing had a symbolic meaning in the Muslim world, and certain formulas contain religious invocations including the name of Allah, the West apparently did not understand it as such. As this writing often occurred on Biblical figures, including the Jewish High Priest, it may have been interpreted as ancient Hebrew script or at least that used by the New Testament figures and by Christian saints. As such, it would have differed from the Hebrew alphabet used by the little-esteemed Jewish contemporaries and so seemingly innocuous enough to be used in a Christian context.[66]

The most salient feature of these "pseudo-inscriptions" is that they are meant to appear correct and believeable. Although illegible, they are designed to look as if they could be read. "They imitate a mystique ... both as ancient documents and simply as text, as words carrying a symbolic significance beyond what they actually say."[67] These types of pseudo-inscriptions thus lend an aura of authenticity to these works by their pseudo-accuracy and their power as (even misunderstood) script symbols.

The invention of exotic and highly-significant-looking lettering also characterizes the work of several later Italian Renaissance artists, perhaps most notably Cosmè Tura (ca. 1430–1495) who served as court painter to the prominent Este family of Ferrara from about 1458 to 1485. Several of his paintings, in addition to those that include legible inscriptions in Latin and Hebrew, feature "strange markings, a kind of cryptic epigraphy"[68] which ranges from scrolling forms to sharp angular shapes reminiscent of Hebrew, Arabic Kufic, and Gothic letter forms. For example, his ca. 1460 *Pietà* (Venice, Museo Correr) well demonstrates many of the stylistic idiosyncrasies of his works (illus. 44). The panel depicts the Virgin Mary

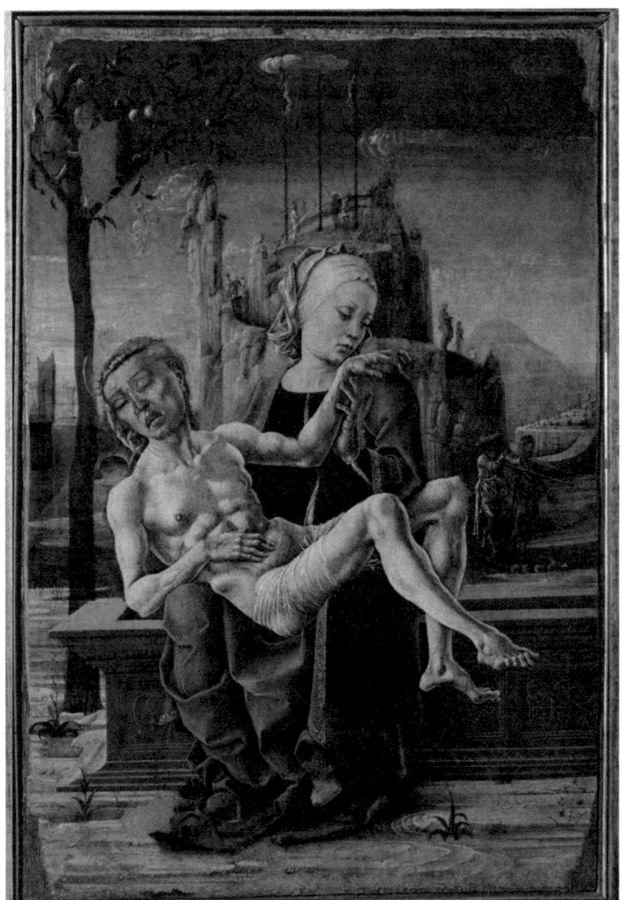

44. Cosmè Tura, *Pietà*, ca. 1460. Museo Correr, Venice, Italy (Cameraphoto Arte, Venice/Art Resource, New York).

seated on the edge of an open sarcophagus supporting the bleeding and ravaged body of Jesus on her lap. "Tura's handling of human proportions has a calculatedly shocking effect,"[69] from the enlarged head of Jesus with his agonizingly contorted facial expression, to his projecting hip bones, knees, and twisted feet and legs. The background shows the site of the Crucifixion on Mount Calvary with the tiny figures of the two thieves elevated on extremely tall crosses. A little monkey clambers up the tall tree on the left side of the composition. The edges of Mary's garment are enriched with golden embroidery in patterns reminiscent of the pseudo-Arabic scripts used by earlier Renaissance artists, but the peculiar raised, script-like forms that appear on the front of the sarcophagus are purely Tura's own calligraphic invention. These scrolling forms, although they "occasionally assume shapes suggestive of the Latin alphabet,"[70] cannot be read. However, they arguably seem to be intended to be seen as inscriptions and not as purely decorative elements, such as appear elsewhere in Tura's works and in his designs for metalwork, medals, sculptures, tomb monuments, and so on.[71] Similar cryptic epigraphy appears in a number of Tura's other works, and while it is possible that "some of these quasi-inscriptions may have had legible meaning for certain members of Tura's audience, their deliberately cryptic nature turns attention away from any content to their formal or pictorial character, to their status as a kind of pure calligraphy ambiguously hovering between writing and patterning."[72] These seem to be more than simply "semi-words,"[73] decorative devices, or "demonstrations of masterly penmanship,"[74] but powerful and mysterious emblems, perhaps symbols of erudition, conjuring up a sense of arcane meaning accessible only to the learned and elite social classes of which Tura preferred to consider himself as a member. There may, in fact, be a whole multitude of meanings behind Tura's enigmatic inscriptions. The artful and erudite lettering he created in several of his works may reflect not only his own personal social aspirations, his interest in creating a "signature style" overall characterized by a linear and calligraphic sense, but also the revived and contemporary debates about the relative merits of writing/writers and painting/visual artists in the courtly culture of later fifteenth-century Ferrara.[75]

Enigmatic inscriptions and pseudoscripts have also been created and used by several other artists for a diversity of reasons. Vincent van Gogh (1853–1890) was, as is well known, enormously enamored of Japanese art and especially Japanese woodblock prints, as were so many other Europeans in the late nineteenth century.[76] Van Gogh was an avid collector of Japanese prints, and he produced several oil paintings that represent copies after examples by renowned nineteenth century Japanese printmakers such as Andō (Utagawa) Hiroshige (1797–1858).[77] In some cases he included Japanese characters as border decorations in these works, such as his 1887 paintings *The Bridge in the Rain* and *The Flowering Plum Tree* (illus. 45), both copies after prints from Hiroshige's series *One Hundred Views of Famous Places in Edo*, ca. 1857. Although Van Gogh more or less accurately copied several of the Japanese *kanji* characters from the original prints, others of the characters are really not accurately

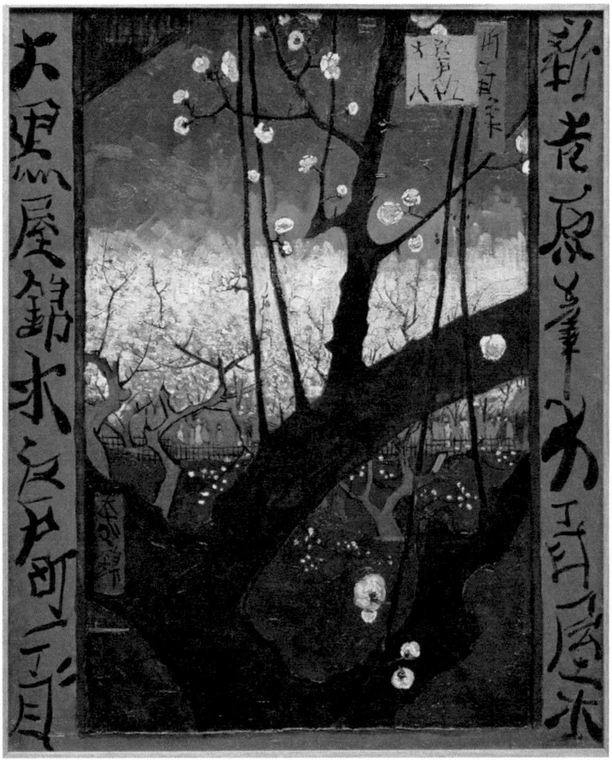

45. Vincent Van Gogh, *The Flowering Plum Tree*, ca. 1887. Van Gogh Museum, Amsterdam, The Netherlands (bpk, Berlin/ Van Gogh Museum/Hermann Buresch/Art Resource, New York).

copied at all and represent rearrangements and additions, especially the characters that he added to the borders of both of these paintings. These calligraphic borders do not appear in Hiroshige's original prints, and Van Gogh otherwise quite creatively replicated the other sections of framed texts that do appear in the original prints, moving them to slightly different placements in his paintings, changing their format, and adding more characters loosely copied from inscriptions on other Japanese prints that he owned.[78] He also painted the frame of his 1887 *Still Life with Quinces, Lemons, Pears and Grapes* with a design of decorative Japanese characters.

Van Gogh was a deep admirer of Japanese *ukiyo-e* prints, he organized several exhibitions of Japanese prints in Paris in 1887, he collected many, and studied them carefully at exhibitions such as organized by the art dealer Siegfried (Samuel) Bing in Paris. Bing was extremely influential in bringing Japanese art to the attention of western audiences in the late nineteenth century. Van Gogh was attracted to the compositions, subject matter, linear quality, and color palettes used by Japanese printmakers; indeed, he regarded Japan as a sort of "utopian dream."[79] His replication of the Japanese calligraphy, used for artists' signatures, titles, and publisher's marks, found on these prints reflects this well. Van Gogh was attracted to the forms, he liked the way they looked, and without trying to study or precisely replicate all of the Japanese characters, he approximated their general appearance, although in some cases his efforts, as has been said, may have resulted in "little more than gobbledygook."[80] In other cases, the characters are "reasonably legible."[81] Above all, the calligraphic motifs he included in his works were intended to give his Japanese-inspired pieces an even greater Japanese "flavor."

Similarly, in the late eighteenth and early nineteenth centuries, the great enthusiasm for all-things-Egyptian characteristic of the Napoleonic era/Empire style saw many works of decorative art, especially furniture, enriched with pseudo-hieroglyphic forms. While some of these pieces copy actual hieroglyphs, many do not, and in any case the often whimsical rearrangement and reinterpretation of the forms was designed not for legibility but to impart an Egyptian ambiance, conjuring up a sense of arcane and enigmatic ancient word/symbols.

Ancient pictograms, as well as Asian calligraphy, have also served as sources of inspiration for many other modern artists, either in their inventions of pseudoscripts or in their use of graphic markings that conjure up foreign, mysterious, or undecipherable symbol systems. For example, Paul Klee (1879–1940),[82] Joan Miró (1893–1983),[83] Henri Michaux (1899–1984),[84] André Masson (1896–1987),[85] and Max Ernst (1891–1976)[86] all created unique personal versions of script-like markings, frequently enlivening their works with what appear to be forms of picture-writing, sometimes interspersed with legible words or word fragments as well as recognizable or semi-recognizable forms plus highly abstract shapes. These sorts of combinations, especially in the works of Klee and Miró, raise deliberately challenging questions about the differences, and if there truly are differences, between pictorial and written symbol systems, between texts and pictures. Viewers may be quite puzzled about how to approach and "read" these pictures because it is often difficult to determine whether the elements included in these works are pictorial images or textual passages, or if these elements are simultaneously both words *and* images. Viewers may wonder if what we customarily perceive as writing cannot also be seen as a form of visual imagery, and what we customarily perceive as visual imagery cannot also represent a form of written textuality.

Both Klee and Miró were deeply interested in these issues and explored "the meeting place of script and image"[87] in their works by using often unexpected combinations of both abstract and recognizable words and images so that the traditional distinctions between writing and pictures are blurred. Miró was extremely fascinated and inspired by prehistoric art and symbols in his own development of a unique sign language based upon "contemporary anthropological theories about 'primitive mentality'" and in his use of pictorial elements "envisioned at a primary, sensory stage wherein form and meaning are undifferentiated."[88] Many of his works use forms and images derived from his studies of Paleolithic painting and sculpture, reinterpreted in his own unique style; others of his works include poetic or evocative or illogical (but legible) inscriptions whose graphic appearance "is as important as their content."[89] For Miró, words and images, and art and poetry, were continuous, one and the same.

Other figures developed highly idiosyncratic forms of illegible picture-writing, such as those of the Belgian author and painter, Henri Michaux, who was inspired by his deep and life-long interest in Asian calligraphy and philosophy, which espe-

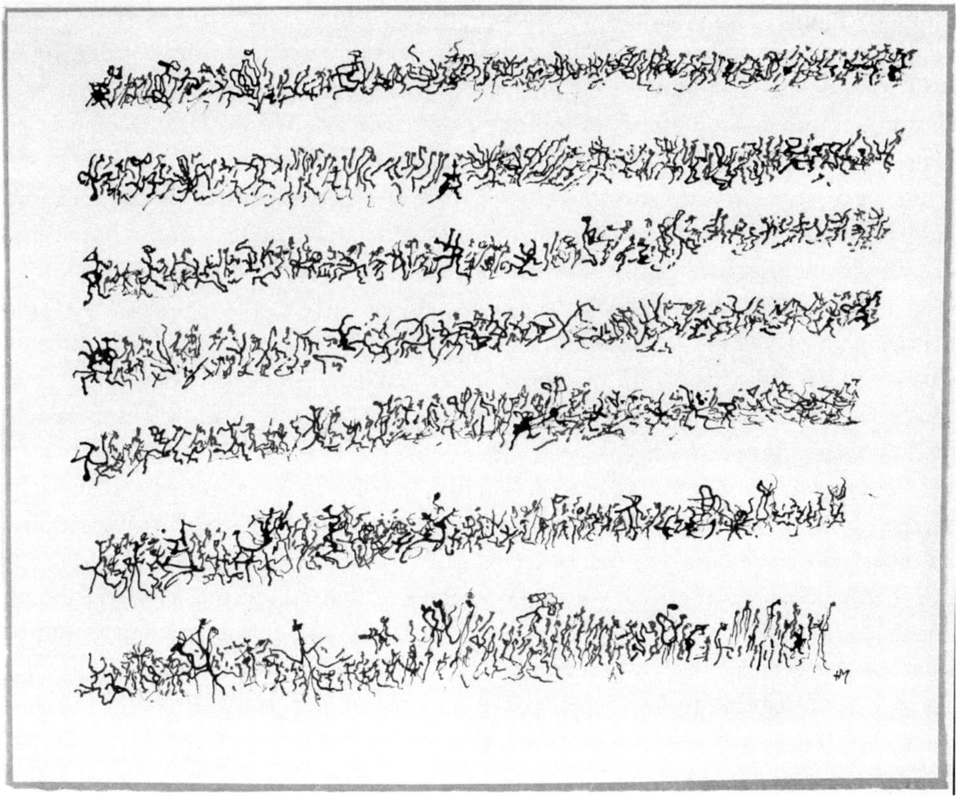

46. Henri Michaux, *India Ink Painting*, 1962. Musée Nationale d'Art Moderne, Centre Georges Pompidou, Paris, France (© CNAC/MNAM/Dist RMN-Grand Palais/Art Resource, New York; © 2013 Artists Rights Society [ARS], New York/ADAGP, Paris).

cially flourished following his travels to Japan, China, and India in the early 1930s. Many of his pen and ink compositions exhibit dense lines or configurations of what appear to be Asian characters but which actually represent his own personal renditions of Asian calligraphic-like forms or ancient pictograms (illus. 46). Some of these works may give viewers the initial impression that they are replications of actual samples of Asian script but, apart from their general appearance, they are wholly creations by Michaux. "Poised at the boundary of verbal and graphic forms of representation, they testify to an impulse to break violently with language as a conventional code."[90] As Michaux wrote, "Who has not wished at some period to create an abecedarium, a bestiary, or even an entire vocabulary, from which the verbal would be entirely excluded?"[91]

The pseudoscript created by the twentieth-century German Surrealist artist, Max Ernst, also conjures up a sense of ancient pictograms and undeciphered or otherwise inaccessible foreign scripts. Ernst, one of the founding members of the Surrealist movement in Paris in the 1920s, has been described as a "*pictor doctus*, or scholarly painter."[92] Extremely well versed in the history of art, and extremely well read in literature, philosophy, and psychology, Ernst created a prolific outpouring of paintings, collage, sculpture, and illustrated books that are of great influence and continue to provide a plethora of topics for scholarly discussion. The German-born Ernst lived in Paris during the 1920s and 1930s, emigrated to the United States in the 1940s, and returned to France in the 1950s. He is well known for his complex and enigmatic works of dream and fantasy, at times witty and erudite, at times horrifying and disturbing. His use of nonconventional techniques such as *frottage* (rubbing surfaces to achieve textures), *grottage* (scraping painted surfaces to create textures), and *decalcomania* (creating textures from paint or ink pressed and pulled away from a surface), as well as his astute juxtapositions of collaged imagery from a variety of illustrative sources, have made Ernst one of the most enigmatic as well as esteemed of twentieth-century artists.

In several of his paintings as well as in his published and illustrated collage/writings, we find "mysterious ciphers invented by Ernst himself, a visible language hiding its meaning or relegating it to another world."[93] In works such as *The World of the Naïve* from 1965, geometrically arranged panels of dense picture script and shapes appear to float in a galactic space, or perhaps a microscopic space such as would be seen via a slide placed for ultraenlarged study in a microscope (illus. 47, in color insert). Is this meant to be "outer space"—a view of stars and planets in the cosmos?—or "inner space"—a view of the amazing complexity of both inorganic and biological forms when viewed through a microscope? Or both? Ernst was extremely interested in science, astronomy, astrology, and alchemy. Perhaps this painting suggests "an alchemical model of divine creation in which galactic and microscopic forms are one."[94]

The oil painting presents a series of fractured and overlapping geometric planes defined by linear white boundaries. Forms resembling stars and planets appear against a hazy dark background that appears to be filled with clouds. Bursts of light appear, as well as linear white shapes placed at diagonals following the confines of the geometric planes. Within these sections, dense lines of script-like markings are included; some of these are small and others are large. Some of the larger markings quite clearly resemble "stick figure" drawings of humans, with arms, legs, and heads. Others appear to be "simply" calligraphic scribbles. The dense and carefully arranged sections of smaller graphic markings also include some of the same humanoid elements interspersed with calligraphic shapes. Thus, the viewer receives the impression that these markings, overall, may represent a type of unknown or "prehistoric" language. Some of the shapes and forms may be recognized as pictographic images or conventional symbols for known forms, whereas others of the markings remain obscure but might be "read" as well, if only the conventions were known.

The viewer is confounded and intrigued by these mysterious texts written in an unknown language.

> The secret writing bridges the gap between a familiar and an unfamiliar world, between the visible and the invisible, composed as it is of ciphers which simultaneously belong to visual and verbal codes. The writing, which functions throughout as a visual sign, creates only momentary illusion that it is decipherable, that the letters may somehow yield a meaning.[95]

Ernst developed this cipher-writing especially in the 1960s, and it notably appears also in his illustrated book published by the avant-garde editor and printer Iliazd (Ilia Zdanevitch, 1894–1975), who was active in Paris in the mid-twentieth century and whose innovative approach to book design, illustration, and typography was highly influential. In the mid–1960s, Ernst and Iliazd collaborated on an illustrated book titled *Maximiliana ou l'exercise illegal de l'astronomie* (*Maximiliana or The Illegal Practice of Astronomy*), which was published in 1964.[96] This book tells of the astronomical discoveries of the late nineteenth-century German astronomer, Ernst Wilhelm Leberecht Tempel (1821–1889), whose career and contributions to the field did not ultimately receive due recognition during his lifetime. Both Iliazd and Ernst were attracted to "voyages of exploration and for quixotic, forgotten heroes."[97] Ernst in particular was intrigued by his shared German ancestry with Tempel, their sharing of names, and by Tempel's naming of one of the minor planets he discovered "Maximiliana" (after the Bavarian king Maximilian II). Tempel was criticized by contemporaries for his use of a nontraditional name for this and others of his planetary discoveries; Maximiliana is today known as Cybele although several comets are still named after Tempel.

In any case, the 1964 book published and typeset by Iliazd and illustrated by Ernst contains many pages filled with Ernst's cipher writing, interspersed with planetary images and selected quotes from Tempel's own writing. These include many "tiny hieroglyphs, vaguely reminiscent of plankton-like living forms," "larger characters of figures of various sizes, suggesting humans or creatures or hybrid Egyptian gods [that] interrupt the flow of hieroglyphs like constellations punctuating the heavens [resembling] at times an underwater scene, at times a nebula or supernova."[98] The page layouts vary widely throughout the volume. In some cases, dense lines of Ernst's cipher writing are shaped into biomorphic forms and geometric blocks; on other pages, the passages are looser and more flowing; and on yet other pages, sections of cipher writing (printed in different colors) are overlaid on top of each other. Many of the little shapes are completely abstract, whereas others bear some resemblance to fish, bird, and human (stick figure) forms. These latter, especially, give the appearance of somewhat frantically gesticulating little figures; they convey the impression of highly active, twittering voices speaking in a mysterious language. Here, however, "text and image [have] become inseparable. Their dual nature has made them immune to decoding, for they have become removed from the sphere of language."[99]

Our traditional perceptions of what constitute "writing" and "pictures" are definitely challenged by such enigmas. Max Ernst's interest in seeking "new ways to represent domains inaccessible to normal perception"[100] by his creation of cryptic script forms is certainly akin to the aims of many other artists/writers who have developed examples of "asemic" writing, that is, abstracted, wordless writing that lacks traditional semantic content. Whether ultimately created by automatic (spontaneous and nondeliberate) means, or loosely inspired by ancient symbols and undeciphered scripts, examples of "invented scripts" appear in the art and literature of many different time periods, from the late medieval "Voynich Manuscript" (Yale University Library MS 408)[101] whose invented script continues to perplex the most astute cryptographers, to the late twentieth-century "Codex Seraphinianus."[102]

In cases where readers/viewers are unfamiliar with the conventions used in either a written language or a pictorial symbol system, what looks like writing may actually be pictures and what appear to be pictures may in fact be a written language. The question is raised: "How do we know when we are looking at writing and not at pictures?"[103] This question resounds especially with specialists in Paleolithic art, some of whom have identified "proto-scripts" among ancient European cultural groups[104] as well as specialists in scripts such as Polynesian *rongo-rongo*, a pictographic writing system that died out in the eighteenth or nineteenth century along with the last people conversant with it.[105] Perhaps it is possible to consider "the relation between pictures and writing: not as a duality with some imbrication, but as an articulated continuum of signs, so that every marked surface will have a measure of pictoriality and a measure of writing."[106]

The investigation of visual/verbal relationships explored by artists such as Magritte, the picture/word puzzles posed by enigmatic texts and pseudoscripts, and the mysterious picture-writing of artists such as Max Ernst may make it "prudent to note how 'word' and 'image' stop making sense as a pair"[107] of separate and distinct communication systems. The following chapter will explore these issues further.

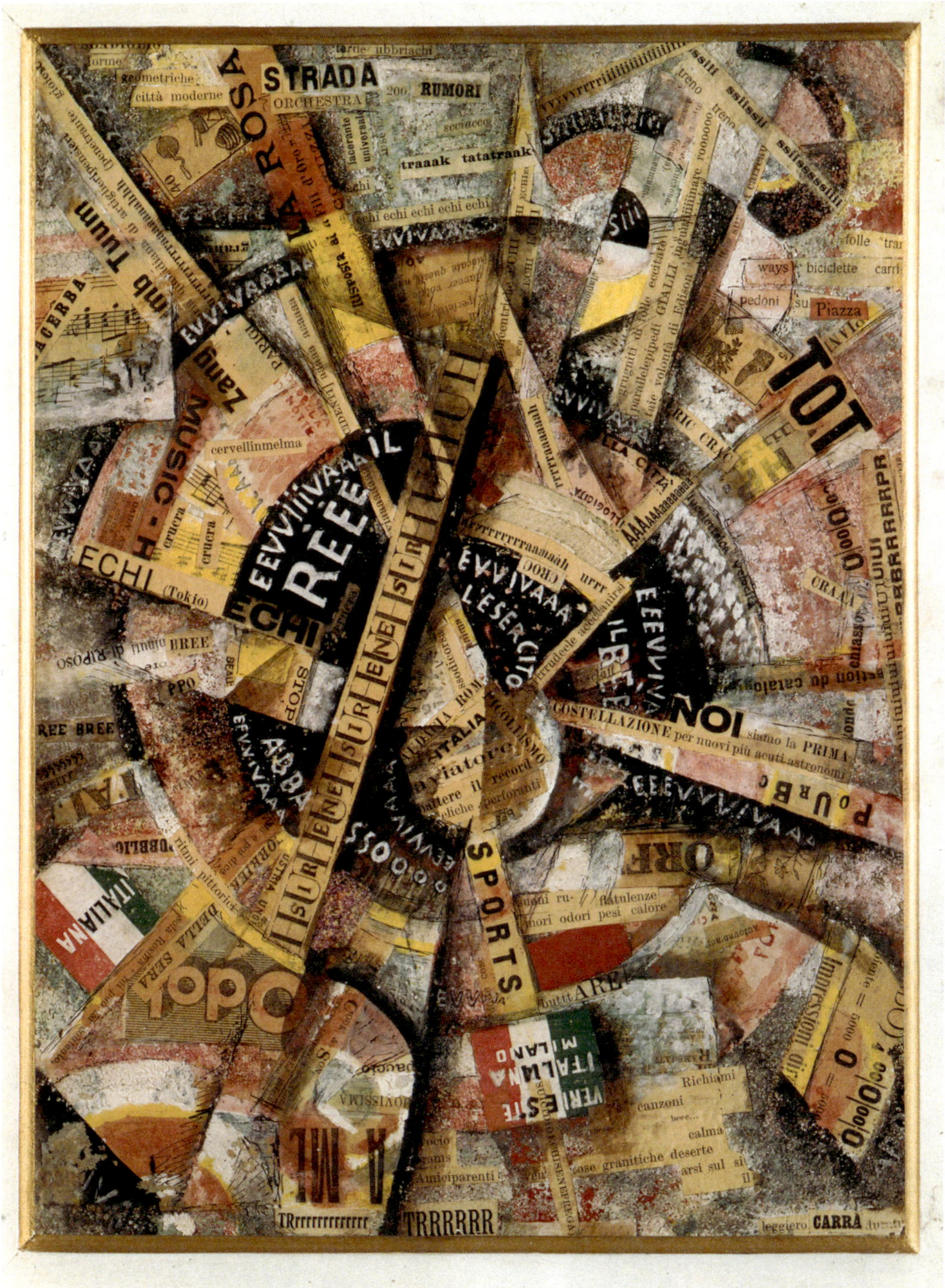

23. Carlo Carrà, *Free Word Painting, Patriotic Celebration,* 1914. Milan, Collection Mattioli (Scala/Art Resource, New York; © 2013 Artists Rights Society [ARS], New York/SIAE, Rome).

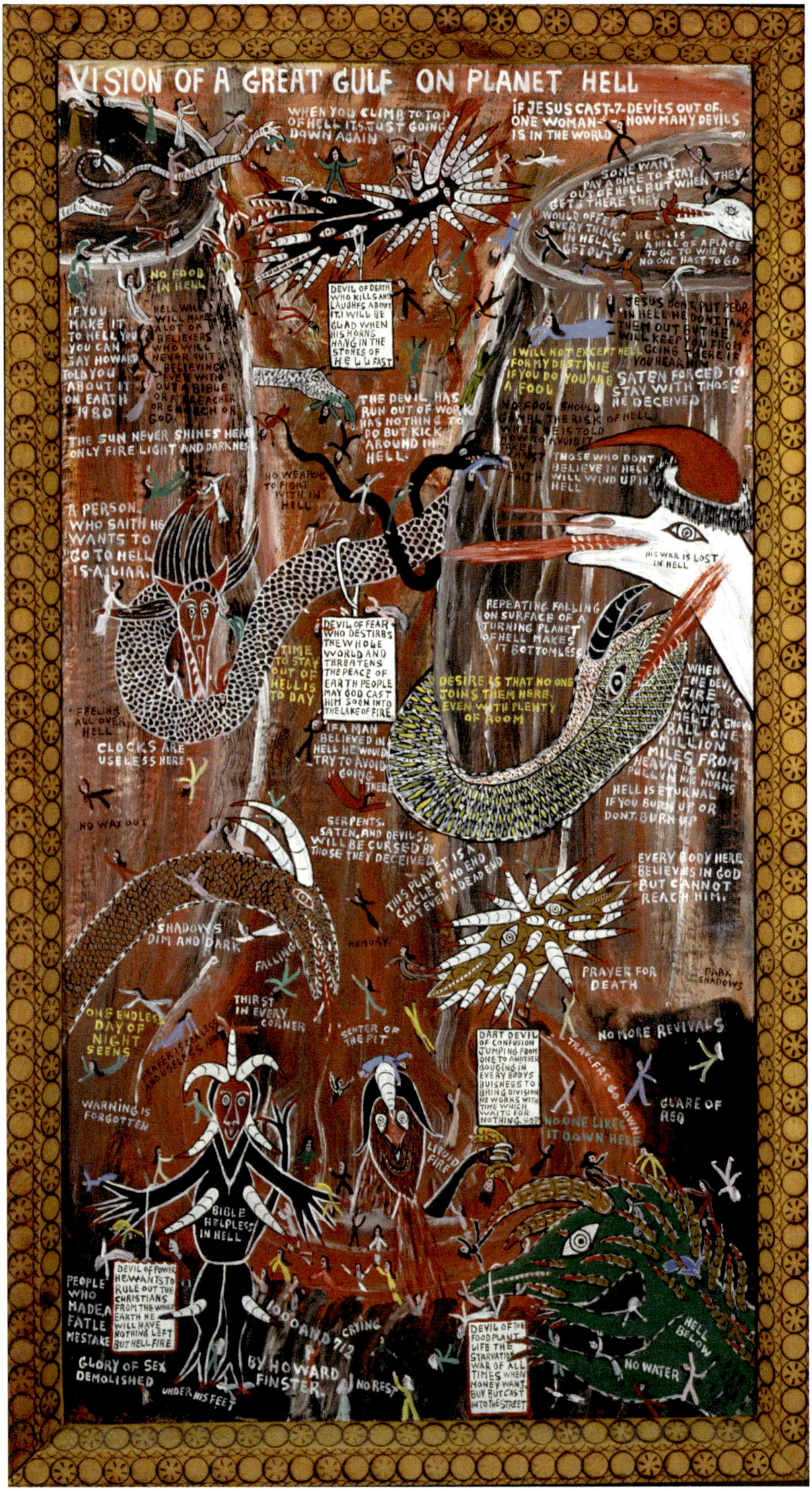
VISION OF A GREAT GULF ON PLANET HELL
WHEN YOU CLIMB TO TOP OF HELL ITS JUST GOING DOWN AGAIN
IF JESUS CAST 7 DEVILS OUT OF ONE WOMAN— HOW MANY DEVILS IS IN THE WORLD
NO FOOD IN HELL
DEVIL OF DEATH WHO KILLS AND LAUGHS ABOUT IT. I WILL BE GLAD WHEN HIS HORNS HANG IN THE STONES OF HELL FAST
HELL IS A HELL OF A PLACE TO GO TO WHEN NO ONE HAST TO GO
SATEN FORCED TO STAY WITH THOSE HE DECEIVED
THE DEVIL HAS RUN OUT OF WORK HAS NOTHING TO DO BUT KICK AROUND IN HELL.
THE SUN NEVER SHINES HERE ONLY FIRE LIGHT AND DARKNESS
THOSE WHO DONT BELIEVE IN HELL WILL WIND UP IN HELL
A PERSON WHO SAITH HE WANTS TO GO TO HELL IS A LIAR.
HIS WAR IS LOST IN HELL
REPEATING FALLING ON SURFACE OF A TURNING PLANET OF HELL MAKES IT BOTTOMLESS
DEVIL OF FEAR WHO DESTIRBS THE WHOLE WORLD AND THREATENS THE PEACE OF EARTH PEOPLE MAY GOD CAST HIM SOON INTO THE LAKE OF FIRE
TIME TO STAY OUT OF HELL IS TO DAY
DESIRE IS THAT NO ONE JOINS THEM HERE. EVEN WITH PLENTY OF ROOM
CLOCKS ARE USELESS HERE
NO WAY OUT
SERPENTS, SATEN, AND DEVILS, WILL BE CURSED BY THOSE THEY DECEIVED
THIS PLANET IS A CIRCLE OF NO END NOT EVEN A DEAD END
EVERY BODY HERE BELIEVES IN GOD BUT CANNOT REACH HIM.
SHADOWS DIM AND DARK
PRAYER FOR DEATH
DARK SHADOWS
NO MORE REVIVALS
ONE ENDLESS DAY OF NIGHT SEEMS
THIRST IN EVERY CORNER
CENTER OF THE PIT
WARNING IS FORGOTTEN
GLARE OF RED
NO ONE LIKES IT DOWN HERE
BIBLE HELPLESS IN HELL
PEOPLE WHO MADE A FATLE MESTAKE
GLORY OF SEX DEMOLISHED
BY HOWARD FINSTER
NO REST
NO WATER
HELL BELOW

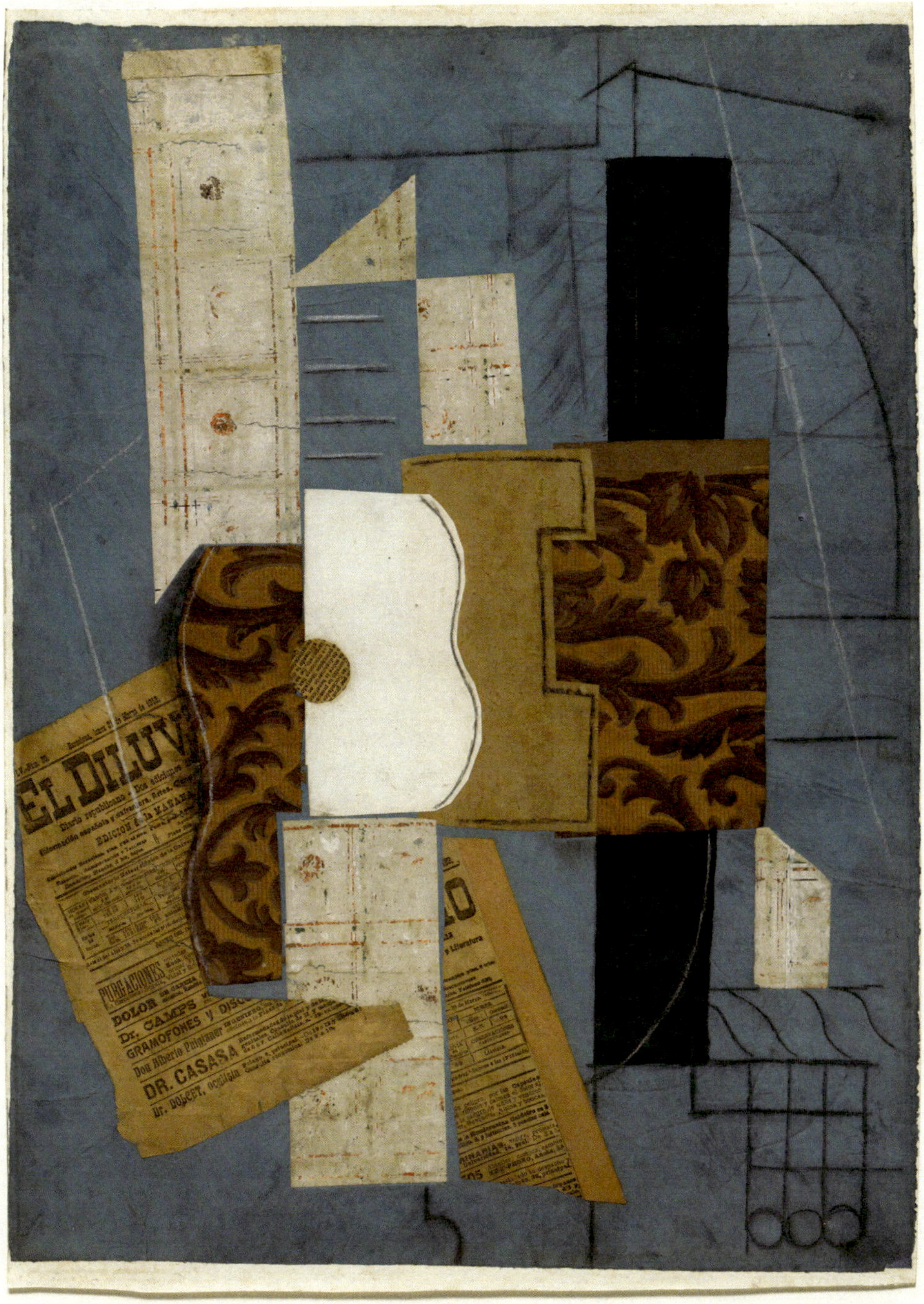

22. Pablo Picasso, *Guitar*, 1913. New York, The Museum of Modern Art (© 2013 Estate of Pablo Picasso/Artists Rights Society [ARS], New York; Digital image © The Museum of Modern Art/ Licensed by Scala/Art Resource, New York).

Opposite: 12. Howard Finster, *VISION OF A GREAT GULF ON PLANET HELL*, 1980. Washington, D.C., Smithsonian American Art Museum (Smithsonian American Art Museum, Washington, D.C./Art Resource, New York; © 2013 Howard Finster/Artists Rights Society [ARS], New York).

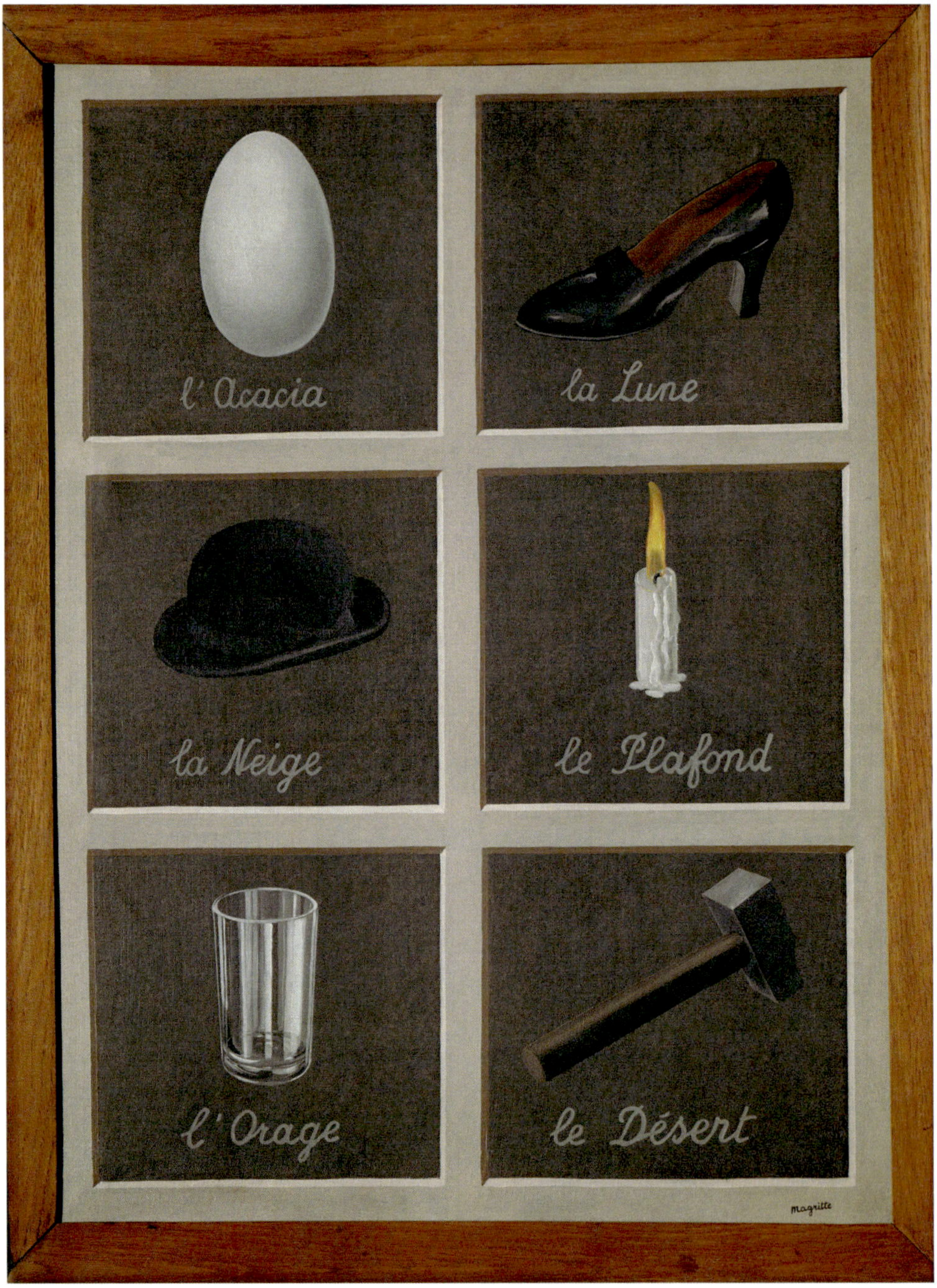

33. René Magritte, *The Interpretation of Dreams*, 1930. Private collection, Vienna (© 2013 C. Herscovici, London/Artists Rights Society [ARS], New York; Erich Lessing/Art Resource, New York).

Opposite top: 52. Deborah Kass, *Enough Already*, 2006 (© 2013 Deborah Kass/Artists Rights Society [ARS], New York; photo courtesy Deborah Kass/Art Resource, New York).

Opposite bottom: 79. René Magritte, *L'Art de la Conversation*, 1950. Private collection (© 2013 C. Herscovici, London/Artists Rights Society [ARS], New York; Herscovici/Art Resource, New York).

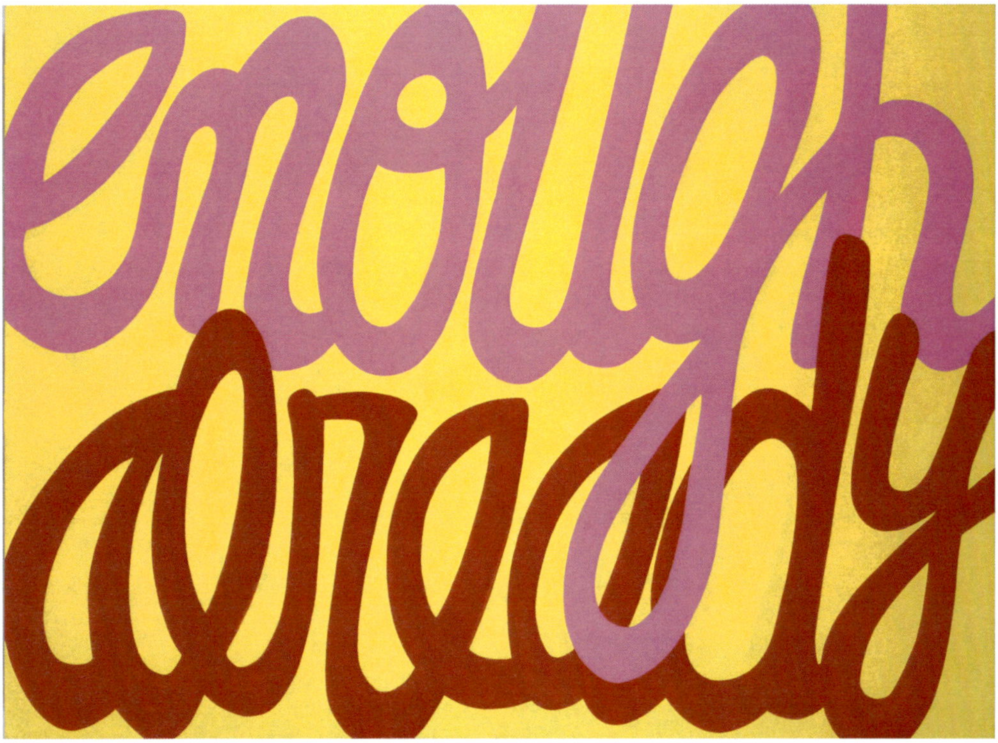
enough
already

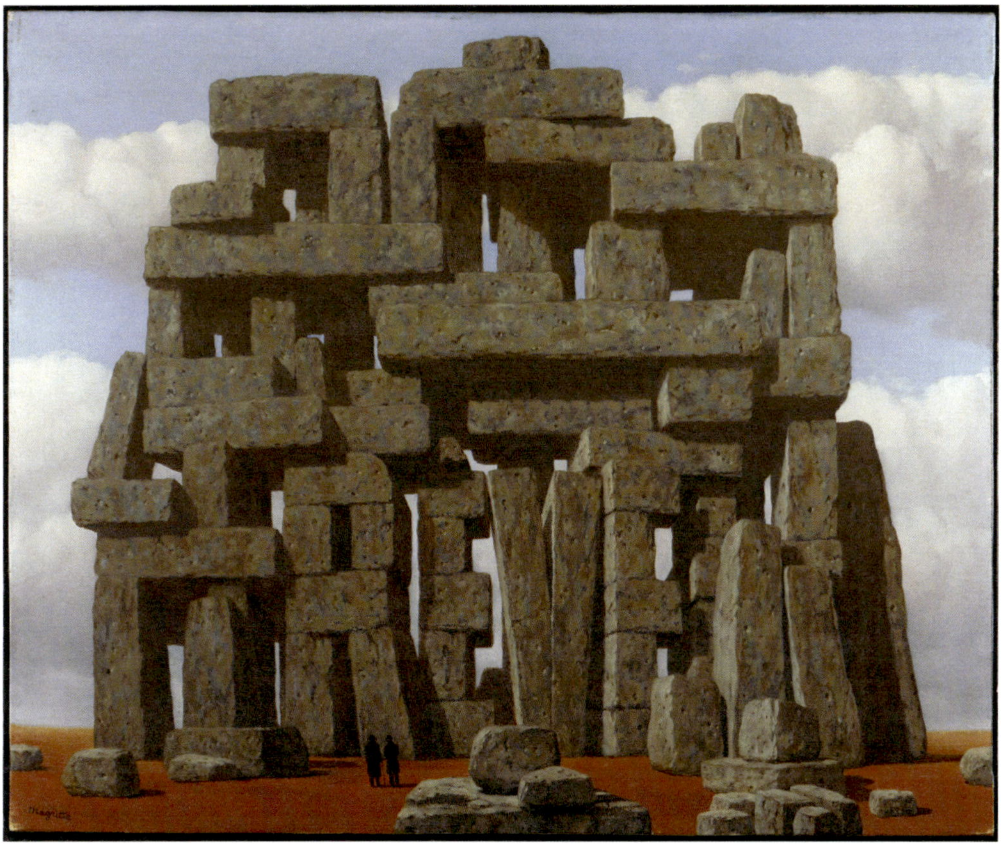

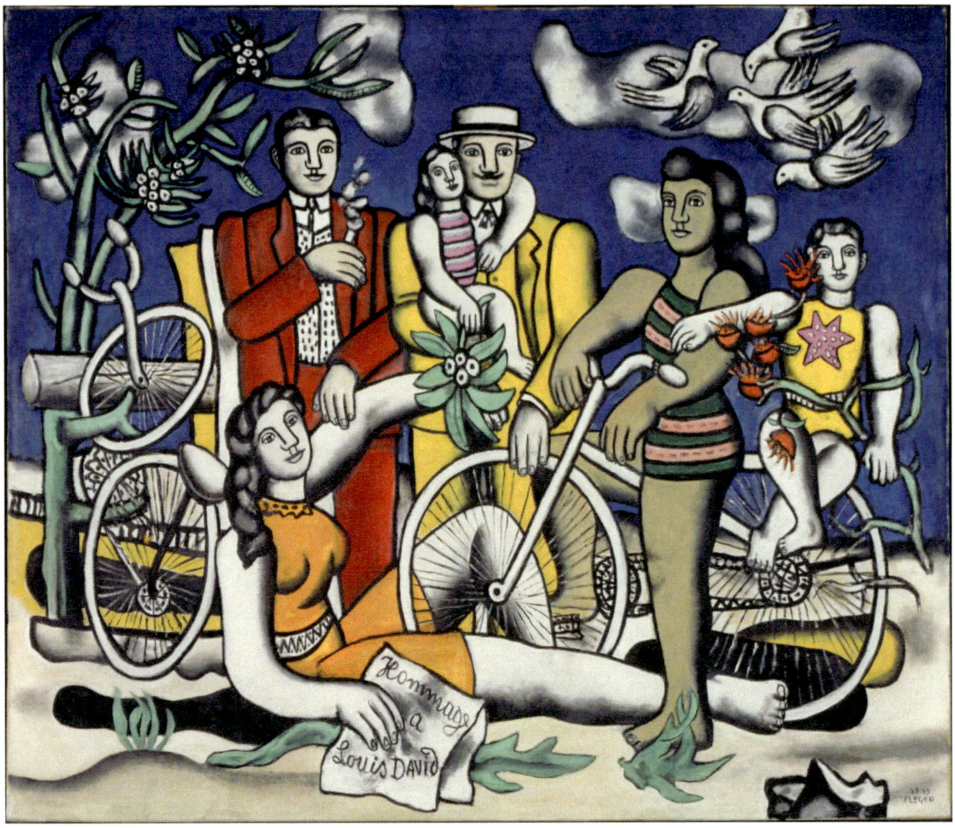
Hommage à Louis DAVID

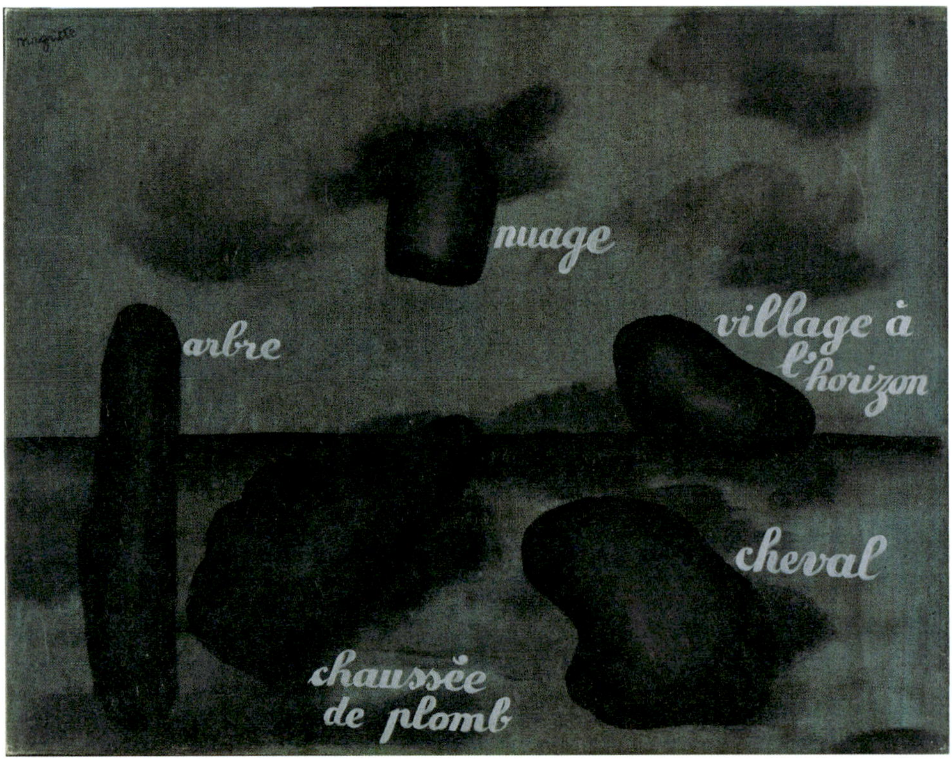
Magritte
nuage
arbre
village à l'horizon
cheval
chaussée de plomb

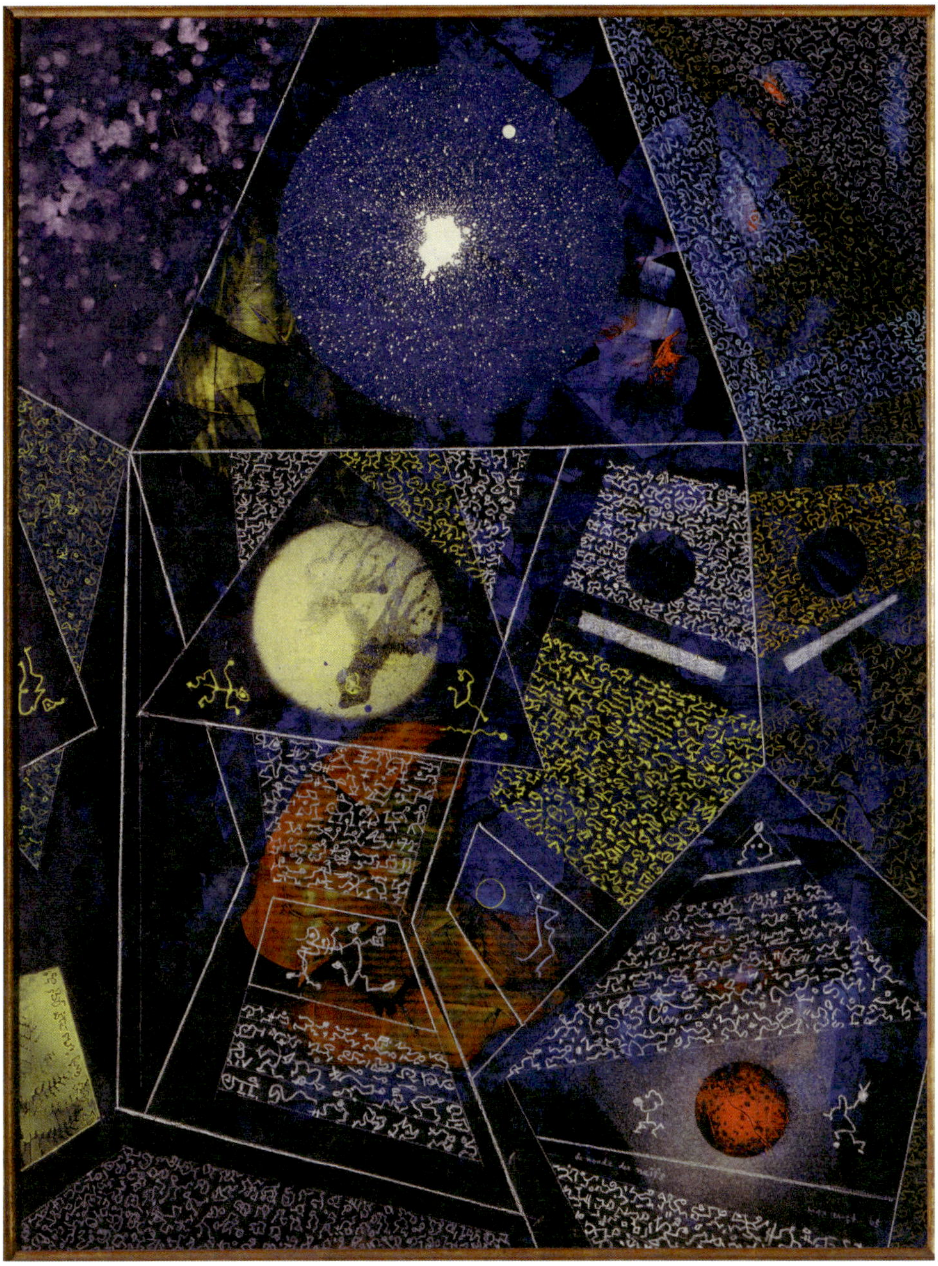

Above: 47. Max Ernst, *The World of the Naïve*, 1965. Musée Nationale d'Art Moderne, Centre Georges Pompidou, Paris (© CNAC/MNAM/Dist RMN–Grand Palais/Art Resource, New York; © 2013 Artists Rights Society [ARS], New York/ADAGP, Paris).

Opposite top: 10. Fernand Léger, *Les Loisirs (Homage to Jacques Louis David)*, 1948. Musée National d'Art Moderne, Centre Georges Pompidou, Paris (©2013 Artists Rights Society [ARS], New York/ADAGP, Paris; Image © CNAC/MNAM/Dist. RMN–Grand Palais/Art Resource, New York).

Opposite bottom: 34. René Magritte, *L'espoir rapide*, 1927–28. Hamburger Kunsthalle, Hamburg (© 2013 C. Herscovici, London/Artists Rights Society [ARS], New York; bpk, Berlin/ Hamburger Kunsthalle/Elke Walford/Art Resource, New York).

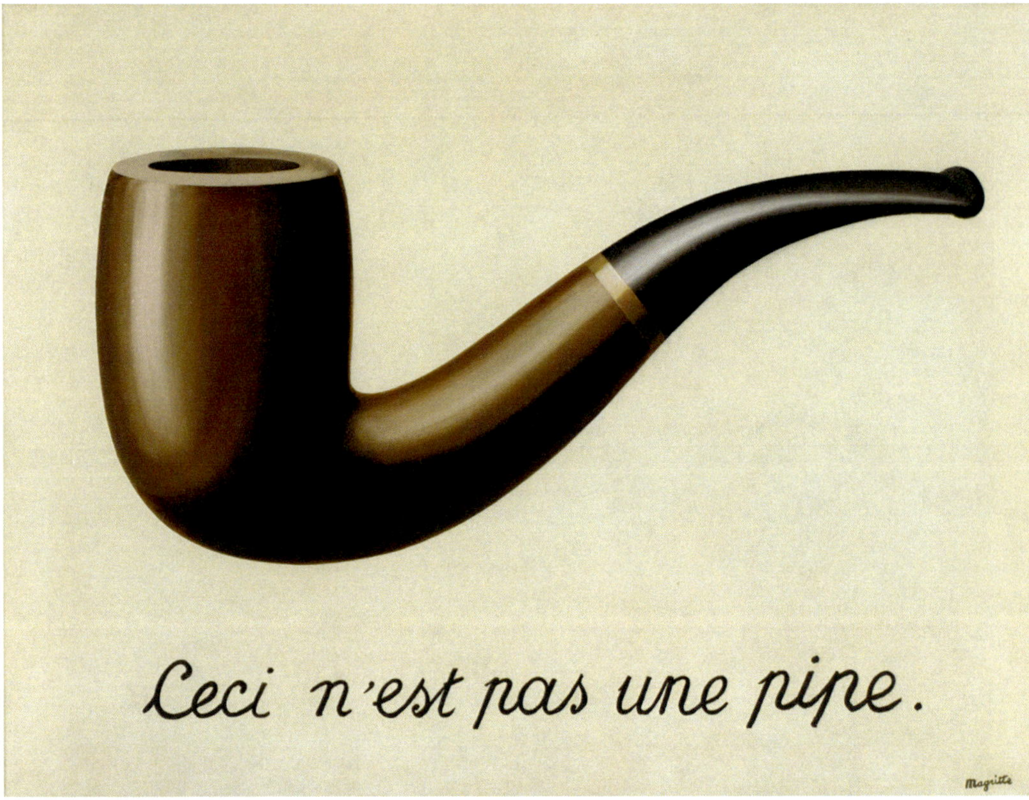

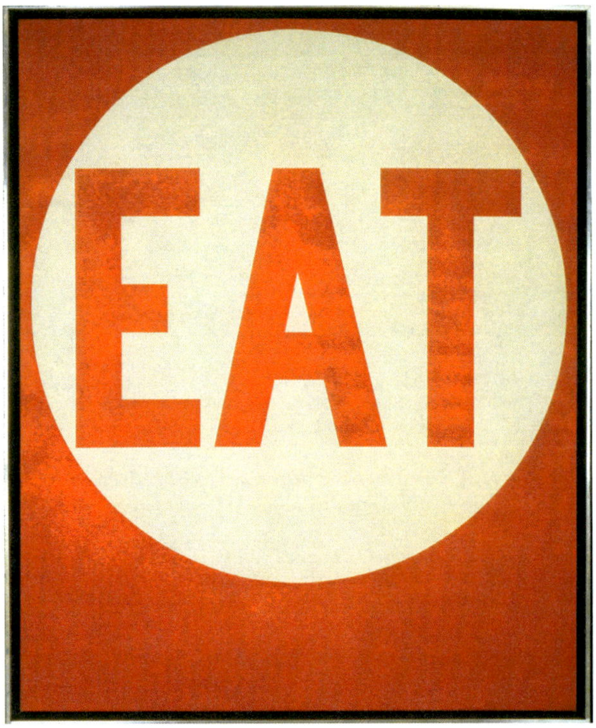

35. René Magritte, *The Treason of Images/Ceci n'est pas une Pipe*, 1929. Los Angeles County Museum of Art, Los Angeles, California (© 2013 C. Herscovici, London/ Artists Rights Society [ARS], New York; digital image © 2013 Museum Associates/ LACMA. Licensed by Art Resource, New York).

50. Robert Indiana, *Eat*, 1962. Private collection, courtesy Simon Salama-Caro (© 2013 Morgan Art Foundation/Artists Rights Society [ARS], New York Morgan Art Foundation SA/Art Resource, New York).

Four

Words as Images

The preceding chapters have offered a highly selected survey of some of the many varieties of word/picture combinations found in works of art from ancient to modern times. In the majority of the forms and examples discussed above, however, words and pictures have been combined. Written texts have appeared along with visual images in these examples, serving to either provide additional information, convey messages, present enigmas, or pose puzzles. In some cases the pictorial imagery in these examples has been quite recognizable, traditionally realistic, or obviously representational. In other cases, the visual images have been more abstract. In some cases the written texts have been legible; in other cases the texts have been cryptic, mysterious, or undecipherable. Although the text/image relationships in these examples range from the direct to the deliberately paradoxical, in most all of the examples previously considered, words and pictures have been employed together to produce a joint reading and viewing experience for the observer.

The provocative question posed at the conclusion of the last chapter ("How do we know when we are looking at writing, and not at pictures?"[1]) provides a thematic starting point for the materials to be discussed in the three sections of this chapter: Artful Words, The Art of the Alphabet, and Words about Words. Here we will be considering examples of words and texts presented as works of visual art, largely, although not exclusively, independent of any accompanying pictorial imagery. The traditional distinction between words and images may be especially challenged by examples of artworks that consist only of words, where words alone might be said to serve as images. There are many variations on this theme, ranging from "imaged words" to "worded images,"[2] with the former representing works that use artfully presented words alone, and the latter representing pictorial compositions in which images are created of words and texts. The use and manipulation of alphabet letters as fields for pictorial imagery is further discussed in this chapter, as well as works of art that use words alone primarily to convey messages that raise questions about the fundamental natures of written language and communication systems.[3]

Artful Words

Works of art that present words alone, without any accompanying pictorial imagery, have become really quite commonplace in modern and contemporary art.[4]

This trend may perhaps be ultimately traceable to the Pop art movement and the use of signs, slogans and advertising logos from popular media presented in and as works of art. Pop artists of the 1950s and 60s challenged the traditional perception that works of art necessarily need to make use of, or make reference to, elevated themes of any historical or literary or religious or mythological importance such as traditionally addressed in works of visual art. Eschewing these norms, Pop artists often selected and reworked images from contemporary culture and re-presented these as art forms. The logos used for advertising products, or the images and texts associated with popular media forms such as cartoons and comic strips, entered the traditional vocabulary of art. This questioning of the inherent nature and forms deemed as art, of course, also followed the explorations of earlier and extremely influential twentieth-century artists such as Marcel Duchamp (1887–1968), whose provocative questioning of traditional art norms more than well led into the many explorations represented by various twentieth-century artists and art movements; these explorations are still on-going in postmodern art forms that may confront the art viewer with unexpected perceptual challenges. Many of these involve words, texts, and letters.

Indeed, in the twentieth- and early twenty-first century, words have become even more ubiquitous in art. In the many variations of the Conceptual art movement, words and texts have continued to be used for any number of purposes: as directions for artworks created *in absentia* by many contemporary artists, or as vocal/visual challenges to our traditional categorization of word and images. In some cases, artists have been clearly and deeply interested in what the words and texts actually say, and they choose their language extremely carefully. In other cases, however, artists may be fundamentally more interested in the appearance of the letters and words, simply in what they look like as visual forms, rather than primarily in any message or meaning that the words or texts may convey to audiences. Although these distinctions may be arguable and difficult to strictly determine or enforce, the contemporary American West Coast artist, Edward Ruscha (b. 1937) may provide an excellent preliminary example for consideration here.

Ed Ruscha works and has worked in a great variety of media and materials, including drawing, painting, photography, film, collage, and book production. Words, often without visual accompaniment, have always played a major role in his art.[5] He began producing his word-paintings in the late 1950s, continually experimenting with different formats through the subsequent decades: single words, phrases, text fragments, and, most recently, palindromes.

Many of his early word-pieces consist of single words, such as *Boss* (1961), *Smash* (1963), *Lisp* (1966–67), *Vaseline* (1967), and *Pool* (1968). Some of these words are depicted as flat, static, and hard-edged. They appear, in upright or slanting format, generally right in the middle of the composition, and they exist alone, without any accompanying imagery to which the viewer might also refer to grasp some meaning behind the choice of these words. In other examples, the words are rendered illusionistically, to appear three dimensional, like twisted pieces of paper or paper ribbons, or as if created from liquid substances poured onto the picture surface, becoming syrupy, bubbly, or gooey. For example, his oil on canvas *Rancho* from 1968 gives the impression that the single word in the composition, "Rancho," has been created of some viscous oily liquid that has been poured onto the surface of the piece, leaving drops of syrupy residue. His graphite and pastel piece *Raw* from 1969 similarly presents this word alone, although it appears to be created of slips of very thin paper standing diagonally and three-dimensionally upright against the background, as does his 1968 gunpowder on paper piece, *Western* (illus. 48). In these cases, the words appear to have become three-dimensional objects; indeed, in some instances, the words appear to be floating above and casting carefully rendered shadows onto the picture surface below. "Whether the 'word' is read as a word or as an illusion of a constructed word-object, there is finally no evidence of what is being signified other than the play of the drawn surface."[6]

Ruscha experimented with a great variety of nontraditional materials especially in the early 1970s, producing paintings, drawings, and prints with gunpowder, ketchup, blood, shellac, and various other organic and vegetable substances such as rubbed rose petals, spinach, egg yolk, blueberry and cherry stain, blackberry juice, and so on. Longer phrases and statements enter his works of the 1970s as well, for example *Listen, I'd Like to Help Out, But* (1973), *Sand in the Vaseline* (1974), *Three Darvons and Two Valiums* (1975) (illus. 49), *Nice, Hot Vegetables* (1976), *He Enjoys the Co. of Women* (1976), and *Honey, I Twisted through More Damn Traffic Today* (1977).

These works, as a whole, exemplify the "peculiarly precarious" and "equivocal" "liquidation of meaning" achieved by Ruscha.[7] Ruscha's word- and phrase-pictures appear to present texts with no contexts. The significance, sense, or meaning of the

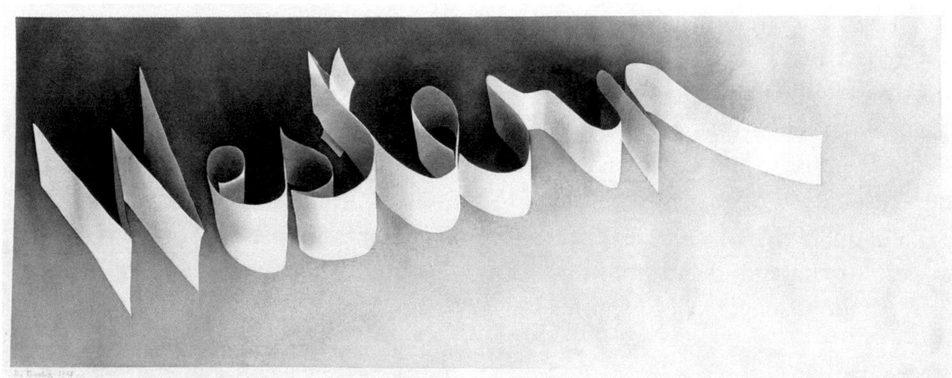

48. Edward Ruscha, *Western*, 1968. McNay Art Museum, San Antonio, Texas (© Ed Ruscha; © McNay Art Museum/Art Resource, New York).

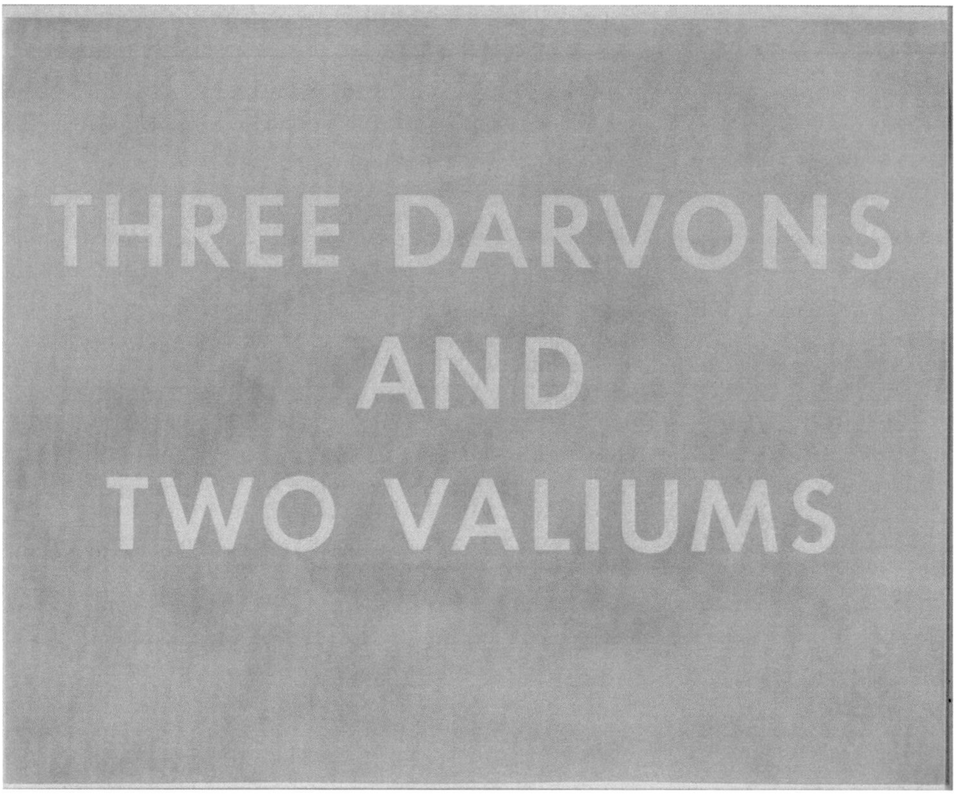

49. Edward Ruscha, *Three Darvons and Two Valiums*, 1975. Private collection (© Ed Ruscha; Jerry L. Thompson/Art Resource, New York).

words seem lost, or in the process of being lost, in spite of their legibility and enlargement. Presented alone, these words and phrases make little sense at all; they appear as if they should be highly significant but the viewer is hard pressed to determine why these selected words and phrases have been singled out for solo presentation. Quoted as always being "dead serious about being nonsensical,"[8] Ruscha's choice of words and phrases ranges from the banal and familiar to the ironic and witty to the disturbingly evocative. Familiar words in his works might indeed be seen as references to modern life and/or wry comments on popular culture. Even so, although viewers may resonate with or bring their own meanings to these words-as-art, Ruscha fundamentally leaves us alone with these words. When asked about some of his early pieces, Ruscha said, "I can't tell you exactly why I picked those words, but I was interested in monosyllabic word sounds that seemed to have a certain comedic value to them."[9]

> These commonplace words gave Ruscha a certain freedom—a desired distance from the subject matter and an open-ended communication or conceit. They give us the same freedom, allowing us to call up images as we like. And of course Ruscha's words contain familiar echoes

and emotions for those of us who may have been in the same places or heard these words ourselves.[10]

Much critical commentary (a "heap of words"[11]) devoted to discussion of Ruscha's art has described the autobiographical hints and especially the Los Angelesness of his idioms. Critics have stated that, "his words deal with the American sense of reality, American everydayness and its preoccupations."[12] But above all, Ruscha's interests in the "decay of language,"[13] and in "the inherent uncertainty of signification"[14] seem to be his major themes. His words and phrases seem "reliably and comfortably but pointlessly there,"[15] requiring reading, but tantalizingly offering no specific narrative or context to which to link these words and phrases. In his works, it seems as if "language has simultaneously assumed the dual roles of word and images,"[16] or as if "the material presence of the letter competes with its role as a carrier of meaning."[17] Ruscha once stated, "I like the idea of a word becoming a picture, almost leaving its body, then coming back and becoming a word again."[18]

In this sense, the artful words of Ed Ruscha pose a contrast to the word-based works of many other modern and contemporary artists whose choice of words and phrases is often far more obviously guided by political or social agendas. Ruscha's works and words differ from the often provocative and highly serious commentaries represented in the works of numerous other language-based artists, to be discussed later, whose interests in challenging, criticizing, or commenting on particular cultural or political issues are far more overt. While Ruscha's words and phrases certainly may carry or convey any number of meanings for viewers, their power and attraction is partially, if not largely, or simultaneously, based on their inherent lack of meaning and context. These quite artfully and painstakingly presented words are to be read, and looked at, at the same time.

The presentation of solo words and fragments of phrases can, of course, easily be found in the works of many other twentieth-century artists as well, especially others associated with the Pop art movement. Robert Indiana (b. 1928), for example, is especially well known for his hard-edged word-images, bold presentations of single words or combinations of words evocative of advertising signs or logos. The words in his works are often "short and isolated and thus assertive as abstract shapes. ... they possess the kind of power that words have in commercial graphics, where they both imply objective narrative and also float free of it and point subjectively, directly, toward the viewer."[19] Described as one of the most "literary" of Pop artists,[20] Indiana created brightly colored, arresting renditions of words and phrases that range from the solo word (for example *Love*, one of his most often repeated in both two- and three-dimensional media) to longer selections of phrases from American literature, poetry, and song lyrics. Much discussion has been devoted to the literary references, social commentary, and Americanness of Indiana's work, as with Ed Ruscha's. Although Indiana's painted words are often terse, his selection and presentation of them reveals and inspires analysis of their larger significance and meaning, a somewhat more conventionally rewarding undertaking than tends to be the case with Ruscha's word-works. Even so, many of Indiana's works can well also be described as "imaged words,"[21] in which the visual and verbal elements are one and the same. They carry "the sense that without a visual dimension the words convey a completely different, if not esthetically negligible experience."[22] These are works that "challenge the difference between reading and seeing."[23]

For example, his 1962 oil on canvas pair *Eat/Die* consists of two large panels, one red, one black, containing the enlarged words EAT and DIE enclosed within large white circles (illus. 50, in color insert, and 51). There is no pictorial imagery, simply these two powerful words rendered in spare, commercial-style, sans-serif lettering. Indiana used these two words frequently; they appear, in repeated variations, colors, and formats, in a great many of his works, sometimes in juxtaposition to other three-letter words, such as HUG and ERR in "his EAT/HUG/ERR/DIE quartet of the cycle of life."[24] Indiana once explained of his works depicting the word EAT, "The word 'eat' is reassuring, it means not only food, but life. When a mother feeds her children, the process makes her indulgent, a giver of life, of love, of kindness."[25] DIE, in contrast, signifies the polar opposite, the end of life. Indiana's word-works are often charged with such drama in presentation as well as implications and references. His visual/verbal lexicon, however, often presents such highly significant words, evoking fundamental human concerns and experiences, as if they were logos or words derived from advertising or popular culture imagery. EAT also makes reference to the enticing signs of roadside diners along the American highways traveled by his struggling parents in his unsettled and difficult youthful years. Many others of his works also include references to these peregrinations and autobiographical details, such as his 1966 piece, *USA 666*, which, he explained, made reference to the famous American highway west (Route 66), Philips 66 gasoline stations, and the number 6 also referring to June, the month of his father's birth.[26]

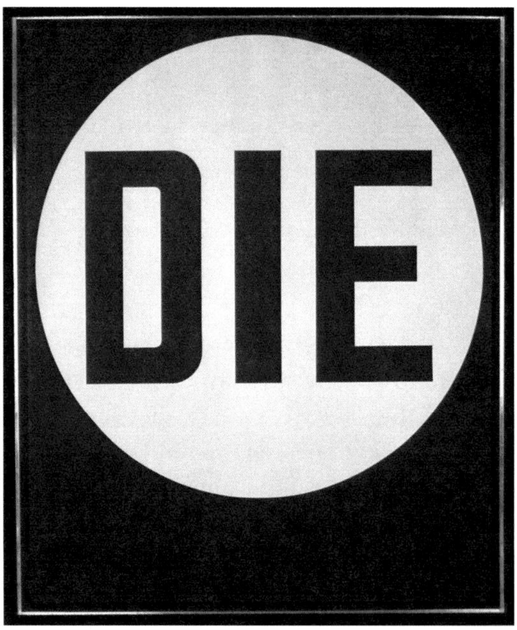

51. Robert Indiana, *Die*, 1962. Private collection, courtesy Simon Salama-Caro (© 2013 Morgan Art Foundation/Artists Rights Society [ARS], New York; Morgan Art Foundation SA/Art Resource, New York).

Singling out, enlarging, and visually presenting words or phrases without any accompanying pictorial imagery creates a viewing experience for the audience that differs significantly from works of art that include both texts and images. Whether the pictorial imagery is abstract or representational, and whether the writing is legible or not, when images are present along with words, viewers logically tend to look at both the writing and the pictures as if their mutual presence may have some sort of a shared purpose. When words alone are presented, however, audiences may be required, or may choose, to adopt different viewing strategies in approaching these imaged words. It is possible, of course, to appreciate and analyze these word-works purely in formal terms, such as color and composition, without much concern about the significance of the words themselves. It might indeed be argued that many of Ruscha's early works, for example, are most interesting on a purely visual level, for his handling of the materials and for his creation of illusionistic or colorful effects in which words appear to be formed of ribbons or thin strips of paper or viscous substances. His word choices, as noted above, often seem to be deliberately bereft of any serious significance, attractive largely due to their banality and absurdity. Similarly, in some early commentary on Robert Indiana "the content of the words was ignored in favor of analyzing their formal use in the composition."[27] Indiana's bold, colorful, graphic style and his repeated use of many of the same short words in his compositions might be appreciated and described largely as his exploration of different color and shape possibilities.

On the other hand, it is also possible for viewers to focus primarily on the words themselves in these imaged word-works. The sense that the words and phrases may indeed have some textual as well as visual substance is difficult to avoid, especially given the traditionally authoritative nature of the written word. In this case, viewers and commentators may derive meaning from many sources, from personal resonances to traditional scholarship exploring the artists' biographies, concerns, and contexts. Some viewers may simply appreciate the seemingly prosaic triviality of Ruscha's words; others may be inclined to see his works as reflective of social values and modern American issues. Some may simply find them annoying. With artists such as Ruscha and Indiana, the level of significance, or deliberate insignificance may also vary from work to work. Many of Indiana's pieces, such as his mid–1960s *Southern States* or *Confederacy* series of paintings, contain strident critiques of racial injustice and brutality, conveying socially concerned messages of a far more serious caliber than, say, Ruscha's 1974 *Sand in the Vaseline.*

Indeed, works such as the 2006 oil and acrylic painting *Enough Already* by the contemporary American East Coast artist, Deborah Kass (b. 1952), can be similarly approached in both visual and textual terms (illus. 52, in color insert). The work consists of words only, rendered in colorful pink and red/orange script against a yellow background. There are no images in the work, just the one bold statement, a common slangy catch-phrase that could be interpreted as a quite serious expression of frustration or just a phrase used in any number of more innocuous and casual conversational interchanges. The work is visually very attractive, with its colorful and overlapping ribbon-like script filling the entire canvas.

It is one in a large series of works that Kass began in 2002, collectively titled *feel good paintings for feel bad times*.[28] The works in this series consist of often very colorful compositions that capture phrases from popular songs of the early to mid-twentieth century, Broadway musicals, movies, and Yiddish expressions, and include versions of *Let the sun shine in* (2006), *Do you wanna funk with me* (2008), *Sing out Louise* (2004), *You can't stop the beat* (2003), *Daddy I Would Love to Dance* (2007), and *C'Mon Get Happy* (2010). Previously acclaimed for her series *The Warhol Project* (1992–2000), in which she replicated Andy Warhol's famous silk-screened portraits of celebrities but instead portrayed people from her own personal list of significant and influential figures (primarily feminist or lesbian or Jewish women such as Gertrude Stein, Barbra Streisand, and so on), Kass created works with an unmistakable political/social agenda replete with references to her own life and identity as a Jewish, lesbian artist living in New York City.[29] She began the *feel good paintings for feel bad times* series in part due to the post–September 11, 2001, American political climate, nostalgically and pointedly selecting catchy and cheerful snippets from earlier twentieth-century songs and upbeat musicals to point out "nostalgia's good past/bad present binary."[30] These works, thus, in spite of their cheery and seemingly innocuous textual content, are filled with associations to the artist's life, times, and identity. These references may not, however, be immediately obvious to viewers whose personal resonances with these catchy phrases may involve simply nostalgic delight, or mystification.

Singling out, enlarging, and visually presenting words or phrases such as in the works of art discussed above creates a highly different viewing experience for the audience than with works of art that include both texts and images, or what we traditionally think of as words and pictures. When legible words alone are offered to us as artworks, our logical impulse may be to read them—*or*—to see them. But, in the cases of the artfully presented word-works described above, we find ourselves needing to do both, without being quite sure about their status as visual images or as texts. Ed Ruscha once said, "I chose words because they have no scale. You can do what you like with them and they still mean the same thing."[31] Ruscha was interested in "finding ways to bring the visual appearance of words into provocative confrontation with their ostensible content."[32] Whether the visually presented words are fraught with drama and substance or are pointedly banal, their enlargement and presentation resembles and evokes diverse other traditions of important public lettering, monumental epigraphy, commercial signage, and graffiti as well, to be discussed further below.[33] In a 1963 interview, Robert Indiana described his works as "verbal-visual."[34] In some senses, these artfully presented words are reminiscent of other very important genres of artful visual/written interchanges as represented by shaped texts, pattern poetry, concrete poetry, and calligrams. These "worded image" forms also make images with words, although they rely upon different means to do and so generally result in different appearances than "imaged words."

The Art of the Alphabet

Artfully shaped texts, or worded images, have a very long history indeed, and examples have been traced back as far as the fourth century BCE, although the form may have originated much earlier.[35] The Greek poet and scholar Simmias of Rhodes (ca. 300 BCE) is often credited with having created the earliest examples of this form in several poetic texts that are shaped in the form of an egg, a pair of wings, and an ax. These figured verses are meant to be read as texts and simultaneously viewed as pictures. The shape of the poem makes reference to the textual content. The texts serve as written descriptions but at the same time serve as visual illustrations. The ax or hatchet-shaped composition is a commemoration of heroism in warfare; the egg-shaped poem celebrates the bounty of nature; and the wing-shaped poem refers to flight, the heavens, and creation. These erudite examples of text-based art also involve specific knowledge on the reader's part about the way in which the lines are to be read. The egg- and the ax-shaped poems are set up in particularly complex patterns, in which the reader is required to read the first line, then the last line, then the second line, then the next-to-last line, and so on until arriving at the concluding lines in the centers of the poems/images.

Several other ancient Greek and Latin authors also created poetic compositions in shapes that reference their textual content. For example, Publilius Optantianus Porfyrius, the court poet of the Roman emperor Constantine (early fourth century CE) is credited with composing poems in the shapes of a syrinx (pan pipes), altar, and other forms, in addition to his complex grid poems discussed above.[36] Like the works by Simmias of Rhodes, these shaped poems simultaneously describe and illustrate their themes. The altar-shaped poem makes reference to an ancient altar to the god Apollo, and the syrinx-shaped poem refers to triumphs and celebrations of successful battles. Porfyrius is best known for his grid poems, which, like those of later medieval authors such as Hrabanus Maurus (discussed previously) often include symbols, shapes, and images superimposed, intertextually, on a foundation grid text. Although grid poems and shaped poems may both be classified within the larger genre of *carmina figurata* (figured poems) or *technopaignia* (literary works that cleverly display the technical skills of their authors), important distinctions can be made between the diverse forms included in this genre.[37] Texts that are actually shaped into images—or worded images—represent a quite distinctive manifestation of the "wish to combine the visual and literary impulses, to tie together the experience of the two areas into an aesthetic whole."[38]

Particularly impressive examples of shaped texts can be found in several medieval copies of the ancient Greek astronomical treatise by Aratus of Soli (ca. 310–245 BCE) known as the *Phaenomena*. This fundamental work was translated into Latin versions by later authors including Cicero (106–43 BCE). It includes descriptions of numerous stars and constellations and was an extremely important reference work for the classical and medieval periods.[39] Several medieval and later illustrated versions exist that include lively diagrams depicting the constellations.[40] For our purposes, the oldest surviving Latin example, a mid-ninth-century Carolingian copy (London, British Library Harley MS 647), is most intriguing for its use of the shaped text format.[41] On several of the illustrated pages in this manuscript, the constellation discussed is simultaneously described and illustrated in a series of figured texts/diagrams in which the written descriptions (extracts from another related Latin text, Gaius Julius Hyginus's *Poeticon Astronomica*) are shaped into the forms of the constellations described. The texts that create the images are written in clear rustic capitals; the stars forming the constellations are clearly indicated with red dots, and painted details fill out the pictorial information, such as heads, feet, and so on. In addition to the word-filled illustrations, sections of the Aratus text appear below many of these diagrams, written in a clear minuscule script.

For example, folio 12, representing the constellation Centaurus, is created of lines of text that read across the arms, body, four legs, and tail of this half-man, half-horse figure (illus. 53).[42] The head, hands, tip of tail, hooves, staff, and the sacrificial animal held by the figure are filled in with painted details, and the stars creating this constellation are indicated with large red dots. The lines of text that create the image describe the various classical myths associated with the figure, the wise centaur Chiron, his relationships with Achilles and Hercules, and Jupiter's honorific positioning of him in the celestial spheres. The unshaped text below the image includes further details about the position of this figure in relation to other constellations. It is generally assumed that the images as well as texts contained in this Carolingian manuscript were copied from a late antique exemplar containing the figured diagrams, of great popularity in classical antiquity. The synthesis of text and image here is remarkable and thought provoking. Are we looking at a picture or reading a text? Are we reading a text or looking at a picture? Both, it seems, can take place at the same time.

Shaped texts, or poems representing objects, were exceedingly popular in the Renaissance period as well, notably with the sixteenth- and seventeenth-century English authors George Puttenham (1529–1590), George Herbert (1593–1633), and Robert Herrick (1591–1674). Puttenham's comprehensive and influential 1589 treatise, *The Art of English Poesie*, contains a series of recommendations on the most pleasing and suitable shapes of poetry, so that the words would please the eye as well as the ear. He believed that "visible symmetry and audible harmony are one and the same,"[43] and he recommended various geometric configurations, such as triangles, spheres, lozenges, pillars, pyramids, and so on, to achieve the greatest subtlety and effectiveness in visual verse. His section, "Of Proportion," for example, includes a tall, column-

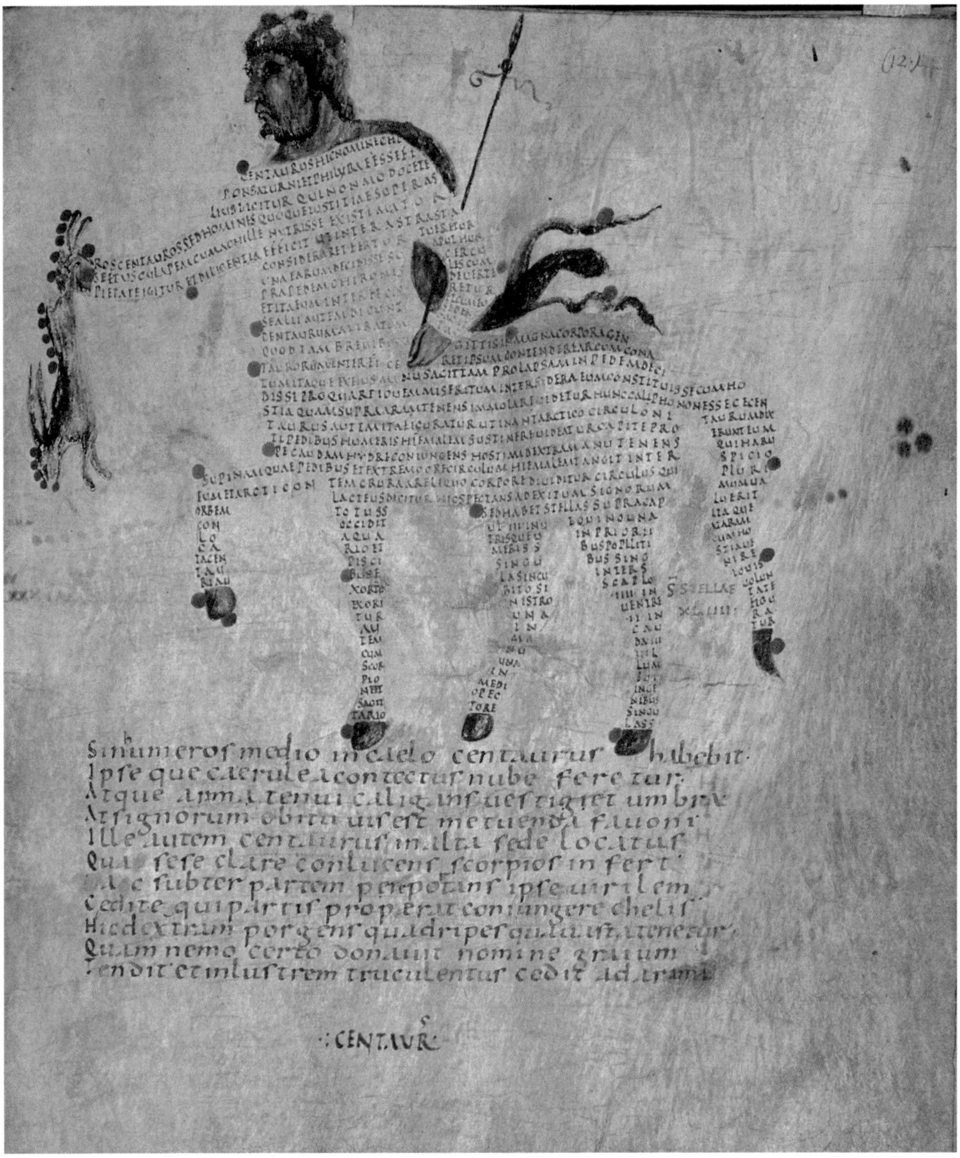

53. Aratus, *Phaenomena*, mid-9th century. London, British Library MS Harley 647, folio 12 (© The British Library Board).

shaped poem with a slightly protruding base and capital. The projecting capital and base are created of lines of text that are just a bit longer than the rest of the tall column of poetic text. This particular poem, dedicated to extolling the magnificence and power of Queen Elizabeth, is meant to be read from bottom to top. Thus the reader begins with the solid base of two introductory lines, and then reads upwards through a series of verses honoring the queen, ultimately reaching the top two lines describing her immortality as an eminent monarch. The words and shape of the poem, as well as the uplifting reading direction, all serve to convey the message about the glory of this ruler. Puttenham's treatise is replete with many further examples of shaped poetic constructions designed to convey written themes in visual forms.

Other authors, such as the poet, orator, and Anglican priest George Herbert, also specialized in shaped poetic constructions. Herbert's poems are primarily, if not exclusively, religious in nature. He used appropriate shapes, such as wings and altars, to convey his spiritual messages. For example, one of his most famous compositions from 1633, "The Altar," simultaneously shows what it describes, referring both visually and verbally to faith and sacrifice.[44] This poem is shaped like an altar, with a solid base and projecting top, each consisting of four lines of text, indented so as to appear architecturally secure. The base and top of the poem are connected by eight lines of text that are meant to be understood as the stand upon which the altar table rests. This poem reads from top to bottom, beginning and ending with a reference to the ALTAR and further containing praises of the Lord's sacrifice, the subject of the poet's ardent and unceasing prayers. Another of Herbert's religious poems, "Easter Wings," is very cleverly shaped so as to appear like the wings of two birds flying next to each other. The poem reads from top to bottom but was deliberately designed to be printed sideways, so that the wings seem to be flying upwards on the page. The poem makes reference to the sacrifice and triumph of Jesus and the desire of believers to also "rise, As larks, harmoniously," in victorious flight.[45]

> Since we are made to *look* at shaped poems even before we begin to read them, they actually begin before their first word is read. This beginning of a verbal experience in the non-verbal is responsible for the form's appropriateness for religious poetry, its affinity with the icon. A Christian poem in the shape of a cross is a beautiful visual corollary of the doctrine of the Incarnation, a poetic demonstration of it: the words, indeed, seem to be made flesh.[46]

The powerful suitability of shaped texts for religious purposes, as emblems and meditative devices, is well demonstrated not only in western European Christian art but in a plethora of world cultures to be further discussed in the next chapter.

Although shaped texts have sometimes been dismissed as simply whimsical conceits, the continued popularity of the form is well demonstrated in the many further explorations and experiments in this genre characteristic of any number of twentieth- century art movements: Dadaism Futurism, Surrealism, and so on.[47] Among the several early twentieth-century exponents of the form, the highly influential French poet, novelist, and art critic Guillaume Apollinaire (1880–1918) certainly stands out as an especially significant figure.[48] After his move to Paris in the late nineteenth century, he eventually became a key player in the Parisian avant-garde art scene, maintained friendships with many of the major artists of the time, and was highly influential on the development and definitions of Surrealism and other new art movements. He served in World War I and was severely wounded, an experience that had a profound effect on him and doubtless shortened his life.

For our purposes, his *Calligrammes* (or *Poems of Peace and War*, 1913–16; published shortly after his death in 1918) represent his experimental combination of textual and visual ideas in highly original manners.[49] "In his experimentation with *calligrammes*—first called 'figurative poems' or 'ideogrammatic poems'—Apollinaire manipulated type into configurations suggestive of a poem's meaning."[50] His use of the term *calligramme* (emphasizing beautiful writing) indicates his unique visual/verbal approach. Unlike the shaped poetry or figured diagrams described above, Apollinaire approached visual poetry in a more free-form but also highly structured and evocative manner. He wanted to "bring poetry alive."[51]

> As he himself noted, the calligrammes are more visually expressive than their antecedents. ...Within the fairly rigid confines of the printer's art, the calligrammes present an astonishing variety of shapes: from the simple lines of everyday objects to visual ballets of complicated counterpoint. Typically, the poems swirl into themselves, swoop into the air, or advance toward the reader. There is a surprising amount of movement, in direct opposition to traditional figurative poetry, which is entirely static.[52]

For example, his oft-reproduced poem, *Il Pleut* (*It Is Raining*; which describes and illustrates rain and the poet's tragic sadness during wartime), is an excellent example of his evocative and movement-filled work, as is *La Colombe Poignardée et le jet d'eau* (*The Stabbed Dove and the Water Jet*) (illus. 54). In *La Columbe Poignardée*, the lines creating the topmost form of the wounded dove with outstretched wings begin with a description of "gentle faces stabbed dear flowering lips"—references to loves lost—and continue with a description of a "fountain (jet of water) that cries and that prays." The dove, a customary symbol of peace, is wounded. The reader/viewer, progressing down the page further, then sees and reads the form of this fountain of water with multiple jets curving up and around. The words here describe the poet's "memories of longing/of my friends gone to war" and poignantly include the names of several other friends whose companionship he is missing, such as the artists Georges Braque and André Derain. One reads down the left side of the water jet first; the lines then continue to be read from top to bottom on the right. These curving, streaming lines and the nostalgia and longing for friends "who may be already dead," concludes with a reference to the "jets of water that weep for the poet's pain." The bottom oval section of the poem grounds and reinforces the painful themes by verses describing "those who left for the war," darkness and fatalities ("Night falls O blood drenched sea"), and concludes with a line describing "gardens where the rose laurel bleeds copiously flower of war."

Apollinaire's *Calligrammes* significantly represent an early-twentieth-century fresh take on the ancient form of shaped poetry or pattern poems.

> ...in place of the funerary monuments, the dreary odes in the form of urns, or the elaborate twisted strands of a love knot entangling the eye as sentiments had entangled the heart, Apollinaire disposed his words in the casual shapes of forms readily scribbled on a napkin from a café—a cigar, a tie, a watch, a heart, the rain. These easy, open forms, when recog-

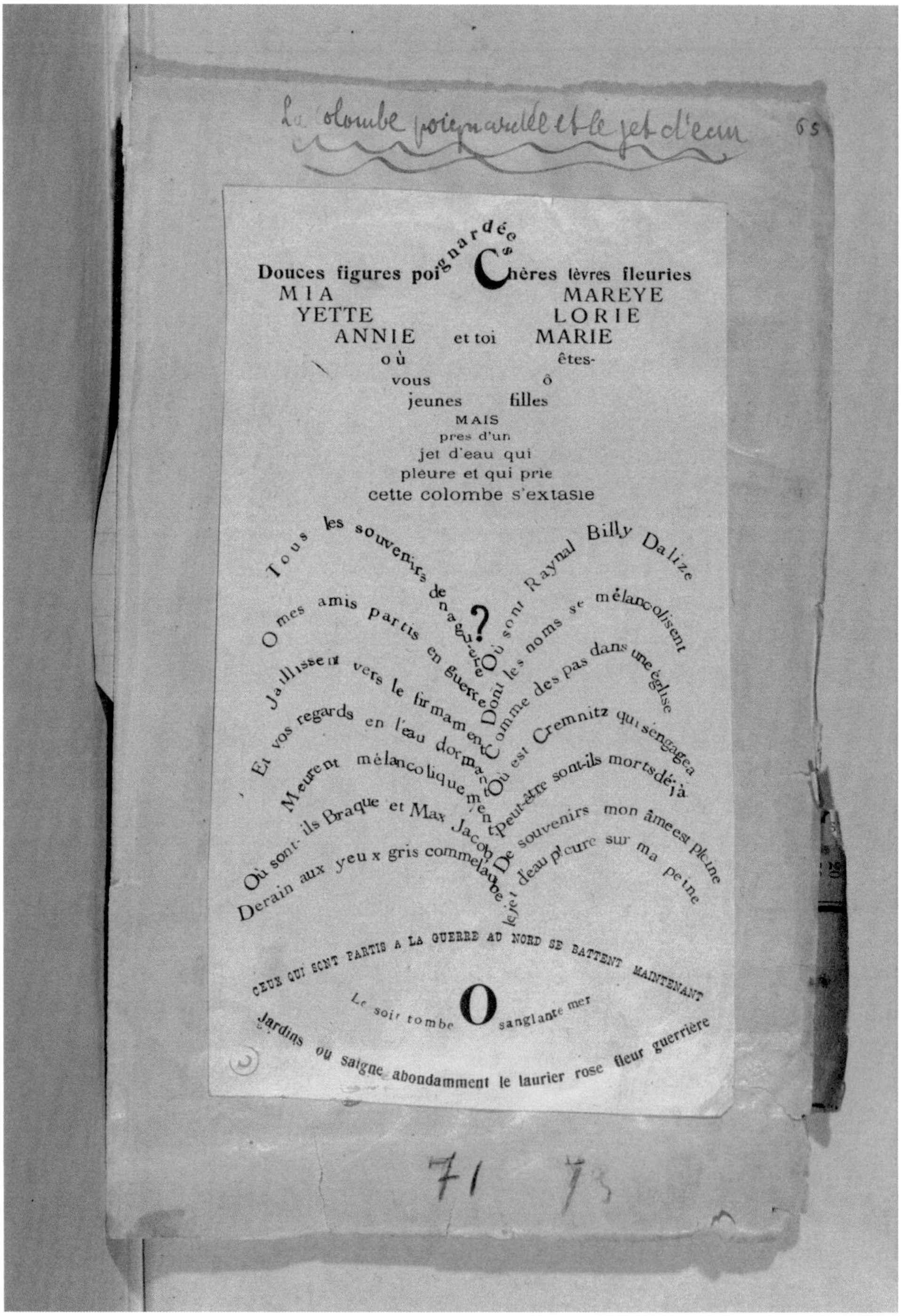

54. Guillaume Apollinaire, *La Colombe Poignardée et le jet d'eau*, 1913–16. Paris, Bibliothèque Litteraire Jacques Doucet (Bridgeman Art Library).

nizable, are sketches, lightly delineating an icon, not building it with cookie-cutter regularity or monumental solidity.[53]

Even so, a number of shared visual/verbal strategies and challenges consistently operate in the vast and diverse realms of shaped texts.[54] All forms in this multifaceted genre require that the reader/viewer be fully, and perhaps also quite patiently, willing to engage with both the written and visual forms at the same time, because the works demand and rely upon this shared viewing/reading experience. These are works that are meant to be seen as visual forms and read as texts, simultaneously, and their success relies upon the ways in which the words evoke images, and the images evoke words.

The viewer's attention focuses first on the format and layout of the text, even in cases where no immediately recognizable image is created by the shaped text, or, where no verbal images mentioned in the text are specifically reproduced in the pictorial image. In the closely related genre of "concrete poetry," especially popular from the 1950s and later, shaped texts may not actually look like specific objects or images, but by placement, layout, and word choice may conjure up themes and concepts.[55] Concrete poems often involve open forms, unconventional layouts, and nontraditional reading directions, requiring the reader/viewer to fill in the blanks. Eugen Gomringer (b. 1925), often called the "father of concrete poetry," described a visual poem as an object that is "memorable and imprints itself upon the mind as a picture."[56] The structure and the meaning, the form and content are one and the same; "the dynamism of the word and letter and of the reality they refer to are stressed in concrete poetry, the poem becoming almost as vital and thinglike as object in the world."[57] Gomringer's often-cited 1963 work "Silencio" is an excellent example of this genre (illus. 55). Each of the five lines of text repeat the word "Silencio" three times, with the exception of the blank space in the very center. The reader/viewer

silencio silencio silencio
silencio silencio silencio
silencio   silencio
silencio silencio silencio
silencio silencio silencio

55. Eugen Gomringer, *Silencio*, 1963 (courtesy Dr. Marvin Sackner, The Sackner Archive of Concrete and Visual Poetry, Florida, with permission from the artist).

may perceive that a word is missing here; however, the deliberate absence of this word more than powerfully evokes the idea of "silence." Not all examples of concrete poetry make use of such minimal design elements. Some involve far more dense configurations of letters and words in all manner of shapes.[58] Regardless, the diverse practitioners of this genre concentrate their attention largely on the optic, phonetic, and kinetic effects of letter layout in their creation of compositional objects made up of written language.

The shaping of words and texts into objects and images—whether recognizable forms or abstract shapes suggestive of ideas and concepts—has a close natural parallel in the shaping and embellishment of individual letters. The examples of decorated and embellished letters in medieval manuscripts, as previously discussed, might well be recalled here. The iconic presentation of sacred letters in medieval religious manuscripts demonstrates how care and attention to individual letter forms may render them as far more than simply letters. Enlarged, decorated, and embellished, they take on an extremely powerful presence, and, especially when narrative images are included within them or as components of the letters' shapes, they function as letters and images simultaneously.

While the embellishment of letters as well as their use as frames for enclosed images is highly typical of the medieval period, the creation of "artful alphabets" has a very long history up to the present day.[59] In the late medieval period, and especially with the advent of printed books in the fifteenth century, a number of artists created alphabet templates that were designed to be copied and used repeatedly. A fascinating pre–Gutenberg example appears in the ca. 1400 "Sketchbook of Giovannino de' Grassi" (Bergamo, Italy, Biblioteca Civica Angelo Mai, Cassaf. 1.21) (illus. 56). Giovannino (d. 1398) was an acclaimed architect, sculptor, and painter active at the Visconti court in Milan in the late fourteenth century. Relatively little is known about his life, although he is documented as having been significantly involved with the architectural, sculptural, and painted designs for the cathedral of Milan in the 1390s. He is generally credited also with having produced at least the first volume of a magnificent prayer book for Gian Galeazzo Visconti in the 1380s. The work for which he is most famous, however, is his "sketchbook," which consists of a compendium of four bound booklets of parchment pages of differing sizes containing intricately detailed and often quite life-like drawings and paintings of people, birds, animals, heraldic devices, and decorative motifs, plus five pages of figured alphabet designs showing cleverly constructed Gothic minuscule letters created of people, animals, and fabulous beasts.[60]

The alphabet designs form a unique section in the "sketchbook," and because their style differs in some respects from the other figural and animal compositions in the compendium, several scholars believe that these are slightly earlier than the other drawings that may be attributed to Giovannino himself, or, that at least two different artists executed these alphabet letters, one of whom may have been Giovannino.[61] Indeed, a number of different hands or styles can be seen in all the sections of the "sketchbook," so the questions of artistic attribution are complex.

In any case, each of the five pages of alphabet designs presents several letters in two rows to be read sequentially across the opening of the manuscript. The letters are constructed of entangled human and animal forms, contorted to fit within and create the angular shapes of the letters. Knights, maidens, peasants playing musical instruments, wooly wild men, horses, bears, dragons, birds, dogs, and insects all cavort in a highly lively fashion in these whimsical alphabetic constructions.

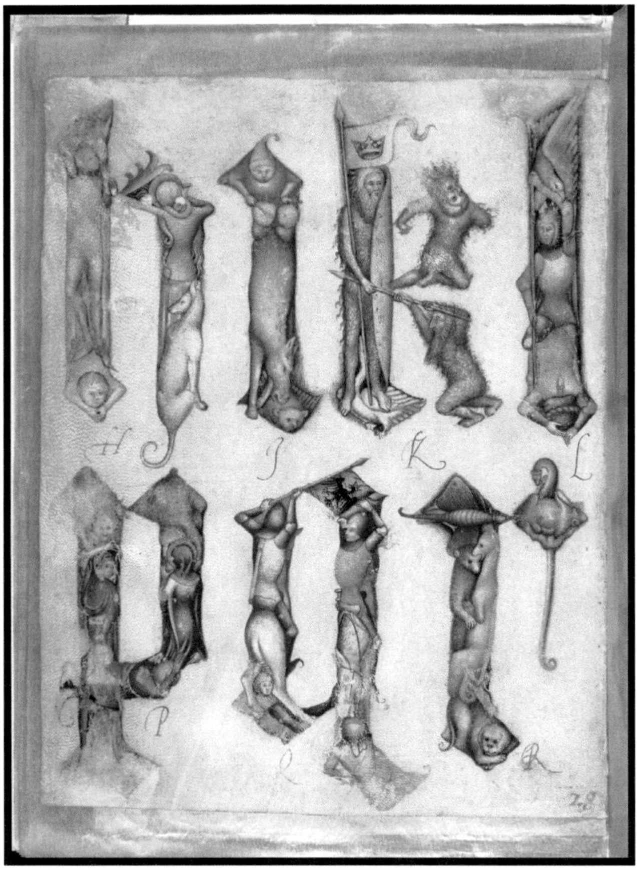

56. Giovannino de' Grassi, sketchbook page with letters of the alphabet, ca. 1400. Biblioteca Civica, Bergamo, Italy (Scala/Art Resource, New York).

> They create the strangest compositions. A donkey, for example, standing on a swan faces a man with a lion on his head. One woman has an eagle on her head, another a flying dwarf. Another woman is kneeling down and stroking a dog while behind her a second woman bares her bottom. The M, meanwhile, shows an Annunciation scene. The figures fill up the whole width of the letters, which stand out boldly from the page as a result.[62]

These are very akin in spirit to earlier medieval and especially Romanesque "inhabited" initials with their zoomorphic, anthropomorphic, and zooanthropomorphic forms. However, unlike earlier examples, these alphabet letters appear to have been designed as a series—presumably to be copied by other artists, perhaps those employed in a workshop directed by the artist. A few of the letters may indeed have been copied from even earlier examples.[63]

These fantastic letters certainly seem to have served as inspiration for several later examples of alphabetic templates, notably those of the figured alphabet created

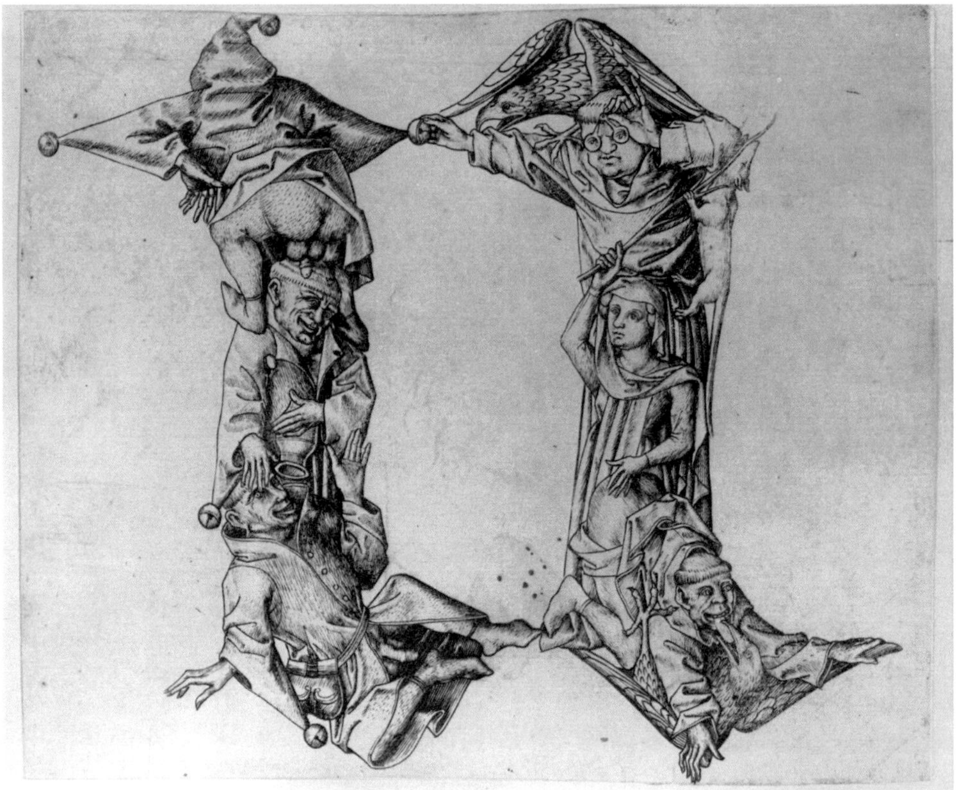

57. "Master E. S.," *Fantastic Alphabet*, ca. 1466–67. Kupferstichkabinett, Staatliche Museen, Berlin, Germany (bpk, Berlin/Staatliche Museen, Berlin/Jörg P. Anders/Art Resource, New York).

by the fifteenth-century German engraver known as "Master E.S." in ca. 1466–67 (illus. 57). This otherwise unidentified German artist was one of the first printmakers to sign his works with his initials, although his specific identity remains confusingly unknown. His engraved series of alphabet letters, like the drawn and painted examples from the Giovannino de' Grassi "sketchbook" close to a century earlier, present the letters of the alphabet in sequential order, as elaborated designs made up of wildly intertwined human and animal forms. People, horses, lions, dogs, winged beasts, lizards, and dragons enliven his densely packed and detailed engraved compositions. Although the shapes of the letters themselves provide the foundational basis for his compositions, Master E.S. creatively used these fundamental letter shapes as vehicles for intense pictorial elaboration. His letters seem to be treated as objects of visual art and as fields for imagery, while still maintaining their function as letters in an alphabetical reading system.

It is generally assumed that the artful and alphabetic constructions found in medieval and Renaissance "model books" were designed to serve as repeatable templates for other artists, students, workshop members, and followers. Indeed, model books and pattern books for artists and printers became increasingly popular with the widespread information dissemination of the Renaissance era.[64] In the Renaissance period and quickly after, the mass production techniques involved with printing continued to inspire many further examples of artful alphabet designs of an amazing variety of forms, including letters created of figural, floral, animal, landscape, and abstract shapes.[65] Ornamental typography is a vast and fascinating field, as is that of Alphabet Books (illustrated reading primers designed for younger readers.) Rather than merely letters whose alphabetic significance rests purely on the sounds they represent, these forms hold inherent and continuing attraction and interest for both visual artists and linguists. Although many ornamental and decorative alphabets are of an extremely whimsical character, it should also be noted that many of the artful alphabet designs of the Renaissance period (and later) represent quite serious religious, emblematic, and symbolic systems as well. Theories regarding the power of letters and the origins and symbolism of individual letter forms are further discussed in the following chapter.

Words About Words

The artful words and letters, the shaped texts, the images created of words, and the words presented as images discussed above altogether represent a variety of specific approaches to text/image relationships with some fundamentally shared features, in spite of their great diversity. In these selected examples, word and letter forms have either been twisted into shapes, made to appear as images or objects, or, in the case of the pictorial alphabets, used as repeatable templates for other works. In many of the examples of the word-based works discussed above, the words and letters seem to have been selected and used primarily as design elements, graphic forms, or shapes with inherent visual interest, irrespective of their textual content. In other cases, the textual content of the selected words has maintained a significant role, to be sure, in conveying either direct or more ambiguous messages capable of multiple readings.

We can now turn our attention to yet another closely related genre of word-based works, those that utilize words to boldly draw attention to words themselves. Although the use of words in art and the presentation of words as art is, as we have seen, a far from new idea, a significant portion of the ubiquitous language-based visual art of the later twentieth century demonstrates a particular interest in investigating the concept of written language itself as a conventional symbol system. This became especially common in postmodern art forms, most notably and often directly associated with the various forms of the Conceptual art movement and related artistic explorations of the second half of the twentieth century.[66] Many late twentieth-century artists have taken language itself as the subject matter for their artworks. Their use of words in their artworks is specifically designed to make statements about language systems, to show how "text acts a visual signifier for the linguistic structure of art."[67] In these cases, "artists use text to refer back to text … to create works of art that point to their own making."[68] "Language in art may become language as art, or art-language."[69]

Precedents for these philosophical and linguistic explorations of visual/verbal communication systems may, of course, easily be traced back to earlier artists, such as René Magritte, whose word-based works, discussed above, posed extremely important questions about the relationships between texts, words, and pictures or images of things. Magritte's word-based works explored the apparent disjuncture or, at least, questionable and thought-provoking relationship between words and images. His paintings depicting images of commonplace objects accompanied by "incorrect" written labels and his paintings with clear labels denoting quite abstract or unrecognizable forms raised highly important questions about the symbol and communication systems represented by both images and words alike. Magritte's profound influence on later twentieth-century art cannot be underestimated, as is especially well demonstrated in the word-based works to be discussed below.[70] A great many later twentieth-century artists, often well read in and very intrigued by modern linguistic theories, have made words/language the subject of their artworks, producing written texts as art forms, and raising even further questions about art and/as language. "The intentionality of Conceptual Art … is language based; therefore, the clarity of the concept as stated through language is a preeminent concern."[71]

Several works of art created in the late 1960s by the highly influential American Conceptual artist and teacher John Baldessari (b. 1931) may serve as representative springboards for this discussion of artful "words about words." Baldessari, an extremely prolific and successful artist, has worked in a great variety of media, including painting, video, printmaking, and performance art.[72] In the 1960s he began to combine photographic images, obtained from a variety of sources, with texts. He also presented painted texts alone as artworks. In examples such as his 19666–68 piece, *Solving Each Problem As It Arises*, the viewer is faced with a black and white surface upon which appears a written description of the traditional artistic processes involved with selecting and choosing subject matter; the care, attention and repeated study required for artists to achieve mastery of their selected subject matter; and how these processes may remain unrecognized by art viewers who simply may be impressed with the final results (illus. 58). Obviously, his text involves simply a written description of artistic subject matter; no visual subject matter accompanies the written text. Visual subjects for art, as the phrases in his painting tell us rather vaguely, could be scenes "of a religious nature" or "a scene in a foreign country." Of course, his work illustrates neither. Baldessari once said, "I guess it's fundamental to my work that I tend to think of words as substitutes for images. I can never seem to figure out what one does that the other doesn't do, so it propels me, this kind of bafflement."[73]

In any number of other works from the same years (1966–68), Baldessari similarly presented pithy statements about art, art making, and critical reception processes. Works such as *Tips for Artists Who Want to Sell*, *Pure Beauty*, *Terms Most Useful in Describing Creative Works of Art*, *What This Painting Aims to Do*, *Exhibiting Paintings*, and *What is Painting* typify his works of these years. These paintings consist of texts alone, largely short statements about art. He recommends, in a series of bullet points, in his *Tips for Artists Who Want to Sell*, that "paintings with light colors sell more quickly than paintings with dark colors," and that paintings that include "bulls and roosters" sell better than pictures that include "cows and hens." In other pieces,

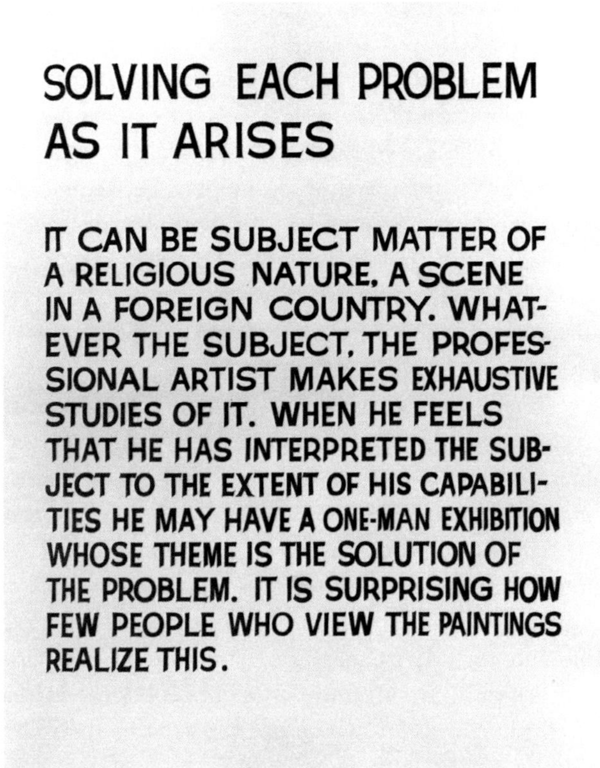

58. John Baldessari, *Solving Each Problem As It Arises*, 1966–68. New Haven, Yale University Art Gallery (courtesy John Baldessari Studio).

his statements tell us that "Quality Material" and "Good Workmanship" can result in a "perfect painting," and that "art is a creation for the eye and can only be hinted at with words." Ironically however, words alone are Baldessari's primary materials in these works. In these pieces, "language operates in the absence of objects, arousing but simultaneously frustrating our desire to see ... who, then, is responsible for creating the image—the artist or the viewer?"[74]

Although Baldessari created many of the texts himself, sometimes basing them upon quotes from or parodies of the type of prosaic recommendations and statements found in basic art instruction manuals as well as statements by art critics, the paintings were executed according to his directions by a professional sign painter whom he directed to use the clearest and least embellished lettering styles, those found in signage of the most basic and direct nature. The lettering style in these works is thus the same as one would find on any simple, professionally created advertising sign that is designed to be clear, legible, and lacking in any frills. Thus he deliberately distanced himself from the traditional processes of art making, while simultaneously using his word-based works to talk about art-creation processes. The results of his explorations are word-based works, presented as visual art, that question the very nature of visual art by using words alone. "His body of work is about perpetual deferral, a celebration of an endless semantic quest for its own sake."[75] These are words about art but also words about words. He once said, "I'm not too interested in this word or that word, but in what happens between these two words when they meet."[76] Additionally, he has stated, "From my own perspective, a word could not be just a substitute for an image, but equal to an image. One could build with words as one would build with imagery."[77] Many of his text pieces seem wryly and intentionally humorous and certainly can be seen as poking fun at the art world and traditional ideas of what constitutes a work of art; nevertheless, by "frustrat[ing] the expectation of an image with a verbal description,"[78] these works raise a number of significant questions, such as: "What is painting? What is art? What is nonart? What are ideas? What is visual, what is verbal, and what is the difference? Could verbal information constitute a visual image? ...Where is the art—in the idea or the object?"[79]

Baldessari's word-based works, although they speak largely, boldly, and primarily about art and art making, also speak about words and the conventions of written language systems. If a carefully painted written description of visual imagery can substitute for said imagery, or if a painting of the words "Pure Beauty" can stand in for this highly complex aesthetic concept, viewers/readers are asked to consider not only the meanings of the words themselves but also how words can or cannot convey meaning.

> What kind of beauty? The signified's relationship to the signifier is uncertain. The signifier, in fact, collapses into a sign; hence, the vagueness of the referent becomes overwhelming. Is beauty merely a concept? A condition in the mind of the beholder? Or is it an absolute dictum (i.e., the standard of taste) as it was in the Salon of the nineteenth century?[80]

This emphasis on words and how they function in relationship to visual imagery (or not) is a particular hallmark of the Conceptual art movement of the 1960s and 70s, as can readily be seen in many other examples such as Joseph Kosuth's famous piece, *One and Three Chairs* from 1965 (illus. 59).

Kosuth's (b. 1945) significance and his influence on later twentieth-century art and art theories really cannot be underestimated.[81] A prolific writer as well as acclaimed artist, Kosuth's work explores the nature of art and language in challenging and thought-provoking ways. His works are also notably lacking in any of the wry humor sensed in Baldessari's works with their tongue-in-cheek statements about art language and art making. Indeed, Kosuth once remarked that he found Baldessari's works to be semi-amusing variations on Pop art rather than more serious and truly Conceptual art pieces.[82] Kosuth's more strict definition of Conceptual art (as dealing with ideas purely) is well demonstrated in his *One and Three Chairs*, an installation piece that comes with specific instructions from the artist. It can be changed or modified each time it is installed, but the work always consists of the same enlarged dic-

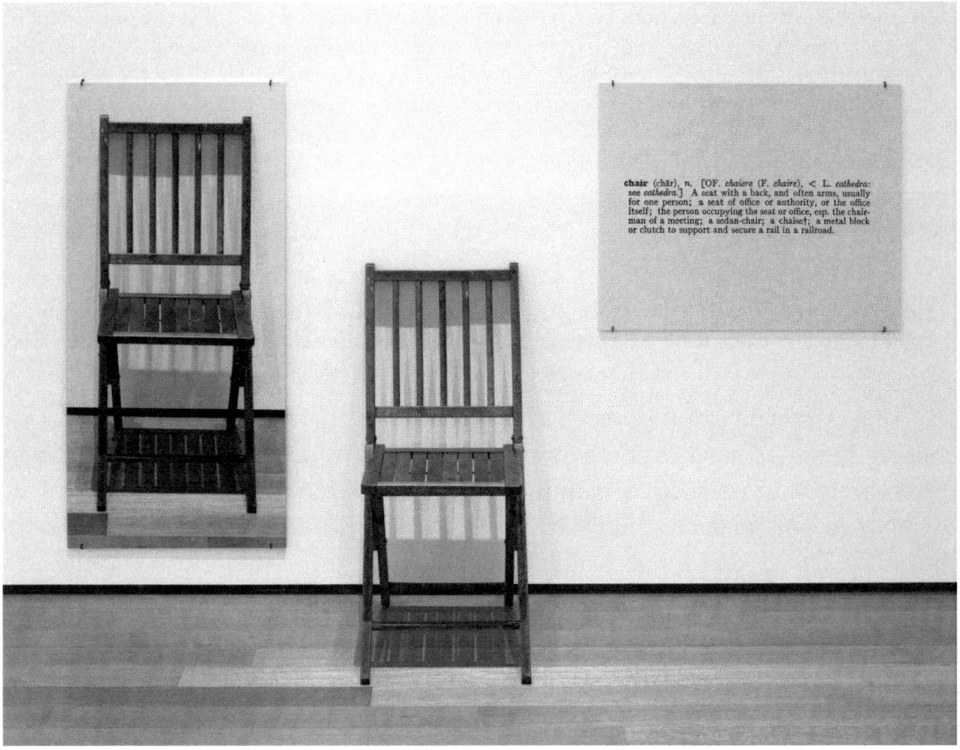

Joseph Kosuth, *One and Three Chairs,* 1965. The Museum of Modern Art, New York (© 2013 Joseph Kosuth/Artists Rights Society [ARS], New York; digital image © The Museum of Modern Art/Licensed by SCALA/Art Resource, New York).

tionary definition of "chair" mounted on the wall and placed to the upper right side of an actual chair. The chair can be chosen by the exhibition installers, who are also directed to take a photograph of the chair, enlarge it to full size, and display the photograph mounted on the wall to the left side of the chair. The upper edges of the photograph and the dictionary definition need to be aligned. Thus, the work consists of a photograph of a chair, the chair itself, and the dictionary description. Kosuth is here questioning the relationship between objects (a chair), images (the photographic representation of the chair), and words (a standard definition of a chair). Viewers may find themselves considering which one of these forms—object, image, or written description—most accurately represents reality. The generic definition of a chair can apply to any and all chairs, whereas the specific chair and photographic image represent only one type of chair, the one selected for display. This demonstrates "the failure of language to capture and contain a real object or its photographic reproduction."[83] Kosuth, in an interview in 1970, stated:

> I used common, functional objects—such as a chair—and to the left of the object would be a full-scale photograph of it and to the right of the object would be a photostat of a definition

> of the object from the dictionary. Everything you saw when you looked at the object had to be the same that you saw in the photograph, so each time the work was exhibited the new installation necessitated a new photograph. I liked that the work itself was something other than simply what you saw. By changing the location, the object, the photograph and still having it remain the same work was *very* interesting. It meant you could have an art work which was that *idea* of an art work, and its formal components weren't important.[84]

In this same interview, he also stated:

> Using a text as art raised questions, using a photograph as art raised questions, the artifact of a dictionary definition raised questions. This was about the time I started reading a lot of language philosophy as well and this paved the way for me to start thinking about art in relation to language. It became clearer to me that the material of the work was these series of contexts or levels. It seems to me that when work works that's how it works.[85]

Closely related are works such as his 1966 series *Titled (Art as Idea as Idea)* that consists simply of enlarged dictionary definitions of various words, many of them terms that refer to art, such as "painting," "image," "thing," "art," "value," "idea," "nothing," "language," "meaning," and "definition." This series quite "neatly demonstrates the philosophy of Conceptual Art,"[86] in that the works themselves represent "the idea of representation *per se*,"[87] using visual language alone to describe ideas of art and to question the idea of art itself. Word-based works of this sort that investigate language systems are largely self-referential. Kosuth's tautological, self-reinforcing statements are quite literally what they say they are: words about words.

Kosuth, well educated in anthropology, philosophy, and psychology, was, along with many other Conceptual artists of the 1960s and 1970s, deeply influenced by his study of the writings of the eminent philosopher Ludwig Wittgenstein (1889–1951) such as the *Tractatus Logico-Philosophicus* (1921) and especially the posthumously published *Philosophical Investigations* (1953). Wittgenstein's works pose questions about language: how words are used, what words mean, and how we understand and misunderstand words. His writings, as well as the language philosophies of Ferdinand de Saussure (1857–1913) and the writings of cultural/literary critics such as Roland Barthes (1913–1980) "destabilize the traditional notions of language."[88] The philosophical/linguistic/semiotic foundation for much word-based Conceptual art of the second half of the twentieth century needs to be understood as reflective of the then-current intellectual discussions and debates about the nature of language.[89] It goes without saying that a number of Conceptual artists of these years were prolific authors/essayists as well, especially Kosuth, Sol Lewitt (b. 1928), and the artists associated with the "Art and Language" group (founded in 1967/8) who published a journal in the late 1960s and early 1970s which Kosuth edited for a period. The headiness and intellectual complexities of their discussions should certainly not be underestimated, nor the important influence of earlier twentieth-century figures such as Marcel Duchamp, mentioned above, whose revolutionary questioning of traditional forms of art provided continued inspiration for so many later twentieth-century movements.

Many further examples of modern text-based art that convey variations on the theme of language itself—words about words—could very easily be multiplied here. In fact, the number of artists using words themselves as the primary focus for their works has escalated more than dramatically since the mid-twentieth century. Foundational examples such as the 1966 piece by Robert Smithson (1938–1973) titled *A Heap of Language* have continued to inspire later artists. This work by Smithson consists of a handwritten pyramid-shaped series of words/terms used for describing language, such as: "phraseology, speech, tongue, lingo," and so on.

> The piece is precisely what it says it is, and yet, in this straightforward simplicity it confounds the problems of presence and reference, managing to collapse them into the same activity. The words are what they say they are and yet they add up to something more—a structure, a form, a materially dense work which describes the materials of the language of which it is made.[90]

Works of art that use language—specifically to raise questions about language—have also been created by a number of highly influential Chinese artists in the twentieth century, notably Xu Bing (b. 1945).[91] Profoundly impacted by the social and political upheavals he experienced growing up in China in the second half of the twentieth century, Xu Bing created works that reflect, in his words, "The jumbled knot of socialism, the Cultural Revolution, the Reform Period, Westernization, modernization."[92] An aspect of the Cultural Revolution of Mao Zedong that had an enormous impact on Xu Bing was the Chinese governmental policy to transform and simplify traditional Chinese characters. "At about the time Xu Bing was old enough to learn to read, the government reformed the language by simplifying characters in an effort to make widespread literacy an obtainable goal. For Xu Bing, however, language began to seem unreliable."[93] Xu Bing has explained:

> When each member of the Chinese cultural community first begins his or her education, he or she must spend years memorizing thousands of characters. This process is a sort of ceremony in homage to the culture, and it leaves all Chinese with an extreme respect for the "written word." My generation, however, was irreparably affected by the campaign to simplify characters. This remolding of my earliest memories—the promulgation of new character after new character, the abandonment of old characters that I had already mastered, the transformation of new characters and their eventual demise, the revival of old characters—shadowed my earliest education and left me confused about the fundamental conceptions of culture.[94]

His installation piece, *Tianshu* (or *Book from the Sky*), first shown in Beijing in 1988, addressed these issues (illus. 60).[95] As regards his original conception of the piece, Xu Bing has said:

> Once in 1986, while thinking of something else, it occurred to me to make a book that no one would ever be able to read.... As to the making of this book I had several ideas that were very clear at the outset: 1) This book would not perform the essential functions of a book; it would be empty of all content, and yet it would very much look like a book. 2) The way of making the book through to its completion, would have to entail an authentic process

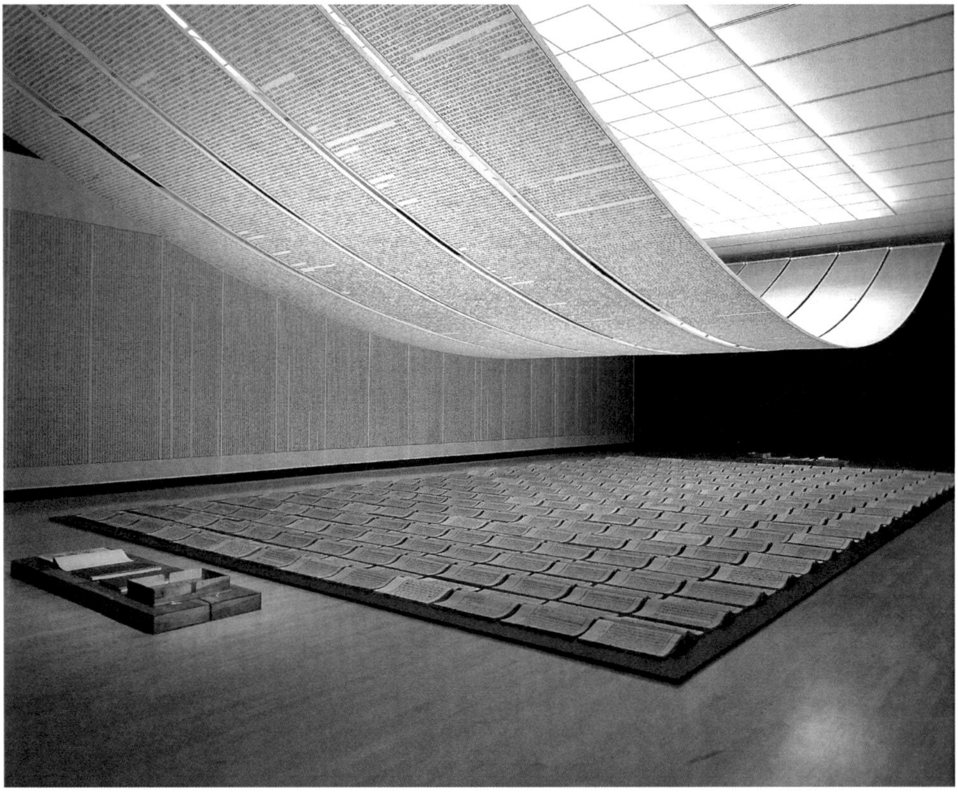

60. Xu Bing, *A Book from the Sky*, 1987–1991. Installation at National Gallery of Canada, Ottawa, 1998 (courtesy Xu Bing Studio).

> proper to book making. 3) In every detail, it would have to be precisely and rigorously executed.[96]

The work includes multiple books printed and bound in traditional Chinese style, massive wall panels, and several huge draping scrolls suspended from the ceiling. All of these were meticulously block printed with thousands of traditional-looking Chinese characters—but all of these characters were newly invented by Xu Bing and set into a moveable type format with his hand-carved wooden blocks. Although the characters give the preliminary impression of potential legibility, they are, in fact, completely unintelligible. They can be read by no one. The exhibition caused an immediate sensation and a variety of responses.

> The installation seemed to suggest that the weight of millennia of Chinese culture oppressed those living at the end of the twentieth century... Visitors to the exhibition remarked that they felt as if they were in a prison, completely hemmed in by unintelligible words. In particular, the scrolls draped from the ceiling seemed to press down on them. For other visitors, the exhibition evoked sensations similar to those felt in a temple or a hall of mourning. Some people felt breathless or frightened. Still others found themselves overwhelmed with a more

positive experience, as the installation inspired them to marvel at the length and wonder of Chinese civilization.[97]

The monumental scale of the work and the incredible amount of meticulous labor involved in its realization[98] are indeed overwhelming, as are the masses of detailed commentary devoted to analysis of the piece. Xu Bing's invented characters are based upon a clear and legible style of Chinese printed writing, but they are "created of elements of real Chinese characters reconfigured in graphs that nobody can read."[99] Interestingly,

> What Xu Bing's work invites is analysis of a theoretical tension embedded in the history of calligraphy, the most tradition-bound of the arts of China. This is the tension between the perception of calligraphy as a system of lexical communication bearing semantic meaning and the perception of calligraphy as a system of pure visual forms.[100]

In some senses, Xu Bing's invented characters might also be seen as examples of "pseudoscripts," such as discussed above. Other past and modern artists, indeed, have invented pseudoscripts or pseudo languages for various reasons and for diverse purposes. These range from artistic attempts to use and copy script patterns derived from unfamiliar or foreign sources as intentional details of decorative embellishment to the more complex artistic invention of arcane symbols evoking ancient pictographs, unknown and indecipherable echoes of ancient communication systems. Xu Bing "seems interested in the complicated mediations involved with any sign-making, concerned not to counterfeit authenticity so much as to disturb authenticity through his own counterfeit."[101]

When Xu Bing left China for the United States in 1990, he had to begin "learning another way of speaking and writing."[102] Highly significant among his works representing his continued investigations of language/communication systems is his 1994–96 creation of "Square Word Calligraphy," a complex system of rendering English letters and words in what appear, at first, to be traditional Chinese characters. "Chinese viewers expect to be able to read Square Word Calligraphy, but cannot. Western viewers, however, are surprised to find out that they *can* read it."[103] Square Word Calligraphy represents "a potential global alphabetic writing that embodies and teaches—as an artwork it is also a pedagogical system—Chinese cultural practices of calligraphy."[104]

Since 1996, installations involving "Square Word Calligraphy" have been featured at various museums around the world. Often these include a computer program that allows visitors to enter texts composed in the Latin alphabet and promptly receive a computer printout with the texts converted into "Square Word Calligraphy."[105] This "enabled western alphabetic writers to generate his more universal Square Word characters without having to trouble themselves with the much longer and more difficult task of learning to write with Chinese brush and ink."[106] Xu Bing's "ultimate goal is to popularize Square Word Calligraphy to such an extent that everyone outside

China can have the opportunity to enjoy practicing calligraphy in a Chinese mode."[107] According to Xu Bing,

> Square Word Calligraphy is on the border between two totally different cultures. Someone asked me, "Do Chinese people find it offensive that you've restructured Chinese into English?" And I've answered, "To the contrary, Chinese people should praise me for having restructured English into Chinese." The absurdity of Square Word Calligraphy is that it takes two different words from two totally unrelated language systems and fuses them into one entity. Through watching people from around the world write Square Word Calligraphy, I can see how it forces their minds to move in nonlinear paths. This opens up so many untouched spaces in our minds and recovers those primal areas of thought and knowledge that have been lost.[108]

In this sense, the message suggested by "Square Word Calligraphy" may be seen as more positive than Xu Bing's earlier language-based work, *Book from the Sky*. "The earlier work presents a view of language as overwhelming and frustrating, and the latter suggests language's power to unify and delight."[109] Indeed, Xu Bing's "interest in the intellectual communicative potential of language art"[110] can also be seen in his *Book from the Ground* project (ongoing since 2003) which uses graphic symbols derived from contemporary universal signage forms as a form of visual language. This work uses logos; icons; insignias; symbols from mathematics, chemistry, music, and corporate advertising; and pictographic-type renditions of human figures and commonly recognizable objects from the modern industrialized world. The narrative presented is "one of modern international life, dealing with clocks, schedules, airports, maps, and the many arrows (sometimes intensified with a '!') that are needed to get the stick figures from one schematic place to another."[111] The artist's intention with this project is to create a legible narrative created of pictorial images that "everyone" should be able to "read."

Most recently, his animation piece *The Character of Characters* (created for the Asian Art Museum of San Francisco, 2012) demonstrates his continued fascination with the history, development, and cultural significance of writing systems.[112] This lively animated work (about 18 minutes long) traces the development of Chinese characters from ancient pictographic symbols, the use of characters in religious ritual and divination practices, the revered nature of the Chinese writing system, the extreme challenges of mastering the art of Chinese calligraphy, and the relationship of characters, political power, and Chinese cultural identity. It has been described as his

> grandest and most comprehensive statement about language ... a summation of his career to date, bringing together elements that were sufficient to animate entire earlier works, touching on them so lightly that their profundity can easily slip by unnoticed. The entire animation is laid out as a narrative of concept, uniting Xu Bing's ideas regarding language with Chinese philosophy and contemporary sociological observations.[113]

Xu Bing's language-based works as a whole indeed represent words about words—but they ultimately speak about the power of words, too. His works investigate the sense of chaos experienced when written and visual language is not understood by anyone—the resultant confusion and sense of disorientation that may take place when, what literate viewers may initially perceive as legible texts turn out to be not so readily accessible or even decipherable. He challenges both western and Asian traditions of written communication by his creation of invented and illegible Chinese characters as well as by his creation of Latin/English letters rendered in a style that appears to be Chinese. His works address not only the forms and structures of written language systems but also the important dimensions of social/political/religious control that may be exerted by language systems held and promulgated by selected and literate members of any society. The power of words—word uses and choices—are themes that have been avidly explored by many other artists too. These themes have many premodern manifestations also, as discussed in the following chapter.

FIVE

The Power of the Word

> Art's about the glorification of *something*; though in my case, it's not necessarily the common object. It may be the power of the word or words that I'm glorifying.—Ed Ruscha[1]

The preceding chapter concluded with a discussion of several of the word-based works by the contemporary Chinese artist, Xu Bing, in which the power of words and the accessibility or inaccessibility of language were dominant themes. His meticulous works, such as *Book from the Sky* (1988), composed of Chinese-like characters that at first appear to be legible but are actually undecipherable, and "Square Word Calligraphy" (1994–96), in which what at first appear to be Chinese characters turn out to actually be English letters rendered in Chinese calligraphic style, use words and letters to raise extremely significant questions about words themselves and language systems in general.

Works of art that use words to comment on the use or abuse of language, especially in social or political contexts, represent an extremely important if not quite prevalent category of modern language-based art. A great many twentieth-century and contemporary artists have created works that use words, often alone, often in conjunction with visual imagery, to produce strident comments about the ways in which language can be used to manipulate, control, dominate, and influence perceptions. The social and political concerns represented by this genre of language-based artworks are very wide ranging: "racism, sexism, bigotry, homophobia, and other forms of prejudice; differences in social classes, including the subjects of poverty and homelessness; social control and the abuse of power"[2] are amongst the many topical issues raised by these works that deploy written language, sometimes alone, sometimes with visual imagery to address these themes.

Many artists, to be further discussed below, have chosen highly specific agendas to consistently explore in their word-based works, such as Barbara Kruger, with her dedicated focus on women's issues and her critiques of the role of traditional popular media in shaping perceptions of women's roles in modern culture. Other artists, such as Martha Rosler, have drawn attention to poverty, homelessness, and the concerns of minorities in contemporary society, focusing upon the ways in which language and/or language combined with visual imagery can be used to create categories of "otherness," isolation, and distance. Some other artists, often working in this same general vein, such as artists Gilbert & George, have chosen to project deliberately shocking words, taken from urban graffiti sources, to challenge viewers and draw their attention to the powerful immediacy of statements found written within the urban environment. These potent and often "impolite" or "bad" words also cause viewers to reflect upon the sources and context for their creation and original appearance.

When words, statements, and phrases that reflect and address contemporary social concerns are presented as works of visual art, viewers are forced to confront the agendas boldly raised by the artists who use words and/or words with images to draw these issues to attention.[3] For these artists, the chosen words and phrases have extremely powerful meanings. Letters, words, and phrases are not primarily shapes to be explored by these artists for their potential aesthetic or visual interest, to be used or perhaps even toyed with artistically, whimsically or playfully, but rather have a power and potency of their own—as conveyers of highly meaningful issues that the artists wish to address and explore with their audiences. These works of visual art that concentrate upon the power and potency of language within the context of highly specific social or cultural concerns are here set apart from other word-based works that may not be so obviously or immediately driven by specific agendas. One further defining characteristic of these socially or politically driven word-works is that the language employed may often be strident, unexpected, deliberately shocking, or controversial in some way. These works often raise singularly important comments about, and critiques of, modern society, by using words and phrases that are designed to be highly provocative, disturbing, and in many cases, quite awful. Both the words/phrases used and the situations these consciousness-raising works address are often extremely upsetting, highly disturbing, and downright hateful. Artists working in this vein utilize powerful and often awful words and phrases to highlight and address awful situations.

The visual presentation of powerful and potent words has also been consistently and importantly utilized in a number of the world's religious traditions as a means to inspire awe. Sacred and holy texts as well as specific phrases and letters have been deemed particularly awesome and powerful in any number of ancient and modern religious and mystical traditions. The significance and power of holy words, letters, texts, and phrases is very well demonstrated in the visual arts by the extreme care and attention to detail given to the creation of works of visual art that include sacred words. This applies quite widely, not only to primarily scripture- or book-based religions. These sacred words and the works of art in which they feature also very much derive their power and potency from the use of a shared visual vocabulary—often transcending the written—to inspire awe and to encourage and stimulate faith adherents.

In both of these genres, those employing "awful words" and "awe-filled" words, the power and potency of words is fully operative. Whether the words/phrases used are awful, disturbing, upsetting, and controversial for some audience members, or comforting, awesome, inspiring, and enlightening for others, works of art in both of these genres fully rely upon the power and potency of written language alone, often but not always in coordination with visual imagery, to make their messages clear.

Awful Words

The old adage, "Sticks and stones will break my bones, but names will never hurt me," precisely bespeaks the naïve approach to the inherent power of language that artists such as Glenn Ligon (b. 1960) point out in their works.[4] Names and words can indeed be extremely powerful, hurtful, and awful indeed. Words can be used to label and define not only objects but also people. Names and definitions can create categories of social "norms" and "otherness." Descriptive words can define classes and types of people as objects cast into misunderstood and negative categories. Ligon, a gay, black, American, East Coast-based artist, came to prominence in the late 1980s and 1990s, especially with his word-based works boldly addressing issues of identity construction, racism, and homophobia, which focused on "how social norms, through language, engage with structures of identity and identification, as well as modes of disidentification."[5] Ligon has worked in a wide range of media including painting, drawing, photography, video, and sculpture, consistently exploring, in a highly sophisticated fashion, the functions, uses, and power of language. His text-based works, however, represent far more than simply "a string of political statements."[6] "There always remains to be negotiated within them a pleasure that has nothing to do with reading."[7] This is a critically important point for Ligon's text-based works generally. His handling is firmly based in highly painterly practices and his works are often characterized by "shamelessly sumptuous paint surfaces."[8] Nevertheless, these works involve the presentation of words.

His carefully selected texts, largely derived from African American literary traditions as well as other modern and contemporary popular sources, are often rendered in very thick stenciled letters using oil stick or another viscous material, which, through his repeated use of the mass-produced, plastic, disposable stencil letter templates, become smeared, blurry, and often ultimately illegible, densely overlaid, and overlapping. In works such as his 1991 *Untitled* ("*I am an Invisible Man*") (illus. 61), the first few lines of the stenciled texts (in black oil stick) can be read, albeit with some difficulty, but as the lines progress down the page, the smeared and overlapping words become denser and denser and eventually impossible to decipher. "Almost no matter how hard one tries, one can neither stop nor go on reading such a picture."[9]

The title and the text of this piece are taken from the prize-winning, experimental 1952 novel *Invisible Man* by Ralph Ellison, in which an unidentified black

61. **Glenn Ligon, *Untitled ("I am an Invisible Man")*, 1991. The Museum of Modern Art, New York (digital image © The Modern of Modern Art/Licensed by SCALA/Art Resource, New York).**

narrator recounts his experiences in mid-twentieth-century America in a disturbing and fantastical manner. The text begins:

> I am an invisible man. No I am not a spook like those who haunted Edgar Allen Poe; Nor am I one of your Hollywood movie ectoplasms. I am a man of substance, of flesh and bone, fiber and liquids—and I might even be said to possess a mind. I am invisible, understand, simply because people refuse to see me…

In Ligon's piece, the stenciled first few lines of Ellison's text are legible at first but then the text becomes increasingly difficult to read and eventually quite illegible due to the smears and markings created by his use of the repeated stencil templates. The lines of text gradually flow together after the first two lines or so, conveying the sense of lost or hidden identity. Invisibility becomes illegibility—with the exception of the two overlaid words "I'm" and "not" that stand out clearly on the upper and lower half in some versions of the piece. "The work appears concerned not simply to present language as a thing, but to make it and its effects on the subject(s) for whom it speaks the point of the representation."[10]

> For the viewer, the entire bottom third of the picture becomes the site of an excavation to resurrect some sense of Ellison's text from the work's coarse, emblackening fracture. Ligon's

> meaningful action appears to be directed at clarifying aspects of the text as *literature*: Ellison's narrator, the clear rendering, and the subject speak together. It seems that what is at stake here is the loss of the subject—even that of the reading self—to the symbolism it becomes when it is written and rewritten.[11]

In other of Ligon's works, stenciled words and phrases are repeated over and over again.[12] Works such as *Untitled (I Am Somebody)* 1991, *Untitled (I Was Somebody)* 1990, *Untitled (I Lost My Voice I Found My Voice)* 1991, *Untitled (I Feel Most Colored When I Am Thrown Against a Sharp White Background)* 1990, and *Untitled (I Am Not Tragically Colored)* 1990, consist of the repetition of the single phrase. Again, the text often begins clearly but ultimately moves down the surface into smeared illegibility. The increasing illegibility of the repeated and overlapping texts strongly conveys the artist's sense of frustration in "saying something over and over and not being heard. The idea of being heard and not being heard."[13] Although the statements are legible at first, the viewer's inability to read the words as the text repeats itself over and over and over again becomes a shared exercise in frustration. The viewer may carefully search to perceive additional words (thinking that perhaps more phrases might be readable in the increasingly smeared texts) while coming to the realization that additional words are simply not there. The same phrase is, mantra-like, repeated to the point where the repetition in itself takes on a powerful meaning. "These works supply us with a kind of interminable, one-line script."[14] In Ligon's own words, his works are "fundamentally about language and an ambivalence and pessimism about the project of communicating, of going back and forth between really wanting to communicate with the viewer and also wanting to withhold things and the aggression of that withholding."[15] He also stated, "It's a very 'Johns-ian' impulse, you know. Jasper Johns and his whole thing about 'Take an object. Do something to it. Do something else to it.' In my case it is 'Take a text. Do something to it. Do something else to it.'"[16]

Ligon's works boldly address the power of words, although they also "derive their vitality from being situated squarely inside a conflict between looking and reading."[17] He "puzzles over the way that language not only shapes literary narratives but also projects social selves and cultural identity across the landscape of the American literary and artistic imagination."[18]

Ligon's interest in the power and also the shock value of words is well demonstrated also in the two groups of paintings he produced from 1993–2004 reproducing jokes told in the 1970s and 1980s by the pioneering black American stand-up comedian Richard Pryor.[19] Pryor is well known for his outrageous and raunchy jokes that both amused and totally shocked audiences by their vulgarity and racial nature. As a black American comedian, Pryor's off-color jokes often shockingly dealt with highly taboo subjects rarely and never so boldly brought to attention at the time—stereotypes of black men and sexuality in extremely crude terms—but terms that were discomfortingly and embarrassingly familiar to the audience.

Ligon's series of *Richard Pryor* paintings are appropriately rendered in garish and bright colors, reflecting the shocking nature of Pryor's jokes. The texts are stenciled in Ligon's typical fashion, becoming increasingly smeared and illegible so that the viewer has to work very hard to actually read these texts.

> As presented by Ligon, the improper grammar, syntax, and spelling of these jokes constitute merely one aspect of their larger "impropriety." For one thing, Pryor's jokes are meant to be heard rather than to be read, listened to rather than looked at. In their original context, the jokes depend on Pryor's vocal performance for their success, on the rhythms and intonations of his particular delivery. Resituated as text paintings, the jokes become dissociated from Pryor's voice and linked instead to the viewer's. It is the viewer who must now read this script, who must mouth, however silently, these words. In rewriting Pryor's jokes as text paintings, Ligon forces us to consider the vehemence of their stereotypes, the rage barely veiled beneath their humor, and the power of their obscenity in the face of a dominant (white) culture that simultaneously desires and dehumanizes black manhood.[20]

A great many other modern artists have taken on the task of critiquing language conventions in works that may include visual imagery as well as words. Glenn Ligon has developed a distinctly recognizable style in his word-based pieces as well as a visual/verbal vocabulary drawn from his own experiences, concerns, desires, and intentions to explore specific social issues in an often highly provocative and thought-provoking manner. The same can be said of other contemporary artists who have also developed unmistakably identifiable styles and who also emphasize the power of words and language in modern social contexts.

For example, Barbara Kruger (b. 1945) is especially notable for the consistency of her agenda, and for her combination of traditional, primarily photographic, imagery with texts that boldly bespeak feminist concerns.[21] Drawing largely from the traditions of twentieth-century advertising imagery, Kruger's works simultaneously poke fun at while also very seriously attacking the words and images promulgated by various visual media—such as television and magazines—primarily as regards the role of women in "modern" American life. "Much of Kruger's work is a feminist critique of representation, namely images of women as they are constructed by the male-dominated media—images that shape the way women view themselves."[22] Kruger's output has been prodigious, and her works have appeared not only in museums and galleries worldwide, but as billboard installations, bus signs, and on T-shirts, mugs, tote bags, and so on. In this manner, she has significantly defied traditional "art" norms and has used "the techniques of mass media to critique mass media."[23]

She worked for several years as a graphic designer and photography editor for Condé Nast publications and has deliberately adopted "the tools of Madison Avenue, of the mass media ... [to create] a strategic use of language as a tool for deconstructive social critique, highlighting the ideological nature of representation and its function in supporting particular interests, values, and systems of power."[24] Her messages are delivered with an economy of means: large, clear texts, usually rendered in the highly legible Bold Futura font, often accompanied by photographic images "selected from

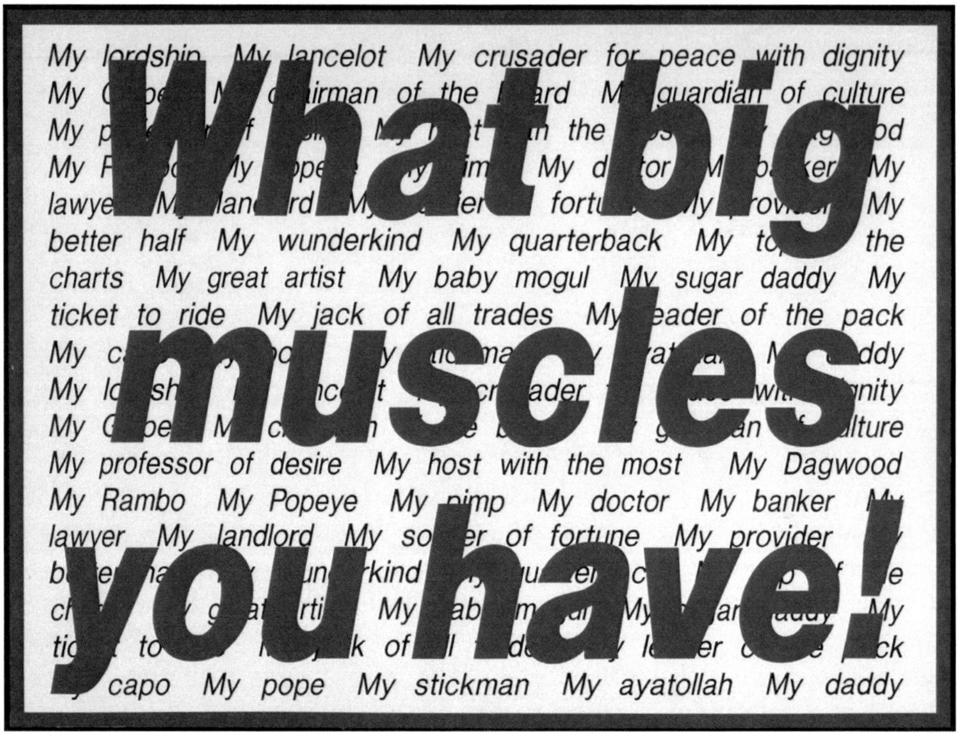

Barbara Kruger, *What Big Muscles You Have!*, 1986. Musée Nationale d'Art Moderne, Centre Georges Pompidou, Paris, France (© CNAC/MNAM/Dist RMN-Grand Palais/Art Resource, New York; © Barbara Kruger, courtesy Mary Boone Gallery, New York).

a variety of sources, all bearing a nostalgic, faded appearance that nurtures the social agenda Kruger attempts to dismantle."[25] Her bold texts and graphics assault the eye with their aggressive clarity and forcefulness and force viewers to consider the specific vocabulary and phrasing of the messages and constructed implications they may recognize all too well.

A work such as her 1986 piece *What Big Muscles You Have!* may serve as an excellent example of her use of language to draw attention to gender relationships and the traditional subordination of women (illus. 62). In her typical color of scheme of red, black, and white, the words of the title are boldly rendered in large bright red letters across a background consisting of trite and slangy words and phrases used by women to define men and traditional male roles: *My lordship My lancelot My better half My pimp My doctor My lawyer My banker My landlord My ticket to ride My soldier of fortune My provider My jack of all trades.* These definitions, in black lettering, are densely arranged in a series of lines filling the entire background space of the composition. In combination with the bold reference to "big muscles," the implication is clearly that the male gender roles represent a dominant, forceful, and oppressive power over women whose traditional labeling of these stereotypes as "*My*" (this or

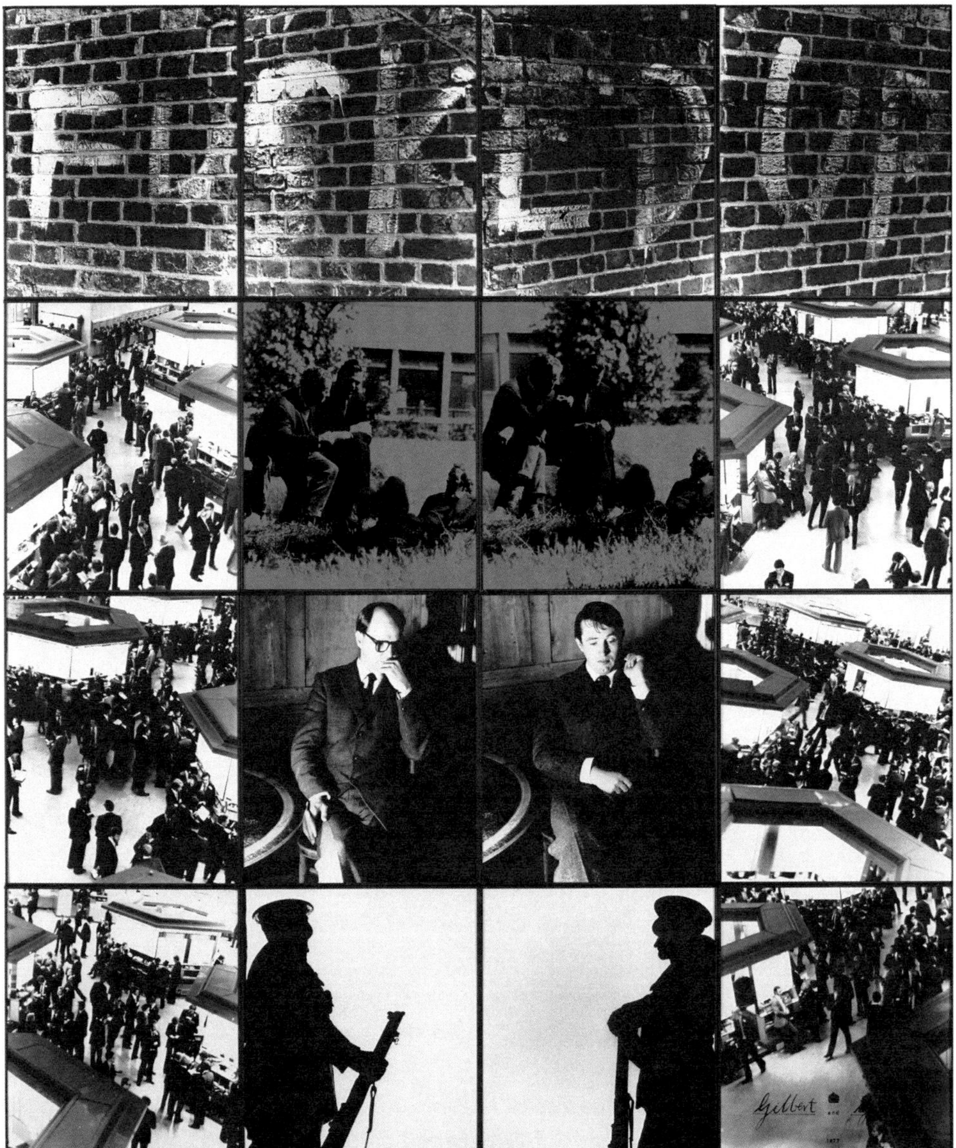

63. **Gilbert & George, *Fucked Up*, 1977 (© the artists, White Cube Gallery, London).**

that endearing term) places women in a weak and passive role. Kruger's work is always direct, bold, and legible, addressing issues of gender, domestic violence, and the power of language to promote as well as to deconstruct stereotypes. Her word-based works are designed to draw attention to specific social issues and the shared language that constructs (and can deconstruct) them.

The power of words to shock and outrage are themes that have been more than well investigated also by the artists Gilbert & George (Gilbert, b. 1943; George, b. 1942). In their 1977 series of *Dirty Words Pictures*, for example, the artists juxtaposed enlargements of "obscene" graffiti with images of "wire mesh fencing and broken windows, soldiers armed with automatic weapons, silhouettes of model soldiers aiming and firing, crowds, the trading floor of the London Stock Exchange, featureless City office blocks, slumped alcoholics, the top deck of night buses, peeling paint, discarded newspapers, glimpsed loners and traffic."[26] The picture titled *Fucked Up* may serve as an excellent example of the works in this series (illus. 63). Typically, as in this example, the artists included images of themselves, well dressed in their highly conservative fashion as per their adopted "artistic" personalities. They are often posed in reflective or pensive stances amidst the total cacophony of verbal and visual violence. All of the graffiti included in this series of twenty-six pictures was found by the artists in London, within a ten-minute walk from their residence. The obscenities and crude sexual scrawls found on buildings, buses, and in the subway represent a characteristic feature of urban reality: awful and "dirty" words encountered on a daily basis by city dwellers. How do we respond to these words when we find them boldly scrawled in public places? What, really, do these "bad" and "awful" words mean? Why are these obscenities prevalent? What causes people to write these words? We may be highly offended by these words, or we may even use a few of them regularly in our own vocabulary. Our degree of comfort or discomfort with these words may not have so much to do with the words themselves, but rather may be due to the fact that our use/abuse of these words may be indicative of our more or less "dignified" status and the way in which we classify ourselves (versus "others") for whom these "dirty words" are "common." What social conventions are at work to make some words "dirtier" than others? "Which is more obscene—social injustice, the quality of contemporary urban life, or dirty words?"[27] These are some of the provocative questions raised by the *Dirty Words Pictures*.

The powerful combination of text and photographic imagery to point out and critique contemporary social problems is also well demonstrated in the work of the American artist Martha Rosler (b. 1943). Rosler works in a variety of media including photo-collage, photo-text, video, installation, and performance, and she has also written extensively and articulately about art and culture.[28] She has consistently concentrated her interest on issues in the modern public realms: housing, homelessness, transportation, urban situations, women's concerns, war, and the role of media in modern life. She has stated, "Art can serve as a condenser of complex matters into symbolic narratives, and a catalytic node for discussion and organizing. It allows for the further germination of ideas through themes that remained unmined or require a more contemporary view."[29] According to Rosler,

> From an early age I felt oppressed by a conspiracy of silences, silences about things in the wider world most of which were perpetually present, unspoken but forming the unmarked boundaries of the possible. ...I soon realized that the work that had the most meaning for

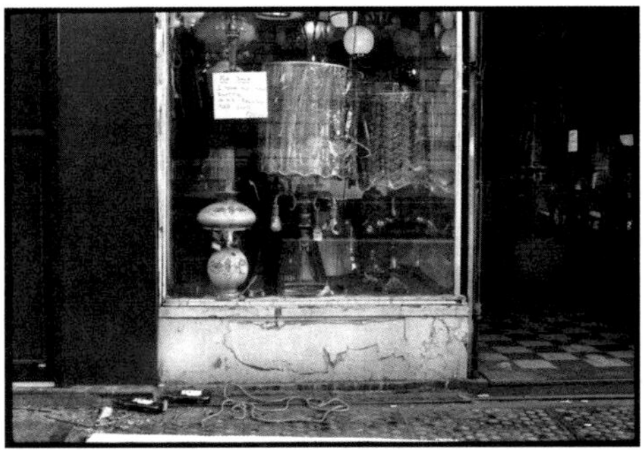

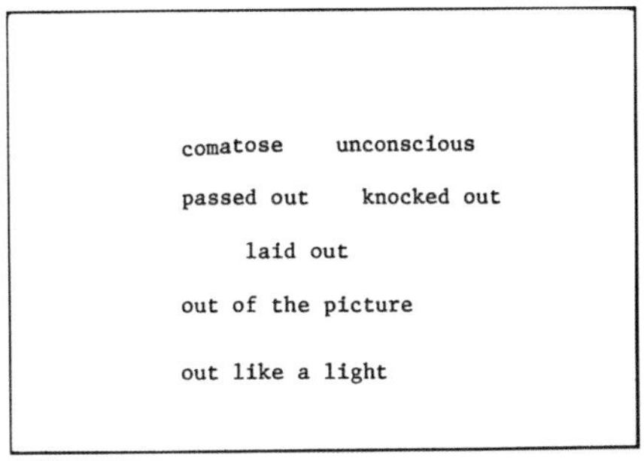

64 a and b. Martha Rosler, *The Bowery in two inadequate descriptive systems*, detail, 1974–75. The Whitney Museum of American Art, New York (courtesy Martha Rosler).

> me, that drew deep, was engaged with the imagery of the "other" world of power, control, and ideological articulation.... [I]n looking at the imagery of the polite world of mainstream magazines, of newspapers and television, I saw worlds of power and wealth on some pages and on other pages, or in other slots, a world of victimized or dispossessed people. I saw men in suits and women in lingerie. I thought of this as the mythologies of everyday life, which kept mental images segregated from one another, serving to shore up ideological absurdities that kept life on an even keel in one neighborhood while around the corner the world was erupting.[30]

One of her most well-known and frequently discussed works is her 1974–75 photo-text installation, *The Bowery in two inadequate descriptive systems.*[31] It consists of twenty-four panels juxtaposing black and white photographs taken on the Bowery—then a notorious skid row area in Manhattan—with a whole series of typed terms referring to alcohol, drunks and drunkenness, and alcoholism (illus. 64). Although no people are shown in the photographs, their presence is amply suggested by empty and discarded bottles, broken bottles, deserted doorways, and gutters and sidewalks littered with debris. These unpeopled images provide only a partial "document" of the inhabitants of this area. Their lives are only hinted at, suggested by what they have left behind. Rosler deliberately chose not to include any people in these pictures, wishing to avoid the traditions often associated with "social documentary" photography where the artist's and viewer's focus may be upon specific individuals as representatives of types, social classes, and ethnic groups: the poor, the disenfranchised, the mentally ill, and so on.[32] Instead, her unpeopled scenes serve as comments upon how photographic images can manipulate and construct social narratives in the same way as written language.

The written component of the piece consists of photographs of a lengthy series of unembellished and simply typed nouns and adjectives describing alcohol and drunks. These panels of written text, placed next to the images, include terms such as "stinko," "blotto," "plastered," "under the table," "boozehound," "souse," and so forth. These words are, as the work's title suggests, fundamentally as "inadequate" as the photographs to serve as a "descriptive system" for the many complex issues related to alcoholism, poverty, and the blighted urban environment represented by the Bowery in New York in the mid-twentieth century.[33] "The two interlaced 'descriptive systems," one linguistic and one verbal, each provide exhaustive details without adequately explaining their subject."[34]

> Some questions seem immediately apposite: what is inadequate about the "two inadequate descriptive systems?" To what do the "systems" refer? Are they visual and verbal, pictures and words, image and text, or perhaps language and photography? Each opposition opens slightly different possibilities. In what sense, if any, are they systems? If they are systems, how systematic are they? With regard to which tasks are they inadequate? To state this slightly differently, how is the inadequacy made manifest in the array of pictures and words set out before the viewer?[35]

The slangy terms and phrases Rosler carefully selected and placed into metamorphic groupings for this piece reveal their power by their "inadequacy." As Rosler describes, the words reveal careful groupings into "food imagery, nautical imagery, the imagery of industrial processes, of militarism, derisive comparisons with animal life, foreignisms, archaisms, and references to still other universes of discourse—applied to a particular state of being, a subculture of sorts, and to the people in it."[36] In some few cases, the verbal and visual pairings can be seen to connect, such as the text panel where the phrases include "out like a light" that is paired with a photograph of a shop window filled with various dusty-looking lamps and lighting fixtures. But the phrases, in general, do not serve as captions for the images, instead, they represent a concurrent and equally inadequate descriptive system.

"The verbal descriptions mix derogatory and endearing phrases for drunks,"[37] ranging from playful and lighthearted to far more antagonistic and negative. In so doing, the written descriptions raise critical issues about the powerful nature of words and how they may be constructed and applied in general and especially in specific social contexts such as alcoholism, poverty, and homelessness. In Rosler's work,

> the words operated as analogues for the mobility of discourses surrounding the bums who populated the Bowery. They loitered next to the poignantly empty spaces, in the accompanying photographs, which the bums themselves should have occupied. ... All we get are deserted doorways, shop fronts, facades—the places in which down-and-outs normally sleep—with the occasional beer or whiskey bottle left as a reminder.[38]

The parallel use of "inadequate" images as well as "inadequate" terms in this celebrated and often discussed work by Rosler points out the powerful manner in which both visual imagery and verbal descriptions can constrain and also manipulate perceptions. She asks us to consider how the constructs and processes involved with selecting purposeful imagery run parallel to the careful (or careless) selection of descriptive words. As viewers and readers, we are asked to more carefully consider our image and word choices and the names that we use to describe our perceptions.

> Naming is crucial. It is the act of naming which gives meaning and significance to the things of this world. The scene in Genesis where Adam names the animals is a key one: in a sense

> he is taking ownership of them. Naming is an almost magical act... Our entry into language as children is marked by our naming of people and things.... It is when we ask questions that we begin to achieve some degree of self-awareness.[39]

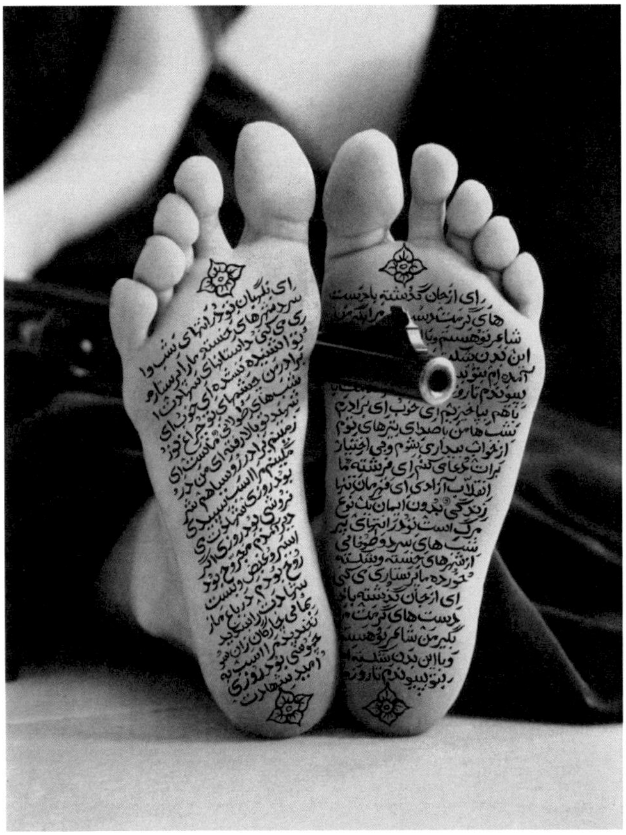

65. Shirin Neshat, *Allegiance with Wakefulness*, 1994. Black and white RC print & ink (photograph taken by Cynthia Preston) (© Shirin Neshat; courtesy Gladstone Gallery, New York and Brussels).

The types of names that we may use to describe our perceptions of images (and indeed our perceptions of unfamiliar written languages too) have also been exceedingly well addressed by the important contemporary Iranian-born, New York–based artist Shirin Neshat (b. 1957), especially in her series of photographs *Women of Allah* that she created between 1993 and 1997.[40] Neshat came to the United States to study at the University of California at Berkeley in 1974 and, due to the political turmoil of the Iranian Revolution, did not return to her homeland even for a visit until 1990. She found the changes that had taken place in Iran during her absence to be profoundly shocking indeed, and she developed her reactions to this changed cultural and political climate notably in her *Women of Allah* series. These images combine powerful themes of violence and sexual and cultural stereotypes and raise discomforting questions about the meaning of both the images and the texts written upon them. They largely present chador-clothed and weapon-bearing women (the artist herself) posed facing the viewer, their hands and faces often covered with Farsi texts written directly onto the photographs. Some examples include only a section of a woman's body—her hands, head, or feet—as in *Allegiance with Wakefulness* that shows a rifle pointing out from between two bare feet, the bottoms of which are inscribed with texts (illus. 65). The texts are excerpts from poems written by the acclaimed twentieth-century Iranian female poet and religious scholar, Tahereh

Saffarzadeh. According to Neshat, "the written text is the voice of the photograph... It breaks the silence of the still woman in the portrait."[41] However, for viewers unfamiliar with the Perso-Arabic script, the texts are illegible, and the voices of the women shown in the photographs remain unheard. The written words combined with the powerful visual images create

> a highly ambiguous text precisely because of the difficulties of translation ... a troubling ambiguity because of its implications. The handwritten texts in the photographs would be fully comprehensible if they were read in Iran or in other Arabic-speaking Islamic countries. But Shirin Neshat's works have never been exhibited in Iran, and in any case in the aforementioned Islamic countries they probably wouldn't be recognized as works of art, given that these cultures are based on an interdiction against iconic language. To us, the writings remain incomprehensible without supplementary information.... Thus clearly the work doesn't speak to us only of the condition of women in Iran, but also of an encounter between cultural universes, at the center of which there is a lack of meaning, a discrepancy, a gap that, while apparently slender, remains unbridgeable.[42]

How viewers perceive these works depends on their personal backgrounds and experience with Islamic cultures, history, and writing. Western viewers may tend to make many assumptions about the images, reading into them any variety of messages and meanings based on their own personal responses. An inability to read the texts essentially contributes to the sense of confusion about the meaning of the images. Neshat was well aware of that when creating the series that also served as her exploration of her own personal reactions to the foreign and changed climate she encountered in her homeland.

> These stereotypes of the Islamic world, as represented by the woman in black, provoke reactions in the West that range from compassion to fear to hatred. Neshat combines these signifying reactions into complex and self-contradictory wholes. Repression, fatalism and passivity, social marginalization, veiled erotic promise, inspiration, heroism, mercilessness and danger converge in a single female figure dressed in a chador. Neshat's aim is not to dispose of the media clichés, but to recompose and reorganize them in ways that produce more flexible and complex meanings.[43]

These works represent the power of language—both visual and verbal—to confuse, challenge, reinforce, or dismantle meaning. Since the late 1990s, Neshat has concentrated primarily on work in video, continuing to address themes that speak of cultural commonalities as well as differences, the challenges of communication between cultures and between men and women.[44]

The influential Conceptual artist, Joseph Kosuth, once stated, "If art is to be more than an expensive decoration, you have to see it as expressing other kinds of philosophical and political meaning."[45] The word-based works sampled above boldly and assuredly demonstrate how many contemporary artists especially have used language in their works to convey singularly important sociopolitical meanings and messages. Often strident and confrontational in nature, these works show how words can be used, abused, and manipulated in constructing roles and norms for gender, ethnic, race, and class relationships. The power of words to create and to convey meaning, to serve as vehicles for alienation and "othering," and the use of words to construct categories of role models and social expectations are all themes especially addressed in these works. These works thus diverge from the word-based art works discussed in the preceding chapter—those that have what might be described as a more philosophical bent in their investigation of language systems. In both cases however, the power of words, and especially words rendered in boldly visual form, is shared by these genres. Whether the artists have engaged with complex philosophical themes or directed their attention to more obviously social/political messages, these works demonstrate the power and potency of the visual word.

Awe-Filled Words

The visual word also plays an absolutely critical role in many religious contexts. Powerful and visually presented words—words designed to inspire and to create awe—are characteristic of a great many of the world's diverse faith traditions, especially but not exclusively those traditions based on sacred scriptural writings. In contrast to the often "awful" and confrontational words selected for visual presentation by many of the socially and politically conscious artists discussed above, the power of words as sacred emblems and symbols of the holy or transcendental can be seen in the "awe-filled" word-based creations characteristic of many faith traditions.

Indeed, a belief in the divine origins of words themselves can be found in many ancient world cultures from Egypt to India to Asia. Many of the world's ancient cultures in which writing systems were initially developed "hold one idea in common: writing is divine, inherently holy, with powers to teach the highest mysteries; writing is the speech of the gods, the ideal form of beauty."[46] Thus, for many world cultures and faith traditions, the written word is inherently vested with a sacred quality, serving as a vehicle for communication with and about the divine. This sacred status of writing is also, of course, reflected in the fact that in preliterate or semiliterate ancient cultures, the abilities to both read and write largely remained the exclusive privilege of the priestly or royal classes, those who were educated in the requisite skills. "From the earliest period of human history ... the power of writing was such that it seemed too profound an invention to have been the product of mere human effort. All early proposals for the origins of the alphabet revolved around the notion of a divine gift."[47]

For the ancient Egyptians, writing was regarded as a gift to humans given by the important and powerful deity Thoth (or Toth). Customarily depicted in art as either ibis- or baboon-headed, the god Thoth was regarded as the font of all knowledge, giving to humankind awareness of all forms of science, philosophy, religion, and magic. He is credited with inventing or conveying the system of hieroglyphic writing used in ancient Egypt. Some ancient Greek traditions tell that the god Hermes was inspired to invent letters when observing the shapes created by the movements of a flock of cranes flying through the sky.[48] Various accounts in Jewish traditions credit either Adam, Abraham, or Moses as having received the gift of letters and writing directly from God. Some Islamic traditions also tell that Allah gave the alphabet to Abraham. In Hindu traditions, the elephant-headed god, Ganesh, is often credited with having invented writing and giving this knowledge to humans. Ancient Chinese legends tell that "Cangjie, the four-eyed dragon-faced wizard, modeled the Chinese characters after the movements of the stars, the footprints of birds, and other patterns that occurred in nature."[49] And of course,

> Christian dogma has in common with certain other Western religious and philosophical belief systems a faith in the concept of the Word. In Christianity, this concept is associated not only with a notion of a Divine Truth ... but also with a notion of embodiment of that Truth. Christ, as Prophet and Saviour, not only delivers the Word, but states that he in effect is the Word as well.[50]

Respect and reverence for the divine word is manifest in a number of religious traditions in a variety of manners directly relevant to our study. For example, this is seen in the care spent in copying and preserving holy texts, as well as in beliefs about the power and sacredness of letters themselves. It has frequently been pointed out that the painstaking care and attention to detail in the copying and embellishing of words in medieval Christian manuscripts, for example, bespeaks the sacredness of the texts themselves as well as the holy nature of the individual letters.[51] For the medieval Christian scribe, the process of copying the holy scriptures was in itself an act of devotion. The "integral spiritual aspect"[52] of the medieval hand-copied book is visibly manifest in the wondrous variety of word treatment and decoration that "played a considerable part in seducing the eye into contemplative engagement with the page."[53] This is most notably the case with lavishly decorated manuscripts, such as those selected examples discussed in chapter 1 above, where text pages are treated as fully artful compositions, where the letters and words themselves are created with enormous care. Decorated, embellished, and artfully positioned on the pages, these sacred letters take on powerful roles as visual symbols as well as written conveyors of sanctified truths. The significance and venerability of the words is reflected by the care with which they were treated and presented by the scribes and artists.

In addition to the diverse forms of embellishment of individual letters and words found in many examples of medieval Christian manuscripts, there are also a number of intriguing and noteworthy examples of manuscripts written by scribes who devoted their attention to shaping holy words into holy images and sacred, symbolic forms. Many of these examples are, of course, akin to the shaped texts and visual poetry discussed earlier by their offsetting of selected words and phrases into patterns that form either geometric or curvilinear shapes. The reader of the text simultaneously sees these as specific shapes as well as lines of words. For instance, several religious manuscripts produced in medieval Byzantium exhibit very impressive variations on this theme: the painstaking process of making shapes with words. In particular, the extensive commentaries compiled and contained in several Byzantine manuscripts of the texts of the biblical prophets appear to have "inspire[d] scribes to remarkable fears of calligraphy"[54] in their creation of complex page layouts. Although some of these are admittedly less creative, more akin to the glossed biblical and other manuscripts of western tradition in which blocks of commentary simply surround blocks of text,[55] some notable Byzantine examples such as the late tenth-century "Bible of Niketas" (Florence, Bibliotheca Medicea-Laurenziana Cod. Plut. 5. 9), exhibit pages with commentaries laid out in an impressive variety of decorative patterns.[56] The "Bible of Niketas" includes texts shaped into crosses, circles, triangles, columnar forms with oval rectangular profiles, and other complex designs.[57]

The medieval Byzantine "delight in shaped text"[58] also takes very impressive form in a mid-twelfth-century Byzantine Gospel Lectionary (New York: Pierpont Morgan Library MS M 692) in which the entire text of the manuscript, every page, is written in the form of the Greek equal-armed cross. This manuscript contains selected readings ("lections") from the gospels arranged according to their use in the Byzantine liturgy and was probably made in an important workshop in Constantinople. Although there are other manuscripts, both western medieval and Byzantine, that include some pages of cross-shaped texts, the "New York Cruciform Lectionary" is virtually unique in using the format consistently throughout the book. This manuscript also includes some figural and narrative illustrations, placed in the four quadrants left in the blank spaces on the sides of the cross-shaped texts. For example, folio 6 contains marginal illustrations of Saint John the Baptist and two of his disciples in the lower left quadrant, and a medallion containing the cruciform-nimbed bust of Jesus Christ in the lower right quadrant (illus. 66). The text comes from John 1:35–52, read on

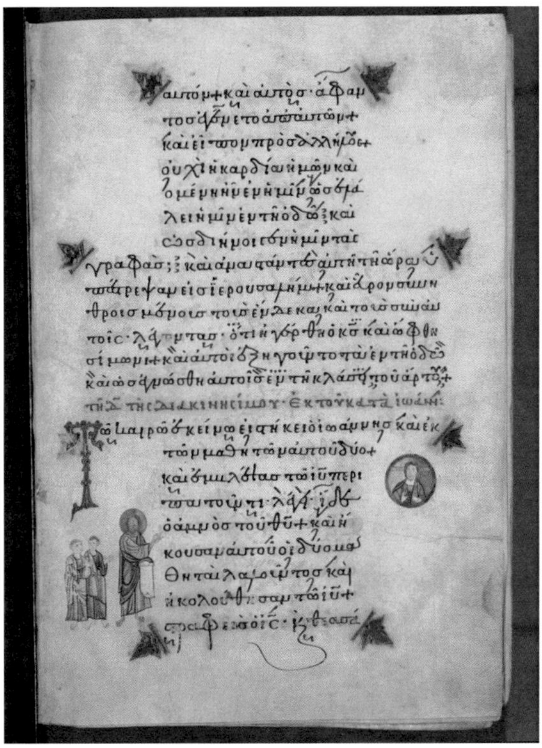

66. Byzantine Cruciform Lectionary, Constantinople, mid-12th century. "The New York Cruciform Lectionary," New York, The Pierpont Morgan Library MS M. 692, folio 6r. Purchased from Mitchell Kennerly, 1925 (The Pierpont Morgan Library, New York).

the Wednesday after Easter, in which Saint John recognizes Jesus and points him out to his companions.

This manuscript was doubtless a luxury production due to the fact that the page layout "left so much expensive parchment empty."[59] This is a singularly important point. Although we can only surmise about the ultimate motivations for this textual design layout, the patron, scribes, and artists involved with the creation of this manuscript must have felt that it was extremely important to have all the texts of the sacred writings contained in this book reflect their Christian significance via their shaping and presentation into the symbolic cross form. This decision clearly bespeaks not only the luxury of the production, but also the powerful nature with which these holy words were regarded. On each page, the reader is simultaneously reminded of the important Christian symbolism of the cross and sees it too in visual form. The visual/written experience is made very powerful indeed, in religious contexts, when both the word and the image share the same goals and forms.

In Jewish religious traditions as well, the process of writing and the forms in which sacred writing appear assume a ritual significance.[60] There are strict rules governing the creation and handling of the Torah scrolls for example, and the reverent attitude towards the Hebrew sacred texts is well demonstrated by the painstaking care with which these scriptures are written and treated. Indeed, "the alphabet and writing have long maintained a symbolic and mystical existence in Jewish folklore and philosophy."[61] In particular, the vast and complex body of Hebrew mystical literature known as the Kabbalah maintains

> a belief in the ineffable character of Divine energy and the sacredness and religious significance of the Hebrew language as an instrument of Divine Power. In the Kabbalah the contemplation and manipulation of the letters is considered a means of approaching God through meditation and esoteric interpretation. For the kabbalist, God's writing is the world.[62]

Texts such as the *Sefir Yetzirah* (*Sefer Yetzirah* or *Sefer Yezira*) (*Book of Creation* or *Book of Formation*) are the major sources for the doctrines of alphabet symbolism in Jewish mystical traditions.[63] The ancient origins of this brief and enigmatic text are obscure but various versions of it, along with other kabbalistic works, became particularly popular and widely studied and commented upon by Jewish scholars, especially in medieval Spain, Germany, and the Near East. Often subtitled "The Alphabet of Our Father Abraham,"[64] the work is primarily "dedicated to a detailed description how the various letters and groups of letters served the process of creation and dominate the various aspects of the universe."[65] "The *Sefir Yetzirah* is both the primary instruction manual for meditative practices using the alphabet and the basic account of the structure of the material world in terms of alphabet symbolism."[66] In this text, the twenty-two letters of the Hebrew alphabet are divided into three groups, and each individual letter is afforded a description explicating the letter's mystical symbolism, properties, roles, and correspondences with passages in the Torah, zodiac signs, parts of the human body, angels, and so on. "The whole of the text is intended as a description of the processes of formation by which the structures and cycles of the material world are brought into being."[67] "Creation itself ... is magical through and through: all things in it live by virtue of the secret names that dwell in them."[68] God's creation of the universe is thus continually manifest in these sacred letters, the study and contemplation of which will result in mystical revelations of "the structure of Divine light, power and wisdom."[69] "The concept that the universe was created by the power of divine speech is an ancient one in Judaism, and the Sefer Yezira developed this idea systematically. The guiding principle seems to have been that if creation is accomplished by language, then the laws of creation are the laws of language."[70] The extreme complexities of kabbalistic theories should not be underestimated; for our purposes here, however, the concept of the divine power of letters as contained in kabbalistic writings is most salient.

Obviously, as well, "preoccupation with the frequency and patterns of letters in the Torah and in specific passages, was an inexhaustible source of kabbalistic interpretation,"[71] and this interest in counting and tracking letters of the Hebrew alphabet in sacred texts is also demonstrated in the system of masoretic notes. This form of marginal textual notation counting, listing, and comparing each word and letter in the Hebrew scriptures appears to have developed around the sixth to eighth centuries CE. The ultimate purpose of the Masorah was "to preserve the text tradition,"[72] to maintain "rules on the reading, writing, and intonation of the biblical text,"[73] and to prevent scribal errors from entering the sacred texts. The masoretes wrote out "lists of biblical words and passages in order to keep track of every word in the Bible. They noted how many times each appeared and where it could be found in the exact same form."[74] Clearly, this was not only a devotional act but also extremely tedious work requiring incredible care and precision. These long lists of letters, words, and notes accompanying biblical texts most usefully appear in the margins of the texts to which they refer, and they are set apart from the main text by being written in much smaller script. The diminutive script used for these notes also gave rise to what has been called a "specifically Jewish form of art,"[75] that of micrography—or miniature writing forming pictures or designs. Although examples of micrography can be widely found in various world cultures, the tradition is notably developed and long-lasting as a Jewish art form. The origins of Hebrew micrography have been traced back to the late ninth century CE and the form is still being practiced today.[76]

The primary and original use of this diminutive writing was for masoretic notes.[77] The scribes engaged with performing this tedious task may have found "an outlet for their creative talents while occupied with the drudgery of copying out the masoreh,"[78] by fashioning the texts into patterns and designs. *Masorah figurata* micrography in Hebrew religious manuscripts takes a variety of forms: marginal decoration as well as carpet pages (full pages of diminutive shaped writing), calligrams (pictures composed of parallel lines of text) and micrograms (where the outlines of images and designs are formed by shaped lines of text). The levels of complexity and sophistication achieved, especially during the thirteenth through fifteenth centuries by scribes working in both the Near East and western Europe, are truly surpassing.[79]

A manuscript of the Pentateuch from the second half of the thirteenth century or early fourteenth century, written either in France or Germany, well demonstrates the enchantment of this word/art form (illus. 67). This manuscript (London, British Library Add. MS 21160) contains numerous pages of micrographic writing of which the folio illustrated here is just one sample. This particular page (folio 300v), at the end of the text of the Book of Ruth, well indicates how the written marginal commentary accompanying the main text, in the center of the page, was creatively shaped by the scribe to form a border of elaborate foliate scrolls and dragons contained within a bounding architectural framework. All of the pictorial details—the pointed arches, the architectural column-forming lines and bases, the dragons and foliage—are created of minuscule writing. At first glance, these forms appear to be simply decorative framing devices, such as well might be expected in important illustrated manuscripts of this time period where significant texts were often enriched and offset with elaborate frames, border designs, and pictorial imagery. However, the framing forms here are actually created of very tiny letters and words, carefully shaped into pictorial patterns. In general with such micrography, the shaping of texts into decorative or figural forms is largely ornamental rather than illustrative. In other words, the designs and forms created of the minuscule words generally are not textually relevant illustrations. This particular manuscript, however, also includes some identifiable figural scenes, such as the image of Jonah and the Whale on folio 292.

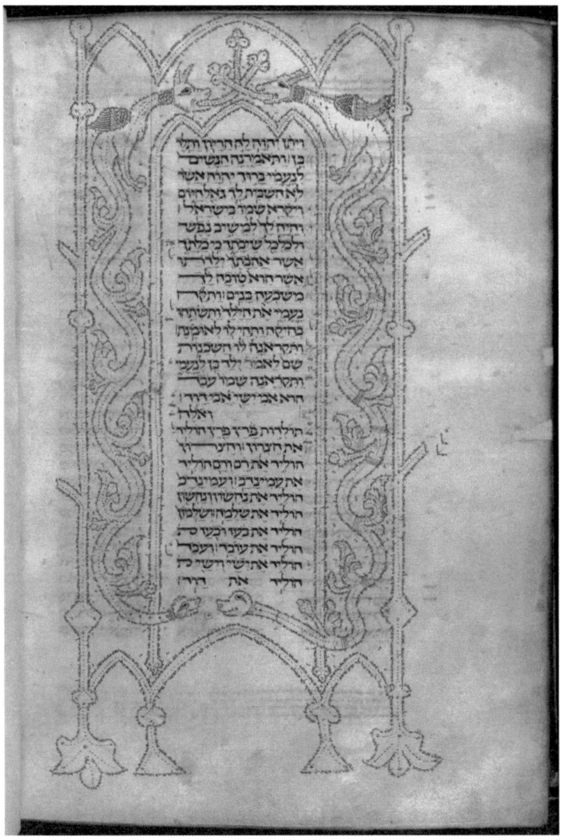

67. Hebrew Pentateuch, 13th–14th century, France or Germany. London, British Library MS Add. 21160, folio 300v (© The British Library Board).

Hebrew micrography flourished in Europe and the Near East primarily during the eleventh through fifteenth centuries. Specific styles and formats are characteristic of particular regions. Manuscripts produced in Yemen, for example, largely employ geometric patterns, whereas manuscripts created in medieval Europe are more likely to draw from the decorative and figural vocabulary of the European Romanesque and Gothic styles. In all examples, however, it should be noted that the extremely small size of the writing sometimes gives the viewer

> the feeling that micrography was sort of a game played by the scribe with the reader. The scribe was intent upon inducing the cerebral condition of alexia, the inability to read written words. As one looks closer and closer at the script to catch a few phrases in order to figure out what text the scribe has used in the micrograph, and as one keeps turning the page around because the lines keep changing direction, the letters seem to melt before one's eyes.[80]

It is indeed quite possible to forget that this actually *is* writing. The mystical symbolism, power, and significance of sacred letters in Hebrew traditions is more than well shown by the special form of micrography, a reverential treatment of holy words.

> Letters and word combinations were first written in decorative, figured form as a means of suggesting all of the potentialities of creation inherent in the letter. Inasmuch as all of creation pre-existed in the letter and its combinations in the Torah, the word and the letter became the only and natural form for expressing all of the creative possibilities of the Word. Decorative, figured, micrographic script should therefore be seen as the visual fulfillment of this concept. The word became the only feasible means of enhancing the Word.[81]

Very similar attitudes about the sacred status of writing may be seen in a variety of other cultural contexts as well. In Islamic traditions, for example, the Arabic script styles that ultimately evolved for the writing of the holy scriptures, the Qur'an, were developed and refined with supreme attention to the sacredness of the task of rendering the direct revelation from Allah to Muhammad (ca. 570–632) in perfectly correct form. Muslims believe that the Qur'an ("the recitation") was verbally revealed to Muhammad through the intermediary of the angel Jibril (Gabriel) over a period of about twenty-three years, from ca. 609 to 632. "According to Islamic teachings, the Qur'an was transmitted to the Prophet Muhammad in the Arabic tongue ... it therefore has the status of divine speech."[82] The sacred recitations were originally shared and preserved orally until quite shortly after the death of Muhammad, when the Qur'an was committed to writing under the direction of the first caliph, Abu Bakr. A codified version was shortly thereafter produced in the mid-seventh century under the direction of the third caliph, Uthman, and this has provided the standard for all later editions. Because the Qur'an was received and ultimately written in Arabic, this language and script represent "the most precious treasure for the Muslim."[83] Language and writing are thus raised to the status of sacred forms of art in Islamic cultures; writing itself becomes an act of reverence.[84] "In Islam, perfect calligraphy is a manifestation of spirituality, of inward perfection which comes from being in harmony with the will and purpose of God."[85]

The general avoidance of visual and especially figurative imagery in much of

Islamic religious art has also contributed to the extreme significance of writing as the preeminent art form in both historical and contemporary Islamic cultures. The art of beautiful writing—calligraphy—appears throughout Islamic art in all contexts, not just in manuscripts but on objects of all types, sizes, and media. Monumental calligraphic inscriptions grace the interiors and exteriors of Islamic architectural structures, both religious and secular. Textiles, ceramics, tiles, glass, metalwork, furniture, and objects for liturgical use as well as daily use are frequently enriched with calligraphic inscriptions. The written word is a preeminent feature in all Islamic arts up to the present day.

Over the centuries, a number of different styles of Arabic script evolved in various geographic regions and cultures. In most fundamental terms, these different styles of script range from the straight-lined to the more curved, cursive, and rounded forms.[86] Certain styles of Arabic script are especially notable for their flexibility in terms of letter forms and letter sequencing, allowing letters to be shaped, curved, elongated, and twisted to form decorative patterns. Sometimes, different styles of script were also combined. As noted above, a number of western European artists in the medieval and Renaissance periods were quite attracted to the decorative possibilities of Arabic script styles as well, often copying these art forms with more—or mostly less—accuracy in their creation of "pseudo-Arabic" scripts.

A carved stucco relief panel from the Hall of the Two Sisters in the Alhambra Palace in Granada, Spain may serve as simply one representative sample here of medieval Islamic calligraphy (illus. 68). The Alhambra Palace was built and occupied by successive Muslim rulers and their courts in medieval Spain from the tenth through the fifteenth centuries. Consistently enlarged and redecorated, it stands today as one of the most impressive exemplars of western medieval Islamic art in terms of its structural plan, gardens, elaborate tile work, and stucco carving. The Hall of the Two Sisters was one of the later additions to this palace complex. This stately room was fully elaborated with a plethora of beautifully carved stucco-work inscriptions and verses from the Qur'an, as well as poems composed by notable fourteenth-century authors. The roundel in the center of the illustration included here contains verses rendered in Thuluth script celebrating the beauty of the building.[87] In many other areas of the palace, the more angular kufic script is, as well, found in combination with the more flowing and Andalusian style of Thuluth script. The phrase "Glory belongs to God" is often repeated over and again in the foliated and interwoven designs found in the calligraphic inscriptions in the Alhambra Palace.

The artful shaping and manipulation of texts and words in Islamic art is well demonstrated also by countless examples of extremely ornate and decoratively shaped texts, mirror writing (in which calligraphic forms are presented as reverse compositions), zoomorphic compositions (in which letters form the shape of animals), and letters that are drawn out to form visual forms of floral or geometric nature. Text compositions in the shape of various objects—musical instruments, urns, and

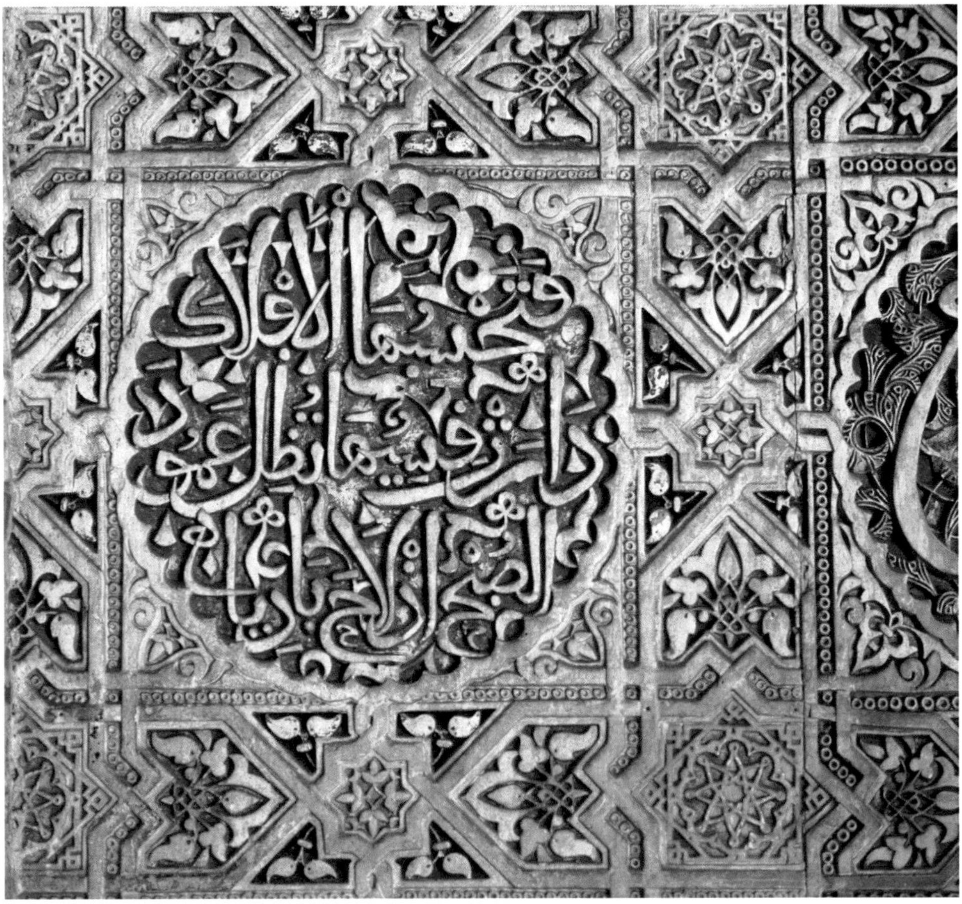

68. Carved stucco relief panel from the Hall of the Two Sisters, the Alhambra, Granada, Spain, 14th century (Album/Art Resource, New York).

ewers—architectural forms, birds, animals, and even human forms and faces demonstrate this Islamic delight in the possibilities of text *as* art.[88] In some extreme cases, the legibility of the texts themselves appears to be quite subsumed to the interest in presenting the letters, words, and phrases purely as potent signs or symbols for sacred themes—rather than as conveyors of "written" information.

The spiritual dimensions of specific letters, as well as the art of writing generally, are especially well expounded in Islamic mystical texts associated with various schools of Sufi thought.[89] Akin to the complexities of Hebrew kabbalistic concepts, "mystical interpretation of each and every letter is a special feature of Islamic Literature."[90]

> The letters of the Koran, even when detached, carry a sanctity of their own. Often letters or holy phrases are duplicated, mirrored, and used as ornamentation. Even seemingly meaningless, unconnected letters can convey some blessing, provided that they have been written with the proper intention.[91]

Calligraphy, one of the most traditional and esteemed forms of Islamic art, has continued to flourish through the centuries up to the present day. A great many contemporary artists, working in or inspired by diverse Islamic cultural contexts, continue to investigate the artistic and expressive use of calligraphy in both traditional and new media. For example, the Syrian-born artist, Mamoun Sakkal, who emigrated to the United States in 1978, specializes in computer-assisted calligraphic pieces, drawing inspiration from the rich visual traditions of his heritage. His 1996 work, *Steps and Shadows* (illus. 69), shows a dense, colorful, three-dimensional rendering of the Islamic profession of faith, the *Shahada*: "There is no God but One God and Muhammad is His messenger." Although this geometric work appears highly abstract—it is difficult to imagine that a "text" is shown—the work derives from examples of mystical writing layouts from earlier Islamic examples in tile work and manuscripts.

While the glorified position and significance of calligraphy is a consistent tradition in Islamic cultures, there is no doubt that "the art of writing well has been treated with greater reverence for longer in China than in any other civilization."[92] The lengthy development and evolution of Chinese writing systems stretches far back in history and represents a fascinating and extremely complex study in and of itself. It is significant to realize that the recognition and usage of calligraphy, especially as a highly regarded art form, is initially associated with the period of the Han dynasty (206 BCE–220 CE), and in all subsequent eras of Chinese history, the art of calligraphy has played a highly significant cultural and political role. This may be partially due to the nature of the Chinese system of writing. Unlike the alphabetic systems developed elsewhere that have a relatively limited set of symbols relating to sounds of the spoken language, Chinese writing consists of a vast number of characters, or ideograms, which essentially serve to signify concepts or words, rather than primarily sounds. "As a concept script Chinese does not depend on the spoken word; it can be read without regards to, or even knowledge of, the spoken language."[93] In other words, "the meanings of written

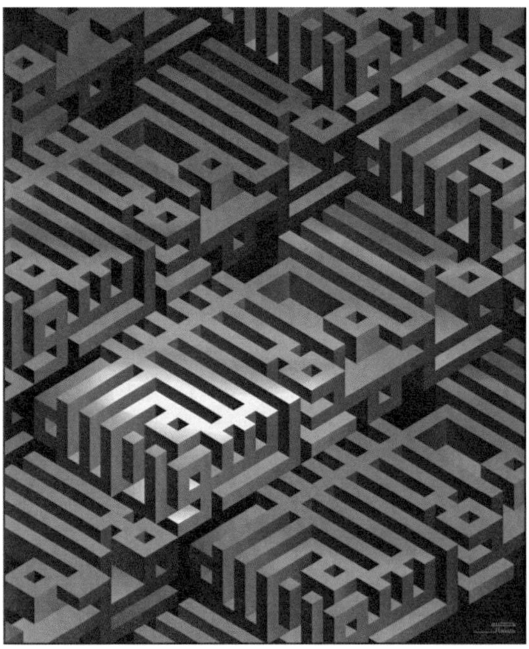

69. Mamoun Sakkal, *Steps and Shadows*, 1996 (© Mamoun Sakkal, image courtesy the artist).

characters with the same pronunciation lie in their visual structure, not in any phonetic rendering."[94] Approximately 50,000 characters exist in the Chinese writing system, although only about 2,000 to 4,000 are commonly employed. The ideographic and pictorial foundation of Chinese characters as a "graphic language"[95] offers "an inexhaustible supply of ideograms that afford the calligrapher immediate access to the entire universe of the senses. That is why, in classical Chinese esthetics, calligraphy is considered not just a major art but the most sublime of the plastic arts."[96]

Chinese calligraphy, performed with brush and ink, is essentially a painterly endeavor. The control of the brush, the size and direction of the strokes, and the order in which the marks are made are the aesthetic criteria that define different historical styles as well as the styles of individual calligraphers and painters. Chinese calligraphy and classical ink painting (or *shuimohua*—water and ink painting—that was developed especially during the Tang dynasty in the eighth century CE) both employ the same materials and techniques. "It is quite common for a Chinese painter to say not that he is 'painting a painting,' but 'writing a painting.'"[97] Conversely then, Chinese calligraphic writing is essentially painting. "The treatment of the brush stroke is the basis for both calligraphy and painting. Whether it is rough or delicate, heavy or light, quick or slow, oblique or regular, curved or straight, the brush stroke must, above all things, be sure and spontaneous, giving an impression of life."[98] Of course, different conventions apply to calligraphy—which is nonrepresentational and created according to the traditional guidelines of stroke order and placement (regardless of script style or era)—and painting, which involves the depiction of visual subject matter. The brushstrokes used in traditional Chinese ink painting may indeed be described as "calligraphic," but they are used for different purposes: the rendering "of something, be it a landscape, a flower, or a stalk of bamboo."[99]

According to an ancient Chinese saying, "Calligraphy is a picture of the mind."[100] Thus, the expressive potential of writing *as* art is emphasized. In traditional Chinese ink paintings, texts and pictures are often combined, handled with the same materials and with the same poetic finesse. An ink painting in the form of a hanging scroll by an anonymous mid-thirteenth-century artist of the Song dynasty, titled *Chan Master Riding a Mule* (illus. 70), "is a perfect example of the way in which images of the real world can be represented in ink, by brushstrokes that are codified like those of ideograms."[101] The fluid ink washes and graceful, minimal brushstrokes that are used to create the pictorial image are mirrored in the easy eloquence of the text characters that provide the poetic epigraph on the upper left of the composition. The text reads: "The rain comes, the mountain becomes misty, the mule takes on the appearance of a horse."[102] In this example, and countless others, we see how "poem and painting are the two perfectly interchangeable faces of the same vision of the world."[103] This particular example is especially representative of the expressive style of Chan (or Zen, in Japanese) Buddhism and has traditionally been attributed to the Chan Master Wuzhun who provided the inscription on the painting.

The Chan or Zen style of Buddhism was introduced to Japan from China in the twelfth century, following the initial introduction of Buddhism to Japan in the sixth century CE. By the seventh century CE, the Japanese had well begun the process of adoption and modification of the Chinese writing system. The history and development of writing in Japan is exceedingly complex. Japanese has been described as "perhaps the most complicated writing system that has ever existed."[104] Happily, in contrast, "Zen calligraphy is perfect simplicity."[105] Or, perhaps it is better to say that Zen calligraphy appears beguilingly simple. Zen practitioners use specific methods and materials in their pursuit of calligraphy as a spiritual practice. Proper attitude, both physical and mental, is critical. "Even when dealing with esoteric themes, the Zen calligrapher cuts through elaborate symbolism, reducing magical doctrines to their original purity."[106] The calligraphic creation of particular symbols/characters—such as the *ichi* (horizontal "I" stroke) and the *enso* (circle of infinity)—are undertaken repeatedly and require years of practice. An *enso* by the calligrapher Onki Jiun (1718–1804) shows this form, profoundly simple but exceedingly difficult to master (illus. 71). The inscription reads: "How many people can pass through?"

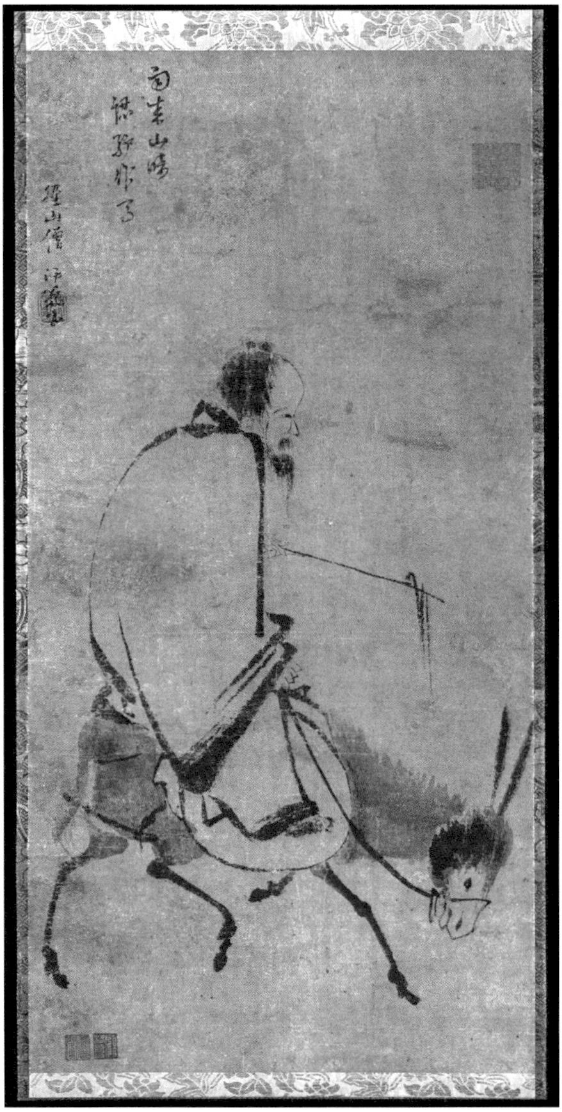

70. Unidentified Chinese artist (active mid–13th century), *Chan Master Riding a Mule*. Southern Song dynasty, before 1249. The Metropolitan Museum of Art, New York (© The Metropolitan Museum of Art; Image source: Art Resource, New York).

A number of twentieth-century western artists have been deeply influenced by the arts of Japanese and Chinese calligraphy, not only from a purely formal or aesthetic point of view but also for their special use in conveying powerful spiritual messages or as forms of religious practice. The American painters Brice Marden (b. 1938) and Mark Tobey (1890–1976) are among the most notable of western artists studiously attracted to Asian calligraphy and spirituality. They do not attempt to replicate Asian calligraphy in their works, but rather have found much inspiration in the forms and functions of calligraphy in Asian religions.

The New York–based artist, Brice Marden, creates linear and calligraphic works that bespeak his attraction to Chinese and Japanese characters and his interest in conveying a sense of essential life energy/life force (*qi* or *chi*) in his works.[107] After travels to Asia in the mid–1980s and his viewing in New York of a major exhibition of Japanese calligraphy, he developed his distinct style of painting in a highly abstract, often large-scale format, with stands of loose, flowing, and overlapping calligraphic markings. These works engulf and engage the viewer with a linear dance; tracing the strands of Marden's calligraphic-style markings can involve and inspire a highly meditative attitude on the part of willing viewers. It is important to note, however, that these works are not precisely based on any actual examples of Asian calligraphy and most viewers would be highly unlikely to make these direct connections. Marden is not interested in replicating specific examples from the Asian traditions that he uses as sources of inspiration, and his works, although seemingly spontaneous, often involve a level of reworking, additions, augmentations, and rearrangements that are decidedly not components of traditional Asian calligraphic

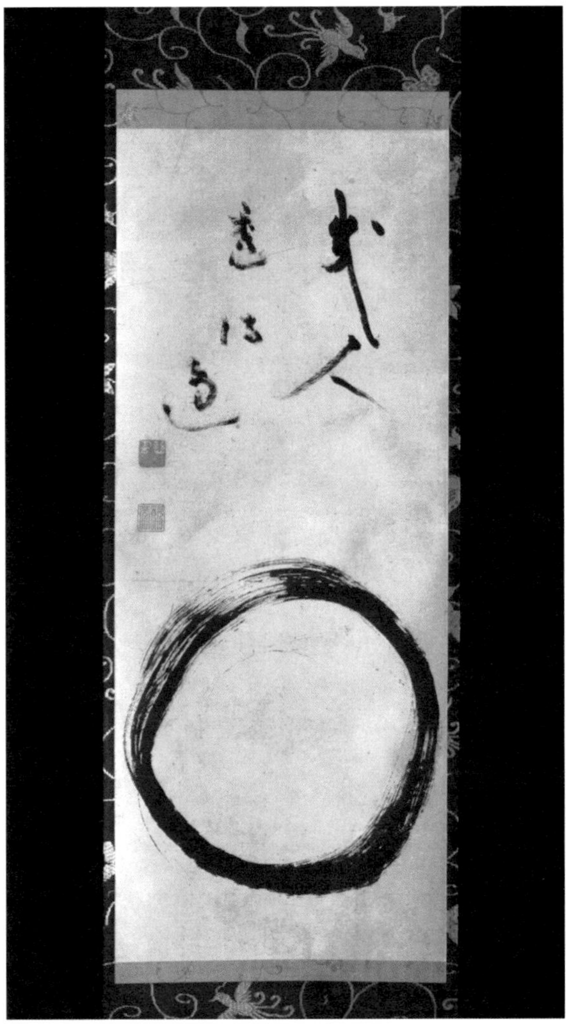

71. Onki Jiun, *Enso*, late 18th century (Sylvan Barnet and William Burto Collection/The Art Archive at Art Resource, New York).

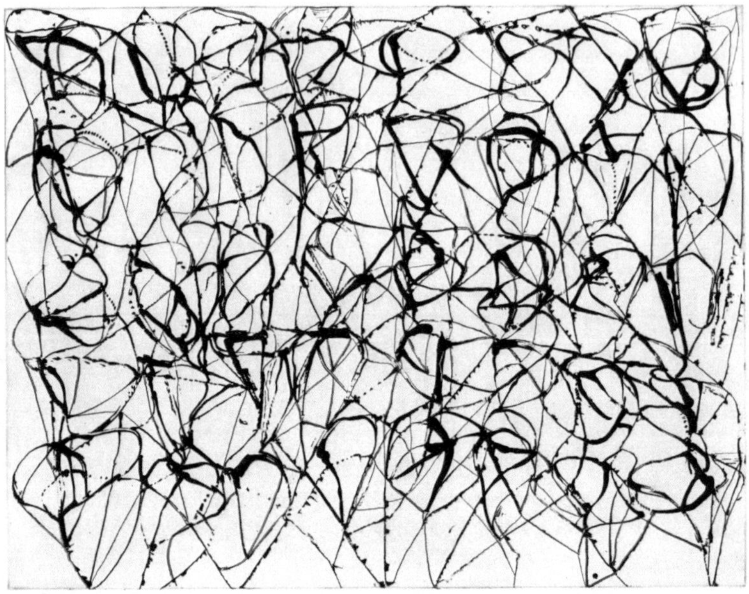

72. Brice Marden, *Zen Study 6*, 1990 (*Cold Mountain* series). New York, The Museum of Modern Art (© 2013 Brice Marden/Artists Rights Society [ARS], New York; Digital image © The Museum of Modern Art/Licensed by SCALA/Art Resource, New York).

practices. Nevertheless, his studies of Asian calligraphy, religion, and literature have wholly contributed to his own unique reinterpretations of the forms. His *Cold Mountain* series of paintings and prints from the early 1990s was inspired in large part by his readings of Zen poetry describing monks meditating in the cold mountains, and the physical and spiritual challenges they faced (illus. 72). His works, certainly those inspired by Asian calligraphy and religion, represent a highly abstract and unique approach to the calligraphic pictorialization of spiritual concepts.

The earlier twentieth-century Northwest coast–based American artist, Mark Tobey, was also highly influenced by Asian spirituality and calligraphic art forms. Tobey's direct studies and practice of Asian calligraphy under the direction of Chinese painter and critic Teng Kwei, whom he met in Seattle in 1923, eventually led him to spend time not only in China but also in Japan. In the early 1930s, Tobey spent a month at a Zen monastery in Kyoto where he studied painting and calligraphy. Tobey's "white writing" paintings, which he first began to produce in the 1930s, convey a remarkable sense of energy, rhythm, and linear complexity, clearly influenced by, but not duplicating, Asian calligraphy. His works in this style are generally

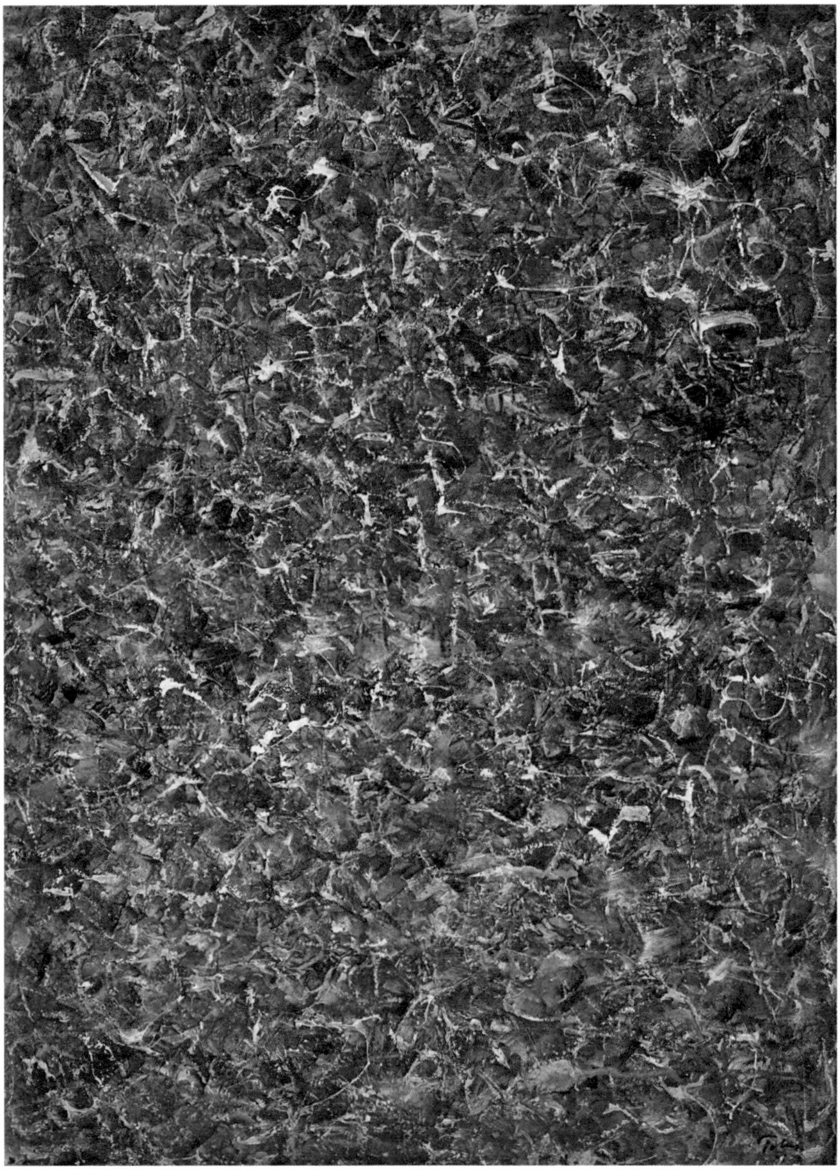

73. Mark Tobey, *Earth Rhythms*, 1961. Museo Thyssen-Bornemisza, Madrid, Spain (© 2013 Estate of Mark Tobey/Artists Rights Society [ARS], New York; Museo Thyssen-Bornemisza/Scala/Art Resource, New York).

quite densely packed by graphic markings which are often so closely overlaid that distinguishing where one mark begins and another ends is impossible. Pieces such as *Earth Rhythms* from 1961 (illus. 73) seem to convey "miraculous hints of a world beyond time and space."[108] Tobey has been quoted as saying, "I have tried to tear out just a few scraps of that beauty which makes up the miracles of the Cosmos and which is the multi-facetedness of life."[109] A dedicated adherent of the Baha'i faith, Tobey consistently produced works dealing with universal themes of spiritual importance: prayer, meditation, and cosmic energy/peace. He has been described as "endow[ing] his work with the 'fragrance of spirituality.'"[110] And in so doing, Tobey masterfully expressed the themes explored especially in the latter half of this chapter: the Power of the (awe-filled) Word.

Six

Monumental and Moving Words

The preceding chapters have concentrated primarily on a discussion of diverse word/image relationships in two-dimensional media, such as painting and the graphic arts, with a few important examples also drawn from metal work, textiles, and other media. This discussion has covered a number of diverse examples of text/picture combinations, representing the immense and thought-provoking variety of ways in which images and writing can be, and have been, used together from the ancient to the modern and contemporary period. Written language, after all, is most essentially a form of communication that appears in handwritten or in mass-produced printed forms on a flat surface—such as a book page, a computer screen, in a painting, an advertisement, or a repeatable print. Paintings and prints are primarily created on flat surfaces such as paper, canvas, board, or walls. The materials discussed above, thus, have primarily concentrated on the use of captions, inscriptions, labels, speech scrolls, and other related forms in the two-dimensional arts, where the graphic markings represented by written language have been deployed either alone or in close coordination with visual imagery.

In some cases, this shared combination of texts and images can be described as mutually elucidating. In other words, the combination of written texts and visual forms may be seen as ultimately working to the same message-conveying purpose. In other cases, such as the various word/picture puzzles and conundrums described earlier, the relationships between the imagery and the written texts included in visual works of art may be less immediately clear if not deliberately cryptic. Also considered have been works of art that consist of words alone, presented in clever or whimsical or artful fashions—or—as extremely powerful and potent conveyors of sociopolitical messages that address issues of language use and abuse and that demonstrate the power of words to shape perceptions and create meanings for readers and viewers alike.

We have also considered some fine examples of monumental relief sculpture where texts and images are combined, such as the inscriptions found in conjunction with imagery on medieval church portals. In these cases, the inscribed words and related images loom overhead for visitors entering the sacred buildings. These are monumental and weighty words—not only via their presence in a large-scale architectural context, but also due to the importance of the messages that they convey. The power of written language in monumental contexts has been explored and utilized in many fashions from ancient epigraphy on public monuments to modern graffiti in public spaces.[1] This chapter focuses upon monumental words, physically big words, and concentrates on examples of artworks that actually render words in three-dimensional fashion, or that create the illusion of such.

Monumental Words

An introduction to the theme of "monumental words" might well begin with any number of examples apart from the first one selected here, but the absolutely enormous inscribed plaque depicted as if floating in the sky in Albrecht Altdorfer's 1528–29 panel painting of *The Battle of Alexander the Great* is a salient example and a fine segue into the larger topic (illus. 74).[2] The German Renaissance artist Altdorfer (ca. 1480–1538) was one of the most highly regarded artists of his time and is especially renowned for his development of landscape subject matter. Associated with the "Danube School" of German landscape painters in Bavaria, he is considered to be one of the first German artists to develop a naturalistic and poetic approach to the native landscape. *The Battle of Alexander* (or: *The Battle of Issus*) was one of his most important commissions. It is one of a series of works depicting famous historical battles and the deeds of heroic men and women from the Hebrew scriptures and antiquity commissioned from various artists by Duke Wilhelm IV of Bavaria to decorate the interior of his residence in Munich. This painting in particular, like the other battle scenes commissioned by Duke Wilhelm, was partially designed to celebrate and commemorate past victories in Europe against eastern invaders, especially relevant at the time in the early sixteenth century when Ottoman Turkish armies led by Suleyman the Magnificent were threatening the region.

Altdorfer's painting has been described as "cosmic."[3] Indeed, "our first impressions on looking at Altdorfer's huge panorama are ones of exhilaration and awe as well as confusion and bewilderment."[4] Apart from the challenges we may face in attempting to make out what is happening in this vast battle scene, or in attempting to identify the two major army leaders (Alexander and Darius), we may also be bewildered by the presence of the huge plaque that is depicted as if it is flying high in the heavens above the scene. The plaque is rendered in perspective and tilted slightly from the picture plane. It is equipped with a pendant tassel and wind-blown drapery and bears a lengthy Latin inscription in formal lettering that identifies the subject below: the famous victory of Alexander the Great over the Persian forces led by Darius in 333 BCE Although the painting has been slightly cut down from its original size,[5] and the original inscription on the tablet was in German, there is little doubt that this huge floating plaque would have been any less impressive even if allowed more panoramic space in which to hover. The viewer cannot help but be highly intrigued by this more than eye-catching monumental form floating over the battle

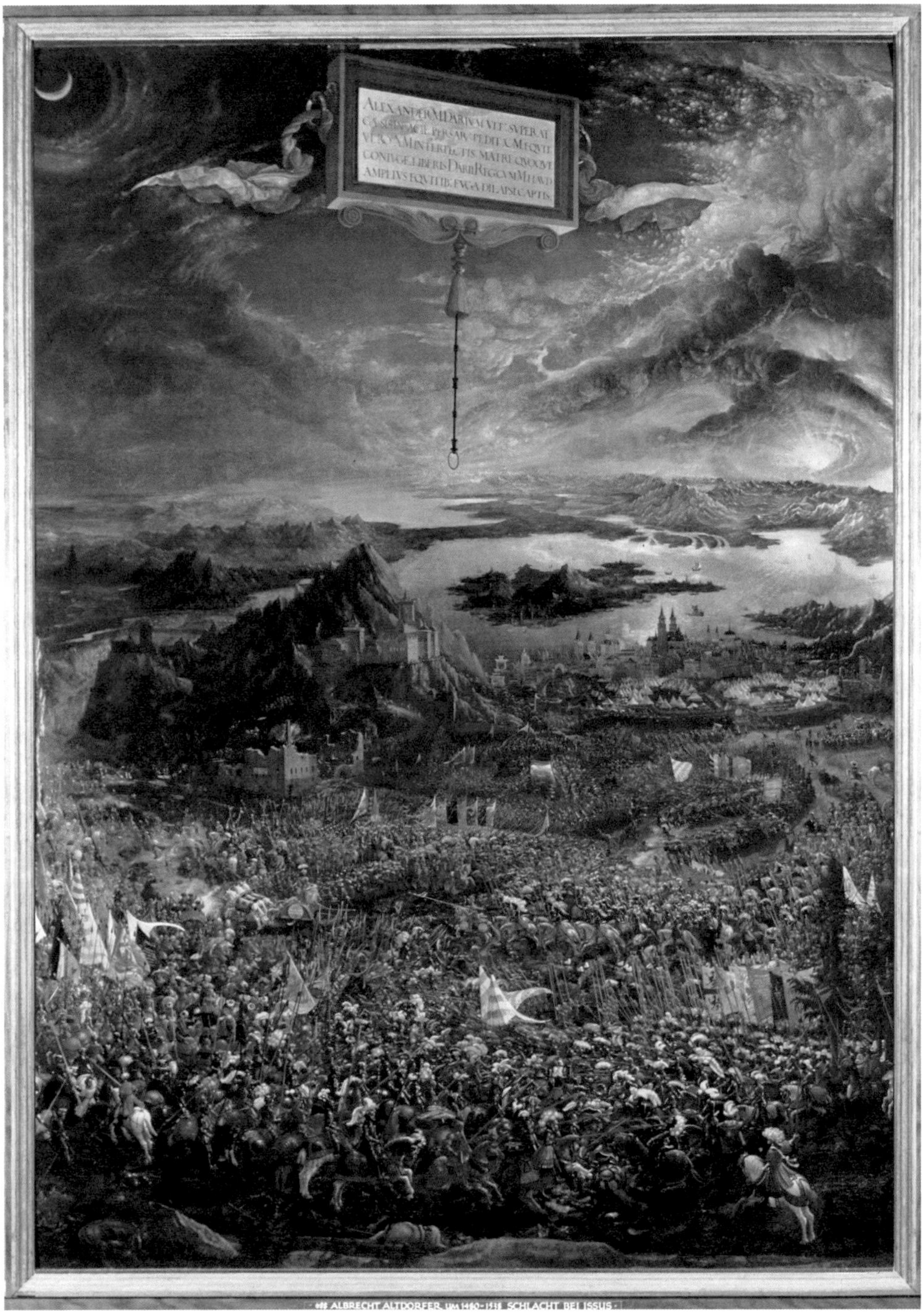

74. Albrecht Altdorfer, *The Battle of Alexander*, 1529. Alte Pinakothek Bayerische Staatsgemaelde-sammlungen, Munich, Germany (Erich Lessing/Art Resource, New York).

scene. A number of questions arise: what is the plaque doing there and where it is meant to be understood in spatial relationship to the vast panoramic landscape below? The combination of the monumental and convincingly rendered plaque with the highly detailed landscape panorama shown from a "bird's eye" view—with hundreds of tiny figures arrayed within a grand scale view of mountains, sea, islands, dramatically lit cloud formations, the setting sun, and the rising moon—altogether give a rather strange combination of visual and spatial perceptions for viewers. Both the text-bearing plaque and the battle scene taking place below it are rendered so as to convince viewers of their substantially realistic, three-dimensional nature. However, the combination of the plaque and the landscape lead viewers to be somewhat perplexed about where exactly the giant inscribed tablet is meant to be located. Its presence seems to peculiarly belie the otherwise magisterial pictorial illusionism of the landscape panorama, while, in itself, the tablet, with its titled perspective, fluttering drapery appendages attached to metal rings on either side, and clear monumental epigraphy also maintains a convincing solidity.

Of the other battle scenes commissioned by Duke Wilhelm, several also include similar devices of tablets suspended by ropes or otherwise hovering over the scenes but none as monumental and eye-catching as Altdorfer's.[6] Generically, these could be termed *tituli*—or informatory captions—a common pictorial device derived from antique traditions and highly popular through the medieval and Renaissance eras as well.[7] In manuscripts and printed books, the term *titulus* generally refers to the introductory words, often written in capital letters, which signal chapter or section headings. Used as an artistic device in painting, sculpture, and architecture, *tituli* in art appear in a variety of forms depending upon the context and era. They function as labels, conventional inscriptions designed to identify the subject matter, much as the informatory texts and captions discussed earlier in this study. *Tituli*, in ancient classical and Christian art, for example, may come in the form of decorative inscribed plaques, sometimes held by putti or cherubs or angels; they may appear as banners or scrolls, or they may appear simply as inscribed tablets lacking any ornament.

For the series of battle scenes commissioned by Duke Wilhelm of Bavaria in the early sixteenth century, the *tituli* or captions served to clearly identify the subject matter in most all of the paintings of famous battles, including Altdorfer's *Battle of Alexander*. Altdorfer's version of this traditional device, however, is notably monumental in appearance. Due to its perspectival treatment and looming solidity suspended over the vast battle scene, it represents an especially noteworthy example of the rendering of a monumental text on a huge tablet that appears to be as fully and illusionistically three-dimensional as the panoramic scene below. However, the spatial relationship between the monumental tablet and the monumental scene remains remarkably visually challenging for viewers due to the fact that the solidity and believability of both the text-inscribed tablet and the battle scene below it seem to exist in two separate but equally convincing spatial arenas. Not unlike the generally significantly smaller *cartellini* forms discussed earlier, this monumental plaque appears to be both within and somehow imposed on the landscape scene. It functions to provide written information about the subject matter and the authorship of the painting, but its appearance involves a puzzling sense of spatial relationships as well.

This type of visual puzzle—the pictorial presentation of monumental texts rendered in spatial ambiguity to accompanying scenes—was indeed a rather favorite device in the Renaissance period, as can easily be noted in a number of other examples drawn from the manuscript/book arts. In handwritten and illustrated manuscripts as well as printed books from the Renaissance period, the naturally close relationship of text and image provided artists of this era many wonderful opportunities to explore their developed and developing expertise and fascination with the creation of perspectival spaces in conjunction with the traditional flat surfaces of a book or manuscript page filled with two-dimensional words. The title pages, especially, of any number of Renaissance- era books often exhibit quite elaborate architectural forms that place the required printed words announcing author, title, and publisher within architectural constructions that appear to be fully three-dimensional.[8] Columns, pediments, pillars and arcades, plaques, tablets, plinths, and arches rendered in linear perspective often enliven these frontispieces, giving viewers the sense that the words exist not on a two-dimensional flat surface but rather in an elaborate and monumental spatial construct.[9] The words are seen as sculptural or architectural elements, as if inscribed on sections or pieces of three-dimensional forms, rather than as flat elements on the page surface. These treatments demonstrate how Renaissance artists were striving "to reconcile their new knowledge of Albertian space with the reality that the printed page is inherently flat."[10]

Other important devices developed by Renaissance book artists also include pictorial illusions of texts suspended on strings, ribbons, or bands and texts that appear to be bent or even shredded or torn, that allow viewers glimpses into pictorial spaces behind the suspended or torn illusions of text surfaces. We have already noted one very intriguing instance of such a format: the letter-strewn torn curtain motif found in the early sixteenth-century Hours of Jean Lallement of Bourges (see chapter 3), although the pictorial illusions in this diminutive manuscript lack the weighty monumentality of the additional examples described below. All told, these illusionistic devices are "literally multilayered,"[11] and the Renaissance fashion for *trompe l'oeil* pictorial "commentary on the nature of the written word"[12] was explored by many artists and book designers in northern Europe and especially in Italy during the late fifteenth and early sixteenth centuries.

An especially fascinating example of the "torn parchment" format can be found, for instance, in the massive two-volume 1483 Venetian vellum incunable of the *Works of Aristotle* (New York: Pierpont Morgan Library 21194, 21195) (illus. 75).[13] Both large volumes were printed on vellum in the workshop of Andrea Torresani and Bartholomaeus de Blavis in Venice. The painted details of the frontispiece to volume one,

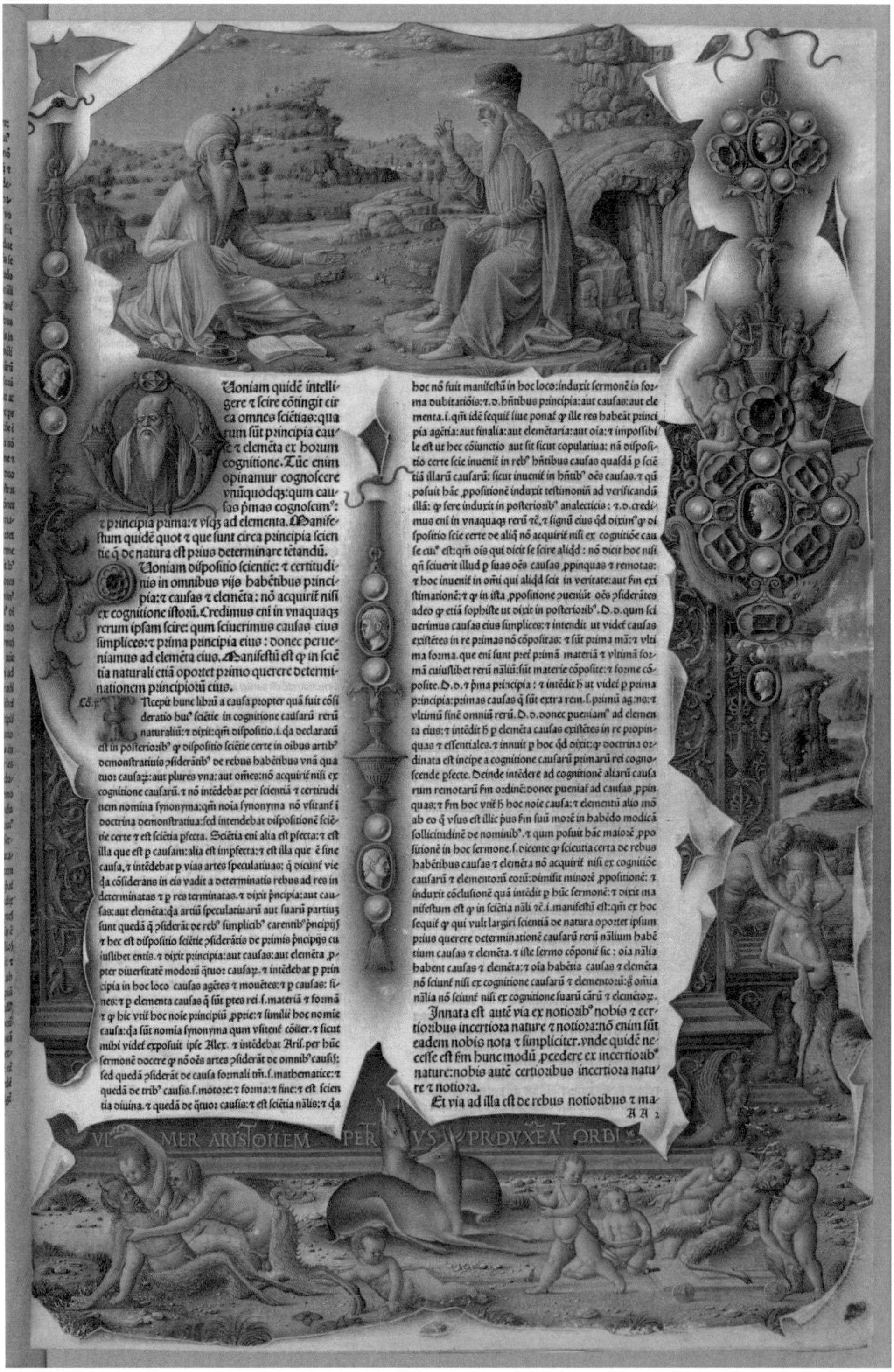

attributed to the artist Girolamo da Cremona, show a dazzling and spatially extremely complex display of printed text and pictorial imagery. The printed surface of the text appears to be split, punched through, and torn in areas; the edges of the parchment appear to be peeling up or becoming unglued from a surface or background. The background, as seen through the illusionistic torn parchment, consists of an expansive landscape with the figures of Aristotle, seated on a rock to the right side, and Averroës, his important Spanish Muslim commentator, seated on the pebbly ground, conversing with each other on the top of the page, while classical putti and satyrs cavort on the bottom of the page. The extensive and brightly lit landscape setting in which the two philosophers are placed consists of meticulously rendered rock formations, trees, and craggy green hills receding into the distance under a blue sky filled with wispy clouds. The same pebbly landscape ground provides the setting for the deer, putti, and satyrs at the base of the page. One satyr appears to have been wounded by an arrow and is depicted falling backwards, tended by another satyr and a putto. Another recumbent satyr appears on a small wheeled cart being pulled by several putti. These "mock-tragic events"[14] are depicted as taking place in front of an elaborate architectural monument that can partially be seen behind the torn parchment and that continues to be glimpsed on the right side of the page, along with the figures of two additional satyrs. This complex pictorial illusion is even further enhanced by the hanging clusters of elaborate gems, pearls, and classical cameos that are depicted as if suspended on strings in front of the printed text. These jeweled clusters hang from little red strings that appear to be tied to the pierced and torn parchment surface.

The overall effect of this complex spatial illusion is truly outstanding. In this, as in other related examples, the text (albeit flat) appears to be printed on a peeling surface that is rendered as a three-dimensional form with shadows carefully cast by the torn edges and ragged, pierced sections. In this sense, the surface on which the text is printed appears sculptural and volumetric, participating in the same degree of pictorial illusionism as the painted figures, jewels, gemstones, landscape background, and classically styled and inscribed architectural monument. The relative locations of all of these compositional elements remain quite spatially ambiguous, however. The landscape scene in which the figures of Aristotle and Averroës are placed appears to be somewhat contingent with the landscape occupied by the carved monument, satyrs and putti, but simultaneously appears to be a separate vignette placed somewhere above the partially revealed sculptural monument. The pierced, torn, and curling surface of the printed text provides the illusion that binds all of the elements together, albeit in a spatially ambiguous fashion. Peter Ugelheimer of Frankfurt, the German merchant and bookseller for whom this book was created and

Opposite: 75. *Works of Aristotle*, Venice, 1483. New York, Pierpont Morgan Library MS 21195 vol. I, folio 2r (title page). The Pierpont Morgan Library, New York, PML 21194–95. Purchased in 1919 (The Pierpont Morgan Library, New York).

whose name appears inscribed in golden classical- style lettering towards the bottom of the architectural monument at the base of the page,[15] appears to have had a well-developed taste for such spatially complex and "most magnificent"[16] productions, as can be seen in other examples of his patronage.[17]

Many other thematic variations and additional examples of this Renaissance fascination with text/image relationships could very easily be cited here.[18] Texts that appear to be suspended in front of pictorial elements or scenes, texts that appear to be positioned behind scenes or behind other texts, and letters or texts that are rendered in three-dimensional forms abound in the book and manuscript arts of the fifteenth and sixteenth centuries. The depiction of texts as three-dimensional forms appearing behind or in front of other compositional elements is doubtless ultimately a manifestation of the Renaissance interest in realism and perspectival construction generally, as a way to solve "the basic problem of a logical discrepancy between two-dimensional letters written on a two-dimensional page, and the three-dimensional imagery which the new linear perspective of the Quattrocento had made mandatory for artists."[19]

As has frequently been noted, this period in the history of manuscript illumination is marked by significant changes in the design and layout of both miniatures and their surrounding margins.[20] Rather than the decorative flatness characteristic of much earlier medieval book illustration, artists in the fifteenth century began "enthusiastic experiments with the uses of illusionism and shifting levels of meaning through the representation of space."[21] *Trompe l'oeil* depictions of flowers, insects, gems, jewelry, pilgrim badges, and other small objects often enliven the borders of late medieval manuscripts. The marginal objects appear tangible, three-dimensional, as if they could be plucked from the page.[22]

Letters that appear to be three-dimensional, that cast shadows, and that appear to be constructed of tangible materials—such as twigs, logs, stone, or metal—show up especially frequently in the border designs of a number of late fifteenth- and early sixteenth-century manuscripts. In some cases, texts written on scrolls appear to be wrapped around poles, branches, or architectural elements that appear to project from the background.[23] In other cases, texts appear to be made of sections of carved wooden logs and leafy twigs. The letters and words are rendered as rounded, three-dimensional objects projecting boldly into space. In the Flemish sixteenth-century "Hours of la Tour and Taxis" (Chantilly, Musée Condé MS 86/1178), for example, the border inscription surrounding the scene of the Adoration of the Magi appears to be constructed of three-dimensional sections of leafy logs (illus. 76). These letter forms appear to be placed solidly on the page border and project a sense of weight and monumentality. They maintain a sense of depth and give the illusion that the border of the page is also a three-dimensional field rather than a flat surface. The border otherwise admits a framed view onto the illusionistic biblical scene of the miniature painting itself that is replete with figures and architectural and landscape elements rendered in a detailed and naturalistic style. Another example of three-dimensional letter forms can be seen in an illuminated letter "A" on a page from another Flemish Book of Hours from ca. 1500 in the Victoria and Albert Museum in London (illus. 77). This letter is made up of crisscrossing, overlapping, and entwined leafy twigs. Along with the accompanying carefully and illusionistically rendered floral motifs and insects, this letter appears highly three-dimensional, as if hovering above the blue background.

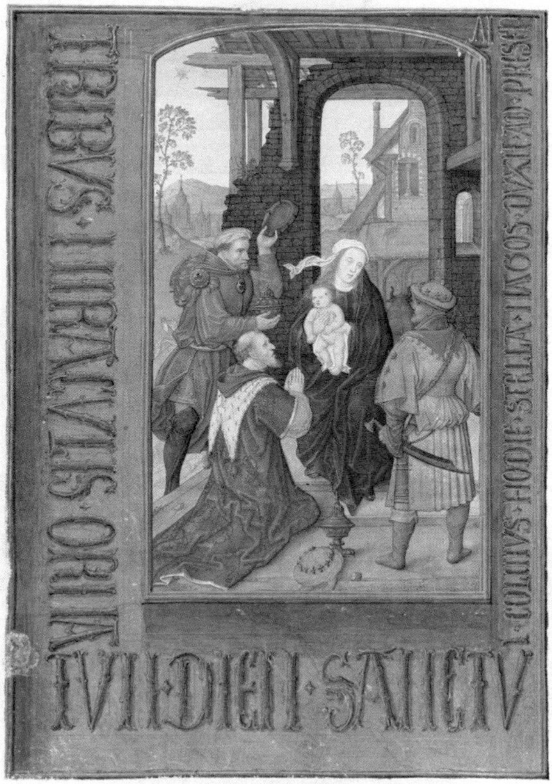

76. Heures de la Tour et Taxis, Flemish, 16th century. The Adoration of the Magi. Chantilly, France: Museé Condé MS 86/1178 folio 3 (Bridgeman Art Library).

Numerous other examples could be cited here of illusionistic letter devices in late medieval and Renaissance manuscript illumination and printed books. The statuesque initial letters that Millard Meiss termed "Littera Mantiniana" and that he credited as an innovation of the important Italian Renaissance painter Andrea Mantegna (1431–1506) also demonstrate a three-dimensional approach to letter forms.[24] For example, the many statuesque initials found in a luxurious and celebrated copy of the ancient Greek historian Strabo's *Geography* produced in northern Italy in the mid-fifteenth century (Albi, Bibliothèque Muncipale MS 77) appear to be carved, free-standing forms, often entwined in luxuriant foliage.[25] Although scholarly opinions diverge as to the exact origins of this "epigraphic capital"[26] form as it appears in fifteenth-century Italian painting and manuscript illumination, the characteristic features of these monumental letters include their "palpably solid and weighty"[27] appearance. "The letters rise like monuments, stony, stable, and finely cut."[28] They appear to be carved out of stone or metal; they are faceted, often cast shadows, and sometimes are entwined in vegetation or floral elements. The classical clarity of these letter forms of course reflects the enthusiastic study of ancient epigraphy carried out by Renaissance humanists generally, and is well documented for Mantegna and his sphere.[29] Variations include the placement of these monumental letters in front of *trompe l'oeil* relief plaques or cameos and their positioning as "free-standing" elements in landscape scenes.[30]

Especially fine examples of this latter format can be seen in a large and elaborate manuscript containing Pliny the Elder's *Historia naturalis*, produced in the early 1480s for the highly important Renaissance scholar, author, and bibliophile Giovanni Pico della Mirandola (1463–94): Venice, Biblioteca Marciana MS lat.VI.245 [coll 2976] (illus. 78).[31] The illuminations are attributed to an anonymous artist known as the "Pico Master," whose style can be seen in several other significant late fifteenth-century hand-illuminated manuscripts and printed books.[32] The *Historia naturalis*, an encyclopedic work composed by the Roman author Pliny the Elder in the first century CE, was considered throughout the medieval and Renaissance periods to be "an invaluable source of information about the universe, the earth, man, plants, animals, minerals, medicine, and art."[33] Illustrated versions, or illustrated excerpts from the lengthy text, had been created before the fifteenth century, with images derived from various traditions of scientific, medical, and botanical illustration.[34] The extremely sumptuous volume commissioned by Pico della Mirandola in 1481 is especially noteworthy for its innovative renditions of stories and anecdotes from Pliny's text, demonstrating great familiarity on the parts of both the artist and patron with the contents of the lengthy work. "It replicates aspects of the earlier visual repertory but it also reveals a much more sophisticated relation between text and images."[35]

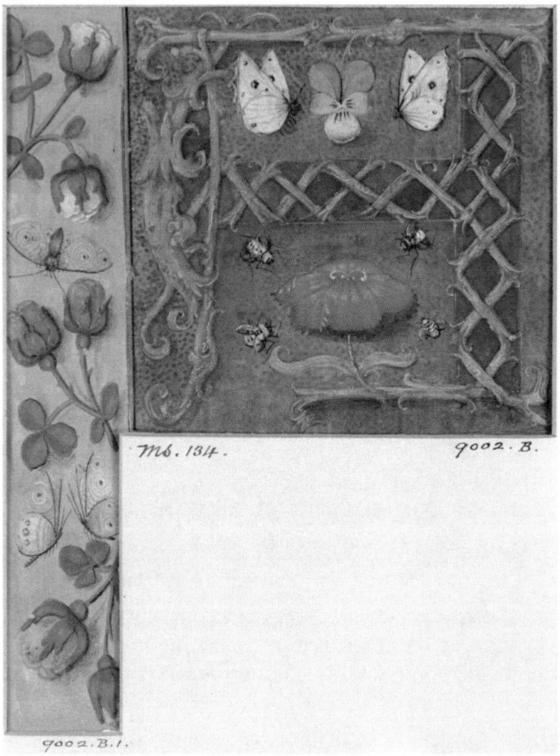

77. Illuminated A from a Flemish Book of Hours, c. 1500. London, Victoria and Albert Museum MS 134 (Bridgeman Art Library).

There are more than thirty illustrated initial letters in the Pico volume serving as openings for each of the books/chapters. These show monumental epigraphic letters placed in landscape settings that are peopled with figures (carrying out various tasks), animals, birds, and various symbolic devices. The enlarged letters have the

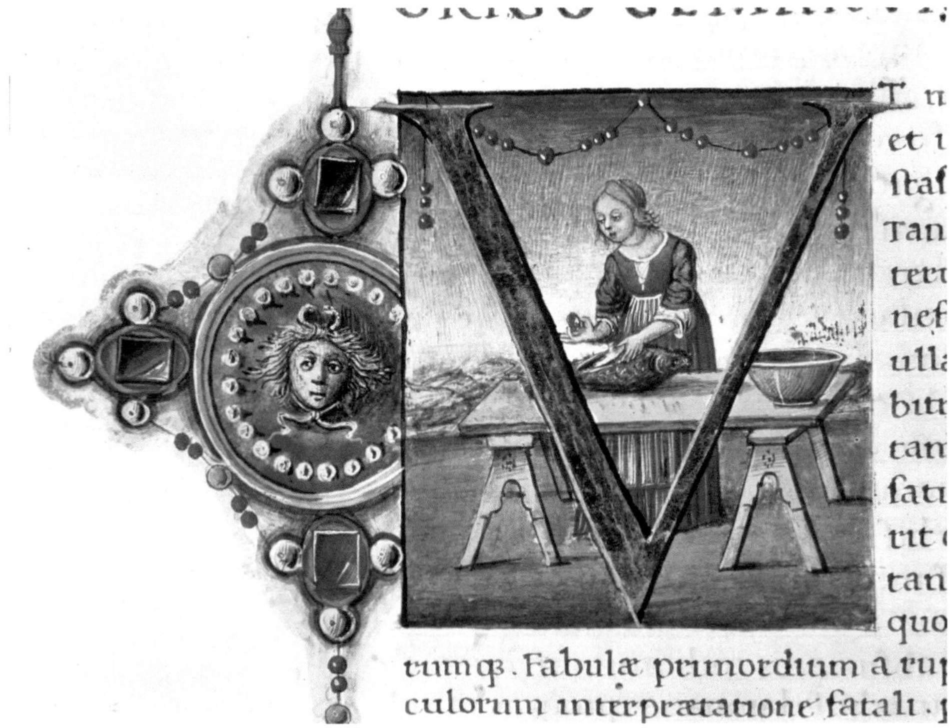

78. Pliny the Elder, *Historia naturalis*, 1481. Venice, Biblioteca Marciana MS Lat. VI. 245 [coll. 2976] (Bridgeman-Giraudon/Art Resource, New York).

appearance of freestanding sculptural forms, three-dimensional elements that are placed solidly within the landscape vignettes or that provide a three-dimensional visual entry into the scenes depicted in the square or rectangular illuminations. Book 37, in which Pliny discusses precious gems, opens with an illuminated "V" initial that partially projects beyond the confines of the scene behind it. This letter, appropriately, is festooned with a string of jewels. To the left of the main miniature, further pearls and gemstones surround the portrait of the Roman general Pompey (first century BCE) who Pliny mentions later in this book as having been unduly distracted by luxury goods and expensive displays of personal adornment. The illuminated vignette behind the monumental "V" initial depicts a woman standing at a trestle table gutting a large fish and removing a substantial red stone from its body. This illustrates Pliny's story about an ancient Greek ruler (Polycrates, mid-sixth century BCE) who, unlike the luxury-loving Pompey, cast away an impressive gemstone only to have it resurface later after it was swallowed by a fish that was eventually served for dinner in Polycrates' own home. The "V" initial introduces Pliny's text in this section and also serves as a visual entry into the illusionistic scene behind it. Both the enlarged letter and the pictorial vignette are rendered realistically. The letter appears solid and weighty, and the scene behind it also includes cast shadows in the abbreviated landscape setting. Elsewhere in the Pico manuscript, these same monumental letter forms consistently appear for the openings of book sections. They often project slightly beyond the scenes behind them or rest firmly with the pictorial vignettes.

The colossal and three-dimensional appearance of these letters poses a significant contrast to earlier medieval treatment of similar forms, such as the decorated and historiated initials discussed earlier in this study. In manuscript illumination of the Romanesque and Gothic periods, initial letters in texts were often very elaborately rendered indeed and sometimes quite filled with figural scenes. Although exceptions can readily be found, generally speaking, the enlarged decorated and historiated letters in Romanesque and Gothic manuscripts served as framing devices or containers for narrative scenes rather than as freestanding elements within a pictorial composition. In some of the most impressive and detailed examples, vast amounts of pictorial materials, including multiple sequential narratives, were compressed into the frame of a single monumental letter. In spite of the sizes of the letters and the complexity of the contained images, these earlier examples lack the sense of physical monumentality and tangible presence as is seen in the later Renaissance epigraphic format. Rather than serving as a frame for a scene, the letters in these later examples serve as colossal elements placed within a scene, or they appear to be projecting boldly from the page surface. The previously contained pictorial elements have now spread beyond the confines of the letters themselves. The individual letter takes on a role as a fully three-dimensional participant in the overall composition.

Variations on this theme multiply rapidly in the later Renaissance and post-Renaissance period. Numerous examples could be cited of woodcut and engraved alphabets where monumental letters dominate the physical space within framed pictorial vignettes. Many inventive engravers and typographers of the seventeenth and eighteenth century in particular created complex and repeatable templates showing huge letters placed within figural or landscape scenes.[36] "It is as if, by placing the typographic letter in the framework of a tableau, artists were endeavouring to evoke its power of resonance, or in other words its specific capacity to carry meaning."[37]

Several twentieth-century artists have also explored this theme of illusionistic alphabetic monumentality. For example, a painting from 1950 by the Belgian Surrealist artist René Magritte titled *L'Art de la Conversation* presents an imposing text rising in a barren landscape (illus. 79, in color insert). A couple of small human figures are depicted in this scene, observing and completely dwarfed by the massive text that appears to be constructed of solid stonework. At first, a viewer may not realize that sections of this monumental stone structure are actually constructed of words but, upon closer look, it becomes more obvious that the monument can be read: the lower stones of the central section make out the word "rêve" (dream). Magritte did several variations on this subject during the early 1950s during a period when he was experimenting with the theme of petrification. Other examples include organic materials and human forms turned to stone, large boulders, and rocky landscapes. The heaviness and solidity of stonework attracted Magritte as a theme during these years, "Magritte did not regard petrification as a process, but as a kind of catastrophe, like that at Pompeii, when lava transfixed the world and brought all movement to a halt."[38] In his typically paradoxical fashion, Magritte has here transformed the word for dream—usually regarded as an insubstantial or fleeting experience—into an imposing and weighty Stonehenge-like monument, placed on a low horizon line against a backdrop of large clouds in a blue sky. The monument casts shadows and fills the entire canvas with its imposing presence. The viewer of course is tempted to see if other words can be additionally made out by the shapes of the stony blocks, several of which may look like other letters; however, only the word "rêve" stands out clearly. Magritte, as previously discussed, was deeply interested in the relationship of words and images throughout his career and frequently combined words and images in perplexing relationships. In the 1950s he also did several other paintings with large-scale words that appear to be cut out from backgrounds, but his *L'Art de la Conversation* series is especially notable for his transformation of words into forms that appear to be monumental and three-dimensional.

Three-Dimensional Words

The examples covered so far in this chapter have concentrated on the various ways in which artists have rendered letters and words to appear as if they are three-dimensional. From Altdorfer's monumental plaque hovering in the heavens above the *Battle of Alexander* to the epigraphic capitals of Renaissance manuscripts and printed books to Magritte's *L'Art de la Conversation* series, these examples have all involved the illusion of alphabetic solidity. The words and letters in these examples have been made to look as if they are solid forms, or, at least, inscribed on surfaces that are tilted, torn, angled, or shaped in some way so as to appear three-dimensional. In this sense, many of these renderings are not wholly dissimilar to materials discussed earlier in this study, such as the *trompe l'oeil* "letter rack" compositions in which printed or handwritten materials are presented as if they are actual objects affixed to a surface, or, the *cartellino* form where small tablets, letters, or scrolls are included as more-or-less believable elements in painted compositions. Indeed, twentieth-century artists such as Ed Ruscha have also avidly explored the potentials of creating letters and texts that appear to be created of various liquid substances or that seem to be created of pieces of paper standing upright or at angles projecting away from a background.

The actual construction of fully three-dimensional texts and letters in sculptural form represents yet another intriguing genre in the realm of word-related art. The idea of presenting letters and words as completely three-dimensional forms has been frequently explored by artists of various eras ranging from the medieval to modern periods. Rather than creating simply the illusion of three dimensions, these further examples, ranging in size from the small to monumental, show how texts and letters have also provided much inspiration for the sculptural arts.

One particularly fascinating example from the medieval period exists in the so-called "A of Charlemagne," housed in the treasury of the abbey church of Conques in southern France (illus. 80). This rather unique object is highly intriguing due not only to its form but also to the alphabetic lore with which it is associated.[39] It consists of a triangular shape constructed on a core of wooden strips covered with gilt silver, and cameos and gemstones set within filigree tracery, standing about sixteen and a half inches tall on a supporting base of about sixteen inches in length. At the apex of the triangle is a circular medallion holding a large rock crystal surrounded by filigree tracery and gemstones, and, on the back, small disks of enamel work. The figures of two angels holding censers are worked in low relief in gilt silver on two wooden plaques standing on the base within the triangular framework. The work appears to be a pastiche of different styles and elements, which is actually not atypical of medieval metalwork objects, but sections of the base especially appear to consist "of scraps which must have been appropriated from other projects of various types and divergent dates."[40] Traditionally described as a reliquary, the original appearance, function, and date of the object remain unclear. A fragmentary inscription along the narrow sides of the triangular arms refers to an abbot Bego (or Bégon) whom some scholars have identified as Bégon III who served as abbot of Conques in the late eleventh and early twelfth centuries, thus giving this work a late eleventh-century date. It should be noted, however, that three abbots named Bégon are recorded in the chronicles of Conques, one from the late ninth century and one from the late tenth century, in addition to the late eleventh-

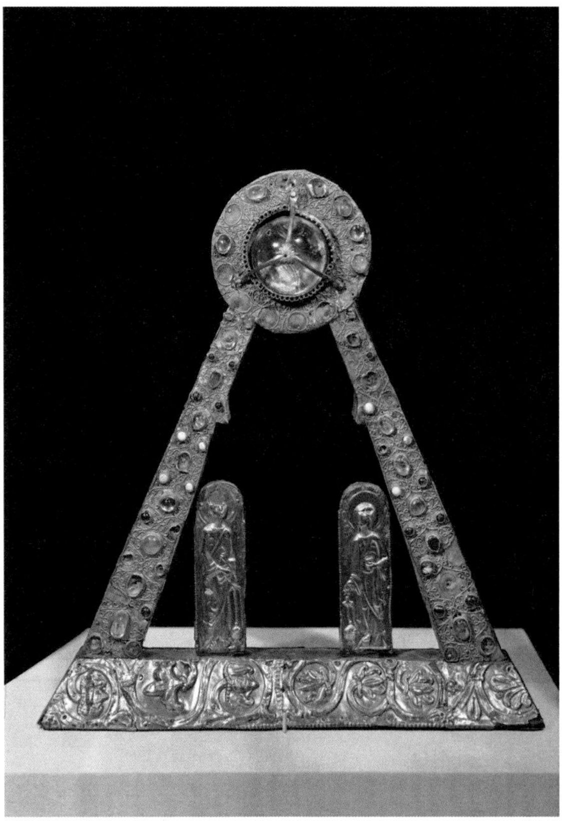

80. The "A" of Conques. Treasury, Abbey Ste. Foy, Conques, France (Erich Lessing/Art Resource, New York).

century Bégon III, so earlier dates for some sections of this work have also been previously proposed.[41]

The chronicles of Conques (the *Liber mirabilis*) as well as other medieval documents contain some intriguing explanations for why this object came to be known as "The A of Charlemagne." According to these legendary accounts, the emperor Charlemagne, in his interest in establishing, supporting, and endowing monastic foundations during his reign and throughout his realm, gifted each of these monastic establishments with letters of the alphabet rendered in silver and gold. These accounts, which exist in various versions, further specify that Charlemagne's foundations eventually numbered a total of twenty-four, one for each letter of the alphabet. The Conques chronicle particularly notes that "Charlemagne singled out Conques among the monasteries he founded through the gift of the first letter of the alphabet."[42] Thus Conques, being given the letter "A," assumed a great deal of priority and prestige in spite of the fact

> that Conques was founded by Charlemagne is not borne out by the sources; that the emperor might rank it as his foremost foundation is exceedingly improbable in light of our historical picture of his reign; and that a Carolingian date for the object now identified as the letter which he is said to have given to the monastery could not be seriously defended.[43]

It should also be noted that this object, at least in present appearance, bears only vague or abstract resemblance to the letter "A." In order to be read as the letter "A," the object would need to have a crossbar of some sort between the two sides of the triangle. The important and often overlooked presence of two small flanges or projections midway up the interior of the sloping triangular bars, however, may be evidence of a missing cross bar. Some scholars believe that this object was indeed originally an "A" (or Alpha), perhaps one suspended from what would have been a quite monumental processional or altar cross with a pendant Omega hanging to the other side. In any case, no other alphabetic letters in metalwork form survive from the medieval period that could in any way be connected with the legends of Charlemagne's monastic foundations and donations of golden letters. Thus, the "A of Charlemagne" remains today as one of the most perplexing and intriguing of medieval objects with the accrued and potent symbolism associated with the letters of the alphabet.

Doubtless far more well known to modern audiences are the several sculptural renditions of Pop artist Robert Indiana's *Love* motif (illus. 81).[44] In addition to his two-dimensional word- and text-based works discussed previously, Indiana also created sculptures of both small and large scale in a variety of media. The *Love* motif first began to feature in his paintings of the mid–1960s, on square canvases with two lines with the two letters "LO" and "VE" each taking up one half of the pictorial space. In the painted versions, "word and image are equal, and figure and ground coextensive."[45] Indiana explored this motif extensively throughout his career, creating many variations in different scales, colors, and materials. He was originally inspired by the inscriptions ("God is love") that he saw in Christian Science churches he was taken to during his childhood, and his hard-edged *Love* compositions ultimately became some of the most popular and iconic images in American art and culture during the second half of the twentieth century. Indeed, *Love* has been described as America's "most plagiarized work of art,"[46] and has been often parodied, appropriated, and re-used. Indiana began to produce small-scale sculptural versions of the motif in the mid-1960s, such as the series of small chunky versions measuring twelve by twelve by six inches, created of aluminum. Some later versions are painted with his typically bright color scheme, especially red and blue. Larger versions followed, measuring thirty-six by thirty-six by eighteen inches, and further larger versions, done in steel, measuring twelve by twelve by six feet, and even larger. The sculptural versions of this motif generally maintain the geometric clarity of the original painted versions on flat canvases or prints, keeping the same four-square ratio, but retranslated into appropriately calculated three dimensions; the depth of these sculptures is often exactly half the dimensions of the height and width. Thus, these sculptures precisely translate the two-dimensional words into three dimensions, maintaining—if not indeed amplifying—the simultaneous verbal-visual impact of Indiana's iconic work.

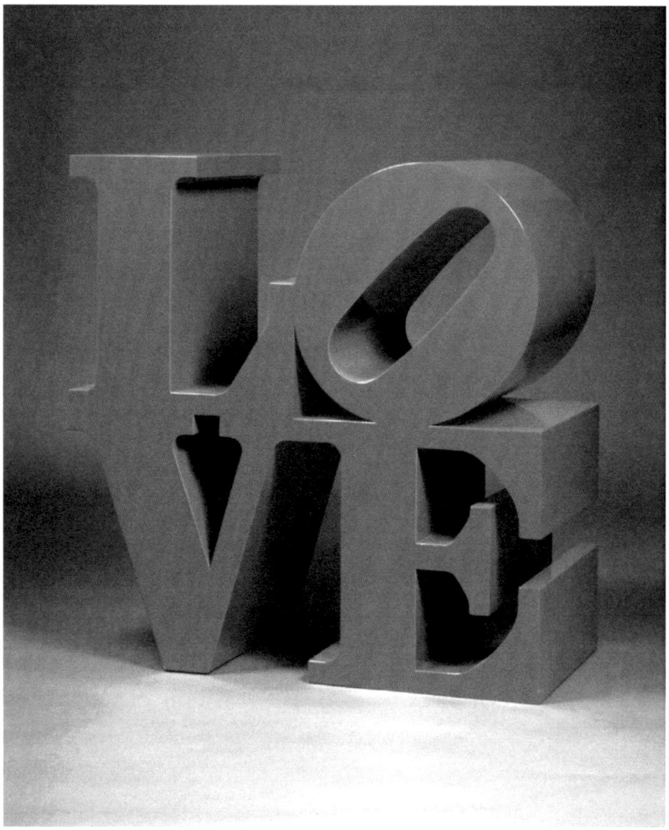

81. Robert Indiana, *Love*, 1966–1995. Private collection, courtesy Simon Calamo-Caro (© 2013 Morgan Art Foundation/Artists Rights Society [ARS], New York; Morgan Art Foundation SA/Art Resource, New York).

The potentially big impact of three-dimensional words has been explored by any number of modern and contemporary artists whose aims and materials are varied. The power of words to shock and disturb, to speak boldly about sociopolitical concerns, to raise questions about language systems and usage, to evoke emotions, to convey mixed messages, and to disguise hidden texts are all themes of word-based art in both two- and three-dimensional media. When these themes are presented in three-dimensional formats, the words and phrases often take on a remarkable degree of solidity and physical presence.

For example, a work such as *Last Chance Lost* (2007) by Jack Pierson (b. 1960) arguably derives much of its impact from its materials (illus. 82). This installation piece consists of an assemblage of mismatched metal, wood, plastic, and neon letters that the artist salvaged from junkyards and garage sales and then placed together to spell out the words. This is one of a large group of "found letter" sculptures that Pierson first began creating in the early 1990s.[47] These works utilize fragments of discarded commercial signage from sources such as old movie marquees, diners, and casinos, placed together in either free-standing or wall-mounted installations. Pierson, also well known for his evocative and often highly erotic photography, has consistently explored themes of "fame, despair, solitude, itinerancy and the existential" in his works that "evoke various states of mind, responses to and impressions of the physical world, and memories of lost time—both personal and universal."[48]

His preliminary explorations with arranging discarded letters from commercial signage sources did not spell out any specific words but rather presented absurd and haphazard letter groupings.[49] He soon turned, however, to creating recognizable and readable words and phrases from the detritus of commercial signage, producing works such as *Stay* (1991), *Helpless Hopeless* (1991), *Solitude* (1995), *Desire Despair* (1996), *Nowhere* (1996), *Tragedie* (1999), *Another Time, Another Place* (2000), *Wasted*

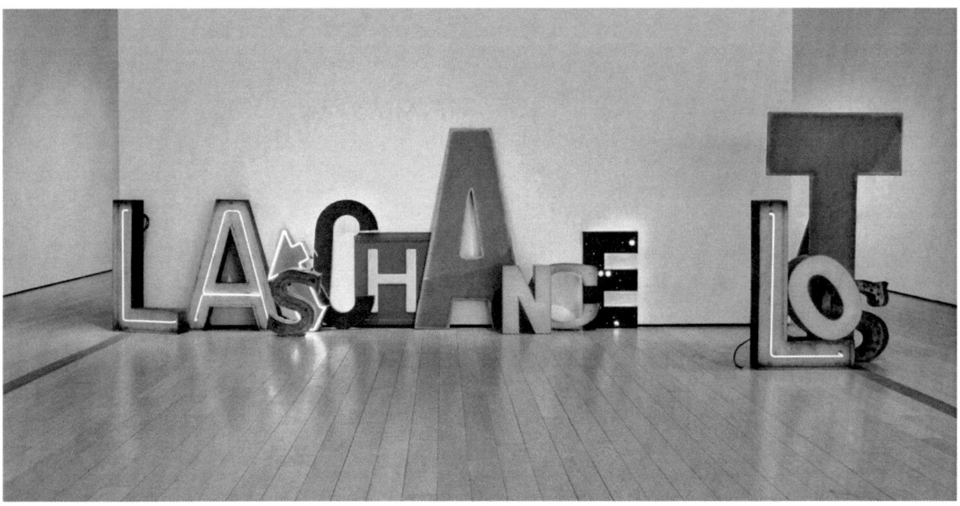

82. Jack Pierson, *Last Chance Lost*, 2007. Los Angeles County Museum of Art, Los Angeles, CA (Digital Image © 2013 Museum Associates/LACMA; Licensed by Art Resource, New York).

Youth (2002), and *Your Face* (2004). Pierson's constructed words and phrases, as in *Last Chance Lost*, bespeak a sense of longing, melancholy, unfulfilled wishes, regrets, nostalgia, disillusionment, and dissatisfaction. According to Pierson, "all art deals with loneliness on some level if it's doing its job."[50] These words evoking "lost chances," time "wasted," "despair," and "desire" are rendered all the more poignant due to the materials from which they are constructed. The bits and pieces, letters from discarded signage, are artifacts from once presumably flourishing businesses whose glory days have long passed. Relegated to junkyards and scrap heaps, these found letters, collected and repurposed by the artist, serve as most tangible reminders and mementos of the passage of time, past glamour, and seduction. The salvaged individual letters from disparate sources, once parts of a whole, are reworked into new compositions by Pierson where "the material, color, size and placement of each letter are crucial to the work's overall effect."[51] His word and phrase choices in these works tend to be evocative rather than specific—universal and not directly clear or purely autobiographical; they inspire multiple interpretations. Viewers may resonate with the nostalgic, poignant, or indeed tragic messages conveyed by the disconnected and salvaged letters he uses in these works—and perhaps even the more so due to their presentation and materials.

Pierson's three-dimensional "found letter" works have, logically, often been compared to the word-based compositions of several other modern artists, such as Ed Ruscha and others.[52] While Ruscha's visual and sometimes illusionistically monumental presentation of words and snippets of conversation may seem, at first glance, to be akin to the constructed words of Pierson, the sense of humor, banality, and cleverness often characteristic of Ruscha's word-based pieces is generally not shared by Pierson. Pierson's word-based sculptures tend to assume a much more serious tone, deriving their power from the actual solidity of the discarded and repurposed materials used. At the same time, Pierson is not so obviously or primarily interested in the semantics of verbal/visual language or language theory so seriously explored by others of his earlier contemporaries of the Conceptual art genre.[53] He creates poignant phrases from discarded words and letters, presenting the audience of viewers/readers with evocative ideas to consider, manifested in tangible objects.

Several of Pierson's installations have also involved seemingly random piles of discarded letters, such as *Psycho Killer* (2000), *Palm Trees* (2000), *Dead Bodies* (2000), *Roses, Roses, Roses* (2005), and *Angst* (2000), this latter representing a mixed-media installation in which a single bed and the floor space around it are strewn with large and broken letters spelling out the word "angst." In these strewn-letter installations, and indeed even more so in the artist's most recent "abstract" letter compositions, textual legibility is discarded in favor of textual chaos or hints of unclear messages conveyed in fragmentary form. The evocative texts can no longer be easily read, and the messages have thus become even more cryptic and hidden. The overlapping piles of letters in his strewn-letter installations leave the viewer with a discomforting sense

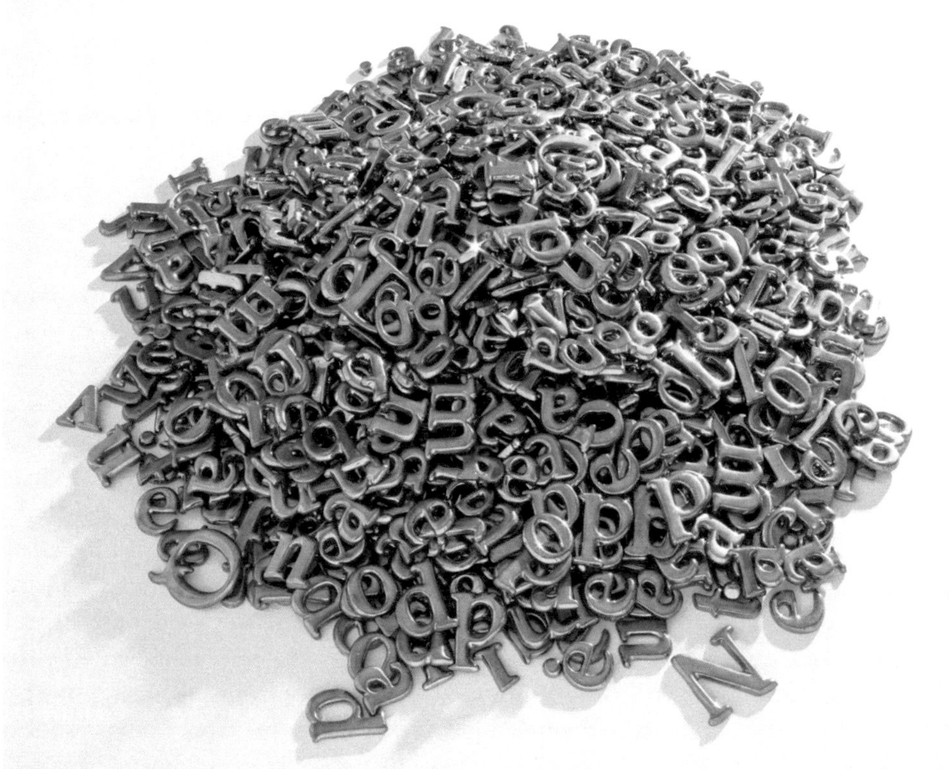

83. Valeska Soares, *Untitled*, 2005. Los Angeles County Museum of Art, Los Angeles, CA (Digital image © 2013 Museum Associates/LACMA; Licensed by Art Resource, New York).

of communication loss, in spite of the fact that the shapes, in many cases, are still recognizable as letter forms. Their sculptural solidity and three-dimensionality make the lost or hidden messages in these works seem to be all the more tragically ungraspable.

A similar—but much more amplified—sense of alphabetic chaos is evoked by Valeska Soares' *Untitled* installation piece from 2005 that consists of a huge pile of platinum-glazed ceramic letters (illus. 83). This pile of letters references a section from the Italian author Italo Calvino's experimental novel of 1972 titled *Invisible Cities*. This complex and poetic literary work is framed in the form of an imaginary conversation between the great Mongol emperor, Kublai Khan, and the thirteenth century Italian explorer, Marco Polo, who describes various cities he visited during his travels. Kublai Khan and Marco Polo do not speak the same language so their initial conversations were largely based on their own interpretations of what was being said or visually demonstrated. As time went on however, they began to understand each other's words a bit better; even so, they discovered that words were less effective in truly conveying the sense of what life was like in the cities they discussed.

The selection of ceramic letters in Soares' installation piece includes the words and punctuation marks from Polo's description of the jumbled and labyrinthine setting of the city of Zobeide, dreamed of by men of various nations and eventually replicated and rearranged into a complex urban form with many traps and dead ends.[54] The pile of letters evokes the maze-like ambiance described in the story by its confusing illegibility.

The Brazilian-born, New York–based Soares (b. 1957) has often used texts, letters, books, and pages from books in her multifaceted and multimedia installation pieces.[55] "Through a seemingly inexhaustible range of techniques, themes and strategies, Valeska's work oscillates between materiality and memory, desire and decay, sensation and intoxication."[56] She explores themes such as the passage of time, memory, and issues of human perception of and reactions to sensory impressions, space and the environment in her complex works. Several of her installations have involved books, book pages, or text fragments, such as her *Love Stories* series of 2009–10 that consisted of books in a variety of romance languages sitting on long white shelves, each including a reference to the word "love" in their titles, and *Timeline* that included a series of book pages all including references to the passage of time strung on a wire and fluttering in the air. Of different sizes, some yellowed and wrinkled, others fresh and crisp, these book pages make viewers aware of the passage of time involved with life, reading, and viewing art. A wall-mounted collage piece from 2007 using similar materials titled *For To* contained about 1000 dedicatory pages from books that the artist collected in bookshops around the world. It comprises "a chorus of wide-ranging voices from the past that, in their various stages of middle age or dusty decrepitude, still manage to hum a faint tune of forgotten passions and sincerely composed affections."[57] In her related 2007 installation piece (*Fragments: Dedication*), she arranged 8000 porcelain letters in a pile on the floor. This disassembled text is taken from an essay by Roland Barthes on the topic of love.

> The delicate alphabetic heap appears to have crumbled in discourse, but the solidity of the random characters seemingly defies the ravages of time, a notion strengthened by the idea that they could conceivably be reassembled and used to construct new vows. The potential for renewal seems to filter through the thousand areas of whiteness, but beyond that not much is certain.[58]

A well-read and scholarly artist, her works often question the ways in which information is conveyed and disseminated and how visual information as well as written texts are created, received, and potentially rearranged and reinterpreted by audiences. She has stated:

> I'm not interested in some sort of monolithic narrative... I'm giving people triggers that activate memories and contexts, and they create their own narratives. So each piece has multiple readings depending upon who is seeing it, or the context in which they are seeing it. There is no fixed meaning. What I want my pieces to be are triggers.[59]

The evocative power as well as the puzzling sense of three-dimensional words are themes that have been well explored by any number of contemporary or earlier twentieth- century artists. For example, the extremely influential twentieth-century Pop artist Claes Oldenburg (1929–2009) also avidly explored the theme of three-dimensional words throughout his career. He is particularly well known for his monumental sculptural enlargements, in a variety of media, of prosaic objects of popular culture and modern life. His interest in three-dimensional words and letters can be traced back to the late 1950s when he created compositions such as *C-E-L-I-N-E, Backwards* (1959), which spells out the name of the French author Celine in mirror writing in puffy letters created of soaked newspaper on a wire frame. The piece "has something sensual and tactile about it; it is a voluminous word that becomes a mouth or a body, a surging forth of a perceptible fragment of the human being."[60] Oldenburg personally described his interest in words and letters as "part of [his] turn to objects, after forsaking representation of the figure."[61]

In subsequent decades, Oldenburg's many alphabetic/textual explorations include his *Alphabet Good Humor Bar* (1970s), *City as Alphabet* projects (1970s), *Inverted Q* series (1970s/1980s), *Torn Notebook* (1990s), *Free Stamp* (1991) for Cleveland, Ohio, and perhaps most notably, *Bottle of Notes*, a monumental painted steel sculpture completed for the city of Middlesbrough, England, in 1993 (illus. 84). The theoretical background and textual complexity of this piece is extremely impressive.[62] The thirty-foot tall form, in the shape of a bottle, consists of two texts and clearly conveys the appropriately nautical motif of a message-filled bottle washed up on the seashore. The external text that actually creates the pierced openwork form of the bottle is taken from the journals of the famous eighteenth-century voyager, Captain Cook, whose birthplace is one of the local attractions in

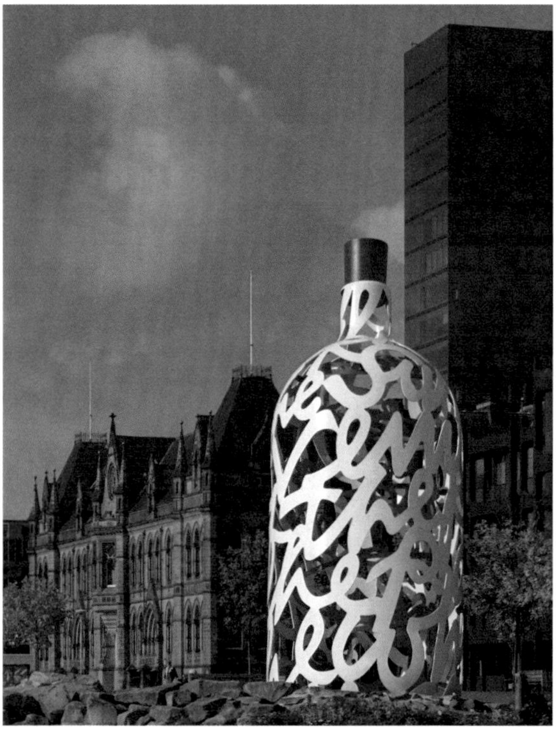

84. Claes Oldenburg and Coosje van Bruggen, *Bottle of Notes*, 1993. Collection Central Gardens, Middlesbrough, England (photograph courtesy Oldenburg van Bruggen Studio; © 1993 Claes Oldenburg and Coosje van Bruggen).

Middlesbrough. This external text consists of an extract from Captain Cook's description of an astronomer's shipboard observation. It is written in large white letters in Oldenburg's script and reads, "We had every advantage we could desire in observing the whole of the passage of the Planet Venus over the sun's disk." The internal text comprises a portion of a poem written by Oldenburg's artistic collaborator, Cossje van Bruggen. Van Bruggen's text, written in her more delicate script, reads, "I like to remember seagulls in flight gliding over the ring of canals."[63] This interior text, painted in blue, spirals upwards within the pierced external frame of the "bottle." "In *Bottle of Notes*, words are a material substance that can be used to form images. By the same token, images become writing."[64] This piece evokes, in a lyrical fashion, motifs of seafaring voyages and adventures, textual fragments, and messages.

> The complex articulation of the sculptural envelope arises from the use of handwriting as a motif. The coincidence between script and object ... underscores a perfect equivalence of languages: that of tale and theory, of vision and image. ...The language that speaks and the language that shows are identified with one another, becoming indistinguishable peers.[65]

The pierced metal openwork that creates the two texts, as well as the large scale of the work as a whole, tend to give more of an impression of writing—a permeable bottle created of short notes—rather than immediately or clearly legible messages. The play of light and shadow on these blue and white cutout metal forms also conjures up the movements of the sea and the motions of clouds in the sky. The piece, although solidly monumental, captures a sense of fleeting moments, incomplete messages, hints of past observations, recollections, and memories. The interior and exterior texts spiral around or within the bottle shape, seemingly in perpetual motion as the weather changes and as the observer moves around the piece. The sense of movement captured in this piece offers a good prelude to further word-based sculptural works that do actually move.

Moving Words

An extremely intriguing variation on the theme of "monumental and moving words" can be seen in several examples, especially by modern and contemporary artists, of *literally* "moving" words. In these cases, words and phrases are not presented as traditionally static forms, but as forms that change shape, appear and disappear, melt, flash on and off, deteriorate, fluctuate, and present themselves to viewers in a variety of fluid formats. Any sense of textual solidity is quite belied in these examples, many of which are ephemeral constructions designed for specific spaces and for limited time durations, using performance, video, and various forms of mixed and technologically based media. These works tend to emphasize the transitory nature of the spoken and written word, the impermanence of language statements, and the challenges involved with the comprehension and interpretation of language, as well as issues of censorship and disappearing texts.

The American artist Jenny Holzer (b. 1950) may serve as a fine example of this genre.[66] Her long-standing interest "in trying to respond to the place of language in art"[67] has taken on a great number of forms throughout her career. Her word-based pieces range from posters and billboards to T-shirts and coffee cups, carved tablets, and fluctuating lighted word projections streaming onto public buildings and landscapes. Holzer's works have largely if not always conveyed messages of intense social or political importance. She has consistently been interested in the power of words to influence perceptions, and she has used her language-based works as vehicles for posing provocative questions about a wide range of topics in modern life: the perception of women and women's roles in modern society, warfare, violence, injustice, politics, and political dissembling. "From the beginning, Holzer has made no bones about her preferred themes, 'sex, death and war.'"[68] Holzer has said, "I used language because I wanted to offer content that people—not necessarily art people—could understand."[69]

She is doubtless most well known for her text works in a variety of technologically based formats, especially her large-scale electronic signage (LED) pieces. For example, her 1989–1990 installation at the Guggenheim Museum in New York used an over-500-foot-long ribbon of electronic signage spiraling around the interior ramp of the museum. Rapidly flashing messages appeared on this text ribbon, sometimes moving back and forth in different directions, in an impressive array of bright colors. The texts consisted of 330 terse statements many of which were taken from her previous *Truisms* (1978), *Inflammatory Essays* (1979), *Living* series (1980s), *Survival* series (1983–85), *Under a Rock* (1986), and *Laments* (1989), combined in a 105-minute continuously running program that bombarded viewers with a dazzling and bewildering array of textual material. The running phrases included such statements as: "When something terrible happens people wake up," "Monomania is a prerequisite of success," "You are a victim of the rules you live by," "Limit time," "Forget truths," "Restrain the senses," and so on. Holzer described her attraction to electronic signage: "Because it's so much like the spoken word; you can emphasize things; you can roll and pause, which is the kinetic equivalent to inflection in the voice. ...Having [the texts] move is an extension of that."[70]

> The propulsive energy of the electronic signboard, the way it can change speed, keeping pace with reading—with thought—and even exceed it; the way that it allows for words to be perceived as images when flashed, and as text when scrolled; the degree to which such words can seem percussive, like music, and explosive, like gunfire; and even decorative, but with a kind of festivity that is on the edge of danger, like fireworks; and ... the way using the signboards makes art analogous to both advertising and mainstream news broadcasts ... all these things recommended the medium to Holzer.[71]

These streaming and moving messages, in a format more often associated with commercial and advertising venues, were carefully designed by the artist to replicate as well as to question the shortness and banality of the prosaic, repeated messages so often promulgated by conventional media sources. Holzer's flowing texts and terse statements run boldly contrary to the messages that viewers normally expect to see, read, notice, or indeed ignore in public spaces filled with the bright flashing display of promotional advertising, company logos, stock market reports, or latest trends. Her calculated and complex use of the electronic signage format, a form well familiar to her modern audiences, represents a brilliant appropriation of this monumental and literally moving form of word-based message conveyance. Her work "masquerades as a public service message of a decidedly subversive type."[72]

Since the mid-1990s, Holzer has been engaged with complex and large-scale projections of texts on buildings. These range from texts projected on public buildings in various cities in Europe and America to texts projected on canals and rivers within the urban environment. These rolling and running texts often change due to their fractured reflections on water, or due to their partially obscured projection on large buildings. "Monumental and ghostly, the scrolling projections pick out architectural details, or leaves, or curls of foam from the obscurity of darkness, while broadcasting enormous words that have an oracular presence tremendously potent even in the photographs that are their only lasting document."[73] These large-scale text projections present provocative, succinct, easily readable, but ever fluctuating messages, briefly but boldly brought to the attention of viewers. "Holzer's art seldom exists as self-contained language; rather it is a symbiotic collage of contextual elements in which language is enhanced by the site and the site is, in turn, charged or energized by the language."[74]

Holzer's most recent work has involved the visually enlarged presentation of sections of declassified U.S. government documents largely from the 1990s containing information about the U.S. military involvement in Iraq and elsewhere in the Middle East. For example, her 2008 LED piece *Thorax* (illus. 85) consists of a curved series of lines of signage that focus on "one incident—the death of a civilian driver in Baghdad. ...Truth is elusive, but the facts of pain and death are solid."[75] The curved shape of the piece evokes the rib cage of a human body. The texts that repeatedly flash across this shape contain fragments of different formal accounts of the death of a civilian noncombatant. Several individuals made reports on the incident presenting the data from different points of view. The texts convey fragments of different versions of the "facts," but the fact of this individual's death remains unquestionable.

In a related group of work, Holzer has also created a series of silk-screened pieces again replicating actual texts from declassified U.S. government documents that are partly blacked out and expunged. Many names, dates, authors, and critical pieces of information originally contained in these documents have been formally

***Opposite:* 85. Jenny Holzer, *Thorax*, 2008. Installation: Cheim and Read, Armory Show, New York, 2008 (© 2013 Jenny Holzer, member Artists Rights Society [ARS], New York; courtesy Jenny Holzer/Art Resource, New York).**

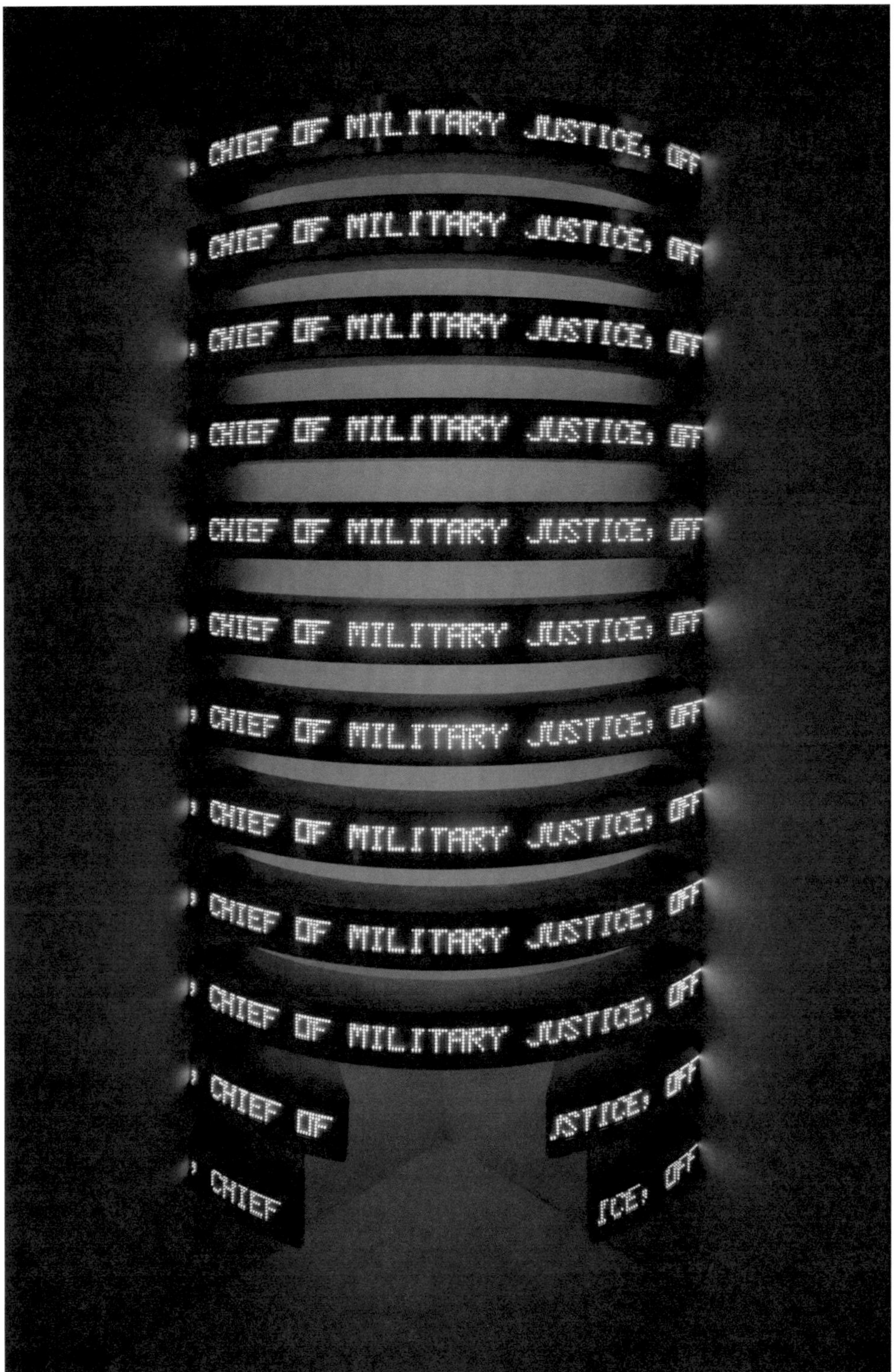
CHIEF OF MILITARY JUSTICE, OFF

obscured by bold sections of black-out markings. In some cases, almost no text remains. These works raise questions about the transmission of information to the public audience—what is withheld, hidden, obscured, or conveyed—and for what purposes this may be the case. The sense that there is a bounty of withheld and protected information otherwise unavailable is boldly addressed in these works that present incomplete and censored texts.

A similar suspicion of authority and decay of information is demonstrated by the disappearing texts created in the ephemeral medium of ice sculpture by the contemporary team of artists Nora Ligorano and Marshall Reese.[76] They have created large-scale words carved from blocks of ice and installed these works outdoors in public spaces where, depending upon the weather conditions, the words ultimately melt away slowly or more rapidly, usually within twenty-four hours. At both the Republican and Democratic National Conventions in 2008, held in Denver and in St. Paul, they created ice sculptures of the word "Democracy." Also in 2008, they installed an ice sculpture of the word "Economy" at Foley Square in New York City, in front of the New York State Supreme Court building. In this installation, the individual letters of ice were about five feet tall and placed atop a fifteen-foot-long platform. In the summer of 2012, they installed an ice sculpture of the phrase "Middle Class" at a public park in Tampa, Florida, also coinciding with the political convention season.

The artists adeptly document, in still photographs and on video, the deterioration processes as the monumental and meaningful words melt and ultimately disappear. Obviously, these works are quite politically strident in dealing with contemporary issues as phrased by the artists: economic meltdown, the erosion of democracy, the disappearance or neglect of the middle class. Their chosen medium, melting ice, serves to convey their messages extremely effectively. As the once solid and blocky letters in these installations melt away, the meanings change as well. Certain letters may disappear more quickly than others, rendering a once solid word incomplete and illegible. As the meltdown process continues, viewers are left with bits and pieces, fragments or hints of words, until only little icy stubs remain. Ultimately, these moving words vanish completely.

CONCLUSION

The Bottom Line

From the elucidatory to the elusive, the puzzling to the profound, the monumental to the melting, the intention of this study has been to demonstrate the diverse ways in which images and writing—two fundamental means of human communication—have so often been combined, through the ages, with quite remarkable and intriguing results. From images that include words to words that include images, and from images created of words, to words created of images, the interplay between the visual and written forms of communication has been consistently explored in a diversity of ways by artists and writers through the ages.

This broadly based study has focused upon the visual and the written—images and writing—whilst also fully acknowledging the verbal communication systems that underlie, augment, and often serve as foundations for both writing systems and image forms.[1] From ancient pictographs to modern multimedia examples, this study has touched upon many carefully selected examples from a variety of time periods and cultural contexts and has arranged this rich material into a series of thematic groupings. This thematic approach has quite deliberately departed from traditional chronological formats in attempting to demonstrate how both visual artists and writers of many eras have long explored the challenges, potentials, and the shared as well as divergent nature of visual and written systems of communication as artistic forms of expression. What quickly becomes so intriguingly apparent with this thematically organized approach to language in the visual arts is that particular ways of thinking about written/visual language systems—or specific manners of combining texts and images—really do not follow a strictly sequential order through history or are *necessarily* representative of particular advances in media, technology, or image/word delivery formats. We find, rather, an ongoing process in which the relationship between images and words has been consistently explored in many of the same ways from antiquity to the present. It indeed even appears that some of the issues and questions "newly" addressed, for example, in modern and postmodern language-based art are paths that have actually been well trodden already, quite logically and interestingly too, in earlier eras and in different formats.

Although language-based art has become exceedingly popular if not indeed quite commonplace in the modern and contemporary periods, this study has intended to show how artists of significantly earlier eras, too, similarly grappled with many of the text-image relationships explored by their modern and postmodern descendants albeit in new media formats. From the medieval period (and earlier) to the modern (and postmodern), artists and writers have explored the relationships between the two fundamentally visual modes of human communication: texts and images, pictures and written words.[2]

This long-standing and continued fascination with the interplay between these two modes of human communication has been demonstrated in the cultural and chronological diversity of materials covered in this study. We see how artists have inserted written texts into pictorial compositions, how artists have taken letters and words and shaped them into forms of visual art, how texts and images have been manipulated by both visual artists and writers to create text-filled images or image-filled texts, how cryptic or mixed messages and hidden texts have been conveyed in word-image combinations, and how quite bold and clear messages of social or political or religious importance have been conveyed by text-based art through the ages. The thematic groupings in this study have been designed to demonstrate how artists of vastly different eras have used both words and images in combination, or artfully presented words alone, to convey messages, to highlight contemporary concerns and issues, and/or to raise questions about the modes, meanings, and roles of visual and written language as related systems of communication.

As demonstrated in the thematic groupings of this study, words and pictures can appear to quite nicely and rather simply "work together," such as when visual images include written devices like explanatory captions, labels, or inscriptions presented within works of pictorial art. In these cases, the viewer/reader is meant to understand that this sort of written information, when it is added to or when it appears with images, is provided in order to offer necessary information about or elucidation of the pictorial subjects depicted. Works of art that include these forms of writing—titles, or captions, inscriptions, and indications of spoken dialogue taking place between the figures represented—seem to present the most obvious and prosaic levels of text/image interplay.

While this may indeed be the case in any number of examples of mutually elucidating text/image combinations, it is also quite clear that the presence of written data in works of pictorial art can result in some very interesting written/visual discontinuity and competition as well, such as when the texts seem to "say" more than the pictures, or when the pictures may illustrate far more than is described in the texts. Issues of verbal/visual literacy on the part of past or present audience members and the structural formats for written and visual narrative presentations are boldly brought into play here, as scholarly researchers attempt to reconstruct the meanings that specific historical audiences may have derived from particular texts or images—or their combinations. Were either the words or the pictures more—or less—accessible for the intended audience? With what degree of visual/verbal knowledge did past audiences approach or understand these text-filled works of art? Did the added writing assist them to better "see" the works of art? Did the presence of written texts lend more "authority" to the visual images? Were written texts included in visual images to impress and/or even to deliberately alienate the nonliterate audience? Or was the visual literacy of viewers in the past more astute than ours—allowing them to quickly recognize particular scenes and topics, pictorially presented, that now have become the purviews of scholarly specialists alone?

These types of questions may seem to be especially appropriate for older works of art, such as the Bayeux Tapestry, with its embroidered and abbreviated running Latin commentary on the visual narrative scenes; or the complex series of inscriptions on the Klosterneuburg altarpiece, with multitudes of texts drawn from Latin biblical literature and commentary; or the remarkable multilingual texts of works such as the Ruthwell Cross and Franks Casket, in which pictorial narrative scenes, presumably of more visual currency to the medieval audience, were enriched and explicated by written texts via graphic markings that are generally quite unfamiliar to present readers, apart of course from specialists in medieval Latin with its system of abbreviations or ancient scripts such as runes.

Although some familiarity with the stories and subjects depicted and/or the writing systems used may be assumed on the part of at least some medieval audience members, it is really not such a very large comparative jump from the medieval to the modern period, when text-filled works of art such as those by Deborah Kass, Ed Ruscha, Glenn Ligon, and many others include snippets from modern dialogue, references to popular songs, and current or traditional slangy catch-phrases as fundamental features. Within a few more years (if not already) many modern audience members may be very much in need of even more detailed explanations to assist them in their understandings of the historical and social contexts for these text-filled works. Image/text combinations may often rely upon specific knowledge (such as visual and/or verbal literacy) on the part of audiences. Even if the words and images are clear and legible, the verbal/visual resonances are ever changing.

Indeed, any number of modern photographic images that capture images as well as texts from the "found environment" often present a startling disjunction between written and visual information, such as is more than well demonstrated, for example, in the "documentary" photographs of American people faced with grave economic challenges during the Great Depression in the early twentieth century that were sponsored by the Works Progress Administration and the Farm Security Administration. Carefully captured images of people waiting in "bread lines" beneath signs with slogans happily pronouncing the "world's highest standard of living," or photographs of people trudging along on foot with small suitcases or knapsacks beneath signs encouraging them to "relax" and "next time, try the train" are quite bold examples of the disjuncture between written texts and visual images that may be mentioned here.[3] The visual and written "realities" thus presented in these types of images well serve to demonstrate how texts and pictures, even if carefully captured or astutely manipulated by photographic means—can be highly evocative and puzzling, or ironically work at crossed purposes to each other.

It is not only the often puzzling relationship between visual and verbal information that is so often at play here, but also issues of pictorial and textual space relationships. When written texts are included *in* visual images, or presented *as* visual images, the viewer/reader is often faced with trying to understand "where" these texts are located in the picture. This may be less the case in the photos or the other artworks mentioned above, but may perhaps be especially well demonstrated by the *cartellino* form in Renaissance and later art, as well as the *trompe l'oeil* devices used by artists from antiquity to the present.

The device of the *cartellino* logically received some detailed coverage in this study because it represents, in its many variant forms, an especially intriguing example of the challenges of text/image relationships. When clever devices such as fictive bits of text-bearing paper are included *in* or appear to be *on* works of art that otherwise may maintain a consistent spatial illusion, viewers/readers may be required to suspend their disbelief in these cases, not insisting that the included texts and the pictorial illusion share the same perceptual plane. The *trompe l'oeil* illusionism of the *cartellino* device, as well as its use in later and related "letter rack," "office board," or *quod libet* compositions demonstrates how very often artists have enjoyed challenging viewers' traditional perceptions of written texts as simply graphic forms on a flat surface. When texts are presented as three-dimensional forms, with curling edges and cast shadows, the viewer is asked to "read" these as texts and simultaneously perceive these as pictorial objects. When words or letters are depicted as three-dimensional forms, or appear to be suspended in space within, in front of, or behind other pictorial devices, the viewer/reader is required to fully engage with this carefully constructed play of word/image relationships.

The selected examples of late medieval and Renaissance manuscripts and printed books discussed in this study well demonstrate the remarkable degrees with which artists have avidly approached the perceptual challenges of text/image relationships. Curling and cut-through texts, texts that might traditionally be perceived as appearing on the surface of a picture, texts that appear to be spatially located behind other written or pictorial elements, and texts that appear to be suspended or hanging in fully three-dimensional form above a landscape scene (such as in Altdorfer's *Battle of Alexander* painting) are all excellent examples.

Of course, the use of actual snippets and textual fragments cut from newspapers or other print sources, such as seen in the early modern collage works as those by Picasso, discussed in this study, similarly challenge traditional perceptions of the relative roles of writing and images. When fragments of actual texts, drawn from various contemporary media sources, are used as compositional elements in the visual arts, readers/viewers may be quite challenged in understanding how to both "read" the texts and "see" the images. Do the artistically selected texts have any particular meaning?—thus fully requiring being read and carefully analyzed as both written and visual elements that contribute to the meaning or messages of the work? Or not? Were Picasso's collaged text fragments carefully selected for their contemporary sociopolitical content or were these just bits of paper that he found ready to hand?

Text/image relationships become even more complicated when artists create or use deliberately cryptic texts, when they hide the meanings of their texts, or create puzzling and enigmatic text/image combinations. In these cases, the viewer/reader is often quite confounded. Although they may be able to see the letters or read the words, the decipherment process requires either astute effort, great admiration, or a willingly appreciative lack of comprehension. The deliberately puzzling word/picture combinations of highly influential twentieth-century artists such as René Magritte, for example, show how words and pictures can often work at crossed purposes. Magritte's "mislabelings" of commonly recognized visual objects with words that convey different (or "incorrect") meanings draw the viewer/reader into a realm where words and images simply do not coincide. We are asked to consider not only the reality but also the authority of visual images, spoken language, and written texts by his artful combinations of these forms. Especially in his word/image compositions of the early twentieth century, Magritte raised a number of issues that have continued to provide great fodder and additional philosophical/linguistically-based materials for later modern artists.

Many other highly intriguing and enigmatic text/image relationships by earlier artists have been explored in this study also. The cryptic and hidden texts found, for example, in the amazingly complex figured-word diagrams created by medieval artists such as Hrabanus Maurus (with his classical precedents) also require and inspire patient viewers/readers to appreciate how very carefully texts can be shaped into images, and vice versa. These classical and medieval forms might indeed, admittedly with a slight stretch, be seen as precedents for more modern forms, such as the word-based, pictorially shaped calligram forms of Guillaume Apollinaire where words are also shaped into evocative images. Forms of art that rely upon both the written and visual modes to convey or suggest meanings and messages to the audience have a long history indeed.

The inclusion of as-yet-undeciphered (and possibly undecipherable) letters and texts in some of the selected examples of medieval and Renaissance manuscripts discussed in this study (such as the Hours of Jean Lallement and the Hours of Marguerite d'Orleans) seem to indicate that letter forms have long been used as hidden codes, or arcane cipher devices accessible to only a few, if indeed these hidden meanings were ever actually designed to be read. While astute decoders have devoted much energy and time to cracking these apparent codes, in some cases we are really not sure if the texts and/or pseudotexts were ever meant to be "read" at all. This may be especially the case with the examples of presumably asemic writing and the pseudoscripts invented and used by artists from the medieval to the modern period, such as the very odd and as-yet-undeciphered "script" in the medieval Voynich Manuscript to the works of Max Ernst, Henri Michaux, and others.

These types of script/image creations also follow in the long tradition of artistically replicating ancient or foreign writing styles, or newly inventing evocative scripts that cannot be really read. The pseudo-Arabic inscriptions so common in medieval and Renaissance art may be seen as similarly involving the artful translation of unfamiliar script systems into design elements. The Asian scripts that provided inspiration for modern artists such as Mark Tobey and Brice Marden are other excellent cases in point. Artists such as Tobey and Marden were really not interested in replicating Asian script styles, but rather more engaged in giving the viewers a "sense" of the calligraphic art forms that inspired them.

Other contemporary artists, such as William T. Wiley, also draw from a highly personal vocabulary of not only textual but also pictorial forms—creating visual/written puzzles in readable forms that require and reward diligent audiences. Many of Wiley's works are clearly based upon references to past art; others of his works involve a personal and semicryptic visual and written vocabulary of his own.

In contrast to this, some words-in-art appear to scream out boldly, making their messages more than clear. From the large-scale epigraphy of ancient monuments to modern installation works such as those by Barbara Kruger, Jenny Holzer, and many others, big, bold words (especially in public spaces) can challenge, assault, or reassure viewers/readers alike with their direct and directive messages. The authority of monumental epigraphy as so carefully and statically (everlastingly) carved on ancient monuments is more than questioned by artists such as Holzer with her bold LED and xenon projections and the word-based installations of Kruger. Presented as bold visual forms, these language-based works may dramatically confront the viewer visually as well as "verbally," requiring them to consider any number of contemporary sociocultural concerns.

The modern art texts projected on or in public spaces, these installations of bold words, might indeed be seen, also with a slight stretch, as somewhat akin to the admonitions and explanatory texts so often carved on medieval church portals where viewers/readers were similarly faced with words and images and experiences. It is really not so great a leap to consider Holzer's bold statements about contemporary issues, projected on public buildings, to be at least somewhat akin to the admonitory messages inscribed on medieval church portals. The materials used and messages conveyed are very different, of course—or are they?

The artful presentation of texts alone (without any accompanying pictorial elements) has a very long history in the language and visual arts as well. From the shaped texts, perhaps especially seen in the Islamic and Hebrew calligraphic traditions, to the word-only art forms of the modern period, artists and writers through the ages have been extremely interested in using text-forms alone as conveyors of meaning—either to promulgate religious beliefs, to point out sociocultural concerns, or to convey political or philosophical messages. Text-based art thus has a very long history to be sure. The philosophically and linguistically based semantic trend in postmodern art thus might be seen as indeed having some significant precedents in earlier art forms that have similarly presented texts alone as visual/written statements.

The bold text-only works by artists such as John Baldessari, especially the text-based works with which he was engaged in the 1960s and 70s, along with the works of several other mid-twentieth century artists, might thus be seen as heirs to a long tradition of artistic image-avoidance (albeit for quite different aims) due to their reliance upon words only. The avoidance of imagery in visual art, the conceptualizing of texts as forms of art, or the use of words alone in artistic compositions actually has a quite long and complex history, as this study hopes to have demonstrated.

Through the ages, written texts have been artfully crafted and shaped into visual formats, and images have been enriched with written texts. From the shaped poems of Simmias of Rhodes to the worded compositions of Deborah Kass, from the cryptic and hidden texts in the compositions of Hrabanus Maurus to the partially revealed texts in Oldenburg and Van Bruggen's *Bottle of Notes*, and from the so-called and quite cobbled together medieval "A" of Charlemagne to Jack Pierson's similar contemporary use of the detritus of commercial signage in his modern works, in the ongoing interplay of language and the visual arts, there is always more than meets the eye.

As the highly influential theorist and modern proponent of effective visual/written interchanges, Edward Tufte, has written:

> We thrive in information-thick worlds because of our marvelous and everyday capacities to select, edit, single out, structure, highlight, group, pair, merge, harmonize, synthesize, focus, organize, condense, reduce, boil down, choose, categorize, catalog, classify, list, abstract, scan, look into, idealize, isolate, discriminate, distinguish, screen, pigeonhole, pick over, sort, integrate, blend, inspect, filter, lump, skip, smooth, chunk, average, approximate, cluster, aggregate, outline, summarize, itemize, review, dip into, flip through, browse, glance into, leaf through, skim, refine, enumerate, glean, synopsize, winnow the wheat from the chaff, and separate the sheep from the goats.[4]

As stated in the introduction to this study, the dangers and potential pitfalls of such a wide-ranging approach are more than obvious. In every single field or area touched upon in this present study, masses of additional and very specialized scholarship exist. Specialists in these diverse fields may well find highly lamentable if not extremely egregious *lacunae* in the materials selected for inclusion here. This is no doubt true. The examples selected for focused discussion in this book admittedly and assuredly could be more than rapidly supplemented by many, many more examples, and perhaps even much better examples. Indeed, any number of important figures and relevant art movements have not been discussed or even mentioned at all. Specialists in particular fields will doubtless find these gaps in information and coverage highly annoying indeed, as well as the summary treatment afforded to ideas and areas that are far more complex than the information offered in this book.

In spite of these glaring gaps and the more or less succinct treatments of the wide-ranging examples chosen for this text, it is hoped that the materials drawn together here will serve as eye openers for modern image readers and text viewers.

Chapter Notes

Introduction

1. John Dixon Hunt, introduction to *Art, Word and Image: Two Thousand Years of Visual/Textual Interaction*, John Dixon Hunt, David Lomas, and Michael Corris (London: Reaktion, 2010), 15.

2. Useful surveys of this complex material include Anne-Marie Christin, ed., *A History of Writing: From Hieroglyph to Multimedia* (Paris: Flammarion, 2001) and Steven Roger Fischer, *A History of Writing* (London: Reaktion, 2001).

3. Dario Covi, *The Inscription in Fifteenth Century Florentine Painting* (New York: Garland, 1986).

4. John Sparrow, *Visible Words: A Study of Inscriptions in and as Books and Works of Art* (Cambridge: Cambridge University Press, 1969).

5. Sparrow, *Visible Words*, 88.

6. Sparrow, *Visible Words*, 49.

7. Mieczyslaw Wallis, "Inscriptions in Paintings," *Semiotica* 9 (1973): 1–28.

8. Wallis, "Inscriptions in Paintings," 1.

9. Wallis, "Inscriptions in Paintings," 9.

10. Wallis, "Inscriptions in Paintings," 27.

11. Omar Calabrese and Betty Gigante, "La Signature du Peintre," *La Part de l'Oeil*, no. 5 (1989): 27–44; André Chastel, "L'Art de la Signature," *Revue de l'Art* 26 (1974): 8–56; Rona Goffen, "Signatures: Inscribing Identity in Italian Renaissance Art," *Viator* 32 (2001): 303–70; Louisa Matthew, "The Painter's Presence: Signatures in Venetian Renaissance Pictures," *The Art Bulletin* 80, no. 4 (1998): 616–48; and Charles Sala, "La signature à la lettre et au figuré," *Poétique* 69 (1987): 119–27.

12. Philipp Fehl, "Death and the Sculptor's Fame: Artists' Signatures on Renaissance Tombs in Rome," *Biuletyn Historii Sztuki* 57 (1997): 196–217; Creighton Gilbert, "A Preface to Signatures (with Some Cases in Venice)," in *Fashioning Identities in Italian Renaissance Art*, ed. Mary Rogers (Aldershot: Ashgate, 2000), 79–89; Creighton Gilbert, "Where Titian's Paintings Are Signed," *The Art Bulletin* 62, no. 1 (1980): 73–75; Lisa Pon, "Michelangelo's First Signature," *Source: Notes in the History of Art* 15 (1996): 16–21; and Patricia Rubin, "Signposts of Invention: Artists' Signatures in Italian Renaissance Art," *Art History* 29, no. 4 (2006): 563–99.

13. Roger Ling, "Inscriptions on Romano-British Mosaics and Wall Paintings," *Britannia* 38 (2007): 63–91 and Beth Cohen, "The Literate Potter: A Tradition of Incised Signatures on Attic Vases," *Metropolitan Museum Journal* 26 (1991): 49–95.

14. Isabelle van Tichelin and Guy Delmarcel, "Marks and Signatures on Ancient Flemish Tapestries: A Methodological Contribution," in *Conservation Research: Studies of Fifteenth- to Nineteenth-Century Tapestry*, ed. Lotus Stack (Washington, DC: National Gallery of Art, 1993), 57–68.

15. James Farquhar, "Identity in an Anonymous Age: Bruges Manuscript Illuminators and Their Signs," *Viator* 2 (1989): 371–85.

16. Chastel, "L'Art de la Signature."

17. R. M. Cook, *Greek Painted Pottery* (London: Methuen, 1960), 253–60.

18. Russell Bowman and Dean Sobel, *Word as Image: American Art 1960–1990* (Milwaukee, WI: Milwaukee Museum of Art, 1990). See also Russell Bowman, "Words and Images: A Persistent Paradox," *The Art Journal* 45, no. 4 (1985): 335–43.

19. Hunt, introduction to *Art, Word and Image*; esp. 17–33.

20. Sparrow, *Visible Words*, 50.

21. Bowman and Sobel, *Word as Image*, 10.

22. Alison Flett, "The Significance of Text Scrolls: Towards a Descriptive Terminology," in *Medieval Texts and Images: Studies of Manuscripts from the Middle Ages*, ed. Margaret Manion and Bernard Muir (Chur, Switzerland: Harwood Academic, 1991), 44.

23. Flett, 53.

24. Richard Kostelanetz, *Imaged Words and Worded Images* (New York: Outerbridge and Dienstfrey, 1970).

Chapter One

1. See for example Hugues Demeude, *The Animated Alphabet* (London: Thames and Hudson, 1996) and Emile-A. van Moé, *The Decorated Letter from the VIIIth to the XIIth Century* (Paris: Editions du Chêne, 1950).

2. Jonathan J. G. Alexander, *The Decorated Letter* (London: Thames and Hudson, 1978); Michelle Brown, *Understanding Illuminated Manuscripts: A*

Guide to Technical Terms (Malibu: J. Paul Getty Museum in association with the British Library Board, 1994); Johanna Drucker, *The Alphabetic Labyrinth: The Letters in History and Imagination* (London: Thames and Hudson, 1995), esp. 93–114; and Otto Pächt, *Book Illumination in the Middle Ages* (London: Harvey Miller, 1986), esp. 45–95.

3. For example, Jonathan J. G. Alexander, "Scribes as Artists: The Arabesque Initial in Twelfth-Century English Manuscripts," in *Medieval Scribes, Manuscripts and Libraries: Essays Presented to N. R. Ker*, ed. M. B. Parkes and Andrew Watson (London: Scolar Press, 1978): 87–116, and Francis Wormald, "Decorated Initials in English Manuscripts from AD 900 to 1100," *Archaeologia* 91 (1945): 107–35.

4. See Michelle Brown, *Understanding Illuminated Manuscripts* for useful and succinct definitions of all of these terms.

5. Alexander, *Decorated Letter*, esp. 9–10 and Pächt, *Book Illumination*, 76–77.

6. Carl Nordenfalk, *Die Spätantiken Zierbuchstaben* (Stockholm: C. G. Röder, 1970).

7. Alexander, *Decorated Letter*, especially 7–13.

8. For the Lindisfarne Gospels, see Michelle Brown, *The Lindisfarne Gospels: Society, Spirituality and the Scribe* (Toronto: University of Toronto Press, 2003) and Janet Backhouse, *The Lindisfarne Gospels* (Ithaca: Cornell University Press, 1981).

9. Michelle Brown, *Lindisfarne Gospels*, esp. ch. 5, 272–394.

10. For a detailed study of another very impressive example—the Chi Rho page in the Book of Kells—see Suzanne Lewis, "Sacred Calligraphy: The Chi Rho Page in the Book of Kells," *Traditio* 36 (1980): 139–59.

11. Robert Calkins, "Liturgical Sequence and Decorative Crescendo in the Drogo Sacaramentary," *Gesta* 25, no. 1 (1986): 17- 23.

12. T.A. Heslop, "Brief in Words but Heavy in the Weight of its Mysteries," *Art History* 9, no. 1 (1986): 1–11.

13. Heslop, "Brief in Words," 3.

14. Conrad Rudolph, *Violence and Daily Life: Reading, Art and Polemics in the Cîteaux Moralia in Job* (Princeton: Princeton University Press, 1997). See also C. Treat Davidson for a discussion of possible pictorial sources and precedents for several of these illustrated letters: C. Treat Davidson, "Sources for the Initials of the Cîteaux Moralia in Job," *Studies in Cistercian Art and Architecture* 3 (Cistercian Studies Series, no. 89; Kalamazoo, MI: Cistercian, 1987): 46–68.

15. Rudolph, *Violence and Daily Life*, 12–13.

16. T.A. Heslop, "Review of Conrad Rudolph, Violence and Daily Life: Reading, Art and Polemics in the Cîteaux Moralia in Job," *Art History* 23, no. 4 (2000): 642.

17. Rudolph, *Violence and Daily Life*, 65–67.

18. Laura Kendrick, *Animating the Letter: The Figurative Embodiment of Writing from Late Antiquity to the Renaissance* (Columbus: Ohio State University Press, 1999), 190.

19. Kendrick, *Animating the Letter*, 17.

20. Kendrick, *Animating the Letter*, 35.

21. Heslop, "Brief in Words," 8.

22. Jonathan J. G. Alexander, James H. Marrow, and Lucy Freeman Sandler, *The Splendor of the Word: Medieval and Renaissance Illuminated Manuscripts at the New York Public Library* (London: Harvey Miller, 2005), 201–207; Donald Drew Egbert, *The Tickhill Psalter and Related Manuscripts: A School of Manuscript Illumination in England during the Early Fourteenth Century* (New York: New York Public Library, 1940); and Lucy Freeman Sandler, *Gothic Manuscripts 1285–1385*, vol. 2 (London: Harvey Miller, 1982), 32–33.

23. See Meyer Schapiro, *Words, Script and Pictures: Semiotics of Visual Language* (New York: George Braziller, 1996), esp. 115–98 and Alison Flett, "The Significance of Text Scrolls: Towards a Descriptive Terminology," in *Medieval Texts and Images: Studies of Manuscripts from the Middle Ages*, ed. Margaret Manion and Bernard Muir (Chur, Switzerland: Harwood Academic, 1991), 43–53.

24. Schapiro, *Words, Script and Pictures*, 181.

25. Drucker, *The Alphabetic Labrynth*, 104.

26. Sources on the Bayeux Tapestry are more than copious: David Bernstein, *The Mystery of the Bayeux Tapestry* (Chicago: University of Chicago Press, 1986); Shirley Ann Brown, *The Bayeux Tapestry: History and Bibliography* (Woodbridge, Suffolk: Boydell Press, 1988); Martin Foys, Karen Overby and Dan Terkla, eds., *The Bayeux Tapestry: New Interpretations* (Woodbridge, Suffolk: Boydell Press, 2009); Richard Gameson, ed., *The Study of the Bayeux Tapestry* (Woodbridge, Suffolk: Boydell Press, 1997); Michael Lewis, Gale Owen-Crocker, and Dan Terkla, eds., *The Bayeux Tapestry: New Approaches. Proceedings of a Conference at the British Museum* (Oxford: Oxbow Books, 2011); J. Bard McNulty, *The Narrative Art of the Bayeux Tapestry Master* (New York: AMS Press, 1989); and David M. Wilson, *The Bayeux Tapestry* (New York: Alfred A. Knopf, 1985). Scholarship specifically focused on the inscriptions includes René Lepelley, "A Contribution to the Study of the Inscriptions in the Bayeux Tapestry: *Bagias* and *Wilgelm*," in *The Study of the Bayeux Tapestry*, ed. Richard Gameson (Woodbridge, Suffolk: Boydell Press, 1997), 39–46; Gale Owen-Crocker, "The Embroidered Word: Text in the Bayeux Tapestry," *Medieval Clothing and Textiles* 2 (2006): 35–59; and Ian Short, "The Language of the Bayeux Tapestry Inscription," *Anglo-Norman Studies* 23 (2000): 267–80.

27. Richard Brilliant, "The Bayeux Tapestry: A Stripped Narrative for their Eyes and Ears," in *The*

Study of the Bayeux Tapestry, ed. Richard Gameson (Woodbridge, Suffolk: Boydell Press, 1997), 111–37.

28. Brilliant, "The Bayeux Tapestry: A Stripped Narrative."

29. Shirley Ann Brown, *The Bayeux Tapestry: History and Bibliography*, 39.

30. Short, "The Language of the Bayeux Tapestry Inscription," 270.

31. Brilliant, "The Bayeux Tapestry: A Stripped Narrative," 132. See also Linda Neagley, "Portals of the Bayeux Tapestry: Visual Experience, Spatial Representation and Oral Performance," in *The Bayeux Tapestry: New Approaches. Proceedings of a Conference at the British Museum*, ed. Michael Lewis, Gale Owen-Crocker, and Dan Terkla (Oxford: Oxbow Books, 2011), 136–46.

32. Helmut Buschhausen, "The Klosterneuburg Altar of Nicholas of Verdun: Art, Theology and Politics," *The Journal of the Warburg and Courtauld Institutes* 37 (1974): 1–32 and Peter Lasko, *Ars Sacra: 800–1200* (New Haven: Yale University Press, 1994).

33. Lasko, *Ars Sacra*, 260.

34. Mieczyslaw Wallis, "Inscriptions in Paintings," *Semiotica* 9 (1973): 1–28.

35. John Sparrow, *Visible Words: A Study of Inscriptions in and as Books and Works of Art* (Cambridge: Cambridge University Press, 1969), 48.

36. Franco and Stefano Borsi, *Paolo Uccello* (New York: Harry N. Abrams, 1994); William Caferro, *John Hawkwood: An English Mercenary in Fourteenth Century Italy* (Baltimore: Johns Hopkins University Press, 2006); Paolo D'Ancona, *Paolo Uccello* (New York: McGraw-Hill, 1960); Rob Hatfield, "Five Early Renaissance Portraits," *The Art Bulletin* 47, no. 3 (1965): 315–34; Hugh Hudson, "The Politics of War: Paolo Uccello's Equestrian Monument for Sir John Hawkwood in the Cathedral of Florence," *Parergon* 23, no. 2 (2006): 1–28; Millard Meiss, "The Original Position of Uccello's John Hawkwood," *The Art Bulletin* 52, no. 3 (1970): 231; and Annarita Paoleri, *Paolo Uccello, Domenico Veneziano, Andrea del Castagno* (Florence: Scala, 1991).

37. Frederick Hartt, *History of Italian Renaissance Art: Painting, Sculpture, Architecture* (New York: Harry N. Abrams, 1994), 252. See also Franco and Stefano Borsi, *Paolo Uccello*, 302–305, for the extremely complex history of the commission, the different versions produced by Uccello, and the subsequent restorations and later additions.

38. Fritz Saxl, "The Classical Inscription in Renaissance Art and Politics: Bartholomaeus Fontius: *Liber monumentorum Romanae urbis*," *Journal of the Warburg and Courtauld Institutes* 4, no. 1–2 (1940): 19–46.

39. See Franco and Stefano Borsi, *Paolo Uccello*, 304, for this inscription.

40. Dario Covi, *The Inscription in Fifteenth Century Florentine Painting* (New York: Garland, 1986); Dario Covi, "Lettering in the Inscriptions of Fifteenth Century Florentine Paintings," *Renaissance News* 7, no. 2 (1954): 46–60; Dario Covi, "Lettering in Fifteenth Century Florentine Painting," *The Art Bulletin* 45, no. 1 (1963): 1–17; and Millard Meiss, "Towards a More Comprehensive Renaissance Palaeography," *The Art Bulletin* 42, no. 2 (1960): 97–112.

41. Saxl, "The Classical Inscription in Renaissance Art and Politics," 28.

42. Eve Borsook and Johannes Offerhaus, *Francesco Sassetti and Ghirlandaio at Santa Trinità, Florence: History and Legend in a Renaissance Chapel* (Doornspijk, Holland: Davaco, 1981), 34.

43. Saxl, "The Classical Inscription in Renaissance Art and Politics," 28.

44. Saxl, "The Classical Inscription in Renaissance Art and Politics," 29.

45. Shapiro, *Words, Script and Pictures*, esp. 119–126, 181–191; and Sparrow, *Visible Words*, 49–50.

46. Anita Brookner, *Jacques-Louis David* (New York: Harper and Row, 1980); Michael Greenhalgh, "David's 'Marat Assassiné' and Its Sources," *Yearbook of English Studies* 19 (1989): 162–80; William Vaughn and Helen Weston, eds., *Jacques-Louis David's Marat* (Cambridge: Cambridge University Press, 2000).

47. Didier Maleuvre, "David Painting Death," *Diacritics* 30, no. 3 (2000): 13.

48. For detailed descriptions of these items, see T. J. Clark, "Painting in the Year Two," *Representations* 47 (1994): 13–63.

49. Helen Weston, "The Corday-Marat Affair: No Place for a Woman," in *Jacques-Louis David's Marat*, ed. William Vaughn and Helen Weston (Cambridge: Cambridge University Press, 2000), 128–52.

50. Gilles Néret, *F. Léger* (New York: BDD Illustrated Books, 1993), 226.

51. Néret, F. Léger, 226.

52. Serge Fauchereau, *Fernand Léger: A Painter in the City* (New York: Rizzoli, 1994), 32.

53. Calvin Kendall, *Allegory of the Church: Romanesque Portals and their Verse Inscriptions* (Toronto: University of Toronto Press, 1998) and Calvin Kendall, "The Voice in the Stone: The Verse Inscriptions of Ste.-Foy of Conques and the Date of the Tympanum," in *Hermeneutics and Medieval Culture*, ed. Patrick Gallacher and Helen Damico (Albany: State University of New York Press, 1989), 163–82.

54. Kendall, *Allegory*, 89.

55. Linda Seidel, *Legends in Limestone: Lazarus, Gislebertus and the Cathedral of Autun* (Chicago: University of Chicago Press, 1999).

56. Denis Grivot and George Zarnecki, *Gislebertus: Sculptor of Autun* (New York: Orion Press, 1961), 26.

57. Kendall, *Allegory*, 90.

58. Kendall, *Allegory*, especially ch. 6: "The Portal as Christ: Personification or Real Presence?" 80–91.

59. Kendall, *Allegory*, 81.

60. The literature in this area is vast. In addition to the sources cited in notes below, see Franz Bäuml, "Varieties and Consequences of Medieval Literacy and Illiteracy," *Speculum* 55 (1989): 237–65; Peter Brown, "Images as a Substitute for Writing," in *East and West: Modes of Communication: Proceedings of the First Plenary Conference at Merida*, ed. Evangelos Chrysos and Ian Wood (Leiden: Brill, 1999), 15–34; Celia Chazelle, "Pictures, Books, and the Illiterate: Pope Gregory I's Letters to Serenus of Marseilles," *Word and Image* 6, no. 2 (1990): 138–53; Walter Cahn, "Romanesque Sculpture and the Spectator," in *The Romanesque Frieze and its Spectator. The Lincoln Symposium Papers*, ed. Deborah Kahn (London: Harvey Miller, 1992), 45–60; Michael Clanchy, *From Memory to Written Record: England 1066–1307* (London: Edward Arnold, 1979); William Diebold, *Word and Image: An Introduction to Early Medieval Art* (Boulder, CO: Westview Press, 2000); Lawrence Duggan, "Was Art Really the 'Book of the Illiterate?'" *Word and Image* 5, no. 3 (1989): 227–51; Walter Ong, *Orality and Literacy: The Technologizing of the Word* (London: Methuen, 1982); Rosamond McKitterick, *The Carolingians and the Written Word* (Cambridge: Cambridge University Press, 1989); Rosamond McKitterick, ed., *The Uses of Literacy in Early Medieval Europe* (Cambridge: Cambridge University Press, 1990); Brian Stock, *The Implications of Literacy: Written Language and Models of Interpretation in the Eleventh and Twelfth Centuries* (Princeton: Princeton University Press, 1983); and Ian Wood, "Images as a Substitute for Writing: A Reply," in *East and West: Modes of Communication*, ed. Evangelos Chrysos and Ian Wood (Leiden: Brill, 1999), 35–36.

For a selection of studies concentrating on medieval Byzantine examples, see Karen Boston, "The Power of Inscriptions and the Trouble with Texts," in *Icon and Word: The Power of Images in Byzantium; Studies Presented to Robin Cormack*, ed. Antony Eastmond and Liz James (Aldershot: Ashgate, 2003), 35–51; Liz James, "'And Shall These Mute Stones Speak?' Text as Art," in *Art and Text in Byzantine Culture*, ed. Liz James (Cambridge: Cambridge University Press, 2007), 188–206; and Amy Papalexandrou, "Echoes of Orality in the Monumental Inscriptions of Byzantium," in *Art and Text in Byzantine Culture*, ed. Liz James (Cambridge: Cambridge University Press, 2007), 161–87.

61. Michael Camille, "Seeing and Reading: Some Visual Implications of Medieval Literacy and Illiteracy," *Art History* 8, no. 1 (1985): 32.

62. Kendall, *Allegory*, 70.

63. John Mitchell, "Literacy Displayed: The Use of Inscriptions in the Monastery of San Vincenzo al Volturno in the Early Ninth Century," in *The Uses of Literacy in Early Medieval Europe*, ed. Rosamond McKitterick (Cambridge: Cambridge University Press, 1990), 186–225.

64. Christine Verzar, "Text and Image in North Italian Romanesque Sculpture," in *The Romanesque Frieze and its Spectator. The Lincoln Symposium Papers*, ed. Deborah Kahn (London: Harvey Miller, 1992), 121.

65. Camille, "Seeing and Reading," 33.

66. Calvin Kendall, "The Verse Inscription of the Tympanum of Jaca and the PAX Anagram," *Mediaevalia* 19 (1996): 410–11.

67. Howard Finster and S. Mee, *Howard Finster: Man of Visions* (Atlanta: Peachtree Publishers, 1989); Howard Finster and Tom Patterson, *Howard Finster: Stranger from Another World, Man of Visions Now on this Earth* (New York: Abbeville, 1989); Lisa Kirwin, "The Reverend Howard Finster: The Last Red Light before the Apocalypse," *American Art* 16, no. 2 (2002): 90–93.

68. See Nancy Grubb, *Revelations: Art of the Apocalypse* (New York: Abbeville Press, 1997) for additional text-laden works with religious themes by other "outsider" artists.

69. Brendan Cassidy, "The Later life of the Ruthwell Cross: From the Seventeenth Century to the Present," in *The Ruthwell Cross*, ed. Brendan Cassidy (Princeton: Princeton University Press, 1992), 3.

70. Fred Orton, Ian Wood, and Clare Lees, *Fragments of History: Rethinking the Ruthwell and Bewcastle Monuments* (Manchester: Manchester University Press, 2007); see also the extensive bibliography complied by Brendan Cassidy and Katherine Kiefer in *The Ruthwell Cross*, ed. Cassidy, 167–199.

71. Ralph Elliott, *Runes: An Introduction* (New York: Philosophical Library, 1959); R. I. Page, *An Introduction to English Runes* (Woodbridge, Suffolk: Boydell Press, 1999); and R. I. Page, *Runes* (Berkeley: University of California Press, 1987).

72. Paul Meyvaert, "A New Perspective on the Ruthwell Cross: *Ecclesia* and *Vita Monastica*," in *The Ruthwell Cross*, ed. Brendan Cassidy (Princeton: Princeton University Press, 1992), 95–166, especially 164–165; Fred Orton, Ian Wood, and Clare Lees, *Fragments of History*, esp. chapter 7: "The Ruthwell Runes and The Dream of the Rood," 144–169; Anne King, "The Ruthwell Cross—A Linguistic Monument (Runes as Evidence for Old English)," *Folia Linguistica Historica* 7, no. 1 (1986): 43–79; John Fleming, "'The Dream of the Rood' and Anglo-Saxon Monasticism," *Traditio* 22 (1966): 43–72; and Robert Burlin, "The Ruthwell Cross, *The Dream of the Rood* and the Vita Contemplativa," *Studies in Philology* 65, no. 1 (1968): 23–43.

73. This translation is quoted from Kendall, *Allegory of the Church*, 84–85.

74. John Higgitt, "Words and Crosses: The Inscribed Stone Slabs in Early Medieval Britain and Ireland," in *Early Medieval Sculpture in Britain and Ireland*, ed. John Higgitt (Oxford: British Archaeological Reports, British Series 152, 1986), 125.

75. For oral reading and delivery in the Middle Ages, see Clanchy, *From Memory to Written Record*, 214–20.

76. It is called the Franks Casket after its nineteenth-century owner, Sir Augustus Wollaston Franks. For a useful, recent, and concise publication on this object see Leslie Webster, *The Franks Casket* (London: British Museum Press, 2012); also Carol Neuman de Vegvar, "Reading the Franks Casket: Contexts and Audiences," in *Intertexts: Studies in Anglo-Saxon Culture Presented to Paul E. Szarmach*, ed. Virginia Blanton and Helene Scheck (Tempe: Arizona Center for Medieval and Renaissance Studies, 2008), 141–59; Richard Abels, "What Has Weland to Do with Christ? The Franks Casket and the Acculturation of Christianity in Early Anglo-Saxon England," *Speculum* 84, no. 3 (2009): 549–81; Leslie Webster, "The Iconographic Programme of the Franks Casket," in *Northumbria's Golden Age*, ed. Jane Hawkes and Susan Mills (Stroud: Sutton, 1999), 227–46; James Lang, "The Imagery of the Franks Casket: Another Approach," in *Northumbria's Golden Age*, ed. Jane Hawkes and Susan Mills (Stoud: Sutton, 1999), 247–55; and Carol Neuman de Vegvar, "The Travelling Twins: Romulus and Remus in Anglo-Saxon England," in *Northumbria's Golden Age*, ed. Jane Hawkes and Susan Mills (Stoud: Sutton, 1999), 256–76.

77. Elliott, *Runes*, 99.

78. Page, *Runes*, 41.

79. Webster, *Franks Casket*, 18.

80. Page, *Runes*, 41.

81. Webster, *Franks Casket*, 9.

82. Webster, *Franks Casket*, 34.

83. Erwin Panofsky, "*Et in Arcadia Ego*: Poussin and the Elegiac Tradition," in *Meaning in the Visual Arts* (New York: Anchor Books, 1955), 195–320; Louis Marin, "Towards a Theory of Reading in the Visual Arts: Poussin's *The Arcadian Shepherds*," in *Calligram*, ed. Norman Bryson (Cambridge: Cambridge University Press, 1988), 63–90; and Lawrence Steefel, "A Neglected Shadow in Poussin's *Et in Arcadia Ego*," *The Art Bulletin* 57, no. 1 (1975): 99–101.

84. Marin, "Towards a Theory of Reading in the Visual Arts," 86.

85. Albert Boime, "Roy Lichtenstein and the Comic Strip," *Art Journal* 28, no. 2 (1968): 155–59; Bradford Collins, "Modern Romance: Lichtenstein's Comic Book Paintings," *American Art* 17, no. 2 (2003): 60–85; and David Carrier, *The Aesthetics of Comics* (University Park: Pennsylvania State University Press, 2000), esp. ch. 2, "The Speech Balloon, Or, the Problem of Representing Other Minds," 27–45.

86. Carrier, *The Aesthetics of Comics*, 29.

87. Lucy Lippard, Lawrence Alloway, Nancy Marmer and Nicolas Calas, *Pop Art* (New York: Praeger, 1966), 95.

88. See Carrier, ch. 3, "The Image Sequence, Or, Moving Modernist Pictures," 47–59 and Scott McCloud, *Understanding Comics: The Invisible Art* (New York: HarperCollins, 1993).

89. Carrier, "The Image Sequence," 57.

Chapter Two

1. Zygmunt Wazbinski, "Le 'Cartellino,' Origine et Avatars d'une Etiquette," *Panthéon* 21, no. 5 (1963): 278–283.

2. Eckhard Hollman and Jürgen Tesch, *A Trick of the Eye: Trompe l'Oeil Masterpieces* (Munich: Prestel, 2004), 7.

3. For a detailed analysis and excellent overview of the issues and problems related to Bellini signatures, see Debra Pincus, "Giovanni Bellini's Humanist Signature: Petro Bembo, Aldus Manutius and Humanism in Early Sixteenth-Century Venice," *Artibus et Historiae* 29, no. 58 (2008): 89–119.

4. Rona Goffen, *Giovanni Bellini* (New Haven: Yale University Press, 1989) and Rona Goffen, "Icon and Vision: Giovanni Bellini's Half-Length Madonnas," *The Art Bulletin* 57, no. 4 (1975): 487–518.

5. Rona Goffen, "Crossing the Alps: Portraiture in Renaissance Venice," in *Renaissance Venice and the North: Crosscurrents in the Time of Bellini, Dürer and Titian*, ed. Bernard Aikema, Beverly Brown and Giovanna Scirè (New York: Rizzoli, 2004), 124.

6. Victoria Sheridan, "The Quattrocento Calling Card: Origins and Intentions of the Italian Renaissance Cartellino," paper delivered at the Bay Area Graduate Art History Colloquium, The Fine Arts Museums of San Francisco, May 2001.

7. Ronald Lightbown, *Carlo Crivelli* (New Haven: Yale University Press, 2004), 264–66.

8. Norman Land, "Giotto's Fly, Cimabue's Gesture, and a 'Madonna and Child' by Carlo Crivelli," *Source: Notes in the History of Art* 15 (1996): 11–15.

9. Goffen, "Crossing the Alps," 125.

10. Helmut Nickel, "Carpaccio's 'Young Knight in a Landscape': Christian Champion and Guardian of Liberty," *Metropolitan Museum Journal* 18 (1983): 85–96 and Vittorio Sgarbi, *Carpaccio* (New York: Abbeville Press, 1994), 154–56.

11. Nickel, "Carpaccio's 'Young Knight in a Landscape,'" 85–89.

12. Millard Meiss, *Andrea Mantegna as Illuminator: An Episode in Renaissance Art, Humanism and Diplomacy* (New York: Columbia University Press, 1957), 28.

13. Jeffrey Ruda, *Fra Filippo Lippi: Life and Work with a Complete Catalogue* (New York: Harry N. Abrams, 1993), 89.

14. Goffen, "Crossing the Alps," 122, note 55; Rona Goffen, "Signatures: Inscribing Identity in Italian Renaissance Art," *Viator* 32 (2001), 315.

15. Goffen, "Signatures," 315.

16. Goffen, "Signatures," 317.

17. For an analysis of this handwriting see Pincus, "Giovanni Bellini's Humanist Signature," 110–12.

18. Rona Goffen, "Lotto's *Lucretia*," *Renaissance Quarterly* 52 (1999): 742–81.

19. Rona Goffen, "Giovanni Bellini's *Nude with Mirror*," *Venezia Cinquecento* I, no. 2 (1991), 196.

20. Louisa Matthew, "The Painter's Presence: Signatures in Venetian Renaissance Pictures," *The Art Bulletin* 80, no. 4 (1998), 633.

21. Anne Umland, *Picasso: Guitars 1912–14* (New York: Museum of Modern Art, 2011) 25–26, figure 75.

22. John Richardson and Marilyn McCully, *A Life of Picasso: Vol. 2: The Cubist Rebel, 1907–1916* (New York: Alfred A Knopf, 1996).

23. Christine Poggi, "Frames of Reference: 'Table' and 'Tableau' in Picasso's Collage Constructions," *Art Journal* 47, no. 4 (1988): 311–22.

24. Lewis Kachur, "Picasso, Popular Music and Collage Cubism (1911–1913)," *The Burlington Magazine* 135, no. 1081 (1993), 253.

25. See for example the lively discussion in William Rubin, Kirk Varnedoe and Lynn Zelevansky, *Picasso and Braque: A Symposium* (New York: Museum of Modern Art, 1992), 75–91.

26. See especially Patricia Leighten, "Picasso's Collages and the Threat of War, 1912–13," *The Art Bulletin* 67, no. 4 (1985): 664–69; Patricia Leighten, *Re-Ordering the Universe: Picasso and Anarchism, 1897–1914* (Princeton: Princeton University Press, 1989); the responses by Richardson, *A Life of Picasso: Vol. 2*, 250; David Cottington, "What the Papers Say: Politics and Ideology in Picasso's Collages of 1912," *Art Journal* 47, no. 4 (1988): 350–59; and Rosalind Krauss, *The Picasso Papers* (New York: Farrar, Straus and Giroux, 1988), esp. "The Circulation of the Sign," 25–85.

27. Umland, Picasso: Guitars 1912–14, 24.

28. Marjorie Perloff, *The Futurist Movement: Avant-Garde, Avant Guerre, and the Language of Rupture* (Chicago: University of Chicago Press, 1986), 49.

29. Ernst Gombrich, "Image and Word in Twentieth-Century Art," *Word and Image* 1, no. 3 (1985), 215.

30. Diane Waldman, *Collage, Assemblage, and the Found Object* (New York: Harry N. Abrams, 1992), 11.

31. Perloff, *The Futurist Movement*, 44; cited from Françoise Gilot and Carlton Lake, *Life with Picasso* (New York: McGraw-Hill, 1964), 70.

32. Among many sources, see Johanna Drucker, *The Visible Word: Experimental Typography and Modern Art, 1909–1923* (Chicago: University of Chicago Press, 1994); Judi Freeman, *The Dada and Surrealist Word-Image* (Cambridge: MIT Press, 1989); Anne Coffin Hanson, *The Futurist Imagination: Word and Image in Italian Futurist Painting, Drawing, Collage, and Free-Word Poetry* (New Haven: Yale University Press, 1983); and John Milner, "On the Fusion of Verbal and Visual Media," *Leonardo* 9, no. 1 (1976): 5–9.

33. Willard Bohn, "Celebrating with Carlo Carrà: 'Festa Patriottica,'" *Zeitschrift für Kunstgeschichte* 57, no. 4 (1994), 670.

34. Waldman, *Collage, Assemblage, and the Found Object*, 63.

35. Willard Bohn, "Circular Poem-Paintings by Apollinaire and Carrà," *Comparative Literature* 31, no. 3 (1979), 266.

36. Bohn, "Celebrating," 674, 679.

37. Perloff, *The Futurist Movement*, 63.

38. A similar composition was used by Guillaume Apollinaire in his 1941 visual poem "Lettre-Océan" which probably served as partial inspiration for Carrá. See Bohn, "Circular Poem-Paintings" and *The Aesthetics of Visual Poetry, 1914–1928* (Cambridge: Cambridge University Press, 1986), 9–15, 24–28.

39. Christine Poggi, "Folla/Follia: Futurism and the Crowd," *Critical Inquiry* 28, no. 3 (2002), 731.

40. Bohn, "Celebrating," 677.

41. Christine Poggi, "Marinetti's Parole in Libertà and the Futurist Collage Aesthetic," in *The Futurist Imagination: Word and Image in Italian Futurist Painting, Drawing, Collage, and Free-Word Poetry*, ed. Anne Coffin Hanson (New Haven: Yale University Art Gallery, 1983), 2–15.

42. Waldman, *Collage, Assemblage, and the Found Object*, 65.

43. Freeman, The Dada and Surrealist Word-Image, 15.

44. Alfred Frankenstein, *After the Hunt: William Harnett and other American Still Life Painters 1870–1900* (Berkeley: University of California Press, 1953; rev. 1975) and Edward Lucie-Smith, *American Realism* (New York: Harry N. Abrams, 1994), esp. chapter 3, "Still-Life and Populist *Trompe l'Oeil*," 40–49.

45. John Wilmerding, *Important Information Inside: The Art of John F. Peto and the Idea of Still-Life Painting in Nineteenth-Century America* (Washington, DC: National Gallery of Art, 1983), figures 194, 202, and 206.

46. For example, Doreen Bolger, "Cards and Letters from his Friends: Mr. Huling's Rack Picture by William Michael Harnett," *The American Art Journal* 22, no. 2 (1990): 5–32; Robert Chirico, "Language and Imagery in Late Nineteenth Century *Trompe l'oeil*," *Arts Magazine* 40, no. 7 (1985): 110–144; Barbara Groseclose, "Vanity and the Artist: Some Still-Life Paintings by William Michael Harnett," *The American Art Journal* 19, no. 1 (1987): 51–59; Johanna Drucker, "Visuality and Artifice Among the Proto-Modern Americans," *The Art Bulletin* 74, no. 1 (1992): 37–50; and the many essays in *William M. Harnett*, ed. Doreen Bolger, Marc Simpson and John

Wilmerding (New York: Metropolitan Museum of Art, 1992).

47. James Elkins, *Why Are Our Pictures Puzzles? On the Modern Origins of Pictorial Complexity* (London: Routledge, 1999).

48. Jean Baudrillard, "The *Trompe l'Oeil*," in *Calligram: Essays in New Art History from France,* ed. Norman Bryson (Cambridge: Cambridge University Press, 1988), 54.

49. Hollmann and Tesch, *A Trick of the Eye.*

50. Penny Howell Jolly, "Jan van Eyck and Saint Jerome: A Study of Eyckian Influence on Colantonio and Antonello da Messina in Quattrocento Naples" (Ph.D. dissertation, University of Pennsylvania, 1976), 142–45 and Herbert Friedmann, *A Bestiary for Saint Jerome: Animal Symbolism in European Religious Art* (Washington, DC: Smithsonian Institution Press, 1980).

51. Jolly, *Jan van Eyck and Saint Jerome*, 95.

52. Millard Meiss, "Scholarship and Penitence in the Early Renaissance Image of Saint Jerome," in Millard Meiss, *The Painter's Choice: Problems in the Interpretation of Renaissance Art* (New York: Harper and Row, 1976), 189–202 and Bernhard Ridderbos, *Saint and Symbol: Images of Saint Jerome in Early Italian Art* (Groningen: Bouma's Boekhuis, 1984).

53. Brian Richardson, *Printing, Writers and Readers in Renaissance Italy* (Cambridge: Cambridge University Press, 1999), figure 14.

54. Friedmann, *Bestiary*, 271; see also Erwin Panofsky, "The Mouse that Michelangelo Failed to Carve," in *Essays in Memory of Karl Lehmann*, ed. Lucy Freedman Sandler (New York: Institute of Fine Arts, New York University, 1964), 242–51.

55. Jolly, *Jan van Eyck and Saint Jerome*, 82, 110.

56. Aikema, Brown and Scirè, *Renaissance Venice and the North*, 214–217. The sixteenth-century scholar and art historian Marcantonio Michiel described this work in 1529, noting: "On the desk is a little label which seems to contain the name of the master, but by looking at it closely, one cannot distinguish any letters, as it is all a deception." Cited in Ridderbos, *Saint and Symbol*, 41.

57. Although not illustrated here, another wonderful example of an early "letter rack" composition can be found on the reverse of Vittore Carpaccio's *Hunting Scene on the Lagoon*, ca. 1493–95; see Aikema, Brown and Scirè, *Renaissance Venice and the North*, 236–39.

58. Thomas Holman, "Holbein's Portraits of the Steelyard Merchants: An Investigation," *Metropolitan Museum Journal* 14 (1979): 152.

59. James Snyder, *Northern Renaissance Art: Painting, Sculpture, the Graphic Arts from 1350 to 1575* (New York: Harry N. Abrams, 1985), 392; see also Charles Cuttler, "Holbein's Inscriptions," *The Sixteenth Century Journal* 24, no. 2 (1993): 369–382.

60. Marie-Louise d'Otrange Mastai, *Illusion in Art: Trompe l'Oeil: A History of Pictorial Illusionism* (New York: Abaris, 1975), 160.

61. See Poul Gammelbo, *Dutch Still-Life Painting, from the 16th to the 18th Centuries in Danish Collections* (Leigh-on-Sea: F. Lewis, 1960), 160–70 for further examples of his work including the companion piece to the 1668 *Letter Rack* or *Trompe l'Oeil* (number 248).

62. Mastai, *Illusion in Art*, 164.

63. Jean Leymarie, *The Spirit of the Letter in Painting* (Lausanne: Skira, 1961), 50.

64. Hollmann and Tesch, *A Trick of the Eye*, 7.

65. Mastai, *Illusion in Art*, 208.

66. Mastai, *Illusion in Art*, 176.

67. Ani Boyajian and Mark Rutkoski, eds., *Stuart Davis: A Catalogue Raisonné*, three vols. (New Haven: Yale University Press, 2007).

68. Stuart Davis Papers, November 1, 1951; cited in Lewis Kachur, "Stuart Davis's Word Pictures," in *Stuart Davis: American Painter*, ed. Lowery Stokes Sims (New York: Metropolitan Museum of Art, 1991), 103.

69. Stuart Davis quoted in Katharine Kuh, *The Artist's Voice: Talks with Seventeen Artists* (New York: Harper and Row, 1962), 52.

70. Boyajian and Rutkoski, eds., *Stuart Davis*, vol. 3, 380.

71. Kachur, "Stuart Davis's Word Pictures," 102.

72. Boyajian and Rutkoski, eds., *Stuart Davis*, vol. 3, 380.

73. Lewis Kachur, "The Language of Stuart Davis: Writing/Drawing," in *The Drawings of Stuart Davis: The Amazing Continuity*, Karen Wilkin and Lewis Kachur (New York: American Federation of Arts, 1992), 42.

74. Sims, Stuart Davis, 280.

75. Kachur, "Stuart Davis's Word Pictures," 97.

76. Freeman, *The Dada and Surrealist Word-Image*, esp. "Layers of Meaning: The Multiple Readings of Dada and Surrealist Word Images," 13–56.

77. Kachur, "Stuart Davis's Word Pictures," 102.

78. Kachur, "The Language of Stuart Davis," 42.

79. John Perreault, "Metaphysical Funk Monk," *Art News* 67 (1968): 52–53, 66–67.

80. Joann Moser, *What's It All Mean: William T. Wiley in Retrospect* (Berkeley: University of California Press, 2009).

81. William T. Wiley, 1979 interview with John Perreault, cited in John Perreault, "Wiley Territory," in *Wiley Territory*, Graham Beal and John Perreault (Minneapolis: Walker Art Center, 1979), 7.

82. Robert Johnson, *Nothing Lost from the Original: William T. Wiley Looks at Art History* (San Francisco: M. H. de Young Memorial Museum, 1996).

83. Graham Beal, "The Beginner's Mind," in Graham Beal and John Perreault, *Wiley Territory* (Minneapolis: Walker Art Center, 1979), 22.

84. Beal, "The Beginner's Mind," 22.

85. See especially Ulrich Ernst, *Carmen Figuratum: Geschichte des Figurengedichts von den antiken Ursprüngen bis zum Augsgang des Mittelalters* (Cologne: Böhlau, 1991); Ulrich Ernst, "The Figured Poem: Towards a Definition of Genre," *Visible Language* 20, no. 1 (1986): 8–17; and Dick Higgins, *Pattern Poetry: Guide to an Unknown Literature* (Albany: State University of New York Press, 1987).

86. William Levitan, "Dancing at the End of the Rope: Optatian Porfyry and the Field of Roman Verse," *Transactions of the American Philological Association* 115 (1985): 268.

87. Ernst, "Figured Poem," 15.

88. Charles Doria, "Visual Writing Forms in Antiquity: The *Versus Intexti*," *West Coast Poetry Review* 19 (1979): 63–92.

89. Ernst, "Figured Poem," 16.

90. Hans-Georg Müller, *Hrabanus Maurus: De laudibus sancta cruces: Studien zur Überlieferung und Geistesgeschicte mit dem Faksimile-Textabdruck aus Codex Reg. Lat. 124 der Vatikanischen Bibliothek* (Ratingen: A. Henn, 1973); Bruno Reudenbach, "Das Verhältnis von Text und Bild in 'De laudibus sanctae crucis' des Hrabanus Maurus," in *Geistliche Denkformen in der Literatur des Mittelalters*, ed. K. Grubmüller (Munich: W. Fink, 1984), 282–320; Bruno Reudenbach, "Imago-Figura: Zum Bildverständis in den Figurendicten von Hrabanus Maurus," *Frümittelalterliche Studien* 20 (1986): 25–35; Robert Massin, *Letter and Image* (New York: Van Nostrand Reinhold, 1970), figures 637–66.

91. Ernst, "Figured Poem," 16.

92. Elizabeth Sears, "Louis the Pious as *Miles Christi*: The Dedicatory Image in Hrabanus Maurus's *De laudibus sanctae crucis*," in *Charlemagne's Heir: New Perspectives on the Reign of Louis the Pious*, ed. Roger Collins and Peter Godman (Oxford: Clarendon Press, 1990): 605–628.

93. Sears, "Louis the Pious," 606.

94. Florentine Mütherich and Joachim Gaehde, *Carolingian Painting* (New York: George Braziller, 1976), 55.

95. Sears, "Louis the Pious," 607.

96. A helpful list of these manuscripts may be found in Ernst, *Carmen Figuratem*, 309–22.

97. Elizabeth Sears, "Word and Image in Carolingian *Carmina Figurata*," in *World Art: Themes of Unity in Diversity*, vol. 2, ed. Irving Lavin (University Park: Pennsylvania State University Press, 1989), 342.

98. Sears, "Word and Image," 343.

99. Laura Kendrick, *Animating the Letter: The Figurative Embodiment of Writing from Late Antiquity to the Renaissance* (Columbus: Ohio State University Press, 1999), 53.

100. Sears, "Word and Image," 343.

Chapter Three

1. Siegfried Gohr, *Magritte* (New York: Harry N. Abrams, 2005), 15.

2. René Magritte, *Magritte: A to Z* (London: Tate Gallery, 2011); Daniel Abadie, ed., *Magritte* (New York: Art Publishers, 2003); and Siegfried Gohr, *Magritte* (San Francisco: San Francisco Museum of Modern Art, 2000).

3. David Sylvester, *Magritte* (Brussels: Mercatorfonds, 2009), esp. ch. 25: "Words as Images," 210–23. Originally published as *Magritte: The Silence of the World* (New York: Harry N. Abrams, 1992).

4. Suzi Gablik, *Magritte* (London: Thames and Hudson, 1970), 137.

5. Gablik, *Magritte*, 127.

6. Judi Freeman, *The Dada and Surrealist Word-Image* (Cambridge: MIT Press, 1989), 44.

7. Simon Morley, *Writing on the Wall: Word and Image in Modern Art* (Berkeley: University of California Press, 2003), 86.

8. Morley, *Writing on the Wall*, 87.

9. Gablik, *Magritte*, 140.

10. Gablik, *Magritte*, 127.

11. Gablik, *Magritte*, 139.

12. A. Hammacher, *Magritte* (New York: Harry N. Abrams, 1974), 27. The section on "The Problem of Magritte's Titles," 25–30, is especially useful.

13. Gablik, *Magritte*, 141.

14. James Harkness, trans. intro. to Michel Foucault, *This Is Not a Pipe* (Berkeley: University of California Press, 1983), 2.

15. Silvano Levy, "Foucault on Magritte on Resemblance," *The Modern Language Review* 85, no. 1 (1990): 50–56.

16. Michel Foucault, *This Is Not a Pipe*, ed. and trans. James Harness.

17. Hammacher, *Magritte*, 32.

18. Gablik, *Magritte*, 127.

19. Randa Dubnick, "Visible Poetry: Metaphor and Metonymy in the Paintings of René Magritte," *Contemporary Literature* 21, no. 3 (1980): 407–19.

20. Stephanie Barron and Michel Draguet, *Magritte and Contemporary Art: The Treachery of Images* (Los Angeles: Los Angeles County Museum of Art, 2006).

21. Roberta Bernstein, *Jasper Johns' Paintings and Sculptures 1954–1974: "The Changing Focus of the Eye"* (Ann Arbor: UMI Research Press, 1985), 40. See also Gary Garrels, ed., *Jasper Johns: Seeing with the Mind's Eye* (San Francisco: San Francisco Museum of Modern Art, 2012).

22. Philip Fisher, *Making and Effacing Art: Modern American Art in a Culture of Museums* (New York: Oxford University Press, 1991), 83.

23. Michael Crichton, *Jasper Johns* (New York: Harry N. Abrams, 1994), 38.

24. Bruce Bower, "Brother Stroop's Enduring Effect," *Science News* 141 (1992): 312–16.

25. Bower, "Brother Stroop's Enduring Effect," 312.

26. Fisher, *Making and Effacing Art*, 86.

27. Roberta Bernstein, "René Magritte and Jasper Johns: Making Thoughts Visible," in *Magritte and Contemporary Art: The Treachery of Images*, ed. Stephanie Barron and Michel Draguet (Los Angeles: Los Angles County Museum of Art, 2012), 117.

28. Bernstein, *Jasper Johns' Paintings and Sculptures*, esp. ch. 2, "Objects and Words: 1954–1962," 31–49.

29. Gablik, *Magritte*, 138.

30. Helen Harrison, *Larry Rivers* (New York: Artnews Books, 1984), 77.

31. Harrison, *Larry Rivers*, 77.

32. Harrison, *Larry Rivers*, 77.

33. Hammacher, *Magritte*, 30.

34. John Harthan, *The Book of Hours* (London: Thames and Hudson, 1970), 150–153; Thomas Kren and Scot McKendrick, *Illuminating the Renaissance: The Triumph of Flemish Manuscript Painting in Europe* (Los Angeles: J. Paul Getty Museum, 2003), 444–46; and Eric Millar, *Les Manuscrits à Peintures des Bibliothèques de Londres; Extrait du Bulletin de la Société Française de Reproduction de Manuscrits à Peintures* (Paris, 1924), 95–108.

35. Folios 31v, 103, and 116v.

36. Eric Millar, writing in the early 1920s, described these words as "apparement dénuées de signification," and further stated that "telles inscriptions sont fréquentes dan les travaux flamandes de l'époque." Millar, 104.

37. Kren and McKendrick, *Illuminating the Renaissance, 174–176 and Thomas Kren, ed., Renaissance Painting in Manuscripts: Treasures from the British Library* (New York: Hudson Hills Press, 1983), 31–39.

38. Kren, *Renaissance Painting in Manuscripts*, 31.

39. Kren, *Renaissance Painting in Manuscripts*, 38, note 5.

40. Anne Van Buren, "The Master of Mary of Burgundy and His Colleagues: The State of Research and Questions of Method," *Zeitschrift für Kunstgeschichte* 38 (1975): 286–309.

41. Kren and McKendrick, *Illuminating the Renaissance*, 134–37 and Jonathan Alexander, *The Master of Mary of Burgundy: A Prayer Book for Engelbert of Nassau* (New York: George Braziller, 1970).

42. Eberhard König, *Les Heures de Marguerite d'Orleans* (Paris: Les Éditions du Cerf/Bibliothèque Nationale, 1991).

43. König, *Les Heures de Marguerite d'Orleans*, 90.

44. Martina Bagnoli, ed., *Prayers in Code: Books of Hours from Renaissance France* (Baltimore: Walters Art Museum, 2009).

45. Robert Schindler, "Jean Lallement's Books of Hours and French Manuscript Illumination," in *Prayers in Code: Books of Hours from Renaissance France*, ed. Martina Bagnoli (Baltimore: Walters Art Museum, 2009), 23.

46. Lillian Randall, *Medieval and Renaissance Manuscripts in the Walters Art Gallery, Vol. II: France, 1420–1540* (Baltimore: Walters Art Gallery, 1992), 540–49; Myra Orth, "Two Books of Hours for Jean Lallement le Jeune," *The Journal of the Walters Art Gallery* 38 (1980): 70–93; and Roger Wieck, *Time Sanctified: The Book of Hours in Medieval Art and Life* (New York: George Braziller, 1988), 206.

47. Orth, "Two Books of Hours for Jean Lallement le Jeune," 78.

48. Orth, "Two Books of Hours for Jean Lallement le Jeune," 79.

49. Rosamond Mack, *Bazaar to Piazza: Islamic Trade and Italian Art, 1300–1600* (Berkeley: University of California Press, 2002), esp. ch. 3, "Oriental Script in Italian Paintings," 51–71.

50. Moshe Barasch, "Some Oriental Pseudo-Inscriptions in Renaissance Art," *Visible Language* 23 (1989): 170–87.

51. Richard Ettinghausen, "The Impact of Muslim Decorative Arts and Painting on the Arts of Europe," in *Richard Ettinghausen: Islamic Art and Archaeology, Collected Papers*, prep. and ed. Myriam Rosen-Ayalon (Berlin: Gebr. Mann Verlag, 1984), 1074–1102.

52. Irene Bierman, "Art and Politics: The Impact of Fatimid Uses of 'Tiraz' Fabrics" (Ph.D. dissertation, University of Chicago, 1980), appendices C-G, 426–461.

53. Mack, *Bazaar to Piazza*, 54–63.

54. Patricia Baker, *Islamic Textiles* (London: British Museum Press, 1995), 53–62.

55. Bierman, "Art and Politics," 161.

56. Bierman, "Art and Politics," 140.

57. Hidemichi Tanaka, "Oriental Scripts in the Paintings of Giotto's Period," *Gazette des Beaux-Arts* 113 (1989): 224.

58. Hidemichi Tanaka, "The Mongolian Script in Giotto's Paintings at the Scrovegni Chapel at Padua," *Acts of the 25th International Congress of the History of Art*, vol. 6 (Vienna: Hermann Böhlaus Nachf, 1983), 167–72.

59. Mack, *Bazaar to Piazza*, 52; Tanaka, "Mongolian Script," 168–69; Tanaka, "Oriental Scripts," 220–21.

60. Tanaka, "Mongolian Script," 169.

61. Richard Ettinghausen, "Kufesque in Byzantine Greece, the Latin West and the Muslim World," in *Collected Papers*, prep. and ed. Myriam Rosen-Ayalon (Berlin: Gebr. Mann Verlag, 1984), 752–771.

62. Tanaka, "Oriental Scripts," 220.

63. Barasch, "Some Oriental Pseudo-Inscriptions in Renaissance Arts," 187.

64. What used, generically, to be called "Pseudo-

Kufic," but which are actually imitations of other more cursive styles of Arabic calligraphy such as Thuluth; see Mack, *Bazaar to Piazza*, 51.

65. Mack, Bazaar to Piazza, 71.

66. Ettinghausen, "Kufesque," in *Collected Papers*, prep. and ed. Myriam Rosen-Ayalon (Berlin: Gebr. Mann Verlag, 1984), 1076–1077.

67. Barasch, "Some Oriental Pseudo-Inscriptions in Renaissance Arts," 187.

68. Stephen Campbell, *Cosmè Tura of Ferrara: Style, Politics and the Renaissance City, 1450–1495* (New Haven: Yale University Press, 1997), 16. See also Stephen Campbell, "*Pictura* and *Scriptura*: Cosmè Tura and Style as Courtly Performance," *Art History* 19, no. 2 (1996): 267–95 and Stephen Campbell and Alan Chong, eds., *Cosmè Tura: Painting and Design in Renaissance Ferrara* (Boston: Isabella Stewart Gardner Museum, 2002).

69. Campbell, *Cosmè Tura of Ferrara*, 18.

70. Campbell, *Cosmè Tura of Ferrara*, 16.

71. Richard Stemp, "Two Sculptures Designed by Cosmè Tura," *The Burlington Magazine* 141, no. 1153 (1999): 208–15, 226–28 and Luke Syson, "Tura and the 'Minor Arts': The School of Ferrara," in *Cosmè Tura: Painting and Design in Renaissance Ferrara*, eds. Stephen Campbell and Alan Chong, (Boston: Isabella Stewart Gardner Museum, 2002), 31–70.

72. Campbell, *Cosmè Tura of Ferrara*, 16.

73. Barasch, "Some Oriental Pseudo-Inscriptions in Renaissance Arts," 182.

74. Campbell, *Cosmè Tura of Ferrara*, 18.

75. Campbell, *Cosmè Tura of Ferrara*, esp. chs. 2, 4, and 5.

76. Michael Sullivan, *The Meeting of Western and Eastern Art from the Sixteenth Century to the Present Day* (Greenwich, CT: New York Graphic Society, 1973), esp. 207–38; Gabriele Fahr-Becker, *Japanese Prints* (Köln: Taschen, 2001); Lionel Lambourne, *Japonisme: Cultural Crossings between Japan and the West* (London: Phaidon, 2005); Karin Breuer, *Japanesque: The Japanese Print in the Era of Impressionism* (San Francisco: Fine Arts Museums of San Francisco, 2010); Tsukasa Kōdera, "Japan as Primitivistic Utopia: Van Gogh's Japonisme Portraits," *Simiolus: Netherlands Quarterly for the History of Art* 14, no. 3–4 (1984): 189–208; Gabriel Weisberg, Phillip Cate, Gerald Needham, Martin Eidelberg, and William Johnston, *Japonisme: Japanese Influence on French Art 1854–1910* (Cleveland: Cleveland Museum of Art, 1975); Mark Roskill, *Van Gogh, Gauguin and the Impressionist Circle* (Greenwich, CT: New York Graphic Society, 1970); and Siegfried Wichmann, *Japonisme: The Japanese Influence on Western Art in the Nineteenth and Twentieth Centuries* (New York: Harmony Books, 1980).

77. Willem van Gulik and Fred Orton, *Japanese Prints Collected by Vincent Van Gogh* (Amsterdam: Rijksmuseum Vincent Van Gogh, 1978).

78. Fahr-Becker, *Japanese Prints*, 32.

79. Lambourne, *Japonisme*, 47.

80. Lambourne, *Japonisme*, 47.

81. Willem van Gulik, "An Introduction to the Japanese Prints Collected by Vincent Van Gogh," in *Japanese Prints Collected by Vincent Van Gogh*, by Willem van Gulik and Fred Orton, (Amsterdam: Rijksmuseum Vincent Van Gogh, 1978), 11.

82. Jeremy Adler, "Paul Klee as 'Poet Painter,'" in *Art, Word and Image: Two Thousand Years of Visual/Textual Interaction*, John Dixon Hunt, David Lomas, and Michael Corris (London: Reaktion, 2010), 178–201.

83. Rosalind Krauss and Margit Rowell, eds., *Joan Miró: Magnetic Fields* (New York: Solomon R. Guggenheim Foundation, 1972) and Sidra Stich, *Joan Miró: The Development of a Sign Language* (St. Louis: Washington University Gallery of Art, 1980).

84. Richard Sieburth, *Signs in Action: Pound/Michaux* and *Of Language* by Henri Michaux, trans. Richard Sieburth (New York: Reddustbooks, 1987) and Henri Michaux, *Stroke by Stroke*, trans. Richard Sieburth (New York: Archipelago Books, 2006).

85. Renée Riese Hubert, "Traces of Transcendence: Masson, Ernst, Tapiès," *Word and Image* 7, no. 2 (1991): 165–76.

86. Werner Spies and Sabine Rewald, eds., *Max Ernst: A Retrospective* (New York: Metropolitan Museum of Art, 2005); Ian Turpin, *Max Ernst* (Oxford: Phaidon, 1979); Ulrich Bischoff, *Max Ernst: 1891–1976: Beyond Painting* (Köln: Taschen, 2003); Max Ernst, *Max Ernst: Beyond Painting and Other Writings by the Artist and his Friends* (New York: Wittenborn, Schultz, 1948).

87. Adler, "Paul Klee as 'Poet Painter,'" 178.

88. Stitch, *Joan Miró*, 8.

89. Margit Rowell, "Magnetic Fields: The Poetics," in *Joan Miró: Magnetic Fields*, ed. Rosalind Krauss and Margit Rowell (New York: Solomon R. Guggenheim Foundation, 1972), 55.

90. David Lomas, " 'New in Art, They are Already Soaked in Humanity': Word and Image, 1900–1945," in *Art, Word and Image: Two Thousand Years of Visual/Textual Interaction*, John Dixon Hunt, David Lomas, and Michael Corris, 155.

91. Michaux, *Stroke by Stroke*, n.p.

92. Thomas Gaehtgens, "Max Ernst and the Great Masters," *in Max Ernst: A Retrospective*, ed. Werner Spies and Sabine Rewald (New York: Metropolitan Museum of Art, 2008), 37.

93. Renée Riese Hubert, "Max Ernst: The Displacement of the Visual and the Verbal," *New Literary History* 25, no. 3 (1984): 575.

94. M. E. Warlick, *Max Ernst and Alchemy: A Magician in Search of Myth* (Austin: University of Texas Press, 2001), 190.

95. Hubert, "Max Ernst: The Displacement," 600.

96. Anne Hyde Greet, "Iliazd and Max Ernst: 65 Maximiliana or the Illegal Practice of Astronomy," *World Literature Today* 56, no. 1 (1982): 10–18; Max Ernst and Peter Schamoni, *Maximiliana: The Illegal Practice of Astronomy* (Boston: New York Graphic Society, 1974); and Renée Riese Hubert, *Surrealism and the Book* (Berkeley: University of California Press, 1988), 308–19.

97. Greet, "Iliard and Max Ernst," 10.

98. Greet, "Iliard and Max Ernst," 16.

99. Hubert, "Traces of Transcendence," 173.

100. Hubert, "Max Ernst: The Displacement," 598.

101. Books and articles on the Voynich Manuscript abound. See, for example, Lawrence and Nancy Goldstone, *The Friar and the Cipher: Roger Bacon and the Unsolved Mystery of the Most Unusual Manuscript in the World* (New York; Doubleday, 2005) and Gerry Kennedy and Rob Churchill, *The Voynich Manuscript* (London: Orion, 2004).

102. Luigi Serafini, *Codex Seraphinianus* (Milan: F. M. Ricci, 1981). This original two-volume publication has since appeared in a number of different printings.

103. James Elkins, *On Pictures and the Words that Fail Them* (Cambridge: Cambridge University Press, 1998), 130. See also James Elkins, "Art History and Images That Are Not Art," *The Art Bulletin* 77, no. 4 (1995): 553–71.

104. Shan Winn, *Pre-Writing in Southeastern Europe: The Sign System of the Vinča Culture* (Calgary: Western, 1981).

105. Steven Roger Fischer, *A History of Writing* (London: Reaktion, 2001), 290–92.

106. Elkins, *On Pictures*, 158.

107. Elkins, *On Pictures*, 129.

Chapter Four

1. James Elkins, *On Pictures and the Words That Fail Them* (Cambridge: Cambridge University Press, 1998), 130.

2. Richard Kostelanetz, *Imaged Words and Worded Images* (New York: Outerbridge and Dienstfrey, 1970).

3. For a thoughtful introduction, see Johanna Drucker, "The Art of the Written Image," in *The Dual Muse: The Writer as Artist, the Artist as Writer*, Cornelia Homburg, Johanna Drucker, and William Gass (Philadelphia: John Benjamins, 1997), 83–117.

4. Useful surveys include Liz Kotz, *Words to Be Looked At: Language in 1960s Art* (Cambridge: MIT Press, 2007); Simon Morley, *Writing on the Wall: Word and Image in Modern Art* (Berkeley: University of California Press, 2003); and Aimee Selby, *Art and Text* (London: Black Dog, 2009).

5. Edward Ruscha et al., *Edward Ruscha: Catalogue Raisonné of the Paintings*, five vols. (New York: Gagosian Gallery, 2003–2011); Siri Engberg and Clive Phillpot, *Edward Ruscha: Editions 1959–1999: Catalogue Raisonné*, two vols. (Minneapolis: Walker Art Center, 1999); Dave Hickey, Peter Plagens, and Anne Livet, *The Works of Edward Ruscha* (New York: Hudson Hills Press, San Francisco Museum of Modern Art, 1982); Margit Rowell and Cornelia Butler, *Cotton Puffs, Q-Tips, Smoke and Mirrors: The Drawings of Ed Ruscha* (New York: Whitney Museum of American Art, 2004); *Edward Ruscha: Powders, Pressures and Other Drawings* (San Francisco: John Berggruen Gallery, 2000); Alexandra Schwartz, ed., *Leave Any Information at the Signal: Writings, Interviews, Bits, Pages* (Cambridge: MIT Press, 2002); Eleanor Antin, "Reading Ruscha," *Art in America* 61, no. 6 (1973): 64–71; and Lisa Pasquariello, "Ed Ruscha and the Language That He Used," *October* 111 (2005): 81–106.

6. Robert Morgan, *Art Into Ideas: Essays on Conceptual Art* (Cambridge: Cambridge University Press, 1996), 191.

7. Donald Kuspit, "Signs in Suspense: Ed Ruscha's Liquidation of Meaning," *Arts Magazine* 65, no. 8 (1991), 54.

8. Patricia Failing, "Ed Ruscha, Young Artist: Dead Serious about Being Nonsensical," *Art News* 81, no. 4 (1982), 77.

9. Failing, "Ed Ruscha, Young Artist," 78.

10. Rowell and Butler, *Cotton Puffs*, 18.

11. David Bourdon, "A Heap of Words about Ed Ruscha," *Art International* 25, no. 9 (1971): 25–38.

12. Kuspit, "Signs in Suspense," 56.

13. Ralph Rugoff, "The Last Word," *Art News* 88, no. 10 (1989), 123.

14. Kuspit, "Signs in Suspense," 54.

15. Kuspit, "Signs in Suspense," 54.

16. Engberg and Phillpot, vol. 2, 14.

17. Simon Morley, *Writing on the Wall*, 135.

18. Edward Ruscha, lecture at the Getty Center in Los Angeles, July 17, 1988; quoted in Engberg and Phillpot, vol. 2, 14.

19. Susan Ryan, *Robert Indiana: Figures of Speech* (New Haven: Yale University Press, 2000), 112.

20. Lucy Lippard, *Pop Art* (London: Thames and Hudson, 1966; second edition, 1988), 122.

21. Kostelanetz, *Imaged Words and Worded Images*, i.

22. Kostelanetz, *Imaged Words and Worded Images*, ii.

23. Ryan, *Robert Indiana*, 5.

24. Ryan, *Robert Indiana*, 182.

25. Interview with Robert Indiana in *Vogue* (March 1, 1965) quoted in Lippard, *Pop Art*, 86.

26. Susan Ryan, 263.

27. G. R. Swenson, "The Horizons of Robert Indiana," in *Pop Art: A Critical Anthology*, ed. Steven

Madoff (Berkeley: University of California Press, 1997), 320.

28. John Waters, *Deborah Kass: Feel Good Paintings for Feel Bad Times* (New York: Paul Kasmin Gallery, 2007); Robert Storr, *Deborah Kass: More! Feel Good Paintings for Feel Bad Times* (New York: Paul Kasmin Gallery, 2010); and Eric Shiner, Robert Storr, Griselda Pollack, Lisa Liebmann and Brooks Adams, *Deborah Kass: Before and Happily Ever After* (New York: Skira/Rizzoli, 2012).

29. Constance Zaytoun, "Enough Already! It's Deborah Kass's Turn to Take the Stage," *TDR: The Drama Review* 55, no. 3 (2011): 110–123.

30. Zaytoun, "Enough Already!" 120.

31. Rowell and Butler, *Cotton Puffs*, 16.

32. Morley, *Writing on the Wall*, 135.

33. Armando Petrucci, *Public Lettering* (Chicago: University of Chicago Press, 1993); Gary Garrels, Jim Lewis, Sandra Phillips, Christopher Phillips, Abigail Solomon-Godeau, Robert Riley, and John Weber *Public Information: Desire, Disaster, Document* (San Francisco: San Francisco Museum of Modern Art, 1994).

34. Quoted in Ryan, *Robert Indiana*, 116.

35. The literature in this area is vast; important sources include Jeremy Adler and Ulrich Ernst, *Text als Figure: Visuelle Poesie von der Antike bis zur Moderne* (Wolfenbüttel: Herzon August Bibliothek, 1987); Charles Boultenhouse, "Poems in the Shapes of Things," *Art News Annual* 28 (1959): 64–83; Berjouhi Bowler, *The Word as Image* (London: Studio Vista, 1970); Elizabeth Cook, "Figured Poetry," *Journal of the Warburg and Courtauld Institutes* 42 (1979): 1–15; Charles Doria, "Visual Writing Forms in Antiquity: The *Versus Intexti*," *West Coast Poetry Review* 19 (1979): 63-92; Ulrich Ernst, *Carmen Figuratem: Geschichte des Figurengedichts von den antiken Ursprüngen bis zum Ausgang des Mittelaters* (Cologne: Böhlau, 1991); Ulrich Ernst, "The Figured Poem: Towards a Definition of Genre," *Visible Language* 20, no. 1 (1986): 8–27; Dick Higgins, *Pattern Poetry: Guide to an Unknown Literature* (Albany: State University of New York, 1986); Milton Klonsky, ed., *Speaking Pictures: A Gallery of Pictorial Poetry from the Sixteenth Century to the Present* (New York: Harmony Books, 1975); Robert Massin, *Letter and Image* (New York: Van Nostrand Reinhold, 1970); and Nicole Mosher, *Le Text Visualisé: Le Calligramme de l'époque Alexandrine à l'époque Cubiste* (New York: Peter Lang, 1990).

36. William Levitan, "Dancing at the End of the Rope: Optatian Porfyry and the Field of Roman Verse," *Transactions of the American Philological Association* 115 (1985): 245–269.

37. See Higgins, *Pattern Poetry*, 230–33 for a useful glossary.

38. Higgins, *Pattern Poetry*, 3.

39. Nick Kanas, *Star Maps: History, Artistry, and Cartography* (Chichester: Praxis, 2009), 108.

40. Patrick McGurk, "Carolingian Astrological Manuscripts," in *Charles the Bald: Court and Kingdom*, ed. Margaret Gibson and Janet Nelson (Oxford: British Archaeological Reports, 1981), 317–332.

41. Janet Backhouse, *The Illuminated Manuscript* (Oxford: Phaidon, 1979), 14; Nicolas Barker, *Treasures of the British Library* (New York: Harry N. Abrams, 1989), 51; André Grabar and Carl Nordenfalk, *Early Medieval Painting* (New York: Skira, 1957), 91–92; John Murdoch, *Album of Science: Antiquity and the Middle Ages* (New York: Charles Scribner's Sons, 1984), 250; Peter Whitfield, *The Mapping of the Heavens* (London: British Library, 1995), 35.

42. For information of the iconography of the centaur in classical and medieval art, see Jacqueline Leclerq-Marx, "Le Centaure dans l'art préroman et roman: Sources d'inspiration et modes de transmission," *Les Cahiers de Saint-Michel de Cuxa* 37 (2006): 33–42.

43. Cook, "Figured Poetry," 8.

44. Dick Higgins, *George Herbert's Pattern Poems: In Their Tradition* (West Glover, VT: Unpublished Editions, 1977).

45. Boultenhouse, "Poems in the Shapes of Things," figure 77.

46. Boultenhouse, "Poems in the Shapes of Things," 83.

47. Judi Freeman, *The Dada and Surrealist Word-Image* (Cambridge: MIT Press, 1989).

48. Francis Steegmuller, *Apollinaire: Poet Among the Painters* (New York: Penguin, 1986) and Willard Bohn, *Apollinaire: Visual Poetry and Art Criticism* (London: Associated University Presses, 1993).

49. Guillaume Apollinaire, *Oeuvres Poétiques* (Paris: Bibliothèque de la Pléide, 1965), 167–314.

50. Freeman, *The Dada and Surrealist Word-Image*, 18.

51. Michael Webster, *Reading Visual Poetry After Futurism: Marinetti, Apollinaire, Schwitters, Cummings* (New York: Peter Lang, 1995), 51.

52. Willard Bohn, *The Aesthetics of Visual Poetry 1914–1928* (Cambridge: Cambridge University Press, 1986), 49.

53. Johanna Drucker, *The Visible Word: Experimental Typography and Modern Art, 1909–1923* (Chicago: University of Chicago Press, 1994), 153–54.

54. Dick Higgins, "The Strategy of Visual Poetry: Three Aspects," in *Visual Literature Criticism, A New Collection*, ed. Richard Kostelanetz (Carbondale: Southern Illinois University Press, 1979), 41–50 and Stephen Galiani, "Words as Art: A New Perspective on Shaped Poetry" (MA thesis, Dominican University of California, 2009). See also the special issue "TextImage" of *ZYZZYVA* 25, no. 1 (2009).

55. Mary Ellen Solt, ed., *Concrete Poetry: A World View* (Bloomington: Indiana University Press, 1968); Johanna Drucker, *Figuring the Word: Essays on*

Books, Writing, and Visual Poetry (New York: Granary Books, 1998), esp. "Experimental/Visual/Concrete," 110–36; and Emmett Williams, ed., *An Anthology of Concrete Poetry* (New York: Something Else Press, 1967).

56. Quoted in Wendy Steiner, "*Res Poetica*: The Problematics of the Concrete Program," *New Literary History* 12, no. 3 (1981), 532.

57. Steiner, "*Res Poetica*," 542.

58. See Mary Ellen Solt, ed., *Concrete Poetry* and Emmett Williams, ed., *An Anthology of Concrete Poetry* for many further examples.

59. The literature in this area is vast. Useful introductory sources include Hugues Demeude, *The Animated Alphabet* (London: Thames and Hudson, 1996) and Richard Firmage, *The Alphabet Abecedarium: Some Notes on Letters* (Boston: David A. Godine, 1993).

60. Jonathan Alexander, *The Decorated Letter* (London: Thames and Hudson, 1978), 111; Robert Scheller, *A Survey of Medieval Model Books* (Haarlem: De Erven F. Bohn N.V., 1963), 142–54; Robert Scheller, *Exemplum: Model-Book Drawings and the Practice of Artistic Transmission in the Middle Ages* (ca. 900-ca. 1470) (Amsterdam: Amsterdam University Press, 1995), 276–91; and Albert Elen, "Italian Late-Medieval and Renaissance Drawing-Books from Giovannino de'Grassi to Palma Giovane" (PhD dissertation, Rijksuniversiteit, Leiden, 1995), 165–69.

61. Scheller, *A Survey of Medieval Model Books*, 149 and Scheller, *Exemplum*, 283.

62. Demeude, *The Animated Alphabet*, 32.

63. Alexander, *The Decorated Letter*, 111 and Scheller, *Survey* and *Exemplum*.

64. Scheller, *Exemplum*.

65. See Hugues Demeude for excellent examples and further bibliography.

66. For a very useful survey of Conceptual art, see Tony Godfrey, *Conceptual Art* (London: Phaidon, 1998). See also Alexander Alberro and Blake Stimson, *Conceptual Art: A Critical Anthology* (Cambridge: MIT Press, 1999); and Robert Morgan, *Art into Ideas: Essays on Conceptual Art* (Cambridge: Cambridge University Press, 1996). For an amusingly critical look at language-art, see Jeff Perrone, "'Words': When Art Takes a Rest," *Artforum* 15, no. 10 (1977): 34–37.

67. Benedict Borthwick, Lisa Dent, Cylena Simonds, and Manon Slome, *Articulations: Forms of Language in Contemporary Art* (New York: Whitney Museum of American Art, 1995), 7.

68. Borthwick, *Articulations*, 7.

69. Morgan, *Art Into Ideas*, 16.

70. Stephanie Barron and Michel Draguet, *Magritte and Contemporary Art: The Treachery of Images* (Los Angeles: Los Angeles County Museum of Art, 2006).

71. Morgan, *Art Into Ideas*, 9.

72. Among the vast number of books, articles, and exhibition catalogues devoted to Baldessari also noted below, see especially Jessica Morgan, Leslie Jones, John Baldessari and Marie de Brugerolle, *John Baldessari: Pure Beauty* (Los Angeles: Los Angeles County Museum of Art, 2009); John Baldessari, *John Baldessari: Somewhere Between Almost Right and Not Quite (With Orange)* (New York: Guggenheim Museum Publications, 2004); Adam Budak and Peter Pakesch, eds., *John Baldessari: Life's Balance, Works 1984-2004* (Cologne: Walther König, 2005); and Rainer Fuchs, ed., *John Baldessari: A Different Kind of Order (Arbeiten 1962-1984)* (Cologne: Walther König, 2005).

73. Meg Cranston, "John Baldessari: Many Worthwhile Aspects," in *Baldessari: While Something Is Happening Here, Something Else Is Happening There, Works 1988–1999*, Thomas Weski, Meg Cranston and Diedrich Diederichsen (Hannover: Sprengel Museum, 1999), 24.

74. Colin Gardner, "A Systematic Bewildering," *Artforum* 28, no. 4 (1989): 108.

75. Gardner, "A Systematic Bewildering," 107.

76. John Baldessari, Ann Goldstein, and Christopher Williams, "The Things We Sweep Under the Rug," in *John Baldessari: Life's Balance, Works 1984–2004*, ed. Adam Budak and Peter Pakesch, (Cologne: Walther König, 2005), 88.

77. Baldessari, *John Baldessari*, 51.

78. Manon Slome, "An I for An Eye: Strategies of Language in Contemporary American Art," in *Articulations*, Benedict Borthwick, Lisa Dent, Cylena Simonds and Manon Slome, (New York: Whitney Museum of American Art, 1995), 12.

79. Irving Sandler, *Art of the Postmodern Era: From the Late 1960s to the Early 1990s* (New York: Icon Editions, 1996), 251.

80. Morgan, *Art Into Ideas*, 21.

81. Joseph Kosuth, "Intention(s)," *The Art Bulletin* 73, no. 3 (1966): 407–412 and Joseph Kosuth, *Art after Philosophy and After: Collected Writings, 1966–1990* (Cambridge: MIT Press, 1991).

82. Leslie Jones, "Art Lesson: A Narrative Chronology of John Baldessari's Life and Work," in *John Baldessari: Pure Beauty*, Jessica Morgan, Leslie Jones, John Baldessari and Marie de Brugerolle (Los Angeles: Los Angeles County Museum of Art, 2009), 49. See also Godfrey, *Conceptual Art*, 163; and Rainer Fuchs, "Written Paintings and Photographed Colors," in *John Baldessari: A Different Kind of Order*, ed. Rainer Fuchs, (Cologne: Walther König, 2005), 15–42.

83. John J. Curley, "Fuzzy Language: Joseph Kosuth's Titled *(Art as Idea as Idea)*, 1967," *Yale University Art Gallery Bulletin* (2005): 125.

84. Joseph Kosuth, "Art as Idea as Idea," in *Artwords: Discourse on the 60s and 70s*, Jeanne Siegel (Ann Arbor: UMI Research Press, 1985), 225.

85. Kosuth, "Art as Idea as Idea," 222.

86. Rachel Barnes, Marin Coomer, Carl Freedman, Tony Godfrey, et al., *The Twentieth Century Art Book* (London: Phaidon, 1998), 251.

87. Catherine Gudis, Mary Jane Jacob, and Ann Goldstein, *A Forest of Signs: Art in the Crisis of Representation* (Cambridge: MIT Press, 1989), 133.

88. Borthwick, *Articulations*, 7.

89. Peter Osborne, "Conceptual Art and/as Philosophy," in *Rewriting Conceptual Art*, ed. Michael Newman and Jon Bird (London: Reaktion, 1999), 47–65.

90. Drucker, *Figuring the Word*, 70.

91. Gordon Barass, *The Art of Calligraphy in Modern China* (Berkeley: University of California Press, 2002); Britta Erickson, *Words without Meaning, Meaning Without Words: The Art of Xu Bing* (Washington, DC: Smithsonian Institution, 2001); Jerome Silbergeld and Dora C. Y. Ching, eds., *Persistence/Transformation: Text as Image in the Art of Xu Bing* (Princeton: Princeton University Press, 2006); and Jeffrey Keough, Eugene Yuejin Wang, and Ann Wilson, *Xu Bing: Language Lost* (Boston: Massachusetts College of Art, 1995).

92. Quoted in Erickson, *Words Without Meaning*, 13.

93. Erickson, *Words Without Meaning*, 33.

94. Quoted in Erickson, *Words Without Meaning*, 14.

95. For this much-discussed work, see also Stanley Abe, "No Questions, No Answers: China and a Book from the Sky," *Boundary 2* 25, no. 3 (1998): 169–192; Robert Harrist, "*Book from the Sky* at Princeton: Reflections on Scale, Sense, and Sound," in *Persistence/Transformation*, ed. Jerome Silbergeld and Dora Y.C. Ching (Princeton: Princeton University Press, 2006), 24–45; Stanley Abe, "Reading the Sky," in *Cross-Cultural Readings of Chineseness: Narratives, Images, and Interpretations of the 1990s*, ed. Wen-Hsien Yeh (Berkeley: University of California Institute for East Asian Studies, 2000), 53–79; Patricia Berger, "Pun Intended: A Response to Stanley Abe, 'Reading the Sky,'" in *Cross-Cultural Readings of Chineseness*, ed. Wen-Hsien Yeh (Berkeley: university of California), 80–99; and Katherine Spears, ed., *Tianshu: Passages in the Making of a Book* (London: Quaritch, 2009).

96. Xu Bing, "The Making of Book from the Sky," in *Tianshu: Passages in the Making of a Book*, ed. Katherine Spears (London: Quaritch, 2009), 51.

97. Erickson, *Words Without Meaning*, 38–39.

98. Xu Bing, "The Making of Book from the Sky," in *Tianshu: Passages in the Making of a Book*, ed. Katherine Spears (London: Quaritch, 2009), 51–63.

99. Harrist, "*Book from the Sky*," 32.

100. Harrist, "*Book from the Sky*," 82.

101. Hal Foster, "Xu Bing: A Western Perspective," in *Persistence/Transformation*, ed. Jerome Sibergeld and Dora C.Y. Ching (Princeton: Princeton University Press, 2006), 91.

102. Quoted in Erickson, *Words Without Meaning*, 14.

103. Erickson, *Words Without Meaning*, 55.

104. John Caley, "His Books," in *Tianshu: Passages in the Making of a Book*, ed. Katherine Spears, (London: Quaritch, 2009), 24.

105. For example at the Pacific Asia Museum in Pasadena, California, in 2003.

106. Caley, "His Books," in *Tianshu: Passages in the Making of a Book*, ed. Katherine Spears (London: Quaritch, 2009), 24.

107. Erickson, *Words Without Meaning*, 70.

108. Xu Bing, "An Artist's View," in *Persistence/Transformation*, ed. Jerome Sibergeld and Dora C.Y. Ching (Princeton: Princeton University Press, 2006), 105.

109. Erickson, *Words Without Meaning*, 55.

110. Caley, "His Books," in 17.

111. Haun Saussey, "Xu Bing and Writing," in *Tianshu: Passages in the Making of a Book*, ed. Katherine Spears, (London: Quaritch, 2009), 83.

112. Xu Bing and Britta Erickson, *The Character of Characters: An Animation by Xu Bing* (San Francisco: Asian Art Museum, 2012).

113. Britta Erickson, "Xu Bing's Journey through Language," in *The Character of Characters: An Animation by Xu Bing*, (San Francisco: Asian Art Museum, 2012), 20–21.

Chapter Five

1. Quoted in Ralph Rugoff, "The Last Word," *Art News* 88, no. 10 (1989), 125.

2. Dean Sobel, "Words as Socio-Political Commentary," in *Word as Image: American Art 1960–1990*, ed. Russell Bowman and Dean Sobel (Milwaukee: Milwaukee Art Museum, 1990), 130.

3. Marjorie Welish, "Who's Afraid of Verbs, Nouns, and Adjectives?" *Arts Magazine* 64, no. 8 (1990): 79–84.

4. Scott Rothkopf, ed., *Glenn Ligon America* (New York: Whitney Museum of American Art, 2011) and Glenn Ligon and Hilton Als, *Glenn Ligon: Stranger* (New York: Studio Museum in Harlem, 2001).

5. Okwui Enwezor, "Text, Subtext, Intertext: Painting, Language, and Signifying in the Work of Glenn Ligon," in *Glenn Ligon America*, ed. Scott Rothkopf (New York: Whitney Museum of American Art, 2011), 51–52.

6. Rothkopf, *Glenn Ligon America*, 15.

7. Darby English, *How to See a Work of Art in Total Darkness* (Cambridge: The MIT Press, 2007), 203.

8. English, *How to See a Work of Art in Total Darkness*, 24.

9. English, *How to See a Work of Art in Total Darkness*, 239.
10. English, *How to See a Work of Art in Total Darkness*, 219.
11. English, *How to See a Work of Art in Total Darkness*, 217–19.
12. For an excellent description of Ligon's working methods in these stenciled pieces, see Rothkopf, *Glenn Ligon America*, 26–27.
13. Quoted in Tony Godfrey, *Conceptual Art* (London: Phaidon, 1998), 372.
14. English, *How to See a Work of Art in Total Darkness*, 220.
15. Ligon and Als, *Glenn Ligon: Stranger*, 28.
16. Glenn Ligon interview with Stephen Andrews in *Glenn Ligon: Some Changes*, Wayne Baerwaldt, Richard Crevier and Thelma Golden (Toronto: The Power Plant, 2005), 179–81.
17. English, *How to See a Work of Art in Total Darkness*, 204.
18. Enwezor, "Text, Subtext, Intertext," 54.
19. Baerwaldt and Golden, *Glenn Ligon: Some Changes*, catalogue numbers 80–87.
20. Richard Meyer, "Borrowed Voices: Glenn Ligon and the Face of Language," in *Glenn Ligon: Un/becoming*, Judith Tannenbaum (Philadelphia: Institute of Contemporary Art, 1988), 18–19.
21. See the excellent series of essays in Ann Goldstein, Rosalyn Deutsche, Katherine Dieckmann, et al., *Thinking of You: Barbara Kruger* (Los Angeles: Museum of Contemporary Art, 1999).
22. Irving Sandler, *Art of the Postmodern Era: From the Late 1960s to the Early 1990s* (New York: Icon Editions, 1996), 391.
23. Steven Heller, "Barbara Kruger, Graphic Designer?" in *Thinking of You: Barbara Kruger*, Ann Goldstein, Rosalyn Deutsche, Katherine Dieckmann, et al., (Los Angeles: Museum of Contemporary Art, 1999), 126.
24. Manon Slome, "An I for an Eye: Strategies of Language in Contemporary Art," in *Articulations: Forms of Language in Contemporary Art*, Benedict Borthwick, Lisa Dent, Cylena Simonds, and Manon Slome (New York: Whitney Museum of American Art, 1995), 11.
25. Catherine Gudis, ed., *A Forest of Signs: Art in the Crisis of Representation* (Cambridge: MIT Press, 1989), 59.
26. Michael Bracewell, "Writing the Modern World," in *Gilbert & George: Dirty Words Pictures*, ed. Lisa Corrin (London: Serpentine Gallery, 2002), 8.
27. Lisa Corrin, "Are You Angry or Are You Boring?" in *Gilbert & George: Dirty Words Pictures*, ed. Lisa Corrin (London: Serpentine Gallery, 2002), 31.
28. Martha Rosler, *Decoys and Disruptions: Selected Writings, 1975-2001* (Cambridge: MIT Press, 2004).
29. Media Farzin, "Still Here: An Interview with Martha Rosler and Anton Vidokle," *Art in America*, interviews, Sept. 9, 2009, http://www.artinamericamagazine.com/news-features/interviews/interview-with-martha-rosler-and-anton-vidokle/.
30. Martha Rosler, "Statement," in *Conceptual Art: A Critical Anthology*, ed. Alexander Alberro and Blake Stimson (Cambridge: MIT Press, 1999), 486–87.
31. For a recent and detailed critical overview, see Steve Edwards, *Martha Rosler: The Bowery in Two Inadequate Descriptive Systems* (London: Afterall, 2012). I am deeply indebted to Martha Rosler for her generous assistance with this section of my text.
32. Martha Rosler, "In, Around, and Afterthoughts (on Documentary Photography)," in *The Contest of Meaning: Critical Histories of Photography*, ed. Richard Bolton (Cambridge: MIT Press, 1992), 303–340. See also Benjamin Buchloh, "A Conversation with Martha Rosler," in *Martha Rosler: Positions in the Life World*, ed. Catherine de Zegher (Cambridge: MIT Press, 1998), 23–55; and Benjamin Buchloh, "Allegorical Procedures: Appropriation and Montage in Contemporary Art," *Artforum* 21, no. 1 (1982): 43–56.
33. Rosler originally considered using the term "insufficient" rather than "inadequate." Edwards, *Martha Rosler: The Bowery*, 130, note 58.
34. Gary Garrels, Jim Lewis, Sandra Phillips, Christopher Phillips, Abigail Solomon-Godeau, Robert Riley and John Weber, *Public Information: Desire, Disaster, Document* (San Francisco: San Francisco Museum of Modern Art, 1994), 116.
35. Edwards, *Martha Rosler: The Bowery*, 19.
36. Rosler, "In, Around, and Afterthoughts," 324.
37. Benedict Borthwick, "Referents and Reflection in Conceptual Art," in *Articulations: Forms of Language in Contemporary Art*, Benedict Borthwick, Lisa Dent, Cylena Simonds, and Manon Slome, (New York: Whitney Museum of American Art, 1995), 19.
38. David Hopkins, " 'Out of it': Drunkenness and Ethics in Martha Rosler and Gillian Wearing," *Art History* 26, no. 3 (2003), 341.
39. Godfrey, *Conceptual Art*, 350.
40. Shadi Sheybani, "Women of Allah: A Conversation with Shirin Neshat," *Michigan Quarterly Review* 38, no. 2 (1999), no pages.
41. Shirin Neshat quoted in RoseLee Goldberg, "Shirin Neshat. Material Witness," in *Shirin Neshat*, ed. Giorgio Verzotti (Milan: Edizioni Charta, 2002), 67.
42. Giorgio Verzotti, "Shirin Neshat. That Which Always Speaks in Silence is the Body," in *Shirin Neshat*, ed. Giorgio Verzotti (Milan: Edizioni Charta, 2002), 76.
43. Igor Zabel, "Women in Black," *Art Journal* 60, no. 4 (2001), 18.
44. Giorgio Verzotto, *Shirin Neshat*; and Bill Hor-

rigan, *Shirin Neshat: Two Installations* (Columbus, OH: Wexner Center for the Arts, 2000) and Eleanor Heartney, "Shirin Neshat: Living between Cultures," in *After the Revolution: Women Who Transformed Contemporary Art*, Eleanor Heartney, Helaine Poser, Nancy Princenthal, and Sue Scott (Munich: Prestel, 2007), 230–51.

45. Quoted in Godfrey, *Conceptual Art*, 407.

46. John Stevens, *Sacred Calligraphy of the East* (Boston: Shambhala, 1995), 2.

47. Johanna Drucker, *The Alphabetic Labyrinth: The Letters in History and Imagination* (London: Thames and Hudson, 1995), 22.

48. Nigel Pennick, *The Secret Lore of Runes and Other Ancient Alphabets* (London: Rider, 1991), 5, 43.

49. Stevens, *Sacred Calligraphy of the East*, 2. This story also provides a critical component in Xu Bing's animation, *The Character of Characters* (discussed in chapter 4).

50. Drucker, *The Alphabetic Labyrinth*, 77.

51. For example, see Rosamond McKitterick, "Text and Images in the Carolingian World," in *The Uses of Literacy in Early Medieval Europe*, ed. Rosamond McKitterick (Cambridge: Cambridge University Press, 1990), 297–318.

52. Otto Pächt, *Book Illumination in the Middle Ages* (London: Harvey Miller, 1986), 10.

53. Drucker, *The Alphabetic Labyrinth*, 104.

54. John Lowden, *Illustrated Prophet Books* (University Park: Pennsylvania State University Press, 1988), 7.

55. Christopher De Hamel, *Glossed Books of the Bible and the Origins of the Paris Booktrade* (Woodbridge, Suffolk: D. S. Brewer, 1984). For some notable and creatively shaped examples, see also William Schipper, "Textual Varieties in Manuscript Margins," in *Signs on the Edge: Space, Text and Margin in Medieval Manuscripts*, ed. Sarah Keefer and Rolf Bremmer (Paris: Peeters, 2007), 25–56.

56. Hans Belting and Guglielmo Cavallo, *Die Bibel des Niketas* (Wiesbaden: Dr. Ludwig Reichert, 1979).

57. Ulrich Ernst, *Carmen Figuratum: Geschichte des Figurengedichts von den antiken Ursprüngen bis zum Ausgang des Mittelalters* (Cologne: Böhlau, 1991), esp. "Figurative Texte in byzantinischen Literatur," 738–65.

58. Jeffrey Anderson, *The New York Cruciform Lectionary* (New York: College Art Association, 1992), 75.

59. Anderson, *The New York Cruciform Lectionary*, 13.

60. Rabbi Yitzchak Ginsburgh, *The Alef-Beit: Jewish Thought Revealed through the Hebrew Letters* (Northvale, NJ: Jason Aronson, 1991).

61. Leila Avrin, "Hebrew Micrography: One Thousand Years of Art in Script," *Visible Language* 18, no. 1 (1984), 94.

62. Drucker, *The Alphabetic Labyrinth*, 129. Additional useful sources on the Kabbalah include David Ariel, *Kabbalah: The Mystic Quest in Judaism* (Lanham, MD: Rowman & Littlefield, 2006); Joseph Dan, *Kabbalah: A Very Short Introduction* (Oxford: Oxford University Press, 2006); Leo Schaya, *The Universal Meaning of the Kabbalah* (London: George Allen and Unwin, 1971); and Gershom Scholem, *On the Kabbalah and Its Symbolism* (New York: Schocken, 1965).

63. Aryeh Kaplan, *Sefer Yetzirah = The Book of Creation: In Theory and Practice* (York Beach, ME: Samuel Weiser, 1997).

64. Scholem, *On the Kabbalah and its Symbolism*, 170.

65. Dan, *Kabbalah*, 19.

66. Drucker, *The Alphabetic Labyrinth*, 140.

67. Drucker, *The Alphabetic Labyrinth*, 144.

68. Scholem, *On the Kabbalah and its Symbolism*, 174.

69. Drucker, *The Alphabetic Labyrinth*, 156.

70. Dan, *Kabbalah*, 19.

71. Drucker, *The Alphabetic Labyrinth*, 143.

72. Page Kelley, Daniel Mynatt, and Timothy Crawford, *The Masorah of Biblia Hebraica Stuttgartensia* (Grand Rapids: William B. Eerdmans, 1988), 23.

73. Ilana Tahan, *Hebrew Manuscripts: The Power of Script and Image* (London: British Library, 2007), 11.

74. Leila Avrin, "Micrography as Art," in *La Lettre Hébraïque et sa Signification*, ed. Colette Sirat (Paris: Editions du Centre National de la Recherche Scientifique, 1981), 45.

75. Stanley Ferber, "Micrography: A Jewish Art Form," *The Journal of Jewish Art* 3/4 (1977): 12–24.

76. Avrin, "Hebrew Micrography," 87–95.

77. Joseph Gutmann, "*Masorah Figurata*: The Origins and Development of a Jewish Art Form," in *Estudios Masorecticos*, ed. Emilia Fernandez and Harry Meyer Orlinsky (Madrid: Instituto Arias Montano, 1983), 49–64.

78. Avrin, "Hebrew Micrography," 90.

79. Additional sources including information on Hebrew micrography include David Goldstein, *Hebrew Manuscript Painting* (London: British Library, 1984); Michel Garel, "Un Ornement propre aux manuscrits hébreux médiévaux: La micrographie," *Bulletin de la Bibliothèque Nationale* 3 (1978): 158–66; Joseph Gutmann, *Hebrew Manuscript Painting* (New York: George Braziller, 1978); Thérèse Metzger, "La Masora Ornementale et la Décor Calligraphique dans les Manuscrits Hébreux Espagnols au Moyen Age," in *La Paléographie Hébraïque Médiévale*, ed. Jean Glénnison (Paris: Centre Nationale de la Recherche Scientifique, 1972), 88–113; and Bezalel Narkiss, *Hebrew Illuminated Manuscripts* (New York: Leon Amiel, 1969).

80. Avrin, "Micrography as Art," 51.
81. Ferber, "Micrography," 21.
82. Yasin Hamid Safadi, *Islamic Calligraphy* (Boulder: Shambhala, 1979), 9. See also Anthony Welch, "Epigraphs as Icons: The Role of the Written Word in Islamic Art," in *The Image and the Word: Confrontations in Judaism, Christianity and Islam*, ed. Joseph Gutmann (Missoula: Scholars Press, 1977), 63–74.
83. Annemarie Schimmel, *Calligraphy and Islamic Culture* (New York: New York University Press, 1984), 81.
84. David Roxburgh, *Writing the Word of God: Calligraphy and the Qur'an* (Houston: Museum of Fine Arts, Houston, 2007).
85. Albertine Gaur, *A History of Writing* (New York: Cross River Press, 1992), 165.
86. For useful discussions of Arabic script styles see Safadi, *Islamic Calligraphy* and Gabriel Mandel Khan, *Arabic Script: Styles, Variants, and Calligraphic Adaptations* (New York: Abbeville, 2001).
87. Safadi, *Islamic Calligraphy*, fig. 41.
88. See Berjouhi Bowler, *The Word as Image* (London: Studio Vista, 1970), figures 28–39 for examples.
89. See Annemarie Schimmel, *Mystical Dimensions of Islam* (Chapel Hill: University of North Carolina Press, 1975), esp. "Letter Symbolism in Sufi Literature," 411–25.
90. Schimmel, *Calligraphy and Islamic Culture*, 94.
91. Schimmel, *Calligraphy and Islamic Culture*, 84.
92. Gordon Barass, *The Art of Calligraphy in Modern China* (Berkeley: University of California Press, 2002), 17.
93. Gaur, *A History of Writing*, 80.
94. Michael Knight, "Introduction: Decoding Chinese Calligraphy," in *Out of Character: Decoding Chinese Calligraphy*, ed. Michael Knight and Joseph Chang (San Francisco: Asian Art Museum, 2012), 27.
95. Leon Vandermeersch, "Writing in China," in *A History of Writing*, ed. Anne-Marie Christin (Paris: Flammarion, 2001), 69.
96. Vandermeersch, "Writing in China," 73.
97. Chang Yee, *Chinese Calligraphy: An Introduction to its Aesthetic and Technique* (Cambridge: Harvard University Press, 1973), 207.
98. Yee, *Chinese Calligraphy*, 207.
99. Knight, "Introduction: Decoding Chinese Calligraphy," 46.
100. Stevens, *Sacred Calligraphy of the East*, 133.
101. Vandermeersch, "Writing in China," 78.
102. Vandermeersch, "Writing in China," 78.
103. Vandermeersch, "Writing in China," 82.
104. Steven Fischer, *A History of Writing* (London: Reaktion, 2001), 195.
105. Stevens, *Sacred Calligraphy of the East*, 147.
106. Stevens, *Sacred Calligraphy of the East*, 147.
107. Yiguo Zhang, "Brice Marden and Chinese Calligraphy: An Interview," in *Brushed Voices: Calligraphy in Contemporary China*, Yiguo Zhang (New York: Columbia University, Miriam and Ira D. Wallach Art Gallery, 1998), 125–32.
108. Michael Sullivan, *The Meeting of Eastern and Western Art from the Sixteenth Century to the Present Day* (Greenwich, CT: New York Graphic Society, 1973), 252.
109. Mark Tobey quoted in *Tobey*, Wieland Schmied (New York: Harry N. Abrams, 1966), 13.
110. Arthur Dahl, "The Fragrance of Spirituality," in *Mark Tobey: Art and Belief*, Arthur Dahl, William Seitz, and Joshua Taylor (Oxford: George Ronald, 1984), 40.

Chapter Six

1. Nicolete Gray, *Lettering on Buildings* (London: Architectural Press, 1960).
2. The bibliography on Altdorfer and this painting in particular is copious. Useful sources include Ernst Buchner, *Albrecht Altdorfer: Die Alexanderschlacht* (Stuttgart: Reclam-Verlag GmbH, 1956); Barbara Eshenburg, "Altdorfer's 'Alexanderschlacht' und ihr Verhältnis zum Historienzklus Wilhems IV," *Zeitschrift des Deutschen Vereins für Kunstwissenschaft* 33 (1979): 36–67; Gisela Goldberg, "Albrecht Altdorfer: The Battle of Alexander the Great," in *Altdorfer and Fantastic Realism in German Art*, ed. Jacqueline and Maurice Guilland (New York: Rizzoli, 1985), 245–268; Gisela Goldberg, "Die ursprüngliche Inschriftentafel der *Alexanderschlacht* Albrecht Altdorfers," *Müncher Jahrbuch des bildenden Kunst* 19 (1968): 121–26; Jörg Krichbaum, *Albrecht Altdorfer: Meister der Alexanderschlacht* (Cologne: DuMont Buchverlag, 1978); Cord Meckseper, "Zur Ikonographie von Altdorfer's Alexanderschlacht," *Zeitschrift des Deutschen Vereins für Kunstwissenschaft* 22 (1968): 178–185; and Larry Silver, "Nature and Nature's God: Landscape and Cosmos of Albrecht Altdorfer," *The Art Bulletin* 81, no. 2 (1999): 194–214. I am deeply indebted to Barbara Luttig-Haber for her research assistance on this piece. Barbara Luttig-Haber, "Drama in the Sky: A Titulus in Action," unpublished graduate research paper, Dominican University of California, 2004.
3. James Snyder, *Northern Renaissance Art: Painting, Sculpture, the Graphic Arts from 1350 to 1575* (New York: Harry N. Abrams, 1985), 363.
4. Snyder, *Northern Renaissance Art*, 362.
5. See the reconstruction in Franz Winzinger, *Albrecht Altdorfer: Die Gemälde* (Munich: R. Piper, 1975), 42, fig. 27.
6. The other paintings of battle scenes in this commissioned series include depictions of the an-

cient Roman battles of Cannae, Zama, and Alesia by artists including Melchior Feselen, Ludwig Refinger, Abraham Schöpfer, Jörg Breu and Hans Burgkmair. Several of the other panels also have *tituli*. See Barbara Eshenburg, "Altdorfer's 'Alexanderschlact' und ihr Verhältnis zum Historienzklus Wilhems IV" and Gisela Goldberg, "Albrecht Altdorfer: The Battle of Alexander the Great" for a description of the complete series of sixteen paintings. The choice of subject matter for this series was presumably directed by the contemporary court historian Jean Aventius.

7. For example, see the discussion of *tituli* in early medieval wall painting by Herbert Kessler, "Pictorial Narrative and Church Mission in Sixth-Century Gaul," in *Pictorial Narrative in Antiquity and the Middle Ages*, ed. Herbert Kessler and Marianna Shreve Simpson (Washington, DC: National Gallery of Art, 1985), 75–91. For *tituli* in classical art see Nicholas Horsfall, "Stesichorus at Bovillae?" *Journal of Hellenic Studies* 99 (1979): 26–48.

8. Margaret M. Smith, *The Title-page, Its Early Development, 1460–1510* (London: British Library, 2000).

9. Margery Corbett, "The Architectural Title Page," *Motif* 12 (1964): 49–62; see also Otto Pächt, "Notes and Observations on the Origin of Humanistic Book Decoration," in *Fritz Saxl 1890–1948: A Volume of Memorial Essays*, ed. D. J. Gordon (London: Thomas Nelson and Sons, 1957), 184–94.

10. Lillian Armstrong, "The Pico Master: A Venetian Miniaturist of the Late Quattrocento," in *Studies of Renaissance Miniaturists in Venice*, vol. 1, Lillian Armstrong (London: Pindar Press, 2003), 250.

11. Jonathan Alexander, ed., *The Painted Page: Italian Renaissance Book Illumination 1450–1550* (London: Royal Academy of Art, 1995), catalogue entry by Lillian Armstrong, 162.

12. Lillian Armstrong, *Renaissance Miniature Painters and Classical Imagery: The Master of the Putti and His Venetian Workshop* (London: Harvey Miller, 1981), 37.

13. Alexander, ed., *The Painted Page*, catalogue entry by Lillian Armstrong, 204–205; Jonathan Alexander, *Italian Renaissance Illuminations* (London: Chatto and Windus, 1977), 72–75.

14. Alexander, ed., *The Painted Page*, catalogue entry by Lillian Armstrong, 204.

15. This inscription reads VLMER ARISTOTILEM PETRVS PRODVX(R)AT ORBIS—"Peter Ugelheimer has brought [this] Aristotle forth to the world." Alexander, ed., *The Painted Page*, catalogue entry by Lillian Armstrong, 205.

16. Henry Yates Thompson, "The Most Magnificent Book in the World?" *Burlington Magazine* 4 (1906): 16–19.

17. See, for example, Alexander, ed., *The Painted Page*, catalogue numbers 96, 97 and 98.

18. Additional sources include Jonathan Alexander, "Notes on Some Veneto-Paduan Illuminated Books of the Renaissance," *Arte Veneta* 23 (1969): 9–20; Lillian Armstrong, "*Opus Petri*: Renaissance Miniatures from Venice and Rome," *Viator* 21 (1990): 385–412; Maurits Smeyers and Jan Van der Stock, eds., *Flemish Illuminated Manuscripts: 1475–1550* (New York: Abrams, 1996); Thomas Kren and Scot McKendrick, eds., *Illuminating the Renaissance: The Triumph of Flemish Manuscript Painting in Europe* (Los Angeles: J. Paul Getty Museum, 2003); and Lillian Armstrong, "The Hand Illumination of Printed Books in Italy 1465–1515," in *The Painted Page*, ed. Alexander, 35–47.

19. Armstrong, *Renaissance Miniature Painters*, 24.

20. Myra Orth, "What Goes Around: Borders and Frames in French Manuscripts," *The Journal of the Walters Art Gallery* 54 (1996): 189–201.

21. Orth, "What Goes Around," 190.

22. Thomas Da Costa Kaufmann and Virginia Roehrig Kaufmann, "The Sanctification of Nature: Observations on the Origins of Trompe l'Oeil in Netherlandish Book Painting of the Fifteenth and Sixteenth Centuries," *The J. Paul Getty Museum Journal* 19 (1991): 43–66. For pilgrim badges—both real and painted—in late medieval prayer books, see Kurt Köster, "Religiöse Medaillen und Wallfahrts-Devotionalien in der flämischen Buchmalerei des 15. und frühen 16. Jahrhunderts," in *Buch und Welt, Festschrift für Gustav Hofmann*, Hans Striedl, Gustav Hofman, and Joachim Wieder (Wiesbaden: O. Harrassowitz, 1965), 459–504, and Kurt Köster, "Kollektionen metallener Wallfahrts-Devotionalien und kleiner Andachtsbilder, eingenäht in spätmitteralterliche Gebetbuch-Handschriften," in *Das Buch und Sein Haus I (Festschrift Gerhard Liebers)*, Rolf Fuhlrott and Bertram Haller (Wiesbaden: Reicher, 1979), 77–130.

23. Such as seen on several folios in a ca. 1470 French Book of Hours (London, British Library MS Add. 25695); Janet Backhouse, *Books of Hours* (London: British Library, 1988), 38; François Avril and N. Reynaud, *Les manuscripts à Peintures en France: 1440–1520* (Paris: Flammarion/Bibliothèque Nationale, 1993), 43–44; Peter Rolfe Monks, "The Rolin Master's Hand in London BL MS Additional 25695," in *Medieval Texts and Images*, ed. Margaret Manion and Bernard Muir (Chur: Harwood Academic, 1991), 57–70.

24. Millard Meiss, *Andrea Mantegna as Illuminator: An Episode in Renaissance Art, Humanism and Diplomacy* (New York: Columbia University Press, 1979), 52–63.

25. The website of the Médiathèque Pierre Amalric in Albi has a magnificent full page and full color display of this manuscript; viewers may page through every folio of the book.

26. Mark Evans, "Italian Manuscript Illumination: 1460–1560," in *Renaissance Painting in Manuscripts: Treasures from the British Library*, ed. Thomas Kren (New York: Hudson Hills Press, 1983), 91.
27. Meiss, *Andrea Mantegna as Illuminator*, 54.
28. Meiss, *Andrea Mantegna as Illuminator*, 54.
29. Meiss, *Andrea Mantegna as Illuminator*, 55–57.
30. Armstrong, *Renaissance Miniature Painters*, 9–18.
31. Sarah Blake McHam, "Erudition on Display: The 'Scientific' Illustrations in Pico della Mirandola's Manuscript of Pliny the Elder's *Natural History*," in *Visualizing Medieval Medicine and Natural History: 1200–1550*, ed. Jean Givens, Karen Reeds, and Alain Touwaide (Aldershot: Ashgate, 2006), 83–114.
32. Lillian Armstrong, "The Pico Master: A Venetian Miniaturist of the Late Quattrocento," in *Studies of Renaissance Miniaturists in Venice*, 233–338.
33. McHam, "Erudition on Display," 83.
34. Lillian Armstrong, "The Illustrations of Pliny's *Historia naturalis*: Manuscripts Before 1430," *Journal of the Warburg and Courtauld Institutes* 46 (1983): 19–39 and Lillian Armstrong, "The Illustration of Pliny's *Historia naturalis* in Venetian Manuscripts and Early Printed Books," in *Manuscripts in the Fifty Years after the Invention of Printing*, ed. J. B. Trapp (London: Warburg Institute, 1983), 97–106.
35. McHam, "Erudition on Display," 86.
36. See Hugues Demeude, *The Animated Alphabet* (London: Thames and Hudson, 1996) for many examples.
37. Demeude, *The Animated Alphabet*, 49.
38. A. M. Hammacher, *Magritte* (New York: Abrams, 1974), 140.
39. Walter Cahn, "Observations on the A of Charlemagne in the Treasure of the Abbey of Conques," *Gesta* 45, no. 2 (2006): 95–107.
40. Cahn, "Observations," 95.
41. Peter Lasko, *Ars Sacra 800–1200* (New Haven: Yale University Press, 1994), 48.
42. Cahn, "Observations," 95.
43. Cahn, "Observations," 95.
44. Susan Ryan, "Eternal Love," in *Love and the American Dream*, Aprile Gallant, Daniel O'Leary, Susan Ryan, and Elizabeth Barry (Portland, ME: Portland Museum of Art, 1999), 76–101.
45. Susan Ryan, *Robert Indiana: Figures of Speech* (New Haven: Yale University Press, 2000), 197.
46. Ryan, *Robert Indiana*, 197. For the complex copyright issues and promulgation of this image, see Ryan, chapter 6, 197–243.
47. Burkhard Riemschneider and Uta Grosenick, eds., *Art at the Turn of the Millennium* (Cologne: Taschen, 1999), 398–401; David Seider, *Artists at Work: Inside the Studios of Today's Most Celebrated Artists* (New York: Rizzoli, 1999), 104–111; Jack Pierson, *Jack Pierson* (Milan: Photology, 2007); and Jack Pierson, *All of a Sudden* (New York: Powerhouse Books, 1995).
48. Richard Marshall and Liz Kotz, *Jack Pierson: Desire Despair* (New York: Rizzoli, 2006), 15.
49. Such as *Deuce Lingo* (1991) and *Scarface* (1991).
50. Pierson quoted in Seider, *Artists at Work*, 104.
51. David Ebony, "Trouble in Paradise," *Art in America* 91, no. 1 (2003): 78.
52. Marshall, *Jack Pierson: Desire Despair*, 10.
53. Ebony, "Trouble in Paradise," 78.
54. Italo Calvino, *Invisible Cities*, trans. William Weaver (New York: Harcourt, 1974), 45–46.
55. Jeffrey Cyphers Wright, "Valeska Soares," *Art Nexus* 77, no. 9 (2010): 112–113.
56. Vik Muniz and Valeska Soares, "Valeska Soares," *BOMB* 74 (2001): 49.
57. Silas Martí, "Valeska Soares," *Frieze* 113 (2008): 3.
58. Martí, "Valeska Soares," 1–2.
59. Muniz and Soares, "Valeska Soares," 55.
60. Germano Celant, "Claes Oldenburg and the Feeling of Things," in *Claes Oldenburg: An Anthology*, Germano Celant, Dieter Koepplin, Marla Prather, and Mark Rosenthal (New York: Guggenheim Museum, 1995), 21.
61. F. Picchi, "Domus 569, April 1977," *Domus* 843 (2001): 154.
62. Germano Celant, *A Bottle of Notes and Some Voyages: Claes Oldenburg and Cossje van Bruggen* (Sunderland: Northern Centre for Contemporary Art, 1988).
63. Claes Oldenburg and Cossje van Bruggen, *Claes Oldenburg and Cossje van Bruggen: Large Scale Projects* (New York: Monacelli Press, 1994), 525.
64. Celant, *A Bottle of Notes and Some Voyages*, 18.
65. Germano Celant, "The Sculptor Versus the Architect," in *Claes Oldenburg: An Anthology*, Germano Celant, Dieter Koepplin, Marla Prather, and Mark Rosenthal (New York: Guggenheim Museum, 1995), 379.
66. Useful sources on Holzer include David Joselit, Joan Simon, and Renata Saleci, *Jenny Holzer* (London: Phaidon, 1998); Nancy Princenthal, "Jenny Holzer: Language Lessons," in *After the Revolution: Women Who Transformed Contemporary Art*, Eleanor Heartney, Helaine Poser, Nancy Princenthal, and Sue Scott (Munich: Prestel, 2007), 144–67; Jenny Holzer, *Jenny Holzer Retro* (New York: Skarstedt Gallery, 2010); Jenny Holzer, David Breslin, Elizabeth A. T. Smith, and Philippe Büttner, *Jenny Holzer* (Ostfildern-Ruit, Germany: Hatje Cantz, 2008); and Söke Dinkla, ed., *Jenny Holzer: Die Macht des Wortes: I Can't Tell You* (Ostfildern-Ruit, Germany: Hatje Cantz, 2006).
67. Jenny Holzer, quoted in Irving Sandler, *Art of the Postmodern Era: From the Late 1960s to the Early 1990s* (Boulder: Westview Press, 1998), 396.

68. Michael Auping, "Reading Holzer or Speaking in Tongues," in *Jenny Holzer: The Venice Installation*, ed. Karen Lee Spaulding (United States Pavilion: The 44th Venice Biennale, 1990), 25.
69. Kiki Smith, "Jenny Holzer," *Interview* 42, no. 3 (2012), 114.
70. Jenny Holzer, quoted in Irving Sandler, *Art of the Postmodern Era*, 398.
71. Princenthal, "Jenny Holzer: Language Lessons," 152–53.
72. Auping, "Reading Holzer or Speaking in Tongues," 26.
73. Princenthal, "Jenny Holzer: Language Lessons," 163.
74. Auping, "Reading Holzer: Language Lessons," 30.
75. Roberta Smith, "Sounding the Alarm in Words and Light," *The New York Times*, March 13, 2009.
76. http://ligoranoreese.net.

Conclusion

1. Ferruccio Rossi-Landi, Raymond Williams, et al., *Contact: Human Communication and its History* (New York: Thames and Hudson, 1981).
2. In addition to the many sources included in the chapters above, see also Claude Gandelman's discussion of the "optic" and "haptic" modes of perception in Claude Gandelman, *Reading Pictures, Viewing Texts* (Bloomington: Indiana State University Press, 1991).
3. Jefferson Hunter, *Image and Word: The Interaction of Twentieth-Century Photographs and Texts* (Cambridge: Harvard University Press, 1987).
4. Edward Tufte, *Envisioning Information* (Cheshire, CT: Graphics Press, 1990), 49–50.

Bibliography

Abadie, Daniel, ed. *Magritte*. New York: Art Publishers, 2003.

Abe, Stanley. "No Questions, No Answers: China and a Book from the Sky." *Boundary 2* 25, no. 3 (1998): 169–192.

Abe, Stanley. "Reading the Sky." In *Cross-Cultural Readings of Chineseness: Narratives, Images, and Interpretations of the 1990s*, ed. Wen-Hsien Yeh, 53–79. Berkeley: University of California Institute for East Asian Studies, 2000.

Abels, Richard. "What Has Weland to Do with Christ? The Franks Casket and the Acculturation of Christianity in Early Anglo-Saxon England." *Speculum* 84, no. 3 (2009): 549–81.

Adler, Jeremy. "Paul Klee as 'Poet Painter.'" In *Art, Word and Image: Two Thousand Years of Visual/Textual Interaction*, John Dixon Hunt, David Lomas, and Michael Corris, 178–201. London: Reaktion, 2010.

Adler, Jeremy, and Ulrich Ernst. *Text als Figure: Visuelle Poesie von der Antike bis zur Moderne*. Wolfenbüttel: Herzon August Bibliothek, 1987.

Aikema, Bernard, Beverly Brown, and Giovanna Scirè, eds. *Renaissance Venice and the North: Crosscurrents in the Time of Bellini, Dürer and Titian*. New York: Rizzoli, 2004.

Alberro, Alexander, and Blake Stimson, eds. *Conceptual Art: A Critical Anthology*. Cambridge: MIT Press, 1999.

Alexander, Jonathan. *The Decorated Letter*. London: Thames and Hudson, 1978.

Alexander, Jonathan. *Italian Renaissance Illuminations*. London: Chatto and Windus, 1977.

Alexander, Jonathan. *The Master of Mary of Burgundy: A Prayer Book for Engelbert of Nassau*. New York: George Braziller, 1970.

Alexander, Jonathan. "Notes on Some Veneto-Paduan Illuminated Books of the Renaissance." *Arte Veneta* 23 (1969): 9–20.

Alexander, Jonathan. "Scribes as Artists: The Arabesque Initial in Twelfth-Century English Manuscripts." In *Medieval Scribes, Manuscripts and Libraries: Essays Presented to N. R. Ker*, ed. M. B. Parkes and Andrew Watson, 87–116. London: Scolar Press, 1978.

Alexander, Jonathan, ed. *The Painted Page: Italian Renaissance Book Illumination 1450–1550*. London: Royal Academy of Art, 1995.

Alexander, Jonathan, James H. Marrow, and Lucy Freeman Sandler. *The Splendor of the Word: Medieval and Renaissance Illuminated Manuscripts at the New York Public Library*. London: Harvey Miller, 2005.

Anderson, Jeffrey. *The New York Cruciform Lectionary*. New York: College Art Association, 1992.

Andrews, Stephen. "Interview with Glenn Ligon." In *Glenn Ligon: Some Changes*, Wayne Baerwaldt, Richard Crevier, and Thelma Golden, 179–81. Toronto: Power Plant, 2005.

Antin, Eleanor. "Reading Ruscha." *Art in America* 61, no. 6 (1973): 64–71.

Apollinaire, Guillaume. *Oeuvres Poétiques*. Paris: Bibliothèque de la Pléide, 1965.

Ariel, David. *Kabbalah: The Mystic Quest in Judaism*. Lanham, MD: Rowman & Littlefield, 2006.

Armstrong, Lillian. "The Hand Illumination of Printed Books in Italy 1465–1515." In *The Painted Page*, ed. Jonathan Alexander, 35–47. London: Royal Academy of Art, 1995.

Armstrong, Lillian. "The Illustration of Pliny's *Historia naturalis* in Venetian Manuscripts and Early Printed Books." In *Manuscripts in the Fifty Years after the Invention of Printing*, ed. J. B. Trapp, 97–106. London: Warburg Institute, 1983.

Armstrong, Lillian. "The Illustrations of Pliny's *Historia naturalis*: Manuscripts before 1430." *Journal of the Warburg and Courtauld Institutes* 46 (1983): 19–39.

Armstrong, Lillian. "*Opus Petri*: Renaissance Miniatures from Venice and Rome." *Viator* 21 (1990): 385–412.

Armstrong, Lillian. "The Pico Master: A Venetian Miniaturist of the Late Quattrocento." In *Studies of Renaissance Miniaturists in Venice*, vol. 1, 233–338. London: Pindar Press, 2003.

Armstrong, Lillian. *Renaissance Miniature Painters and Classical Imagery: The Master of the Putti and his Venetian Workshop*. London: Harvey Miller, 1981.

Auping, Michael. "Reading Holzer or Speaking in Tongues." In *Jenny Holzer: The Venice Installation*, ed. Karen Lee Spaulding, 25–37. United States Pavilion: The 44th Venice Biennale, 1990.

Avril, François, and N. Reynaud. *Les manuscripts à Peintures en France: 1440–1520*. Paris: Flammarion/Bibliothèque Nationale, 1993.

Avrin, Leila. "Hebrew Micrography: One Thousand Years of Art in Script." *Visible Language* 18, no. 1 (1984): 87–95.

Avrin, Leila. "Micrography as Art." In *La Lettre Hébraïque et sa Signification*, ed. Colette Sirat, 43–80. Paris: Editions du Centre National de la Recherche Scientifique, 1981.

Backhouse, Janet. *Books of Hours*. London: British Library, 1988.

Backhouse, Janet. *The Illuminated Manuscript*. Oxford: Phaidon, 1979.

Backhouse, Janet. *The Lindisfarne Gospels*. Ithaca: Cornell University Press, 1981.

Baerwaldt, Wayne, Richard Crevier, and Thelma Golden. *Glenn Ligon: Some Changes*. Toronto: Power Plant, 2005.

Bagnoli, Martina, ed. *Prayers in Code: Books of Hours from Renaissance France*. Baltimore: Walters Art Museum, 2009.

Baker, Patricia. *Islamic Textiles*. London: British Museum Press, 1995.

Baldessari, John. *John Baldessari: Somewhere Between Almost Right and Not Quite (With Orange)*. New York: Guggenheim Museum Publications, 2004.

Baldessari, John, Ann Goldstein, and Christopher Williams. "The Things We Sweep Under the Rug." In *John Baldessari: Life's Balance, Works 1984–2004*, ed. Adam Budak and Peter Pakesch, 80–98. Cologne: Walther König, 2005.

Barasch, Moshe. "Some Oriental Pseudo-Inscriptions in Renaissance Art." *Visible Language* 23 (1989): 170–87.

Barass, Gordon. *The Art of Calligraphy in Modern China*. Berkeley: University of California Press, 2002.

Barker, Nicolas. *Treasures of the British Library*. New York: Harry N. Abrams, 1989.

Barnes, Rachel, Martin Coomer, Carl Freedman, et al. *The Twentieth Century Art Book*. London: Phaidon, 1996.

Barron, Stephanie, and Michel Draguet. *Magritte and Contemporary Art: The Treachery of Images*. Los Angeles: Los Angeles County Museum of Art, 2006.

Baudrillard, Jean. "The *Trompe l'Oeil*." In *Calligram: Essays in New Art History from France*, ed. Norman Bryson, 53–62. Cambridge: Cambridge University Press, 1988.

Bäuml, Franz. "Varieties and Consequences of Medieval Literacy and Illiteracy." *Speculum* 55 (1989): 237–65.

Beal, Graham. "The Beginner's Mind." In *Wiley Territory*, Graham Beal and John Perreault, 15–47. Minneapolis: Walker Art Center, 1979.

Beal, Graham, and John Perreault. *Wiley Territory*. Minneapolis: Walker Art Center, 1979.

Belting, Hans, and Guglielmo Cavallo. *Die Bibel des Niketas*. Wiesbaden: Dr. Ludwig Reichert, 1979.

Berger, Patrica. "Pun Intended: A Response to Stanley Abe, 'Reading the Sky.'" In *Cross-Cultural Readings of Chineseness: Narratives, Images, and Interpretations of the 1990s*, ed. Wen-Hsien Yeh, 80–99. Berkeley: University of California Institute for East Asian Studies, 2000.

Berggruen, John. *Edward Ruscha: Powders, Pressures and Other Drawings*. San Francisco: John Berggruen Gallery, 2000.

Bernstein, David. *The Mystery of the Bayeux Tapestry*. Chicago: University of Chicago Press, 1986.

Bernstein, Roberta. *Jasper Johns' Paintings and Sculptures 1954–1974: "The Changing Focus of the Eye."* Ann Arbor: UMI Research Press, 1985.

Bernstein, Roberta. "René Magritte and Jasper Johns: Making Thoughts Visible." In *Magritte and Contemporary Art: The Treachery of Images*, Stephanie Barron and Michel Draguet, 109–23. Los Angeles: Los Angeles County Museum of Art, 2006.

Bierman, Irene. "Art and Politics: The Impact of Fatimid Uses of 'Tiraz' Fabrics." Ph.D. dissertation, University of Chicago, 1980.

Bing, Xu. "An Artist's View." In *Persistence/Transformation: Text as Image in the Art of Xu Bing*, ed. Jerome Silbergeld and Dora C. Y. Ching, 99–111. Princeton: Princeton University Press, 2006.

Bing, Xu. "The Making of Book From the Sky." In *Tianshu: Passages in the Making of a Book*, ed. Katherine Spears, 51–63. London: Quaritch, 2009.

Bing, Xu, and Britta Erickson. *The Character of Characters: An Animation by Xu Bing*. San Francisco: Asian Art Museum, 2012.

Bischoff, Ulrich. *Max Ernst: 1891–1976: Beyond Painting*. Köln: Taschen, 2003.

Blanton, Virginia, and Helene Scheck, eds. *Intertexts: Studies in Anglo-Saxon Culture Presented to Paul E. Szarmach*. Tempe: Arizona Center for Medieval and Renaissance Studies, 2008.

Bohn, Willard. *The Aesthetics of Visual Poetry 1914–1928*. Cambridge: Cambridge University Press, 1986.

Bohn, Willard. *Apollinaire: Visual Poetry and Art Criticism*. London: Associated University Presses, 1993.

Bohn, Willard. "Celebrating with Carlo Carrà: 'Festa Patriottica.'" *Zeitschrift für Kunstgeschichte* 57, no. 4 (1994): 670–81.

Bohn, Willard. "Circular Poem-Paintings by Apollinaire and Carrà." *Comparative Literature* 31, no. 3 (1979): 246–71.

Boime, Albert. "Roy Lichtenstein and the Comic Strip." *Art Journal* 28, no. 2 (1968): 155–59.

Bolger, Doreen. "Cards and Letters from His Friends: Mr. Huling's Rack Picture by William Michael Harnett." *The American Art Journal* 22, no. 2 (1990): 5–32.

Bolger, Doreen, Marc Simpson, and John Wilmerding, eds. *William M. Harnett*. New York: Metropolitan Museum of Art, 1992.

Bolton, Richard, ed. *The Contest of Meaning: Critical Histories of Photography*. Cambridge: MIT Press, 1992.

Borsi, Franco, and Stefano Borsi. *Paolo Uccello*. New York: Harry N. Abrams, 1994.

Borsook, Eve, and Johannes Offerhaus, *Francesco Sassetti and Ghirlandaio at Santa Trinità, Florence: History and Legend in a Renaissance Chapel*. Doornspijk: Davaco, 1981.

Borthwick, Benedict. "Referents and Reflection in Conceptual Art." In *Articulations: Forms of Language in Contemporary Art*, Benedict Borthwick, Lisa Dent, Cylena Simonds, and Manon Slome, 15–19. New York: Whitney Museum of American Art, 1995.

Borthwick, Benedict, Lisa Dent, Cylena Simonds, and Manon Slome. *Articulations: Forms of Language in Contemporary Art*. New York: Whitney Museum of American Art, 1995.

Boston, Karen. "The Power of Inscriptions and the Trouble with Texts." In *Icon and Word: The Power of Images in Byzantium; Studies Presented to Robin Cormack*, ed. Antony Eastmond and Liz James, 35–51. Aldershot: Ashgate, 2003.

Boultenhouse, Charles. "Poems in the Shapes of Things." *Art News Annual* 28 (1959): 64–83.

Bourdon, David. "A Heap of Words about Ed Ruscha." *Art International* 25, no. 9 (1971): 25–38.

Bower, Bruce. "Brother Stroop's Enduring Effect." *Science News* 141 (1992): 312–16.

Bowler, Berjouhi. *The Word as Image*. London: Studio Vista, 1970.

Bowman, Russell. "Words and Images: A Persistent Paradox." *The Art Journal* 45, no. 4 (1985): 335–43.

Bowman, Russell, and Dean Sobel, eds. *Word as Image: American Art 1960–1990*. Milwaukee: Milwaukee Art Museum, 1990.

Boyajian, Ani, and Mark Rutkoski, eds. *Stuart Davis: A Catalogue Raisonné*, 3 vols. New Haven: Yale University Press, 2007.

Bracewell, Michael. "Writing the Modern World." In *Gilbert & George: Dirty Words Pictures*, ed. Lisa Corrin, 8–18. London: Serpentine Gallery, 2002.

Breuer, Karin. *Japanesque: The Japanese Print in the Era of Impressionism*. San Francisco: Fine Arts Museums of San Francisco, 2010.

Brilliant, Richard. "The Bayeux Tapestry: A Stripped Narrative for Their Eyes and Ears." In *The Study of the Bayeux Tapestry*, ed. Richard Gameson, 111–37. Woodbridge, Suffolk: Boydell Press, 1997.

Brookner, Anita. *Jacques-Louis David*. New York: Harper & Row, 1980.

Brown, Michelle. *The Lindisfarne Gospels: Society, Spirituality and the Scribe*. Toronto: University of Toronto Press, 2003.

Brown, Michelle. *Understanding Illuminated Manuscripts: A Guide to Technical Terms*. Malibu: J. Paul Getty Museum in association with the British Library Board, 1994.

Brown, Peter. "Images as a Substitute for Writing." In *East and West: Modes of Communication: Proceedings of the First Plenary Conference at Merida*, ed. Evangelos Chrysos and Ian Wood, 15–34. Leiden: Brill, 1999.

Brown, Shirley Ann. *The Bayeux Tapestry: History and Bibliography*. Woodbridge, Suffolk: Boydell Press, 1988.

Bryson, Norman, ed. *Calligram: Essays in New Art History from France*. Cambridge: Cambridge University Press, 1988.

Buchloh, Benjamin. "Allegorical Procedures: Appropriation and Montage in Contemporary Art." *Artforum* 21, no. 1 (1982): 43–56.

Buchloh, Benjamin. "A Conversation with Martha Rosler." In *Martha Rosler: Positions in the Life World*, ed. Catherine de Zegher, 23–55. Cambridge: MIT Press, 1998.

Buchner, Ernst. *Albrecht Altdorfer: Die Alexanderschlacht*. Stuttgart: Reclam-Verlag GmbH, 1956.

Budak, Adam, and Peter Pakesch, eds. *John Baldessari: Life's Balance, Works 1984–2004.* Cologne: Walther König, 2005.
Burlin, Robert. "The Ruthwell Cross, *The Dream of the Rood* and the Vita Contemplativa." *Studies in Philology* 65, no. 1 (1968): 23–43.
Buschhausen, Helmut. "The Klosterneuburg Altar of Nicholas of Verdun: Art, Theology and Politics." *The Journal of the Warburg and Courtauld Institutes* 37 (1974): 1–32.
Caferro, William. *John Hawkwood: An English Mercenary in Fourteenth Century Italy.* Baltimore: Johns Hopkins University Press, 2006.
Cahn, Walter. "Observations on the A of Charlemagne in the Treasure of the Abbey of Conques." *Gesta* 45, no. 2 (2006): 95–107.
Cahn, Walter. "Romanesque Sculpture and the Spectator." In *The Romanesque Frieze and its Spectator. The Lincoln Symposium Papers*, ed. Deborah Kahn, 45–60. London: Harvey Miller, 1992.
Calabrese, Omar, and Betty Gigante. "La Signature du Peintre." *La Part de l'Oeil*, no. 5 (1989): 27–44.
Caley, John. "His Books." In *Tianshu: Passages in the Making of a Book*, ed. Katherine Spears, 1–37. London: Quaritch, 2009.
Calkins, Robert. "Liturgical Sequence and Decorative Crescendo in the Drogo Sacaramentary." *Gesta* 25, no. 1 (1986): 17- 23.
Calvino, Italo. *Invisible Cities.* Trans. William Weaver. New York: Harcourt, 1974.
Camille, Michael. "Seeing and Reading: Some Visual Implications of Medieval Literacy and Illiteracy." *Art History* 8, no. 1 (1985): 1–49.
Campbell, Stephen. *Cosmè Tura of Ferrara: Style, Politics and the Renaissance City, 1450–1495.* New Haven: Yale University Press, 1997.
Campbell, Stephen. "*Pictura* and *Scriptura*: Cosmè Tura and Style as Courtly Performance." *Art History* 19, no. 2 (1996): 267–95.
Campbell, Stephen, and Alan Chong, eds. *Cosmè Tura: Painting and Design in Renaissance Ferrara.* Boston: Isabella Stewart Gardner Museum, 2002.
Carrier, David. *The Aesthetics of Comics.* University Park: Pennsylvania State University Press, 2000.
Cassidy, Brendan. "The Later life of the Ruthwell Cross: From the Seventeenth Century to the Present." In *The Ruthwell Cross*, ed. Brendan Cassidy, 3–34. Princeton: Princeton University Press, 1992.
Cassidy, Brendan, ed. *The Ruthwell Cross.* Princeton: Princeton University Press, 1992.
Celant, Germano. *A Bottle of Notes and Some Voyages: Claes Oldenburg and Cossje van Bruggen.* Sunderland: Northern Centre for Contemporary Art, 1988.
Celant, Germano. "Claes Oldenburg and the Feeling of Things." In *Claes Oldenburg: An Anthology*, Germano Celant, Dieter Koepplin, Marla Prather and Mark Rosenthal, 13–31. New York: Guggenheim Museum, 1995.
Celant, Germano. "The Sculptor Versus the Architect." In *Claes Oldenburg: An Anthology*, Germano Celant, Dieter Koepplin, Marla Prather and Mark Rosenthal, 365–80. New York: Guggenheim Museum, 1995.
Celant, Germano, Dieter Koepplin, Marla Prather, and Mark Rosenthal. *Claes Oldenburg: An Anthology.* New York: Guggenheim Museum, 1995.
Chastel, André. "L'Art de la Signature." *Revue de l'Art* 26 (1974): 8–56.
Chazelle, Celia. "Pictures, Books, and the Illiterate: Pope Gregory I's Letters to Serenus of Marseilles." *Word and Image* 6, no. 2 (1990): 138–53.
Chirico, Robert. "Language and Imagery in Late Nineteenth Century *Trompe l'oeil*." *Arts Magazine* 40, no. 7 (1985): 110–44.
Christin, Anne-Marie, ed. *A History of Writing.* Paris: Flammarion, 2001.
Chrysos, Evangelos, and Ian Wood Brown, eds. *East and West: Modes of Communication: Proceedings of the First Plenary Conference at Merida.* Leiden: Brill, 1999.
Clanchy, Michael. *From Memory to Written Record: England 1066–1307.* London: Edward Arnold, 1979.
Clark, T. J. "Painting in the Year Two." *Representations* 47 (1994): 13–63.
Cohen, Beth. "The Literate Potter: A Tradition of Incised Signatures on Attic Vases." *Metropolitan Museum Journal* 26 (1991): 49–95.
Collins, Bradford. "Modern Romance: Lichtenstein's Comic Book Paintings." *American Art* 17, no. 2 (2003): 60–85.
Collins, Roger, and Peter Godman, eds. *Charlemagne's Heir: New Perspectives on the Reign of Louis the Pious.* Oxford: Clarendon Press, 1990.
Cook, Elizabeth. "Figured Poetry." *Journal of the Warburg and Courtauld Institutes* 42 (1979): 1–15.
Cook, R. M. *Greek Painted Pottery.* London: Methuen, 1960.
Corbett, Margery. "The Architectural Title Page." *Motif* 12 (1964): 49–62.
Corrin, Lisa. "Are You Angry or Are You Boring?"

In *Gilbert & George: Dirty Words Pictures*, ed. Lisa Corrin, 20–33. London: Serpentine Gallery, 2002.

Corrin, Lisa, ed. *Gilbert & George: Dirty Words Pictures*. London: Serpentine Gallery, 2002.

Cottington, David. "What the Papers Say: Politics and Ideology in Picasso's Collages of 1912." *Art Journal* 47, no. 4 (1988): 350–59.

Covi, Dario. *The Inscription in Fifteenth Century Florentine Painting*. New York: Garland, 1986.

Covi, Dario. "Lettering in Fifteenth Century Florentine Painting." *The Art Bulletin* 45, 1 (1963): 1–17.

Covi, Dario. "Lettering in the Inscriptions of Fifteenth Century Florentine Paintings." *Renaissance News* 7, no. 2 (1954): 46–60.

Cranston, Meg. "John Baldessari: Many Worthwhile Aspects." In *Baldessari: While Something is Happening Here, Something Else is Happening There, Works 1988–1999*, Thomas Weski, Meg Cranston, and Diedrich Diederichsen, 13–34. Hannover: Sprengel Museum, 1999.

Crichton, Michael. *Jasper Johns*. New York: Harry N. Abrams, 1994.

Curley, John J. "Fuzzy Language: Joseph Kosuth's Titled *(Art as Idea as Idea)*, 1967." *Yale University Art Gallery Bulletin* (2005): 125–29.

Cuttler, Charles. "Holbein's Inscriptions." *The Sixteenth Century Journal* 24, no. 2 (1993): 369–82.

Dahl, Arthur. "The Fragrance of Spirituality." In *Mark Tobey: Art and Belief*, Arthur Dahl, William Seitz, and Joshua Taylor, 32–40. Oxford: George Ronald, 1984.

Dahl, Arthur, William Seitz, and Joshua Taylor. *Mark Tobey: Art and Belief*. Oxford: George Ronald, 1984.

Dan, Joseph. *Kabbalah: A Very Short Introduction*. Oxford: Oxford University Press, 2006.

D'Ancona, Paolo. *Paolo Uccello*. New York: McGraw-Hill, 1960.

Davidson, C. Treat. "Sources for the Initials of the Cîteaux Moralia in Job." *Studies in Cistercian Art and Architecture* 3 (Cistercian Studies Series, no. 89): 46–68. Kalamazoo, MI: Cistercian, 1987.

De Hamel, Christopher. *Glossed Books of the Bible and the Origins of the Paris Booktrade*. Woodbridge, Suffolk: D. S. Brewer, 1984.

Demeude, Hugues. *The Animated Alphabet*. London: Thames and Hudson, 1996.

De Zegher, Catherine, ed. *Martha Rosler: Positions in the Life World*. Cambridge: Massachusetts Institute of Technology, 1998.

Diebold, William. *Word and Image: An Introduction to Early Medieval Art*. Boulder: Westview Press, 2000.

Dinkla, Söke, ed. *Jenny Holzer: Die Macht des Wortes: I Can't Tell You*. Ostfildern-Ruit, Germany: Hatje Cantz, 2006.

Doria, Charles. "Visual Writing Forms in Antiquity: The *Versus Intexti*." *West Coast Poetry Review* 19 (1979): 63–92.

Drucker, Johanna. *The Alphabetic Labyrinth: The Letters in History and Imagination*. London: Thames and Hudson, 1995.

Drucker, Johanna. "The Art of the Written Image." In *The Dual Muse: The Writer as Artist, the Artist as Writer*, Cornelia Homburg, Johanna Drucker, and William Gass, 83–117. Philadelphia: John Benjamins, 1997.

Drucker, Johanna. *Figuring the Word: Essays on Books, Writing, and Visual Poetry*. New York: Granary, 1998.

Drucker, Johanna. *The Visible Word: Experimental Typography and Modern Art, 1909–1923*. Chicago: University of Chicago Press, 1994.

Drucker, Johanna. "Visuality and Artifice among the Proto-Modern Americans." *The Art Bulletin* 74, no. 1 (1992): 37–50.

Dubnick, Randa. "Visible Poetry: Metaphor and Metonymy in the Paintings of René Magritte." *Contemporary Literature* 21, no. 3 (1980): 407–19.

Duggan, Lawrence. "Was Art Really the 'Book of the Illiterate?'" *Word and Image* 5, no. 3 (1989): 227–51.

Eastmond, Antony, and Liz James, eds. *Icon and Word: The Power of Images in Byzantium; Studies Presented to Robin Cormack*. Aldershot: Ashgate, 2003.

Ebony, David. "Trouble in Paradise." *Art in America* 91, no. 1 (2003): 74–79.

Edwards, Steve. *Martha Rosler: The Bowery in Two Inadequate Descriptive Systems*. London: Afterall, 2012.

Egbert, Donald Drew. *The Tickhill Psalter and Related Manuscripts: A School of Manuscript Illumination in England During the Early Fourteenth Century*. New York: New York Public Library, 1940.

Elen, Albert. Italian "Late-Medieval and Renaissance Drawing-Books from Giovannino de'Grassi to Palma Giovane." Ph.D. dissertation, Rijksuniversiteit, Leiden, 1995.

Elkins, James. "Art History and Images That Are Not Art." *The Art Bulletin* 77, no. 4 (1995): 553–71.

Elkins, James. *On Pictures and the Words That Fail Them*. Cambridge: Cambridge University Press, 1998.

Elkins, James. *Why Are Our Pictures Puzzles? On the Modern Origins of Pictorial Complexity*. London: Routledge, 1999.

Elliott, Ralph. *Runes: An Introduction*. New York: Philosophical Library, 1959.

Engberg, Siri, and Clive Phillpot. *Edward Ruscha: Editions 1959–1999: Catalogue Raisonné*, 2 vols. Minneapolis: Walker Art Center, 1999.

English, Darby. *How to See a Work of Art in Total Darkness*. Cambridge: MIT Press, 2007.

Enwezor, Okwui. "Text, Subtext, Intertext: Painting, Language, and Signifying in the Work of Glenn Ligon." In *Glenn Ligon America*, ed. Scott Rothkopf, 51–63. New York: Whitney Museum of American Art, 2011.

Erickson, Britta. *Words without Meaning, Meaning without Words: The Art of Xu Bing*. Washington, D.C.: Smithsonian Institution, 2001.

Erickson, Britta. "Xu Bing's Journey through Language." In *The Character of Characters: An Animation by Xu Bing*, Xu Bing and Britta Erickson, 13–22. San Francisco: Asian Art Museum, 2012.

Ernst, Max. *Max Ernst: Beyond Painting and Other Writings by the Artist and his Friends*. New York: Wittenborn, Schultz, 1948.

Ernst, Max, and Peter Schamoni. *Maximiliana: The Illegal Practice of Astronomy*. Boston: New York Graphic Society, 1974.

Ernst, Ulrich. *Carmen Figuratum: Geschichte des Figurengedichts von den antiken Ursprüngen bis zum Ausgang des Mittelalters*. Cologne: Böhlau, 1991.

Ernst, Ulrich. "The Figured Poem: Towards a Definition of Genre." *Visible Language* 20, no. 1 (1986): 8–27.

Eshenburg, Barbara. "Altdorfer's 'Alexanderschlacht' und ihr Verhältnis zum Historienzklus Wilhems IV." *Zeitschrift des Deutschen Vereins für Kunstwissenschaft* 33 (1979): 36–67.

Ettinghausen, Richard. "The Impact of Muslim Decorative Arts and Painting on the Arts of Europe." In *Richard Ettinghausen: Islamic Art and Archaeology, Collected Papers*, ed. Myriam Rosen-Ayalon, 1074–1102. Berlin: Gebr. Mann Verlag, 1984.

Ettinghausen, Richard. "Kufesque in Byzantine Greece, the Latin West and the Muslim World." In *Richard Ettinghausen: Islamic Art and Archaeology, Collected Papers*, ed. Myriam Rosen-Ayalon, 752–771. Berlin: Gebr. Mann Verlag, 1984.

Evans, Mark. "Italian Manuscript Illumination: 1460–1560." In *Renaissance Painting in Manuscripts: Treasures from the British Library*, ed. Thomas Kren, 89–141. New York: Hudson Hills Press, 1983.

Fahr-Becker, Gabriele. *Japanese Prints*. Köln: Taschen, 2001.

Failing, Patricia. "Ed Ruscha, Young Artist: Dead Serious about Being Nonsensical." *Art News* 81, no. 4 (1982): 74–81.

Farquhar, James. "Identity in an Anonymous Age: Bruges Manuscript Illuminators and their Signs." *Viator* 2 (1989): 371–85.

Farzin, Media. "Still Here: An Interview with Martha Rosler and Anton Vidokle." *Art in America*, interviews, Sept. 9, 2009. http://www.artinamericamagazine.com/ news-features/interviews/interview-with-martha-rosler-and-anton-vidokle/.

Fauchereau, Serge. *Fernand Léger: A Painter in the City*. New York: Rizzoli, 1994.

Fehl, Philipp. "Death and the Sculptor's Fame: Artists' Signatures on Renaissance Tombs in Rome." *Biuletyn Historii Sztuki* 57 (1997): 196–217.

Ferber, Stanley. "Micrography: A Jewish Art Form." *The Journal of Jewish Art* 3/4 (1977): 12–24.

Fernandez, Emilia, and Harry Meyer Orlinsky, eds. *Estudios Masorecticos*. Madrid: Instituto Arias Montano, 1983.

Finster, Howard, and S. Mee. *Howard Finster: Man of Visions*. Atlanta: Peachtree, 1989.

Finster, Howard, and Tom Patterson. *Howard Finster: Stranger from Another World, Man of Visions Now on this Earth*. New York: Abbeville, 1989.

Firmage, Richard. *The Alphabet Abecedarium: Some Notes on Letters*. Boston: David A. Godine, 1993.

Fischer, Steven Roger. *A History of Writing*. London: Reaktion, 2001.

Fisher, Philip. *Making and Effacing Art: Modern American Art in a Culture of Museums*. New York: Oxford University Press, 1991.

Fleming, John. " 'The Dream of the Rood' and Anglo-Saxon Monasticism." *Traditio* 22 (1966): 43–72.

Flett, Alison. "The Significance of Text Scrolls: Towards a Descriptive Terminology." In *Medieval Texts and Images: Studies of Manuscripts from the Middle Ages*, ed. Margaret Manion and Bernard Muir, 43–53. Chur, Switzerland: Harwood Academic, 1991.

Foster, Hal. "Xu Bing: A Western Perspective." In *Persistence/Transformation: Text as Image in the Art of Xu Bing*, ed. Jerome Silbergeld and Dora C. Y. Ching, 87–97. Princeton: Princeton University Press, 2006.

Foucault, Michael. *This is Not a Pipe*. Trans. James Harkness. Berkeley: University of California Press, 1983.

Foys, Martin, Karen Overby, and Dan Terkla, eds. *The Bayeux Tapestry: New Interpretations*. Woodbridge, Suffolk: Boydell Press, 2009.

Frankenstein, Alfred. *After the Hunt: William Harnett and other American Still Life Painters 1870–1900*. Berkeley: University of California Press, 1953; revised 1975.

Freeman, Judi. *The Dada and Surrealist Word-Image*. Cambridge: Massachusetts Institute of Technology Press, 1989.

Friedmann, Herbert. *A Bestiary for Saint Jerome: Animal Symbolism in European Religious Art*. Washington, DC: Smithsonian Institution Press, 1980.

Fuchs, Rainer, ed. *John Baldessari: A Different Kind of Order (Arbeiten 1962–1984)*. Cologne: Walther König, 2005.

Fuchs, Rainer. "Written Paintings and Photographed Colors." In *John Baldessari: A Different Kind of Order (Arbeiten 1962–1984)*, ed. Rainer Fuchs, 15–42. Cologne: Walther König, 2005.

Fuhlrott, Rolf, and Bertram Haller. *Das Buch und Sein Haus I (Festschrift Gerhard Liebers)*. Wiesbaden: Reicher, 1979.

Gablik, Suzi. *Magritte*. London: Thames and Hudson, 1970.

Gaehtgens, Thomas. "Max Ernst and the Great Masters." In *Max Ernst: A Retrospective*, ed. Werner Spies and Sabine Rewald, 37–49. New York: Metropolitan Museum of Art, 2005.

Galiani, Stephen. "Words as Art: A New Perspective on Shaped Poetry." MA thesis, San Rafael: Dominican University of California, 2009.

Gallacher, Patrick, and Helen Damico, eds. *Hermeneutics and Medieval Culture*. Albany: State University of New York Press, 1989.

Gallant, Aprile, Daniel O'Leary, Susan Ryan, and Elizabeth Barry. *Love and the American Dream*. Portland, ME: Portland Museum of Art, 1999.

Gameson, Richard, ed. *The Study of the Bayeux Tapestry*. Woodbridge, Suffolk: Boydell Press, 1997.

Gammelbo, Poul. *Dutch Still-Life Painting, from the 16th to the 18th Centuries in Danish Collections*. Leigh-on-Sea: F. Lewis, 1960.

Gandelman, Claude. *Reading Pictures, Viewing Texts*. Bloomington: Indiana State University Press, 1991.

Gardner, Colin. "A Systematic Bewildering." *Artforum* 28, no. 4 (1989): 106–12.

Garel, Michel. "Un Ornement propre aux manuscrits hébreux médiévaux: La Micrographie." *Bulletin de la Bibliothèque Nationale* 3 (1978): 158–66.

Garrels, Gary, ed. *Jasper Johns: Seeing with the Mind's Eye*. San Francisco: San Francisco Museum of Modern Art, 2012.

Garrels, Gary, Jim Lewis, Sandra Phillips, Christopher Phillips, Abigail Solomon-Godeau, Robert Riley, and John Weber. *Public Information: Desire, Disaster, Document*. San Francisco: San Francisco Museum of Modern Art, 1994.

Gaur, Albertine. *A History of Writing*. New York: Cross River Press, 1992.

Gibson, Margaret, and Janet Nelson, eds. *Charles the Bald: Court and Kingdom*. Oxford: British Archaeological Reports, 1981.

Gilbert, Creighton. "A Preface to Signatures (with Some Cases in Venice)." In *Fashioning Identities in Italian Renaissance Art*, ed. Mary Rogers, 79–89. Aldershot: Ashgate, 2000.

Gilbert, Creighton. "Where Titian's Paintings Are Signed." *The Art Bulletin* 62, no. 1 (1980): 73–75.

Gilot, Françoise, and Carlton Lake. *Life with Picasso*. New York: McGraw-Hill, 1964.

Ginsburgh, Rabbi Yitzchak. *The Alef-Beit: Jewish Thought Revealed through the Hebrew Letters*. Northvale, NJ: Jason Aronson, 1991.

Givens, Jean, Karen Reeds, and Alain Touwaide, eds. *Visualizing Medieval Medicine and Natural History: 1200–1550*. Aldershot: Ashgate, 2006.

Godfrey, Tony. *Conceptual Art*. London: Phaidon, 1998.

Goffen, Rona. "Crossing the Alps: Portraiture in Renaissance Venice." In *Renaissance Venice and the North: Crosscurrents in the Time of Bellini, Dürer and Titian*, ed. Bernard Aikema, Beverly Brown and Giovanna Scirè, 115–31. New York: Rizzoli, 2004.

Goffen, Rona. *Giovanni Bellini*. New Haven: Yale University Press, 1989.

Goffen, Rona. "Giovanni Bellini's *Nude with Mirror*." *Venezia Cinquecento* I, no. 2 (1991): 185–202.

Goffen, Rona. "Icon and Vision: Giovanni Bellini's Half-Length Madonnas." *The Art Bulletin* 57, no. 4 (1975): 487–518.

Goffen, Rona. "Lotto's *Lucretia*." *Renaissance Quarterly* 52 (1999): 742–81.

Goffen, Rona. "Signatures: Inscribing Identity in Italian Renaissance Art." *Viator* 32 (2001): 303–70.

Gohr, Siegfried. *Magritte*. New York: Harry N. Abrams, 2005.

Goldberg, Gisela. "Albrecht Altdorfer: The Battle

of Alexander the Great." In *Altdorfer and Fantastic Realism in German Art*, ed. Jacqueline and Maurice Guilland, 245–68. New York: Rizzoli, 1985.

Goldberg, Gisela. "Die ursprüngliche Inschriftentafel der *Alexanderschlacht* Albrecht Altdorfers." *Müncher Jahrbuch des bildenden Kunst* 19 (1968): 121–26.

Goldberg, RoseLee. "Shirin Neshat. Material Witness." In *Shirin Neshat*, ed. Giorgio Verzotti, 66–69. Milan: Edizioni Charta, 2002.

Goldstein, Ann, Rosalyn Deutsche, Katherine Dieckmann, et al. *Thinking of You: Barbara Kruger*. Los Angeles: Museum of Contemporary Art, 1999.

Goldstein, David. *Hebrew Manuscript Painting*. London: British Library, 1984.

Goldstone, Lawrence, and Nancy Goldstone. *The Friar and the Cipher: Roger Bacon and the Unsolved Mystery of the Most Unusual Manuscript in the World*. New York: Doubleday, 2005.

Gombrich, Ernst. "Image and Word in Twentieth-Century Art." *Word and Image* 1, no. 3 (1985): 213–41.

Gordon, D. J., ed. *Fritz Saxl 1890–1948: A Volume of Memorial Essays*. London: Thomas Nelson and Sons, 1957.

Grabar, André, and Carl Nordenfalk. *Early Medieval Painting*. New York: Skira, 1957. Reprinted as *Book Illumination: Early Middle Ages*, 1995.

Gray, Nicolete. *Lettering on Buildings*. London: Architectural Press, 1960.

Greenhalgh, Michael. "David's 'Marat Assassiné' and Its Sources." *Yearbook of English Studies* 19 (1989): 162–80.

Greet, Anne Hyde. "Iliazd and Max Ernst: 65 Maximiliana or the Illegal Practice of Astronomy." *World Literature Today* 56, no. 1 (1982): 10–18.

Grivot, Denis, and George Zarnecki. *Gislebertus: Sculptor of Autun*. New York: Orion Press, 1961.

Groseclose, Barbara. "Vanity and the Artist: Some Still-Life Paintings by William Michael Harnett." *The American Art Journal* 19, no. 1 (1987): 51–59.

Grubb, Nancy. *Revelations: Art of the Apocalypse*. New York: Abbeville Press, 1997.

Grubmüller, K., ed. *Geistliche Denkformen in der Literatur des Mittelalters*. Munich: W. Fink, 1984.

Gudis, Catherine, Mary Jane Jacob, and Ann Goldstein. *A Forest of Signs: Art in the Crisis of Representation*. Cambridge: Massachusetts Institute of Technology Press, 1989.

Gutmann, Joseph. *Hebrew Manuscript Painting*. New York: George Braziller, 1978.

Gutmann, Joseph. "*Masorah Figurata*: The Origins and Development of a Jewish Art Form." In *Estudios Masorecticos*, ed. Emilia Fernandez and Harry Meyer Orlinsky, 49–64. Madrid: Instituto Arias Montano, 1983.

Gutmann, Joseph, ed. *The Image and the Word: Confrontations in Judaism, Christianity and Islam*. Missoula: Scholars Press, 1977.

Hammacher, A. M. *Magritte*. New York: Harry N. Abrams, 1974.

Hanson, Anne Coffin. *The Futurist Imagination: Word and Image in Italian Futurist Painting, Drawing, Collage, and Free-Word Poetry*. New Haven: Yale University Press, 1983.

Harrison, Helen. *Larry Rivers*. New York: Artnews Books, 1984.

Harrist, Robert. "*Book from the Sky* at Princeton: Reflections on Scale, Sense, and Sound." In *Persistence/Transformation: Text as Image in the Art of Xu Bing*, ed. Jerome Silbergeld and Dora C. Y. Ching, 24–45. Princeton: Princeton University Press, 2006.

Harthan, John. *The Book of Hours*. London: Thames and Hudson, 1970.

Hartt, Frederick. *History of Italian Renaissance Art: Painting, Sculpture, Architecture*. New York: Harry N. Abrams, 1994.

Hatfield, Rob. "Five Early Renaissance Portraits." *The Art Bulletin* 47, no. 3 (1965): 315–34.

Hawkes, Jane, and Susan Mills, eds. *Northumbria's Golden Age*. Stroud: Sutton, 1999.

Heartney, Eleanor. "Shirin Neshat: Living between Cultures." In *After the Revolution: Women Who Transformed Contemporary Art*, Eleanor Heartney, Helaine Poser, Nancy Princenthal and Sue Scott, 230–51. Munich: Prestel, 2007.

Heartney, Eleanor, Helaine Poser, Nancy Princenthal, and Sue Scott. *After the Revolution: Women Who Transformed Contemporary Art*. Munich: Prestel, 2007.

Heller, Steven. "Barbara Kruger, Graphic Designer?" In *Thinking of You: Barbara Kruger*, Ann Goldstein, et al., 108–16. Los Angeles: Museum of Contemporary Art, 1999.

Heslop, T.A. "Brief in Words but Heavy in the Weight of its Mysteries." *Art History* 9, no. 1 (1986):1–11.

Heslop, T.A. "Review of Conrad Rudolph, *Violence and Daily Life: Reading, Art and Polemics in the Cîteaux Moralia in Job*." *Art History* 23, no. 4 (2000): 642–43.

Hickey, Dave, Peter Plagens, and Anne Livet. *The Works of Edward Ruscha*. New York: Hudson

Hills Press, San Francisco Museum of Modern Art, 1982.

Higgins, Dick. *George Herbert's Pattern Poems: In Their Tradition*. West Glover, VT: Unpublished Editions, 1977.

Higgins, Dick. *Pattern Poetry: Guide to an Unknown Literature*. Albany: State University of New York Press, 1986.

Higgins, Dick. "The Strategy of Visual Poetry: Three Aspects." In *Visual Literature Criticism, A New Collection*, ed. Richard Kostelanetz, 41–50. Carbondale: Southern Illinois University Press, 1979.

Higgitt, John. "Words and Crosses: The Inscribed Stone Slabs in Early Medieval Britain and Ireland." In *Early Medieval Sculpture in Britain and Ireland*, ed. John Higgitt, 125–52. Oxford: British Archaeological Reports, British Series 152, 1986.

Higgitt, John, ed. *Early Medieval Sculpture in Britain and Ireland*. Oxford: British Archaeological Reports, British Series 152, 1986.

Hollman, Eckhard and Jürgen Tesch, *A Trick of the Eye: Trompe l'Oeil Masterpieces*. Munich: Prestel, 2004.

Holman, Thomas. "Holbein's Portraits of the Steelyard Merchants: An Investigation." *Metropolitan Museum Journal* 14 (1979): 139–58.

Holzer, Jenny. *Jenny Holzer Retro*. New York: Skarstedt Gallery, 2010.

Holzer, Jenny, David Breslin, Elizabeth A. T. Smith, and Philippe Büttner. *Jenny Holzer*. Ostfildern-Ruit, Germany: Hatje Cantz, 2008.

Homburg, Cornelia, Johanna Drucker, and William Gass. *The Dual Muse: The Writer as Artist, the Artist as Writer*. Philadelphia: John Benjamins, 1997.

Hopkins, David. " 'Out of it': Drunkenness and Ethics in Martha Rosler and Gillian Wearing." *Art History* 26, no. 3 (2003): 340–63.

Horrigan, Bill. *Shirin Neshat: Two Installations*. Columbus, OH: Wexner Center for the Arts, 2000.

Horsfall, Nicholas. "Stesichorus at Bovillae?" *Journal of Hellenic Studies* 99 (1979): 26–48.

Hubert, Renée Riese. "Max Ernst: The Displacement of the Visual and the Verbal." *New Literary History* 25, no. 3 (1984): 575–606.

Hubert, Renée Riese. *Surrealism and the Book*. Berkeley: University of California Press, 1988.

Hubert, Renée Riese. "Traces of Transcendence: Masson, Ernst, Tapiès." *Word and Image* 7, no. 2 (1991): 165–76.

Hudson, Hugh. "The Politics of War: Paolo Uccello's Equestrian Monument for Sir John Hawkwood in the Cathedral of Florence." *Parergon* 23, no. 2 (2006): 1–28.

Hunt, John Dixon, David Lomas, and Michael Corris. *Art, Word and Image: Two Thousand Years of Visual/Textual Interaction*. London: Reaktion, 2010.

Hunter, Jefferson. *Image and Word: The Interaction of Twentieth-Century Photographs and Texts*. Cambridge: Harvard University Press, 1987.

James, Liz. "'And Shall These Mute Stones Speak?' Text as Art." In *Art and Text in Byzantine Culture*, ed. Liz James, 188–206. Cambridge: Cambridge University Press, 2007.

James, Liz, ed. *Art and Text in Byzantine Culture*. Cambridge: Cambridge University Press, 2007.

Johnson, Robert. *Nothing Lost from the Original: William T. Wiley Looks at Art History*. San Francisco: M. H. de Young Memorial Museum, 1996.

Jolly, Penny Howell. "Jan van Eyck and Saint Jerome: A Study of Eyckian Influence on Colantonio and Antonello da Messina in Quattrocento Naples." Ph.D. dissertation, University of Pennsylvania, 1976.

Jones, Leslie. "Art Lesson: A Narrative Chronology of John Baldessari's Life and Work." In *John Baldessari: Pure Beauty*, John Baldessari, Jessica Morgan, Leslie Jones, Marie de Brugerolle, 46–60. Los Angeles: Los Angeles County Museum of Art, 2009.

Joselit, David, Joan Simon, and Renata Saleci. *Jenny Holzer*. London: Phaidon, 1998.

Kachur, Lewis. "The Language of Stuart Davis: Writing/Drawing." In *The Drawings of Stuart Davis: The Amazing Continuity*, Karen Wilkin and Lewis Kachur, 30–42. New York: American Federation of Arts, 1992.

Kachur, Lewis. "Picasso, Popular Music and Collage Cubism (1911–1913)." *The Burlington Magazine* 135, no. 1081 (1993): 252–60.

Kachur, Lewis. "Stuart Davis's Word Pictures." In *Stuart Davis: American Painter*, ed. Lowery Stokes Sims, 97–108. New York: Metropolitan Museum of Art, 1991.

Kahn, Deborah, ed. *The Romanesque Frieze and its Spectator. The Lincoln Symposium Papers*. London: Harvey Miller, 1992.

Kanas, Nick. *Star Maps: History, Artistry, and Cartography*. Chichester: Praxis, 2009.

Kaplan, Aryeh. *Sefer Yetzirah = The Book of Creation: In Theory and Practice*. York Beach, ME: Samuel Weiser, 1997.

Kaufmann, Thomas Da Costa, and Virginia Roehrig Kaufmann. "The Sanctification of Nature: Observations on the Origins of Trompe l'Oeil in Netherlandish Book Painting of the Fifteenth and Sixteenth Centuries." *The J. Paul Getty Museum Journal* 19 (1991): 43–66.

Keefer, Sarah, and Rolf Bremmer, eds. *Signs on the Edge: Space, Text and Margin in Medieval Manuscripts*. Paris: Peeters, 2007.

Kelley, Page, Daniel Mynatt, and Timothy Crawford. *The Masorah of Biblia Hebraica Stuttgartensia*. Grand Rapids: William B. Eerdmans, 1988.

Kendall, Calvin. *Allegory of the Church: Romanesque Portals and their Verse Inscriptions*. Toronto: University of Toronto Press, 1998.

Kendall, Calvin. "The Verse Inscription of the Tympanum of Jaca and the PAX Anagram." *Mediaevalia* 19 (1996): 405–34.

Kendall, Calvin. "The Voice in the Stone: the Verse Inscriptions of Ste.-Foy of Conques and the Date of the Tympanum." In *Hermeneutics and Medieval Culture*, ed. Patrick Gallacher and Helen Damico, 163–82. Albany: State University of New York Press, 1989.

Kendrick, Laura. *Animating the Letter: The Figurative Embodiment of Writing from Late Antiquity to the Renaissance*. Columbus: Ohio State University Press, 1999.

Kennedy, Gerry, and Rob Churchill. *The Voynich Manuscript*. London: Orion, 2004.

Keough, Jeffrey, Eugene Yuejin Wang, and Ann Wilson. *Xu Bing: Language Lost*. Boston: Massachusetts College of Art, 1995.

Kessler, Herbert. "Pictorial Narrative and Church Mission in Sixth-Century Gaul." In *Pictorial Narrative in Antiquity and the Middle Ages*, ed. Herbert Kessler and Marianna Shreve Simpson, 75–91. Washington, DC: National Gallery of Art, 1985.

Kessler, Herbert, and Marianna Shreve Simpson, eds. *Pictorial Narrative in Antiquity and the Middle Ages*. Washington, DC: National Gallery of Art, 1985.

Khan, Gabriel Mandel. *Arabic Script: Styles, Variants, and Calligraphic Adaptations*. New York: Abbeville, 2001.

King, Anne. "The Ruthwell Cross—A Linguistic Monument (Runes as Evidence for Old English)." *Folia Linguistica Historica* 7, no. 1 (1986): 43–79.

Kirwin, Lisa. "The Reverend Howard Finster: The Last Red Light before the Apocalypse." *American Art* 16, no. 2 (2002): 90–93.

Klonsky, Milton, ed. *Speaking Pictures: A Gallery of Pictorial Poetry from the Sixteenth Century to the Present*. New York: Harmony Books, 1975.

Knight, Michael. "Introduction: Decoding Chinese Calligraphy." In *Out of Character: Decoding Chinese Calligraphy*, ed. Michael Knight and Joseph Chang, 17–50. San Francisco: Asian Art Museum, 2012.

Knight, Michael, and Joseph Chang, eds. *Out of Character: Decoding Chinese Calligraphy*. San Francisco: Asian Art Museum, 2012.

Kōdera, Tsukasa. "Japan as Primitivistic Utopia: Van Gogh's Japonisme Portraits." *Simiolus: Netherlands Quarterly for the History of Art* 14, no. 3–4 (1984): 189–208.

König, Eberhard. *Les Heures de Marguerite d'Orleans*. Paris: Les Éditions du Cerf/Bibliothèque Nationale, 1991.

Kostelanetz, Richard. *Imaged Words and Worded Images*. New York: Outerbridge and Dienstfrey, 1970.

Kostelanetz, Richard, ed. *Visual Literature Criticism, A New Collection*. Carbondale: Southern Illinois University Press, 1979.

Köster, Kurt. "Kollektionen metallener Wallfahrts-Devotionalien und kleiner Andachtsbilder, eingenäht in spätmitteralterliche Gebetbuch-Handschriften." In *Das Buch und Sein Haus I (Festschrift Gerhard Liebers)*, Rolf Fuhlrott and Bertram Haller, 77–130. Wiesbaden: Reicher, 1979.

Köster, Kurt. "Religiöse Medaillen und Wallfahrts-Devotionalien in der flämischen Buchmalerei des 15. und frühen 16. Jahrhunderts." In *Buch und Welt, Festschrift für Gustav Hofmann*, Hans Striedl, Gustav Hofman, and Joachim Wieder, 459–504. Wiesbaden: O. Harrassowitz, 1965.

Kosuth, Joseph. *Art After Philosophy and After: Collected Writings, 1966–1990*. Cambridge: MIT Press, 1991.

Kosuth, Joseph. "Art as Idea as Idea." In *Artwords: Discourse on the 60s and 70s*, Jeanne Siegel, 221–31. Ann Arbor: UMI Research Press, 1985.

Kosuth, Joseph. "Intention(s)." *The Art Bulletin* 73, no. 3 (1966): 407–412.

Kotz, Liz. *Words to Be Looked At: Language in 1960s Art*. Cambridge: MIT Press, 2007.

Krauss, Rosalind. *The Picasso Papers*. New York: Farrar, Straus and Giroux, 1988.

Krauss, Rosalind, and Margit Rowell. *Joan Miró: Magnetic Fields*. New York: Solomon R. Guggenheim Foundation, 1972.

Kren, Thomas, ed. *Renaissance Painting in Manuscripts: Treasures from the British Library*. New York: Hudson Hills Press, 1983.

Kren, Thomas, and Scot McKendrick, eds. *Illuminating the Renaissance: The Triumph of*

Flemish Manuscript Painting in Europe. Los Angeles: J. Paul Getty Museum, 2003.

Krichbaum, Jörg. *Albrecht Altdorfer: Meister der Alexanderschlacht*. Cologne: DuMont Buchverlag, 1978.

Kuh, Katharine. *The Artist's Voice: Talks with Seventeen Artists*. New York: Harper & Row, 1962.

Kuspit, Donald. "Signs in Suspense: Ed Ruscha's Liquidation of Meaning." *Arts Magazine* 65, no. 8 (1991): 54–58.

Lambourne, Lionel. *Japonisme: Cultural Crossings between Japan and the West*. London: Phaidon, 2005.

Land, Norman. "Giotto's Fly, Cimabue's Gesture, and a 'Madonna and Child' by Carlo Crivelli." *Source: Notes in the History of Art* 15 (1996): 11–15.

Lang, James. "The Imagery of the Franks Casket: Another Approach." In *Northumbria's Golden Age*, ed. Jane Hawkes and Susan Mills, 247–55. Stroud: Sutton, 1999.

Lasko, Peter. *Ars Sacra 800–1200*. New Haven: Yale University Press, 1994.

Lavin, Irving, ed. *World Art: Themes of Unity in Diversity*, vol. 2. University Park: Pennsylvania State University Press, 1989.

Leclerq-Marx, Jacqueline. "Le Centaure dans l'art preroman et roman: Sources d'inspiration et modes de transmission." *Les Cahiers de Saint-Michel de Cuxa* 37 (2006): 33–42.

Leighten, Patricia. "Picasso's Collages and the Threat of War, 1912–13." *The Art Bulletin* 67, no. 4 (1985): 664–69.

Leighten, Patricia. *Re-Ordering the Universe: Picasso and Anarchism,1897–1914*. Princeton: Princeton University Press, 1989.

Lepelley, René. "A Contribution to the Study of the Inscriptions in the Bayeux Tapestry: *Bagias* and *Wilgelm*." In *The Study of the Bayeux Tapestry*, ed. Richard Gameson, 39–46. Woodbridge, Suffolk: Boydell Press, 1997.

Levitan, William. "Dancing at the End of the Rope: Optatian Porfyry and the Field of Roman Verse." *Transactions of the American Philological Association* 115 (1985): 245–69.

Levy, Silvano. "Foucault on Magritte on Resemblance." *The Modern Language Review* 85, no. 1 (1990): 50–56.

Lewis, Michael, Gale Owen-Crocker, and Dan Terkla, eds. *The Bayeux Tapestry: New Approaches. Proceedings of a Conference at the British Museum*. Oxford: Oxbow Books, 2011.

Lewis, Suzanne. "Sacred Calligraphy: The Chi Rho Page in the Book of Kells." *Traditio* 36 (1980): 139–59.

Leymarie, Jean. *The Spirit of the Letter in Painting*. Lausanne: Skira, 1961.

Lightbown, Ronald. *Carlo Crivelli*. New Haven: Yale University Press, 2004.

Ligon, Glenn, and Hilton Als. *Glenn Ligon: Stranger*. New York: Studio Museum in Harlem, 2001.

Ling, Roger. "Inscriptions on Romano-British Mosaics and Wall Paintings." *Britannia* 38 (2007): 63–91.

Lippard, Lucy, Lawrence Alloway, Nancy Marmer, and Nicolas Calas. *Pop Art*. London: Thames and Hudson, 1966; 2d ed., 1988.

Lomas, David. " 'New in Art, They are Already Soaked in Humanity': Word and Image, 1900–1945." In *Art, Word and Image: Two Thousand Years of Visual/Textual Interaction*, John Dixon Hunt, David Lomas, and Michael Corris, 111–77. London: Reaktion, 2010.

Lowden, John. *Illustrated Prophet Books*. University Park: Pennsylvania State University Press, 1988.

Lucie-Smith, Edward. *American Realism*. New York: Harry N. Abrams, 1994.

Mack, Rosamond. *Bazaar to Piazza: Islamic Trade and Italian Art, 1300–1600*. Berkeley: University of California Press, 2002.

Madoff, Steven, ed. *Pop Art: A Critical Anthology*. Berkeley: University of California Press, 1997.

Magritte, René. *Magritte: A to Z*. London: Tate Gallery, 2011.

Maleuvre, Didier. "David Painting Death." *Diacritics* 30, no. 3 (2000): 13–27.

Manion, Margaret, and Bernard Muir, eds. *Medieval Texts and Images*. Chur, Switzerland: Harwood Academic, 1991.

Marin, Louis. "Towards a Theory of Reading in the Visual Arts: Poussin's *The Arcadian Shepherds*." In *Calligram: Essays in New Art History from France*, ed. Norman Bryson, 63–90. Cambridge: Cambridge University Press, 1988.

Marshall, Richard, and Liz Kotz. *Jack Pierson: Desire Despair*. New York: Rizzoli, 2006.

Martí, Silas. "Valeska Soares." *Frieze* 113 (2008): 1–3.

Massin, Robert. *Letter and Image*. New York: Van Nostrand Reinhold, 1970.

Mastai, Marie-Louise d'Otrange. *Illusion in Art: Trompe l'Oeil: A History of Pictorial Illusionism*. New York: Abaris, 1975.

Matthew, Louisa. "The Painter's Presence: Signatures in Venetian Renaissance Pictures." *The Art Bulletin* 80, no. 4 (1998): 616–48.

McCloud, Scott. *Understanding Comics: The Invisible Art*. New York: HarperCollins, 1993.

McGurk, Patrick. "Carolingian Astrological Manuscripts." In *Charles the Bald: Court and Kingdom*, ed. Margaret Gibson and Janet Nelson, 317–32. Oxford: British Archaeological Reports, 1981.

McHam, Sarah Blake. "Erudition on Display: The 'Scientific' Illustrations in Pico della Mirandola's Manuscript of Pliny the Elder's *Natural History*." In *Visualizing Medieval Medicine and Natural History: 1200–1550*, ed. Jean Givens, Karen Reeds, and Alain Touwaide, 83–114. Aldershot: Ashgate, 2006.

McKitterick, Rosamond. *The Carolingians and the Written Word*. Cambridge: Cambridge University Press, 1989.

McKitterick, Rosamond. "Text and Image in the Carolingian World." In *The Uses of Literacy in Early Medieval Europe*, ed. Rosamond McKitterick, 297–318. Cambridge: Cambridge University Press, 1990.

McKitterick, Rosamond, ed. *The Uses of Literacy in Early Medieval Europe*. Cambridge: Cambridge University Press, 1990.

McNulty, J. Bard. *The Narrative Art of the Bayeux Tapestry Master*. New York: AMS Press, 1989.

Meckseper, Cord. "Zur Ikonographie von Altdorfer's Alexanderschlacht." *Zeitschrift des Deutschen Vereins für Kunstwissenschaft* 22 (1968): 178–85.

Meiss, Millard. *Andrea Mantegna as Illuminator: An Episode in Renaissance Art, Humanism and Diplomacy*. New York: Columbia University Press, 1979.

Meiss, Millard. "The Original Position of Uccello's John Hawkwood." *The Art Bulletin* 52, no. 3 (1970): 231.

Meiss, Millard. *The Painter's Choice: Problems in the Interpretation of Renaissance Art*. New York: Harper & Row, 1976.

Meiss, Millard. "Scholarship and Penitence in the Early Renaissance Image of Saint Jerome." In *The Painter's Choice: Problems in the Interpretation of Renaissance Art*, Millard Meiss, 189–202. New York: Harper & Row, 1976.

Meiss, Millard. "Towards a More Comprehensive Renaissance Palaeography." *The Art Bulletin* 42, 2 (1960): 97–112.

Meyer, Richard. "Borrowed Voices: Glenn Ligon and the Face of Language." In *Glenn Ligon: Un/becoming*, Judith Tannenbaum, 13–35. Philadelphia: Institute of Contemporary Art, 1988.

Meyvaert, Paul. "A New Perspective on the Ruthwell Cross: *Ecclesia* and *Vita Monastica*." In *The Ruthwell Cross*, ed. Brendan Cassidy, 95–166. Princeton: Princeton University Press, 1992.

Michaux, Henri. *Stroke by Stroke*. Trans. Richard Sieburth. New York: Archipelago Books, 2006.

Millar, Eric. *Les Manuscrits à Peintures des Bibliothèques de Londres; Extrait du Bulletin de la Société Française de Reproduction de Manuscrits à Peintures*. Paris, 1924.

Milner, John. "On the Fusion of Verbal and Visual Media." *Leonardo* 9, no. 1 (1976): 5–9.

Mitchell, John. "Literacy Displayed: The Use of Inscriptions in the Monastery of San Vincenzo al Volturno in the Early Ninth Century." In *The Uses of Literacy in Early Medieval Europe*, ed. Rosamond McKitterick, 186–225. Cambridge: Cambridge University Press, 1990.

Monks, Peter Rolfe. "The Rolin Master's Hand in London BL MS Additional 25695." In *Medieval Texts and Images*, ed. Margaret Manion and Bernard Muir, 57–70. Chur, Switzerland: Harwood Academic, 1991.

Morgan, Jessica, Leslie Jones, John Baldessari, Marie de Brugerelle. *John Baldessari: Pure Beauty*. Los Angeles: Los Angeles County Museum of Art, 2009.

Morgan, Robert. *Art into Ideas: Essays on Conceptual Art*. Cambridge: Cambridge University Press, 1996.

Morley, Simon. *Writing on the Wall: Word and Images in Modern Art*. Berkeley: University of California Press, 2003.

Moser, Joann. *What's It All Mean: William T. Wiley in Retrospect*. Berkeley: University of California Press, 2009.

Mosher, Nicole. *Le Text Visualisé: Le Calligramme de l'époque Alexandrine à l'époque Cubiste*. New York: Peter Lang, 1990.

Müller, Hans-Georg. *Hrabanus Maurus: De laudibus sancta cruces: Studien zur Überlieferung und Geistesgeschicte mit dem Faksimile-Textabdruck aus Codex Reg. Lat. 124 der Vatikanischen Bibliothek*. Ratingen: A. Henn, 1973.

Muniz, Vik, and Valeska Soares. "Valeska Soares." *BOMB* 74 (2001): 48–55.

Murdoch, John. *Album of Science: Antiquity and the Middle Ages*. New York: Charles Scribner's Sons, 1984.

Mütherich, Florentine, and Joachim Gaehde. *Carolingian Painting*. New York: George Braziller, 1976.

Neagley, Linda. "Portals of the Bayeux Tapestry: Visual Experience, Spatial Representation and Oral Performance." In *The Bayeux Tapestry: New Approaches. Proceedings of a Conference at the British Museum*, ed. Michael Lewis, Gale Owen-Crocker, and Dan Terkla, 136–46. Oxford: Oxbow Books, 2011.

Néret, Gilles. *F. Léger*. New York: BDD Illustrated Books, 1993.

Neuman de Vegvar, Carol. "Reading the Franks Casket: Contexts and Audiences." In *Intertexts: Studies in Anglo-Saxon Culture Presented to Paul E. Szarmach*, ed. Virginia Blanton and Helene Scheck, 141–59. Tempe: Arizona Center for Medieval and Renaissance Studies, 2008.

Neuman de Vegvar, Carol. "The Travelling Twins: Romulus and Remus in Anglo-Saxon England." In *Northumbria's Golden Age*, ed. Jane Hawkes and Susan Mills, 256–76. Stroud: Sutton, 1999.

Newman, Michael, and Jon Bird, eds. *Rewriting Conceptual Art*. London: Reaktion, 1999.

Nickel, Helmut. "Carpaccio's 'Young Knight in a Landscape': Christian Champion and Guardian of Liberty." *Metropolitan Museum Journal* 18 (1983): 85–96.

Nordenfalk, Carl. *Die Spätantiken Zierbuchstaben*. Stockholm: C. G. Röder, 1970.

Oldenburg, Claes and Cossje van Bruggen. *Claes Oldenburg and Cossje van Bruggen: Large Scale Projects*. New York: Monacelli Press, 1994.

Ong, Walter. *Orality and Literacy: The Technologizing of the Word*. London: Methuen, 1982.

Orth, Myra. "Two Books of Hours for Jean Lallement le Jeune." *The Journal of the Walters Art Gallery* 38 (1980): 70–93.

Orth, Myra. "What Goes Around: Borders and Frames in French Manuscripts." *The Journal of the Walters Art Gallery* 54 (1996): 189–201.

Orton, Fred, Ian Wood, and Clare Lees. *Fragments of History: Rethinking the Ruthwell and Bewcastle Monuments*. Manchester: Manchester University Press, 2007.

Osborne, Peter. "Conceptual Art and/as Philosophy." In *Rewriting Conceptual Art*, ed. Michael Newman and Jon Bird, 47–65. London: Reaktion, 1999.

Owen-Crocker, Gale. "The Embroidered Word: Text in the Bayeux Tapestry." *Medieval Clothing and Textiles* 2 (2006): 35–59.

Pächt, Otto. *Book Illumination in the Middle Ages*. London: Harvey Miller, 1986.

Pächt, Otto. "Notes and Observations on the Origin of Humanistic Book Decoration." In *Fritz Saxl 1890–1948: A Volume of Memorial Essays*, ed. D. J. Gordon, 184–94. London: Thomas Nelson and Sons, 1957.

Page, R. I. *An Introduction to English Runes*. Woodbridge, Suffolk: Boydell Press, 1999.

Page, R. I. *Runes*. Berkeley: University of California Press, 1987.

Panofsky, Erwin. "*Et in Arcadia Ego*: Poussin and the Elegiac Tradition." In *Meaning in the Visual Arts*, 195–320. New York: Anchor Books, 1955.

Panofsky, Erwin. *Meaning in the Visual Arts*. New York: Anchor Books, 1955.

Panofsky, Erwin. "The Mouse that Michelangelo Failed to Carve." In *Essays in Memory of Karl Lehmann*, ed. Lucy Freedman Sandler, 242–51. New York: Institute of Fine Arts, New York University, 1964.

Paoleri, Annarita. *Paolo Uccello, Domenico Veneziano, Andrea del Castagno*. Florence: Scala, 1991.

Papalexandrou, Amy. "Echoes of Orality in the Monumental Inscriptions of Byzantium." In *Art and Text in Byzantine Culture*, ed. Liz James, 161–87. Cambridge: Cambridge University Press, 2007.

Parkes, M. B., and Andrew Watson, eds. *Medieval Scribes, Manuscripts and Libraries: Essays Presented to N. R. Ker*. London: Scolar Press, 1978.

Pasquariello, Lisa. "Ed Ruscha and the Language That He Used." *October* 111 (2005): 81–106.

Pennick, Nigel. *The Secret Lore of Runes and Other Ancient Alphabets*. London: Rider, 1991.

Perloff, Marjorie. *The Futurist Movement: Avant-Garde, Avant Guerre, and the Language of Rupture*. Chicago: University of Chicago Press, 1986.

Perreault, John. "Metaphysical Funk Monk." *Art News* 67 (1968): 52–53, 66–67.

Perreault, John. "Wiley Territory." In *Wiley Territory*, Graham Beal, and John Perreault, 7–13. Minneapolis: Walker Art Center, 1979.

Perrone, Jeff. " 'Words': When Art Takes a Rest." *Artforum* 15, no. 10 (1977): 34–37.

Petrucci, Armando. *Public Lettering*. Chicago: University of Chicago Press, 1993.

Picchi, F. "Domus 569, April 1977." *Domus* 843 (2001): 154.

Pierson, Jack. *All of a Sudden*. New York: Powerhouse Books, 1995.

Pierson, Jack. *Jack Pierson*. Milan: Photology, 2007.

Pincus, Debra. "Giovanni Bellini's Humanist Signature: Petro Bembo, Aldus Manutius and Humanism in Early Sixteenth-Century Venice." *Artibus et Historiae* 29, no. 58 (2008): 89–119.

Poggi, Christine. "Folla/Follia: Futurism and the Crowd." *Critical Inquiry* 28, no. 3 (2002): 709–48.

Poggi, Christine. "Frames of Reference: 'Table' and 'Tableau' in Picasso's Collage Constructions." *Art Journal* 47, no. 4 (1988): 311–22.

Poggi, Christine. "Marinetti's Parole in Libertà and the Futurist Collage Aesthetic." In *The Fu-*

turist Imagination: Word and Image in Italian Futurist Painting, Drawing, Collage, and Free-Word Poetry, ed. Anne Coffin Hanson, 2–15. New Haven: Yale University Art Gallery, 1983.

Pon, Lisa. "Michelangelo's First Signature." *Source: Notes in the History of Art* 15 (1996): 16–21.

Princenthal, Nancy. "Jenny Holzer: Language Lessons." In *After the Revolution: Women Who Transformed Contemporary Art*, Eleanor Heartney, Helaine Poser, Nancy Princenthal and Sue Scott, 144–67. Munich: Prestel, 2007.

Randall, Lillian. *Medieval and Renaissance Manuscripts in the Walters Art Gallery, Vol. II: France, 1420-1540*. Baltimore: Walters Art Gallery, 1992.

Reudenbach, Bruno. "Imago-Figura: Zum Bildverständis in den Figurendicten von Hrabanus Maurus." *Frümittelalterliche Studien 20* (1986): 25–35.

Reudenbach, Bruno. "Das Verhältnis von Text und Bild in 'De laudibus sanctae crucis' des Hrabanus Maurus." In *Geistliche Denkformen in der Literatur des Mittelalters*, ed. K. Grubmüller, 282–320. Munich: W. Fink, 1984.

Richardson, Brian. *Printing, Writers and Readers in Renaissance Italy*. Cambridge: Cambridge University Press, 1999.

Richardson, John, and Marilyn McCully. *A Life of Picasso: Vol. 2: The Cubist Rebel, 1907-1916*. New York: Alfred A. Knopf, 1996.

Ridderbos, Bernhard. *Saint and Symbol: Images of Saint Jerome in Early Italian Art*. Groningen: Bouma's Boekhuis, 1984.

Riemschneider, Burkhard, and Uta Grosenick, eds. *Art at the Turn of the Millennium*. Cologne: Taschen, 1999.

Rogers, Mary, ed. *Fashioning Identities in Italian Renaissance Art*. Aldershot: Ashgate, 2000.

Rosen-Ayalon, Myriam, ed. *Richard Ettinghausen: Islamic Art and Archaeology, Collected Papers*. Berlin: Gebr. Mann Verlag, 1984.

Roskill, Mark. *Van Gogh, Gauguin and the Impressionist Circle*. Greenwich, CT: New York Graphic Society, 1970.

Rosler, Martha. *Decoys and Disruptions: Selected Writings, 1975-2001*. Cambridge: MIT Press, 2004.

Rosler, Martha. "In, Around, and Afterthoughts (on Documentary Photography)." In *The Contest of Meaning: Critical Histories of Photography*, ed. Richard Bolton, 303–340. Cambridge: MIT Press, 1992.

Rosler, Martha. "Statement." In *Conceptual Art: A Critical Anthology*, ed. Alexander Alberro and Blake Stimson, 486–87. Cambridge: Massachusetts Institute of Technology Press, 1999.

Rossi-Landi, Ferruccio, and Raymond Williams, et al. *Contact: Human Communication and its History*. New York: Thames and Hudson, 1981.

Rothkopf, Scott, ed. *Glenn Ligon America*. New York: Whitney Museum of American Art, 2011.

Rowell, Margit. "Magnetic Fields: The Poetics." In *Joan Miró: Magnetic Fields*, ed. Rosalind Krauss and Margit Rowell, 39–67. New York: Solomon R. Guggenheim Foundation, 1972.

Rowell, Margit, and Cornelia Butler. *Cotton Puffs, Q-Tips, Smoke and Mirrors: The Drawings of Ed Ruscha*. New York: Whitney Museum of American Art, 2004.

Roxburgh, David. *Writing the Word of God: Calligraphy and the Qur'an*. Houston: The Museum of Fine Arts, Houston, 2007.

Rubin, Patricia. "Signposts of Invention: Artists' Signatures in Italian Renaissance Art." *Art History* 29, no. 4 (2006): 563–99.

Rubin, William, Kirk Varnedoe, and Lynn Zelevansky. *Picasso and Braque: A Symposium*. New York: Museum of Modern Art, 1992.

Ruda, Jeffrey. *Fra Filippo Lippi: Life and Work with a Complete Catalogue*. New York: Harry N. Abrams, 1993.

Rudolph, Conrad. *Violence and Daily Life: Reading, Art and Polemics in the Cîteaux Moralia in Job*. Princeton: Princeton University Press, 1997.

Rugoff, Ralph. "The Last Word." *Art News* 88, no. 10 (1989): 120–25.

Ruscha, Edward, Pat Poncy, Robert Dean, Lisa Turvey. *Edward Ruscha: Catalogue Raisonné of the Paintings*, five volumes. New York: Gagosian Gallery, 2003–2011.

Ryan, Susan. "Eternal Love." In *Love and the American Dream*, Aprile Gallant, Daniel O'Leary, Susan Ryan, and Elizabeth Barry, 76–101. Portland, ME: Portland Museum of Art, 1999.

Ryan, Susan. *Robert Indiana: Figures of Speech*. New Haven: Yale University Press, 2000.

Safadi, Yasin Hamid. *Islamic Calligraphy*. Boulder: Shambhala, 1979.

Sala, Charles. "La signature à la lettre et au figure." *Poétique* 69 (1987): 119–27.

Sandler, Irving. *Art of the Postmodern Era: From the Late 1960s to the Early 1990s*. Boulder: Westview Press, 1998.

Sandler, Lucy Freeman. *Gothic Manuscripts 1285–1385*. London: Harvey Miller, 1982.

Sandler, Lucy Freeman, ed. *Essays in Memory of Karl Lehmann*. New York: Institute of Fine Arts, New York University, 1964.

Saussey, Haun. "Xu Bing and Writing." In *Tianshu: Passages in the Making of a Book*, ed. Katherine Spears, 81–85. London: Quaritch, 2009.

Saxl, Fritz. "The Classical Inscription in Renaissance Art and Politics: Bartholomaeus Fontius: *Liber monumentorum Romanae urbis*." *Journal of the Warburg and Courtauld Institutes* 4, no. 1–2 (1940): 19–46.

Schapiro, Meyer. *Words, Script and Pictures: Semiotics of Visual Language*. New York: George Braziller, 1996.

Schaya, Leo. *The Universal Meaning of the Kabbalah*. London: George Allen and Unwin, 1971.

Scheller, Robert. *Exemplum: Model-Book Drawings and the Practice of Artistic Transmission in the Middle Ages* (ca. 900-ca. 1470). Amsterdam: Amsterdam University Press, 1995.

Scheller, Robert. *A Survey of Medieval Model Books*. Haarlem: De Erven F. Bohn N.V., 1963.

Schimmel, Annemarie. *Calligraphy and Islamic Culture*. New York: New York University Press, 1984.

Schimmel, Annemarie. *Mystical Dimensions of Islam*. Chapel Hill: University of North Carolina Press, 1975.

Schindler, Robert. "Jean Lallement's Books of Hours and French Manuscript Illumination." In *Prayers in Code: Books of Hours from Renaissance France*, ed. Martina Bagnoli, 15–32. Baltimore: Walters Art Museum, 2009.

Schipper, William. "Textual Varieties in Manuscript Margins." In *Signs on the Edge: Space, Text and Margin in Medieval Manuscripts*, ed. Sarah Keefer and Rolf Bremmer, 25–56. Paris: Peeters, 2007.

Schmied, Wieland. *Tobey*. New York: Harry N. Abrams, 1966.

Scholem, Gershom. *On the Kabbalah and its Symbolism*. New York: Schocken, 1965.

Schwartz, Alexandra, ed. *Leave Any Information at the Signal: Writings, Interviews, Bits, Pages*. Cambridge: MIT Press, 2002.

Sears, Elizabeth. "Louis the Pious as *Miles Christi*: The Dedicatory Image in Hrabanus Maurus's *De laudibus sanctae cruces*." In *Charlemagne's Heir: New Perspectives on the Reign of Louis the Pious*, ed. Roger Collins and Peter Godman, 605–28. Oxford: Clarendon Press, 1990.

Sears, Elizabeth. "Word and Image in Carolingian *Carmina Figurata*." In *World Art: Themes of Unity in Diversity*, vol. 2, ed. Irving Lavin, 341–48. University Park: Pennsylvania State University Press, 1989.

Seidel, Linda. *Legends in Limestone: Lazarus, Gislebertus and the Cathedral of Autun*. Chicago: University of Chicago Press, 1999.

Seider, David. *Artists at Work: Inside the Studios of Today's Most Celebrated Artists*. New York: Rizzoli, 1999.

Selby, Aimee. *Art and Text*. London: Black Dog, 2009.

Serafini, Luigi. *Codex Seraphinianus*. Milan: F. M. Ricci, 1981.

Sgarbi, Vittorio. *Carpaccio*. New York: Abbeville Press, 1994.

Sheridan, Victoria. "The Quattrocento Calling Card: Origins and Intentions of the Italian Renaissance Cartellino." Paper delivered at the Bay Area Graduate Art History Colloquium, Fine Arts Museums of San Francisco, May 2001.

Sheybani, Shadi. "Women of Allah: A Conversation with Shirin Neshat." *Michigan Quarterly Review* 38, no. 2 (1999).

Shiner, Eric, Robert Storr, Griselda Pollack, Lisa Liebmann, and Brooks Adams. *Deborah Kass: Before and Happily Ever After*. New York: Skira/Rizzoli, 2012.

Short, Ian. "The Language of the Bayeux Tapestry Inscription." *Anglo-Norman Studies* 23 (2000): 267–80.

Sieburth, Richard. *Signs in Action: Pound/Michaux* and *Of Language* by Henri Michaux. Trans. Richard Sieburth. New York: Reddustbooks, 1987.

Siegel, Jeanne. *Artwords: Discourse on the 60s and 70s*. Ann Arbor: UMI Research Press, 1985.

Silbergeld, Jerome, and Dora C. Y. Ching, eds. *Persistence/Transformation: Text as Image in the Art of Xu Bing*. Princeton: Princeton University Press, 2006.

Silver, Larry. "Nature and Nature's God: Landscape and Cosmos of Albrecht Altdorfer." *The Art Bulletin* 81, no. 2 (1999): 194–214.

Sims, Lowery Stokes, ed. *Stuart Davis: American Painter*. New York: Metropolitan Museum of Art, 1991.

Sirat, Colette, ed. *La Lettre Hébraïque et sa Signification*. Paris: Editions du Centre National de la Recherche Scientifique, 1981.

Slome, Manon. "An I for An Eye: Strategies of Language in Contemporary Art." In *Articulations: Forms of Language in Contemporary Art*, Benedict Borthwick, Lisa Dent, Cylena Simonds, and Manon Slome, 9–13. New York: Whitney Museum of American Art, 1995.

Smeyers, Maurits, and Jan Van der Stock, eds. *Flemish Illuminated Manuscripts: 1475–1550*. New York: Abrams, 1996.

Smith, Kiki. "Jenny Holzer." *Interview* 42, no. 3 (2012): 108–50.

Smith, Margaret M. *The Title-page, Its Early De-*

velopment, 1460–1510. London: British Library, 2000.

Smith, Roberta. "Sounding the Alarm in Words and Light." *The New York Times*, March 13, 2009.

Snyder, James. *Northern Renaissance Art: Painting, Sculpture, the Graphic Arts from 1350 to 1575*. New York: Harry N. Abrams, 1985.

Sobel, Dean. "Words as Socio-Political Commentary." In *Word as Image: American Art 1960–1990*, ed. Russell Bowman and Dean Sobel, 130–33. Milwaukee: Milwaukee Art Museum, 1990.

Solt, Mary Ellen, ed. *Concrete Poetry: A World View*. Bloomington: Indiana University Press, 1968.

Sparrow, John. *Visible Words: A Study of Inscriptions in and as Books and Works of Art*. Cambridge: Cambridge University Press, 1969.

Spaulding, Karen Lee, ed. *Jenny Holzer: The Venice Installation*. United States Pavilion: The 44th Venice Biennale, 1990.

Spears, Katherine, ed. *Tianshu: Passages in the Making of a Book*. London: Quaritch, 2009.

Spies, Werner, and Sabine Rewald, eds. *Max Ernst: A Retrospective*. New York: Metropolitan Museum of Art, 2005.

Stack, Lotus, ed. *Conservation Research: Studies of Fifteenth- to Nineteenth-Century Tapestry*. Washington, DC: National Gallery of Art, 1993.

Steefel, Lawrence. "A Neglected Shadow in Poussin's *Et in Arcadia Ego*." *The Art Bulletin* 57, no. 1 (1975): 99–101.

Steegmuller, Francis. *Apollinaire: Poet Among the Painters*. New York: Penguin, 1986.

Steiner, Wendy. "*Res Poetica*: The Problematics of the Concrete Program." *New Literary History* 12, no. 3 (1981): 529–45.

Stemp, Richard. "Two Sculptures Designed by Cosmè Tura." *The Burlington Magazine* 141, no. 1153 (1999): 208–15, 226–28.

Stevens, John. *Sacred Calligraphy of the East*. Boston: Shambhala, 1995.

Stich, Sidra. *Joan Miró: The Development of a Sign Language*. St. Louis: Washington University Gallery of Art, 1980.

Stock, Brian. *The Implications of Literacy: Written Language and Models of Interpretation in the Eleventh and Twelfth Centuries*. Princeton: Princeton University Press, 1983.

Storr, Robert. *Deborah Kass: More! Feel Good Paintings for Feel Bad Times*. New York: Paul Kasmin Gallery, 2010.

Striedl, Hans, Gustav Hofman, and Joachim Wieder. *Buch und Welt, Festschrift für Gustav Hofmann*. Wiesbaden: O. Harrassowitz, 1965.

Sullivan, Michael. *The Meeting of Eastern and Western Art from the Sixteenth Century to the Present Day*. Greenwich, CT: New York Graphic Society, 1973.

Swenson, G. R. "The Horizons of Robert Indiana." In *Pop Art: A Critical Anthology*, ed. Steven Madoff, 318–21. Berkeley: University of California Press, 1997.

Sylvester, David. *Magritte*. Brussels: Mercatorfonds, 2009.

Syson, Luke. "Tura and the 'Minor Arts': The School of Ferrara." In *Cosmè Tura: Painting and Design in Renaissance Ferrara*, ed. Stephen Campbell and Alan Chong, 31–70. Boston: Isabella Stewart Gardner Museum, 2002.

Tahan, Ilana. *Hebrew Manuscripts: The Power of Script and Image*. London: British Library, 2007.

Tanaka, Hidemichi. "The Mongolian Script in Giotto's Paintings at the Scrovegni Chapel at Padua." *Acts of the 25th International Congress of the History of Art*, vol. 6, 167–72. Vienna: Hermann Böhlaus Nachf, 1983.

Tanaka, Hidemichi. "Oriental Scripts in the Paintings of Giotto's Period." *Gazette des Beaux-Arts* 113 (1989): 214–26.

Tannenbaum, Judith. *Glenn Ligon: Un/becoming*. Philadelphia: Institute of Contemporary Art, 1988.

Thompson, Henry Yates. "The Most Magnificent Book in the World?" *Burlington Magazine* 4 (1906): 16–19.

Trapp, J. B., ed. *Manuscripts in the Fifty Years after the Invention of Printing*. London: Warburg Institute, 1983.

Turpin, Ian. *Max Ernst*. Oxford: Phaidon, 1979.

Umland, Anne. *Picasso: Guitars 1912–14*. New York: Museum of Modern Art, 2011.

Van Buren, Anne. "The Master of Mary of Burgundy and His Colleagues: The State of Research and Questions of Method." *Zeitschrift für Kunstgeschichte* 38 (1975): 286–309.

Vandermeersch, Leon. "Writing in China." In *A History of Writing*, ed. Anne-Marie Christin, 66–85. Paris: Flammarion, 2001.

Van Gulik, Willem, and Fred Orton. *Japanese Prints Collected by Vincent Van Gogh*. Amsterdam: Rijksmuseum Vincent Van Gogh, 1978.

Van Moé, Emile-A. *The Decorated Letter from the VIIIth to the XIIth Century*. Paris: Editions du Chêne, 1950.

Van Tichelin, Isabelle, and Guy Delmarcel. "Marks and Signatures on Ancient Flemish Tapestries: A Methodological Contribution." In *Conservation Research: Studies of Fifteenth-*

to *Nineteenth-Century Tapestry*, ed. Lotus Stack, 57–68. Washington, DC: National Gallery of Art, 1993.

Vaughn, William, and Helen Weston, eds. *Jacques-Louis David's Marat*. Cambridge: Cambridge University Press, 2000.

Verzar, Christine. "Text and Image in North Italian Romanesque Sculpture." In *The Romanesque Frieze and its Spectator. The Lincoln Symposium Papers*, ed. Deborah Kahn, 121–40. London: Harvey Miller, 1992.

Verzotti, Giorgio. "Shirin Neshat. That Which Always Speaks in Silence is the Body." In *Shirin Neshat*, ed. Giorgio Verzotti, 75–78. Milan: Edizioni Charta, 2002.

Verzotti, Giorgio, ed. *Shirin Neshat*. Milan: Edizioni Charta, 2002.

Waldman, Diane. *Collage, Assemblage, and the Found Object*. New York: Harry N. Abrams, 1992.

Wallis, Mieczyslaw. "Inscriptions in Paintings." *Semiotica* 9 (1973): 1–28.

Warlick, M. E. *Max Ernst and Alchemy: A Magician in Search of Myth*. Austin: University of Texas Press, 2001.

Waters, John. *Deborah Kass: Feel Good Paintings for Feel Bad Times*. New York: Paul Kasmin Gallery, 2007.

Wazbinski, Zygmunt. "Le 'Cartellino,' Origine et Avatars d'une Etiquette." *Panthéon* 21, no. 5 (1963): 278–83.

Webster, Leslie. *The Franks Casket*. London: British Museum Press, 2012.

Webster, Leslie. "The Iconographic Programme of the Franks Casket." In *Northumbria's Golden Age*, ed. Jane Hawkes and Susan Mills, 227–46. Stroud: Sutton, 1999.

Webster, Michael. *Reading Visual Poetry After Futurism: Marinetti, Apollinaire, Schwitters, Cummings*. New York: Peter Lang, 1995.

Weisberg, Gabriel, Phillip Cate, Gerald Needham, Martin Eidelberg, and William Johnston. *Japonisme: Japanese Influence on French Art 1854–1910*. Cleveland: Cleveland Museum of Art, 1975.

Welch, Anthony. "Epigraphs as Icons: The Role of the Written Word in Islamic Art." In *The Image and the Word: Confrontations in Judaism, Christianity and Islam*, ed. Joseph Gutmann, 63–74. Missoula: Scholars Press, 1977.

Welish, Marjorie. "Who's Afraid of Verbs, Nouns, and Adjectives?" *Arts Magazine* 64, no. 8 (1990): 79–84.

Weski, Thomas, Meg Cranston, and Diedrich Diederichsen. *Baldessari: While Something is Happening Here, Something Else is Happening There, Works 1988–1999*. Hannover: Sprengel Museum, 1999.

Weston, Helen. "The Corday-Marat Affair: No Place for a Woman." In *Jacques-Louis David's Marat*, ed. William Vaughn and Helen Weston, 128–52. Cambridge: Cambridge University Press, 2000.

Whitfield, Peter. *The Mapping of the Heavens*. London: British Library, 1995.

Wichmann, Siegfried. *Japonisme: The Japanese Influence on Western Art in the Nineteenth and Twentieth Centuries*. New York: Harmony Books, 1980.

Wieck, Roger. *Time Sanctified: The Book of Hours in Medieval Art and Life*. New York: George Braziller, 1988.

Wilkin, Karen, and Lewis Kachur. *The Drawings of Stuart Davis: The Amazing Continuity*. New York: American Federation of Arts, 1992.

Williams, Emmett, ed. *An Anthology of Concrete Poetry*. New York: Something Else Press, 1967.

Wilmerding, John. *Important Information Inside: The Art of John F. Peto and the Idea of Still-Life Painting in Nineteenth-Century America*. Washington, DC: National Gallery of Art, 1983.

Wilson, David M. *The Bayeux Tapestry*. New York: Alfred A. Knopf, 1985.

Winn, Shan. *Pre-Writing in Southeastern Europe: The Sign System of the Vinča Culture*. Calgary: Western, 1981.

Winzinger, Franz. *Albrecht Altdorfer: Die Gemälde*. Munich: R. Piper, 1975.

Wood, Ian. "Images as a Substitute for Writing: A Reply." In *East and West: Modes of Communication*, ed. Evangelos Chrysos and Ian Wood, 35–36. Leiden: Brill, 1999.

Wormald, Francis. "Decorated Initials in English Manuscripts from AD 900 to 1100." *Archaeologia* 91 (1945): 107–35.

Wright, Jeffrey Cyphers. "Valeska Soares." *Art Nexus* 77, no. 9 (2010): 112–13.

Yee, Chang. *Chinese Calligraphy: An Introduction to its Aesthetic and Technique*. Cambridge: Harvard University Press, 1973.

Yeh, Wen-Hsien, ed. *Cross-Cultural Readings of Chineseness: Narratives, Images, and Interpretations of the 1990s*. Berkeley: University of California Institute for East Asian Studies, 2000.

Zabel, Igor. "Women in Black." *Art Journal* 60, no. 4 (2001): 17–25.

Zaytoun, Constance. "Enough Already! It's Deborah Kass's Turn to Take the Stage." *TDR: The Drama Review* 55, no. 3 (2011): 110–23.

Zhang, Yiguo. "Brice Marden and Chinese Calligraphy: An Interview." In *Brushed Voices: Calligraphy in Contemporary China*, Yiguo Zhang, 125–32. New York: Columbia University, Miriam and Ira D. Wallach Art Gallery, 1998.

Zhang, Yiguo. *Brushed Voices: Calligraphy in Contemporary China*. New York: Columbia University, Miriam and Ira D. Wallach Art Gallery, 1998.

Index